Illustrated C Programming (ANSI)

J. Emmett Beam

Wordware Publishing, Inc.

Library of Congress Cataloging-in-Publication Data

Beam, J. Emmett.
Illustrated C programming.

Includes index.
1. C (Computer program language). I. Title.
QA76.73.C15B424 1989 005.13'13 89-5270
ISBN 1-55622-068-5

1506 Capital Ave.
Plano, Texas 75074

Printed in the United States of America

ISBN 1-55622-068-5

10 9 8 7 6 5 4 3 2 1
V8902

All inquiries for volume purchases of this book should be addressed to Wordware Publishing, Inc., at the above address. Telephone inquiries may be made by calling:

(214) 423-0090

Dedication

This book is dedicated to my parents, John and Gladys Beam, for their love throughout the years.

Acknowledgements

This book would not have been possible without assistance from the following companies (in alphabetical sequence). Their C compilers, operating systems, debuggers, and documentation allowed this book to speak with authority about the C programming Language. My wholehearted thanks goes to all of them, and I salute them all for their excellent products.

BD Software	The BD Software C Compiler by Leor Zolman for the CP/M-80 Operating System, and the CDB Debugger for BDS C by David Kirkland.
Borland International	The TURBO C Compiler for MS-DOS Operating System.
C WARE	The DeSmet C88 C Compiler for the MS-DOS Operating System.
c-systems	The c-system C Compiler and their C-window source level debugger for the MS-DOS Operating System.
Computer Innovations	The C86 C compiler for the MS-DOS Operating System.
CONTROL-C SOFTWARE	The Mark Williams (Johnson-Laird, Inc) Company C Compiler for the CP/M-86 Operating System.
Digital Research	The C compiler for the CP/M-86 Operating System.
Digital Research	The C compiler for the CP/M-68K Operating System.
Digital Research	The CP/M-68K Operating System.
Gimple Software	C-terp for Microsoft C.
Gimple Software	C-terp for Turbo C.
IBM and Microsoft Corp.	The IBM Xenix Operating System for the IBM PC/AT.
IBM and Microsoft Corp.	The IBM C Compiler for the Xenix Operating System for the IBM PC/AT.

Lattice, Inc.	The Lattice 8086/8088 C Compiler for the PC-DOS Operating System.
Lifeboat Associates	The Lattice/Microsoft 8086/8088 C Compiler for the MS-DOS Operating System.
Microsoft Corp.	The Microsoft C Compiler for the MS-DOS and OS/2 Operating Systems.
MIX Software	The Mix C compiler.
Phase One Systems	The C compiler for the Oasis-80 Multi-user Operating system.
Phase One Systems	The C compiler for the Oasis-16 Multi-user Operating system for the IBM-PC/XT.
Phase One Systems	The Oasis-16 Multi-user Operating System for the IBM-PC/XT.
Santa Cruz Operation	The XENIX Operating System for the IBM PC/XT.
Santa Cruz Operation	The XENIX C Compiler for the IBM PC/XT.
Santa Cruz Operation and Microsoft Corp.	The XENIX Text Processing Package for the IBM PC/XT.
SuperSoft	The SuperSoft C Compiler for the MS-DOS Operating System.
Trisoft	The CP/M-68K Operating System implementation for the Motorola 68000 based TRS-80 Model 16 computer.
WATCOM System, Inc.	The WATCOM C Compiler for the MS-DOS Operating System.

My thanks also goes to Russ and Dianne Stultz and Jana Koch of WORDWARE PUBLISHING for securing most of the tools required to write this book.

Thanks also to Jeff Barton who did a wonderful job as editorial consultant for the first edition of this book. Thank you, Becky Lormor; I appreciate your editorial assistance on the revised edition.

Thanks to Charlie Key and Ramesh Modi with the Xerox Corporation, who allowed me to exercise and hone my C programming skills.

Thanks to IBM, Jon Oelrich, Cindy Corn, and Keith Carter with IBM for allowing me to code some rather difficult tasks for them in C.

My whole hearted thanks to Ken Branscome, EASTFIELD College in Dallas, and the students at EASTFIELD College who used and critiqued the book. Ken and his students' comments and evaluations helped improve immeasurably the final product.

My gratitude to Burt Gearhart and the other reviewers for an excelent job. The author is making the final edit and is responsible for the final content and any mistakes that may remain.

Preface

This book teaches you to program in the C Programming Language. To do this, many examples are provided in the sample programs that can be entered, compiled, and executed by the reader. To gain maximum benefit it is suggested that the reader experiment with C by modifying and expanding the examples.

C has had many critics in the past and their assessments have discouraged many people from learning and using the C language. A recent experience with C has shown me that an inexperienced person can learn C and become very productive and effective with it in a short period of time. A Co-op student was assigned to me to use on a project that was being coded in C. She had no coding experience and had only a couple of introductory computer courses when she joined the project. By the end of the semester, she had become very proficient in coding and debugging C programs. She is now looking for C for her Commodore since she does not know BASIC.

This book was partially inspired by her success.

Contents

Contents (Continued)

Contents (Continued)

Recommended Learning Sequence

Recommended Learning Sequence (Cont.)

Module 1

ABOUT THIS BOOK

INTRODUCTION

This book describes the C programming language and teaches you to program in the C language. It presents detailed information about the C language and is designed to conform with the ANSI standard for C. The text covers all the C statements and the major functions in the ANSI standard library. The low-level file system functions, even though not in the ANSI standard library, are still included in this current revision of the book since so many C programs that use them are still in existence.

This book is designed for a broad range of users. It is for programmers who have never used C and wish to learn it "from scratch." It is for intermediate and advanced programmers who need a quick reference to the many aspects of C. And, finally, it is for the classroom instructor who needs an instructionally designed C textbook.

C is a sophisticated programming language which may seem a little overwhelming at first. But it is not as bad as it first appears to be. As you start learning the elements and aspects of C you will find it easy to use. By the time you finish the book, you will find that it is a very flexible and powerful language.

Throughout the book, examples illustrate the elements being described in each module. The text encourages you to enter the examples and experiment with C. There are no long, extensive C programs in this book. The examples are to *illustrate* the new concept, not to distract you from the concept being covered, and not to provide precoded software that you would blindly enter and run without learning the new concept. This book adheres to the adage: "If you give me a fish, I can eat today. If you teach me to fish, I can eat everyday." This book aims to teach you to 'fish.' It can teach you how to program in C.

ORGANIZATION

The text is divided into small, easy-to-read, bite-sized *modules*. After the beginning introductory modules, the rest of the modules present the elements alphabetically. The alphabetical sequence was chosen so the text can serve as a quick reference for the experienced user and for the student after the learning sequence has been completed. After the introductory modules, the remaining modules each have three main sections: Description, Application, and Typical Operation. Because each module depends on the mastering of the other modules, the best way to use this text is to follow the Recommended Learning Sequence presented at the front of the book.

This book divides some of the elements of C into two modules. The first module is to introduce and familiarize you with the element. The second module usually requires some knowledge of an element that comes later in the learning sequence, so must be saved till the dependent element has been covered. Don't worry about it; the examples keep you on the right track.

RECOMMENDED LEARNING SEQUENCE The learning sequence begins with an introduction to C and your first C program. It then describes numbering systems and converting numbers between bases. It then describes C naming conventions and data types for variables and constants. The next module describes the C operators and how they direct the manipulation of the data.

Following the introductory modules, the learning sequence directs you to a set of modules describing the nine statements that make up the C language. These are followed by a description of the use of functions in C and a set of modules describing more data types, arrays, strings, structures, and pointers. The next module in the learning sequence describes the "stack" and how it works. Data storage classes are then described.

Next the learning sequence moves from general concepts of C towards more detailed information about C. These modules contain part 2 of the descriptions of data types, operators, arrays, structures, pointers, and functions.

The next module describes the C preprocessor.

The next large section of modules in the learning sequence describes both the low-level and the high-level filing system in C, and the functions that make up both filing systems.

The next large section of modules in the learning sequence describes both the low-level and the high-level filing system in C and the functions that make up both filing systems.

APPENDIXES The appendixes are made up of the following:

Appendix A.	Reserved Keywords in C
Appendix B.	ASCII Codes
Appendix C.	Hexadecimal to Decimal Integer Conversion Chart
Appendix D.	Numbers 0 to 255 in Decimal, Binary, Octal, Hex
Appendix E.	Powers of Two
Appendix F.	Powers of Sixteen & Powers of Ten in Hex
Appendix G.	Addition facts for Binary, Octal, and Hex
Appendix H.	Precedence & Associativity of the Operators in C
Appendix I.	Formatted Output Charts
Appendix J.	Summary of Storage Classes and Scope
Appendix K.	Microsoft C version 5.1 Standard Header Files
Appendix L.	Turbo C version 1.5 Standard Header Files
Appendix M.	Representative C Data Type Conversions
Appendix N.	Exercises

CONVENTIONS

Each module which describes a C function begins with a sample of the function calling sequence as it would appear in a program, complete with sample arguments (parameters) and returns. This description is boxed to separate it from the text which follows. The description also identifies which include file contains the corresponding function prototype and provides the ANSI synopsis. Experienced users should find these samples to be a comprehensive, quick reference.

Each module also includes an example, that usually is a complete C program. The examples are followed by a line-by-line description and explanation of the new concept being presented.

Throughout the text, C statements, variables, constants and data types, as well as key concepts, are *italicized*. This is not merely for immediate emphasis, but also to reinforce the exact working of these names. This helps you develop immediate recall of key C names and concepts. Moreover, since many C names are common words, like *main* and *switch*, the distinctive treatment helps prevent confusion.

BEFORE YOU START

This book can be used with any computer and operating system that supports the C programming language. To receive the most benefit from this book, you should have access to a computer with the C compiler installed on it, and you should be familiar with a text editor in order to enter the examples provided in this book.

Keep in mind the fact that C is a modular, extremely portable language. Since it runs on so many different computers, and since there are a number of very good C compilers, no C textbook can hope to cover them all. The approach we take in this book is to describe the key C concepts, and dozens of C functions, which are common to these compilers. Consult your C compiler manual frequently as you work your way through this book. This will help you learn both C and your particular compiler efficiently.

This book is based on the ANSI standard for the programming language C. This book does not cover compiler extentions above and beyond the ANSI standard with the one exception of the low-level file i/o sub-system.

Turn to Module 2 to continue the learning sequence.

Module 2

C OVERVIEW

The C programming language is one of the smallest programming languages available today. If you look back in Appendix A at the reserved words in C, you can see that there are only 33 words reserved as keywords. The size of the C language is one reason it is easy (relatively speaking) to bring up (port) C to a new computer.

Now, don't let the size of the language fool you into thinking that any language this small must restrict and cramp your programming style. Quite the opposite! C is one of the most flexible and versatile of all programming languages. It is being used to develop operating systems, business applications, text processing, data-base applications, spreadsheets, C compilers, and communication packages. Even a COBOL compiler is written in C.

Due to the rapidly expanding use of the C programming language and a large variety of C compilers without a clearly defined standard, the American National Standards Institute responded and addressed the problem by developing the ANSI standard for C. The ANSI standard specifies the form and establishes the interpretation of programs expressed in the program language C. Its purpose is to promote portability, reliability, maintainability, and efficient execution of C language programs on a variety of computing systems. Now developers can develop code in C that will compile and execute as expected in different environments.

C's strength lies in 4 main areas:

1) It contains a powerful data definition method (that is, a way to tell the computer what kind of data it will be working with). The data types supported are alphanumeric characters, character strings, integer numbers (numbers without a decimal point), and floating point numbers (numbers with a decimal point).
2) It contains a powerful instruction set of data operators that tells the computer how to manipulate the data within a program.
3) It contains the modern methods of coding loops (that is, repeating a section of computer instructions a prescribed number of times).
4) It was designed to allow the user to add instructions (called functions) to the language. The user can actually extend the language with custom functions. All C compilers have included with them about 145 functions that are available to be used by the C programmer.

Turn to Module 3 to continue the learning sequence.

Module 3

BASIC ELEMENTS OF A C PROGRAM

This module introduces the basic elements of the C programming language. You will explore the minimum requirements of a C program and learn the basic structure of a C program. You will learn the reasons behind using functions in programs. You will learn about the functions that are provided for you in the standard library that is included with your C compiler.

FORM OF A C PROGRAM

The following example illustrates the generalized form of a C program. A line-by-line explanation describing the meaning of each line in the program follows the example. The example may appear oversimplified, but it implies many things about the C language and the way C source programs are entered into the computer. Look at the example form of a C program now:

```
#include <stdio.h>                                  /* line 1 */
main()                                              /* line 2 */
{    /* start of main    */                         /* line 3 */
int  a ;                                            /* line 4 */

     /*  program body    */                         /* line 5 */

     a = 10 ;                                       /* line 6 */

}    /* end of main      */                         /* line 7 */
```

Line 1 tells the C compiler to include the file STDIO.H as part of this program. The STDIO.H file is included because it contains information that the C compiler needs to compile most programs. The STDIO.H file is provided with each C compiler when purchased. It includes information that is unique for each particular computer and C compiler.

Line 2 is the special name normally used in C to indicate where the program begins executing. Many compilers require that the function where execution begins be named *main*. The open and closed parentheses following *main* are required. In Module 16 you will learn that parameters can be declared between the parentheses.

Line 3 is the open brace that indicates to C the beginning of the *main* function in the program.

Line 4 is an example of the declaration of a variable in C. The variable declared is an integer named "a."

Line 5 represents the body of C statements that accomplishes the purpose of the *main* function.

Line 6 is an example of a program statement in the body of the *main* function.

Line 7 is the close brace that indicates to the C compiler the end of the *main* function. Everything between the braces is a part of the *main* function.

C PROGRAM STRUCTURE

Each computer program has a goal. Before you begin to write a program, you must plan and design how the program is going to accomplish its goal. Some programs are large and complicated. A successful method used in designing a program is to divide and conquer — divide the large program into small pieces and develop it piece by piece. Sometimes a piece must be divided again and again to be conquered. When all the finished pieces are combined, the complete program is produced.

It is important that you understand the concept of a C *function*, the key element in the structure of a C program. The small pieces of the program are placed in functions. They are called functions as they accomplish a small but definite task (its task is to do a particular function). A C program consists of one or more functions. One function within a program is called "main," and this is where the program begins execution. The use of functions allows you to add organizational structure to your programs, making them easier to write and easier to read.

The functions for a C program can be grouped in a single source file or multiple source files. A typical single source file C program structure is represented in the following block diagram:

```
/* compiler header/include files placed here */
/* global data placed here */

function1()
{
    /* local data & C code placed here */
}

function2()
{
    /* local data & C code placed here */
}

        :
        :

functionN()
{
    /* local data & C code placed here */
}

main()              /* entry point - required */
{
    /* local data & C code placed here */
}
```

When you divide functions into multiple source files, each source file is compiled separately. After each source file is compiled error free, they can be combined, or *linked*, to form one execution unit.

```
    }
```

Source File #2

```
/* compiler header/include files placed here */
/* global data placed here */

function3()
{
    /* local data & C code placed here */
}

        :
        :
        :

functionN()
{
    /* local data & C code placed here */
}
```

Source File #3

```
/* compiler header/include files placed here */
/* global data placed here */

functionX()
{
    /* local data & C code placed here */
}

    :
    :
    :

functionZ()
{
    /* local data & C code placed here */
}

main()              /* entry point - required */
{
    /* local data & C code placed here */
}
```

CREATING C SOURCE FILES

You create C source files using your favorite text editor or word processor. The source files can have just about any form you want, because C is a free-form language. The only aspect of C that has any positioning requirements is the preprocessor directives which must begin in the first column on a line. The preprocessor directives are discussed in detail in Module 60. Everything else in a C source file can be spaced as you desire.

The C compiler ignores:

- spaces
- tabs
- carriage returns
- line feeds
- form feeds
- comments

Most programmers use lots of white space in their programs to make them more readable and understandable. Module 6, Naming in C, further explains the use of white space characters.

SYNTAX C does have a defined syntax. *Syntax* means a set of rules to define the proper content and construction of the C statements, similar to the grammar rules of a natural human language. As each aspect of C is presented in this book, the form and syntax of that aspect is defined and explained with an example.

COMMENTS Line 4 in the opening example illustrates a *comment* in C. Comments begin with the /* and end with the */ characters. Since comments are ignored by the compiler, they can be placed anywhere within a C program.

C STATEMENTS A statement in C is an expression that is terminated with a semicolon. The semicolon (terminator) must be present to indicate the end of a C statement. Preprocessor directives, covered in Module 60, do not require a semicolon at the end of a line, but all other C statements always end with a semicolon.

C PROGRAM EXECUTION C programs begin execution with the first instruction in the *main* function. C programs execute from top to bottom one statement at a time. A program executes from the first instruction in the *main* function to the last statement in the *main* function unless control is transferred to another point in the program. When control is transferred to another point, the program continues to execute from the new point toward the bottom, one C statement at a time. C programs execute until they reach the closing brace of the *main* function or until one of the program-terminating instructions is executed.

BRACES Braces are important and are used extensively in C programming. Braces are used in C statements for grouping purposes. Items placed between a paired set of braces are always treated as a unit in a C program. Anywhere one statement is allowed in C, a group of statements placed between braces is also allowed.

INCLUDE FILES The ability to include other files into a C program at compile time is a very valuable C concept. It says that the parts of C programs can be kept small, separate, and manageable. It also says that common pieces of C programs can be created once and used over and over again in many different C programs. This concept prevents many programming errors and discrepancies because of the use of the same code and data definitions.

CASE In the C programming language, uppercase and lowercase letters are different and distinct, just like a spelling difference. C programmers have adopted some suggested guidelines for the usage of case in C programs, and these guideliness will be noted as they are encountered throughout this text.

Turn to Module 4 to continue the learning sequence.

Module 4

YOUR FIRST REAL C PROGRAM

DESCRIPTION

Take a look at the following program:

Example 4.1: YOUR FIRST REAL C PROGRAM

```
/*                        program name:    hello.c              Line 1 */
#include <stdio.h>                                           /* Line 2 */
main()                                                       /* Line 3 */
{                                                            /* Line 4 */
     printf( "Hello World from C" ); /* display sign on message  Line 5 */

}    /* end of main */                                       /* Line 6 */
```

The program output when executed is:

```
Hello World from C
```

Compare this real program with the generalized form of a C program in the previous module to see that it follows the model, the rules, and the programming suggestions already discussed.

EXAMINING THE PROGRAM The stdio.h file is included as part of this example even though it is not necessary in this instance. It is a good idea to include the stdio.h file because most programs do not compile without it. This file contains information that is usually unique to each C compiler and computer, and it is always provided with each C compiler when purchased. The printf statement ended with a semicolon and was followed by a comment. You may have noticed that the printf statement is not included in the reserved word list in Appendix A. Printf is not a reserved word. The printf statement is actually a function call to the printf function included in the C compiler's standard library of functions (provided with each C compiler when purchased).

The printf statement also tells you more about the C language.

Following the word printf are:

- an open parenthesis
- some text in double quotes
- a close parenthesis

Parentheses always enclose the argument(s) of a function call. In this case, the text "Hello World from C" is the argument that is enclosed in parentheses.

As you have probably determined, the purpose of printf is to display on the terminal the argument that is passed to it, which in this case is the text in double quotes. Note that only the text di .plays on the terminal; the double quotes do not.

Braces surround the entire body of the C program, in this case one statement.

When the program starts executing it begins with the first C statement following main, which is the printf function call in this case. After it executes this statement it goes to the next statement in the program. However, in this program, there are no more statements, so it reaches the closing brace. The C compiler recognizes the closing brace as the end of the program. It then stops executing the program and transfers control back to the computer's operating system.

DIRECTING OUTPUT TO THE PRINTER The printf() function used in Example 4.1 sends the string constant in the format string ("Hello World from C") to the computer display. If the C statement is written as follows:

```
fprintf ( stdprn, "Hello World from C");
```

the output is sent to the line printer. Note that everything to the right of 'fprintf(stdprn,' is exactly the same as the printf() statement. Later in the book you are given many more commands and control codes to use with the format string in the printf() function. All of these additional codes and commands apply equally to the fprintf(stdprn,"") function.

Example 4.2:

```
/*                          program name:     hello2.c          */
#include <stdio.h>
main()
{
     fprintf ( stdprn, "Hello World from C" );   /* print sign on message */

}    /* end of main */
```

Note that the *stdprn* is not in the ANSI standard and may not work on your compiler.

TYPICAL OPERATION

In this operation you enter, compile, and run the program in Example 4.1. Begin at the DOS prompt, in your C source code directory. (The C source code for this book is stored in a directory called C on my computer.)

1. Type the C program in Example 4.1, just like it is listed, with your favorite text editor. Call the program HELLO.C. Note that you do not have to enter the comments. You may want to enter the comments so that you can compare your input program to the program in the book if your program does not compile error free.
2. Compile and link the program with your C compiler, in the manner described in your compiler manual.

3. Type **HELLO** and press **Enter**. Notice the following output on your screen:

```
C:\C>HELLO
Hello World from C
C:\C>_
```

NOTE

If this output does not appear on your screen make sure that the program you typed in exactly matches the listing in Example 4.1. Repeat steps 1, 2, and 3 until your output matches the output on the above screen.

4. Turn to Module 5 to continue the learning sequence.

Module 5
STANDARD LIBRARY FUNCTIONS

DESCRIPTION

In the C program in Module 4 you used printf, one of the preprogrammed functions in the standard library. C was designed to use functions. A *function* can be described as a generalized, programmed routine with a definite, but limited, purpose.

For example, the purpose of the printf function is to control the output display. It controls things like how many characters to display in an alpha field (like a person's name), how many decimal places to display in a number (like pi), or how the field is justified, either right or left. All the options of printf are discussed in detail in Module 61.

With any C compiler comes a library of about 145 standard preprogrammed functions. These functions, their names, and purposes, have evolved and are now set by the ANSI standard.

The standard library has evolved because C does not have instructions for I/O (input and output). The standard library includes I/O functions for keyboard input, screen output, printer output, and disk reading/writing. These are provided in the standard library with each C compiler. Many C compilers include the C source code of the functions in the standard library. The source code can provide many excellent examples of good C code and techniques.

Each library function is declared in a header file, whose contents are made available by an #include preprocessor directive. The header file declares a set of related functions plus any necessary types needed to facilitate their use.

The standard header files are:

assert.h	locale.h	stddef.h
ctype.h	math.h	stdio.h
errno.h	setjmp.h	stdlib.h
float.h	signal.h	string.h
limits.h	stdarg.h	time.h

Complete listings of the above-mentioned header files for Microsoft C Compiler version 5.1 and for the Borland Turbo C Compiler version 1.5 are included in Appendixes K & L, respectively.

The functions in the standard library can be summarized generally as:

1.	Character Handling Functions	< ctype.h>
2.	General Utilities Functions	< stdlib.h>
3.	Input/Output Functions	< stdio.h>
4.	String Handling Functions	< string.h>
5.	Date and Time Functions	< time.h>
6.	Mathematics Functions	< math.h>
7.	Other	< errno.h> < stddef.h> < assert.h> < ctype.h> < locale.h> < setjmp.h> < stdarg.h> < float.h> < limits.h>

CHARACTER HANDLING FUNCTIONS The Character Handling Functions include the following:

1. Is the character a digit (isdigit)
2. Is the character a control character (iscntrl)
3. Is the character an alphabetic character (isalpha)
4. Is the character an upper case character (isupper)

GENERAL UTILITIES FUNCTIONS The General Utilities Functions include the following:

1. Get the absolute value of a number (abs)
2. Get a random number (rand)
3. Move a block of memory to another block of memory (memcpy)
4. Make an operating system call (system)

INPUT/OUTPUT FUNCTIONS The Input/output Functions include:

1. Get a character from the standard input device (getchar)
2. Get a line of text from the standard input device (gets)
3. Write a character to the standard output device (putchar)
4. Write a line of text to the standard output device (puts)
5. Write a line of formatted text to the standard output device (printf)
6. Get a line of formatted text from the standard input device (scanf)
7. Open a file for reading, writing, or both (fopen)
8. Close a file (fclose)
9. Read a character from a file (fgetc)
10. Write a character to a file (fputc)
11. Read a block of data from a file (fread)
12. Position to a location within a file (fseek)

STRING HANDLING FUNCTIONS The String Handling Functions include:

1. Function to measure the length of a string (strlen)
2. Function to copy one string over another string (strcpy)
3. Function to add one string to the end of another string, called concatenate (strcat)
4. Function to compare two strings (strcpy)
5. Convert a string of text to upper case (upper)
6. Convert a string of text to lower case (lower)
7. Convert a number in text to an integer number (atoi)

DATE AND TIME FUNCTIONS The Date and Time Functions include:

1. Determine the current time (time)
2. Calculate the diffence between two times (difftime)

MATHEMATICAL FUNCTIONS The Mathematical functions include:

1. Compute the sin, cosine, and tangent of x (sin)(cos)(tan)
2. Compute the natural logarithm (log)
3. Compute x raised to the power y (pow)

OTHER FUNCTIONS The *other* functions include:

1. Functions for errors
2. Common definitions
3. Diagnostics (assert)
4. Localization
5. Non-local jumps
6. Signal handling
7. Variable arguments
8. Implementation limits

Turn to Module 6 to continue the learning sequence.

Module 6

NAMING IN C

DESCRIPTION

This module identifies the C character set, lists the reserved words, and describes the naming requirements for functions, constants and variables.

CHARACTER SET The character set of C is composed of letters, numbers, punctuation marks, and special characters. The letters and numbers are used to form constants, variables, identifiers, and keywords. The punctuation marks and special characters have explicit meanings in C and can only be used as defined in C.

The following are the Letters and Numbers in the C character set (62):

A B C D E F G H I J K L M N O P Q R S T U V W X Y Z
a b c d e f g h i j k l m n o p q r s t u v w x y z
0 1 2 3 4 5 6 7 8 9

The following are the Punctuation and Special Characters in the C character set (29):

,	comma	.	period
;	semicolon	:	colon
?	question mark	!	exclamation mark
"	double quote mark	'	single quote mark
(	left parenthesis	)	right parenthesis
[	left bracket	]	right bracket
{	left brace	}	right brace
<	left angle bracket	>	right angle bracket
/	slash	\	backslash
¦	vertical bar	~	tilde
+	plus sign	-	minus sign
#	pound sign	%	percent sign
_	underscore	^	caret
&	ampersand	*	asterisk
=	equal sign		

MORE SPECIAL CHARACTERS: WHITESPACE CHARACTERS Any character that produces blank space when printed is called a *whitespace* character. The whitespace characters are spaces, tabs, newlines, and comments. Whitespace characters separate otherwise adjacent words in C. Use them freely to make programs easier to read and understand.

NAMING REQUIREMENTS

The names of functions, variables, and constants must follow specific rules. A name consists of a letter, followed by 0 or more letters, underscores, or digits. Remember that uppercase letters are different from lowercase letters in C. The number of significant characters in a name is 31 characters. Names can be longer than 31 characters, but only the first 31 is used by the C compiler.

A name must not be a word reserved as a keyword.

KEYWORDS This is the list of the 33 words reserved as keywords in C:

auto	continue	else	for	long	sizeof	typedef
break	default	enum	goto	register	static	union
case	do	extern	if	return	struct	unsigned
char	double	float	int	short	switch	while
const	volatile	noalias	void	signed		

Keywords have special meaning to the C compiler. Do not use other than as a keyword.

NAMING RULES

TOKENS When the C compiler is processing the source code of a C program, each group of characters separated by whitespace is called a *token*. There are six classes of tokens: Keywords, identifiers, constants, strings, operators, and other separators.

IDENTIFIERS The term *Identifier* is used to describe the names of variables, constants, and functions in C. All are assigned names to identify the variable, constant, or function. The names of identifiers must follow the naming requirements presented in the above section of this module. Constants, variables, and functions are described fully in Modules 17, 86, and 39.

VARIABLES A *variable* is a data object whose value can change during the execution of a program. The variable is referred to by the name that is assigned to it.

FUNCTIONS *Functions* are independent routines that can be called from a different or the same routine to perform an operation and then return a value to the calling routine. A function is referred to by the name that is assigned to it.

CONSTANTS A *constant* is a data object whose value does not change during program execution. A constant that is assigned a name is considered an identifier and follows the naming requirements described above.

NAMING SUMMARY The C language has rules for naming the identifiers of constants, variables, and functions. As you proceed to learn about naming and data types, you should be familiar with the following summary of the naming rules:

1. Identifiers must start with a letter (uppercase or lowercase, A-Z, a-z) or an underscore (_). Note that it is an unwritten rule to not use the underscore as the first character of an identifier, that these are reserved for the C compiler writers.
2. An identifier cannot consist of the underscore alone.
3. All other characters in the identifier can be letters (A-Z,a-z), underscores (_), or numbers (0-9).
4. Identifiers can be 31 characters in length; however, only the first eight characters are significant for global names on most compilers. Note that the underscores also count as characters.
5. Certain words have special meaning to the compiler. These words are known as keywords or reserved words. The keywords must be entered in lowercase. Keywords or reserved words cannot be used as a variable or constant identifier.
6. All symbols used in C are referred to as *punctuation*, such as comma, question mark, ampersand sign.
7. The newline, blank (space), and tab characters are referred to as *whitespace*.

Some examples of valid identifiers:

```
cost , Cost , Pay_rate , total , TOTAL , x12345 , k9 , x , y ,
ThisIsALongIdentifier , SHORT , INT , LONG , Gross_Pay
```

Some examples of *invalid* identifiers:

`Stop!`	(includes a punctuation character)
`1stQuarter`	(starts with a number)
`_`	(underscore alone)
`Gross-Pay`	(includes a punctuation character)
`Gross Pay`	(includes a space)
`long`	(C keyword)
`\q`	(starts with punctuation character)

Turn to Module 51 to continue the learning sequence.

Module 7
ABORT

```
NAME

   abort — terminates a program abnormally

USAGE

  void    abort ( void );

PROTOTYPE in      stdlib.h   process.h

ANSI Synopsis

    #include <stdlib.h>
    void   abort(void);

RETURNS
          no return value
```

DESCRIPTION

The *abort* function immediately terminates the program that is executing and prints an "abnormal termination" message to stderr. This function does not close any open files; it immediately stops executing the program and returns control to the computer's operating system.

There is no return value.

Example 7.1, an example using the *abort* function:

```
/*                              program name:     abort1.c         */
#include <stdlib.h>
main()
{
 int     fatal_error ;

   fatal_error = 1 ;

   /* coding here .... */

   if ( fatal_error )
   {
        printf ( "fatal error, program aborting...\n" );
        abort();                                        /* line 1 */
   }
}    /* end of main */
```

Line 1 is an exmaple of the *abort* function call. The program immediately returns to the computer's operating system without closing any open files after writing a message on stderr.

APPLICATIONS

The typical use of the abort function is when some catastrophic error occurs during the exectution of a program and it needs to terminate execution immediately. One example of a catastrophic error is if a required data file for a program cannot be read from a disk, then the program must terminate, since it cannot read the required data file.

TYPICAL OPERATION

In this operation you enter, compile, and execute the program given in Example 7.1.

1. Begin at the DOS prompt, in your C source code directory. Invoke your text editor.
2. Type the C program given in Example 7.1, just like it is listed. Call the program ABORT1.C.
3. Compile and link the program with your C compiler.
4. Type **ABORT1** and press **Enter**. Notice the following output on your screen:

```
C:\C>ABORT1
fatal error, program aborting...
C:\C>_
```

5. Turn to Module 9 to continue the learning sequence.

Module 8

ABS

```
NAME

   abs --  returns the absolute value of an integer

USAGE

   int    abs ( int i ) ;

PROTOTYPE in      stdlib.h   math.h

ANSI Synopsis

    #include <stdlib.h>
    int      abs(int j);

RETURNS
       returns the absolute value of the integer argument
```

DESCRIPTION

The *abs* function returns the absolute value of the integer argument passed to it.

Example 8.1, an example using the *abs* function:

```
/*                    program name:     abs1.c              */
#include <stdlib.h>
main()
{

   int       j , i = -5 ;

       j = abs( i ) ;                                     /* line 1 */

       printf( " i = %d, abs(i) = %d\n", i , j );         /* line 2 */

}  /* end  of main */


/* sample source for   abs  function:    abs2.c */
int abs ( int i )
{
    if ( i < 0 )   return ( -i ) ;

    return ( i );
}                  end of abs */
```

Line 1 is an example of the *abs* function. In this example the *abs* function would return a value of +5.

Line 2 outputs this line:

```
i = -5, abs(i) = 5
```

APPLICATIONS

Use the abs function anytime you need the absolute value of an integer.

TYPICAL OPERATION

In this operation you enter, compile, and execute the program given in Example 8.1.

1. Begin at the DOS prompt, in your C source code directory. Invoke your text editor.
2. Type the C program given in Example 8.1, just like it is listed. Call the program ABS1.C.
3. Compile and link the program with your C compiler.
4. Type **ABS1** and press **Enter**. Notice the following output on your screen:

```
C:\C>ABS1
i = -5, abs(i) = 5
C:\C>_
```

5. Turn to Module 24 to continue the learning sequence.

Module 9

ARRAYS

DESCRIPTION

This module describes the declaration and usage of arrays.

ARRAY DEFINITION An *array* is the grouping of repetitive data (of the same type) that shares the same name. Arrays are useful when manipulating lists of data. The data shares the same name but each element in the array can be accessed individually. An array can be of any data type.

The elements of an array are accessed by specifying a subscript after the array variable name. The first element of the array has a subscript of 0, the next 1, and so on. The last element has a subscript of n-1 where n is the number of elements in the array.

When an array name is referenced without a subscript, the result is the same as referencing the first element in the array. The name of an array without a subscript is also used as a pointer to that array. That is, it contains the address of the first element of the array. This will be explained in more detail in Module 56, Pointers. Arrays cannot be passed by value (i.e., the whole array) as an argument in a function call. They are always passed by reference (i.e., a pointer to the origional array).

The form for declaring arrays is the same as for simple variable declarations except that the number of elements in the array is placed within square brackets behind the variable's name. The number of elements must be a positive integer constant. The elements in an array start with the number zero, not one.

The form for declaring arrays is:

```
data_type       data_name [  number_elements_in_array ] ;
```

The names of the individual elements are:

```
data_name [ 0 ] ,  data_name [ 1 ] , data_name [ 3 ] , ... ,
          through   data_name [ number_elements_in_array - 1 ]
```

ARRAY USAGE One group of data that is useful to place into an array is the number of days in each month. In this form, the data is easily accessed.

Example of the declaration of an array of integers:

```
int     days_in_each_month[ 12 ];
```

The names of the elements in the above array are:

```
days_in_each_month[ 0 ]     days_in_each_month[ 1 ]
days_in_each_month[ 2 ]     days_in_each_month[ 3 ]
days_in_each_month[ 4 ]     days_in_each_month[ 5 ]
days_in_each_month[ 6 ]     days_in_each_month[ 7 ]
days_in_each_month[ 8 ]     days_in_each_month[ 9 ]
days_in_each_month[ 10]     days_in_each_month[ 11]
```

This example tells us that there is a group of 12 integers that has the name days_in_each_month. To access one of the group, use the variable name with the square brackets, but put the index number of the item you wish to access between the square brackets.

For example to access an individual array element:

```
days_in_this_month  = days_in_each_month[ this_month_no - 1 ] ;
```

Since our months are numbered 1 through 12, we had to subtract one from this_month_no to get the proper index into the array of days_in_each_month. Usually in a situation like this, most programmers declare an extra item in the array (by declaring 13 elements and not using the element 0). This example was picked to reinforce the point that arrays start with element 0.

Example 9.1, an example to calculate the number of days in a non-leap year:

```
/*  program name:        arrays1.c                 */
#include <stdio.h>
main()
{

int     count , i ;
int     days_in_each_month [ 12 ] ;

        days_in_each_month [ 0  ]  = 31 ;      /* jan */
        days_in_each_month [ 1  ]  = 28 ;      /* feb */
        days_in_each_month [ 2  ]  = 31 ;      /* mar */
        days_in_each_month [ 3  ]  = 30 ;      /* apr */
        days_in_each_month [ 4  ]  = 31 ;      /* may */
        days_in_each_month [ 5  ]  = 30 ;      /* jun */
        days_in_each_month [ 6  ]  = 31 ;      /* jul */
        days_in_each_month [ 7  ]  = 31 ;      /* aug */
        days_in_each_month [ 8  ]  = 30 ;      /* sep */
        days_in_each_month [ 9  ]  = 31 ;      /* oct */
        days_in_each_month [ 10 ]  = 30 ;      /* nov */
        days_in_each_month [ 11 ]  = 31 ;      /* dec */


        for( count = i = 0 ; i < 12 ; i++ )
        {
            count += days_in_each_month[ i ] ;                  /* line 1 */
        }

        printf( "number of days in this year is %d \n", count );

}       /* end of main */
```

Line 1 is an example of using each element in an array.

The output of ARRAYS1.C is:

```
number of days in this year is 365
```

The C statement *for* works great with arrays. You simply initialize the index to zero and have the *for* loop execute while the index is less than the number of items in the array. If an error occurs in coding with the *for* in an array, it is relatively easy to spot.

DATA TYPES All *data types* can be used in arrays.

An array of *char* type is called a *string* in C. *Strings* are described in detail in Module 77.

Example 9.2 is another programmed example using arrays:

```
/* Program Name:          SEQDAY.C                          */
/* Purpose: give sequential day number of a day in a year   */
int daysinmonth ( int , int ) ;
main()
{
int   day , month , year , seq_count ;
int  i ;
int   days_in_months [ 13 ] ;                               /* line 1 */

      printf ( "Enter month (01-12)    ... " );
      scanf ( "%d" , &month );
      printf ( "Enter day (01-31)      ... " );
      scanf ( "%d" , &day ) ;
      printf ( "Enter year (1800->)    ... " );
      scanf  ( "%d" , &year );
      for ( i = 1 ; i <= 12 ; i++ )                         /* line 2 */
            days_in_months [ i ] = daysinmonth( i , year ) ;  /* line 3 */
      seq_count = 0 ;
      for ( i = 1 ; i <= ( month - 1 ) ; i++ )              /* line 4 */
            seq_count += days_in_months [ i ] ;             /* line 5 */
      seq_count += day ;                                    /* line 6 */
      printf ( "Today is the %d sequential day of the year.", seq_count );
}

int daysinmonth ( int month , int year )
{
int days ;

      if ( month == 2 )
      {
            if (    ( year % 4 == 0 && year % 100 != 0 )
                 || ( year % 400 == 0 )                    )
                 days = 29 ;    /* leap year */
            else days = 28 ;
      }
      else
      {
            if ( month == 4 || month == 6 || month == 9 || month == 11 )
                 days = 30 ;
            else days = 31 ;
      }
      return ( days );
}
```

Line 1 is the declaration of the array of integers. There are only 12 months, but for simplicity array element 0 is not used. Month 1 (January) number of days is stored in days_in_months[1], February in days_in_months[2], etc. The array has 13 elements and does not use the element 0.

Lines 2 and 3 are the lines used to initialize the array. Notice how nicely the array work with the loop instruction. The loop will execute 12 times, calling the daysinmonth function once for each month, and storing the result in the proper array element.

Lines 4 and 5 are used again with a loop instruction to sum the number of days in the previous months.

Line 6 makes the final calculation by adding in the day number in the requested month.

MULTIDIMENSIONAL ARRAYS Arrays of arrays are possible in C. They are called *multidimensional arrays.* A two-dimensional array has two indexes, a three-dimensional has three, and so on.

The form required for two-dimensional arrays is:

```
data_type      data_name [ no_in_index1 ] [ no_in_index2  ] ;
```

For other dimensional arrays, just include a set of square brackets and number of elements for each dimension.

Example of a two by four array:

```
float     x [ 2 ] [ 4 ] ;
```

The names of the elements in the above array are:

```
x[ 0 ] [ 0 ]      x[ 0 ] [ 1 ]      x[ 0 ] [ 2 ]      x[ 0 ] [ 3 ]
x[ 1 ] [ 0 ]      x[ 1 ] [ 1 ]      x[ 1 ] [ 2 ]      x[ 1 ] [ 3 ]
```

ARRAYS AND THE BUBBLE SORT Many algorithms have been developed for sorting arrays. Some algorithms are superior to others in terms of the average time required to complete the sorting. The bubble sort is not very efficient in regard to time required to sort, but the algorithm is rather simple. Since it is simple and rather easy to implement, look at an example using this algorithm.

The essence of the bubble sort is to start with the first entry and compare its value with the value in each of the other entries in the array. The smallest value is moved into the first entry. Next, start with the second entry and compare its value with the value in each of the following entries and move the lowest value into the second entry. This procedure is followed until each entry has been compared to all entries following the entry. When all entries have been compared the sorting process is complete.

Example 9.3, a programmed bubble sort example using arrays:

```
/* Program Name:    BSORT.C                                 */
/* Purpose:  bubble sort function */
/* Usage:    input a list of numbers, sort into ascending sequence, and
             display in sorted sequence */
void bubble_sort ( int *number   , count )                    /* line 1 */
{
int i , j , hold ;

     for ( i = 0 ; i < count - 1 ; i++ )
     {
          for ( j = i + 1 ; j < count ; j++ )
          {
               if ( number [ i ] > number [ j ] )              /* line 2 */
               {
                    hold         = number [ i ] ;              /* line 3 */
                    number [ i ] = number [ j ] ;              /* line 4 */
                    number [ j ] = hold ;                      /* line 5 */
               }
          }
     }
}  /* end bubble_sort function */

/* display numbers function */
void show_numbers ( int *number   , int count )
{
int  i ;

     for ( i = 0 ; i < count ; i++ )
         printf ( "%d " , number [ i ] );                      /* line 6 */

} /* end of show_numbers */

main()                                      /* main function */
{
int   number [ 10 ] ;
int   i ;

     printf ( "Enter 10 numbers " );
     for ( i = 0 ; i < 10 ; i++ )
     {
          printf ( "\nEnter entry %d .....", i );
          scanf  ( "%d" , &number [ i ] ) ;                    /* line 7 */
     }
     printf ( "\nInput numbers are:\n" );
     show_numbers ( number , 10 ) ;                            /* line 8 */
     bubble_sort  ( number , 10 ) ;                            /* line 9 */
     printf ( "\nSorted numbers are:\n" );
     show_numbers ( number , 10 ) ;                            /* line 10 */
} /* end of main */
```

Line 1 shows an example of the definition of an array of integers as parameters for a function. An array can be defined as a pointer when used as a parameter.

Line 2 is an example showing that array elements can be used as other integer values with relational and equality operators in looping statements.

Line 3 through line 5 are examples of array elements used in assignment statements.

Line 6 is an example of an array element used with the printf statement.

Line 7 is an example of an array element used with the scanf statement.

Line 8 through line 10 are examples of how to pass an array as function parameters. Note that just the name of the array is required when passing a whole array as a parameter.

APPLICATIONS

Arrays are well suited for list processing. Arrays are one-of-a-kind lists, where each element in the array is always the same data type; each item in the list is the same data type.

One example of using arrays in mathematics is in manipulating matrices. Matrix addition is one of the operations commonly performed when manipulating matrices. To be added together, two matrices must have the same number of rows and columns. The sum of two matrices is a matrix. The sum is computed by adding each element in the first matrix with the corresponding element in the second matrix, giving the element in the same position in the final matrix. For example,

$$\begin{bmatrix} 1 & 2 & 3 \\ 4 & 5 & 6 \end{bmatrix} + \begin{bmatrix} 1 & 2 & 3 \\ 1 & 2 & 3 \end{bmatrix} = \begin{bmatrix} 1+1 & 2+2 & 3+3 \\ 4+1 & 5+2 & 6+3 \end{bmatrix} = \begin{bmatrix} 2 & 4 & 6 \\ 5 & 7 & 9 \end{bmatrix}$$

Since there are rows and columns, this requires the use of two-dimensional arrays. In this example the matrices have two rows and three columns. If the two matrices to be added are named matrix1 and matrix2, and the result placed into matrix3, our code can be written as:

```
add_matrix_2_by_3 ( int matrix1[2][3], int matrix2[2][3], int matrix3[2][3] )
{
int row , col ;

     for ( row = 0 ; row < 2 ; row++ )
     {
          for ( col = 0 ; col < 3 ; col++ )
          {
               matrix3[row][col] = matrix1[row][col] + matrix2[row][col] ;
          }
     }
}
```

This function is not a general-purpose function as it only handles matrices that are 2 rows and 3 columns. However, it is a fairly straightforward matter to make a general-purpose function that can add any size matrix up to and including some maximum size. This is left as an exercise for you.

TYPICAL OPERATION

In this operation you enter, compile, and execute the programs given in Example 9.1 and Example 9.2.

1. Begin at the DOS prompt, in your C source code directory. Invoke your text editor.

2. Type the C program given in Example 9.1, just like it is listed. Call the program ARRAYS1.C.
3. Compile and link the program with your C compiler.
4. Type **ARRAYS1** and press **Enter**. Notice the following output on your screen:

```
C:\C>ARRAYS1
number of days in this year is 365
C:\C>_
```

5. Type the C program given in Example 9.2, just like it is listed. Call the program SEQDAY.C.
6. Compile and link the program with your C compiler.
7. Type **SEQDAY** and press **Enter**. Type **1** and press **Enter**, type **5** and press **Enter**, and type **1988** and press **Enter**. Notice the following output on your screen:

```
C:\C>SEQDAY
Enter month (01-12)    ... 1
Enter day (01-31)      ... 5
Enter year (1800->)    ... 1988
Today is the 5 sequential day of the year.
C:\C>_
```

8. Enter, compile, link, and execute the BSORT.C program given in Example 9.3, and verify that it executes properly.
9. Turn to Module 77 to continue the learning sequence.

Module 10

ARRAYS — PART 2

DESCRIPTION

This module explains initializing of arrays and passing arrays as function arguments.

ARRAY INITIALIZATION When arrays are declared they can be assigned an initial value. This is called *initialization*. Only *static* and *global* arrays can be initialized. Initialization is performed once at the beginning of program execution.

Example 10.1, an example of Array initialization:

```
/*                  program name:    arrays21.c         */
#include <stdio.h>

    int         row_column [ 3 ] [ 4 ]  =                  /* line 1 */
    {
                { 1 , 2 , 3 , 4 } ,
                { 6 , 5 , 4 , 0 } ,
                { 9 , 1 , 8 , 3 }
     } ;

     int        dim_3 [ 4 ] [ 3 ] [ 2 ] =                  /* line 2 */
     {
                {   { 1 , 2 } , { 3 , 4 } , { 5 , 6 }   } ,
                {   { 9 , 8 } , { 7 , 6 } , { 5 , 4 }   } ,
                {   { 2 , 4 } , { 6 , 8 } , { 2 , 4 }   } ,
                {   { 1 , 3 } , { 5 , 7 } , { 1 , 3 }   }
      } ;

main()
{
static  char    title [] = "   Customer Inquiry   ";       /* line 3 */

      /* coding ...  */

      printf( "row_column [2] [2]= %d\n", row_column[2][2] );
      printf( "dim_3 [1][1][1]   = %d\n", dim_3 [1][1][1]  );
      printf( "title             = %s\n", title            );

}   /* end of main */
```

Line 1 is the initialization of a two-dimensional global array of *int* type. Since a two-dimensional array is considered an array of arrays, each array is initialized separately. In this example, the *int* array has four elements. This array of 4 elements occurs three times in the first dimension.

The elements of the second-dimension array are initialized first, repeating for each array in the first dimension.

The variable row_column [2] [2] is initialized to the value of 8.

Line 2 is the initialization of a three-dimensional array.

Line 3 is the initialization of a one-dimensional *char* array. Notice that the length of the array is missing. The compiler determines the length from the initialization string automatically.

The output from the preceding example is:

```
row_column [2] [2]= 8
dim_3 [1][1][1]   = 6
title             =    Customer Inquiry
```

ARRAYS AS FUNCTION ARGUMENTS When an array is used as a function argument, C passes a pointer to the array but does not place the entire array on the stack. Arrays are passed by reference (a pointer to the array) and not by value. The called function modifies the actual array since it does not get its own copy of the array. Array elements can also be used as function arguments. If the array element is one of the *int* types, it is passed by value, otherwise it is passed by reference only.

Example 10.2, an example of arrays as function arguments:

```
/*                  program name:     arrays22.c          */
#include <stdio.h>

#define DECEMBER  12

main()
{
     char           name [ 30 ] ;
     int            days_in_months [ 12 ] ;
     float          month_end_balances [ 12 ] [ 5 ] ;

     funct1( name );                                        /* line 1 */

     funct1( &name[ 0 ] );                                  /* line 2 */

     funct2( days_in_months );                              /* line 3 */

     funct3( days_in_months [ DECEMBER -1 ] );              /* line 4 */

     funct4( month_end_balances ) ;                         /* line 5 */

}    /* end of main */

funct1 ( char name[] )
{
         /* coding ... */

}    /* end of function1 */
```

```
funct2 ( int days[] )
{
        /* coding ... */

}   /* end of function2 */

funct3 ( int days )
{
       /* coding ... */

}  /* end of function3 */

funct4 ( month_end_balances )
float    month_end_balances[ ] [ 5 ] ;                   /* line 6 */
{
    /* coding ...        */

}   /* end of function4 */

/* end of module */
```

Line 1 passes an array to a function argument. All that is required is the name of the array. The C compiler passes the address of array element 0 to the function. The *value* of the array is not placed on the stack.

Line 2 passes the address of an array element to a function argument. The C compiler passes only the address to the array element. The value of the array is not placed on the stack.

Line 3 passes the address of an array of *int* types to a function argument.

Line 4 passes an *int* parameter to a function. The value of the variable is placed on the stack and passed to the function.

Line 5 passes the address of the beginning of a two-dimensional array to a function argument.

Line 6 shows how the function must declare its arguments when they are arrays. The first dimension of an array can be left blank, but all further dimensions of the array must be declared, so the program can access the data properly.

Example 10.3, another example of passing an array as a function argument:

```
/*                    program name:    arrays23.c        */
#include <stdio.h>
char     array1 [ 5000 ] [ 2 ] ;                          /* line 1 */
main()
{
     update_array ( &array1[0][0] );                      /* line 2 */
     update_array (  array1       );                      /* line 3 */
} /* end main */

update_array( a )
char            a[5000][2] ;                              /* line 4 */
{
     a[5][1] = 777 ;                                      /* line 5 */
}  /* end update_array */
```

Line 1 is an example of the declaration of a large array.

Line 2 is an example of passing the array to another function. Note that the address operator is used to specify that the address of the array is passed as the parameter; C does not do this automatically for you.

Line 3 is another example of passing an array to another function. When the name of an array is used without the subscripts, then the compiler knows that you are referencing the whole array and, therefore, the address of the first element is passed as the parameter.

Line 4 is an example of the declaration of the array as a function parameter.

Line 5 is an example of the update_array function modifing an element in the original array declared in Line 1.

CALCULATE THE LENGTH OF AN ARRAY You can use the sizeof operator to calculate the number of members of an array. Use the following:

```
members = (sizeof array_name) / (sizeof array_name[0] ) ;
```

The size of the whole array divided by the size of one member yields the number of members of an array.

APPLICATIONS

Arrays are often used in programs to convert error numbers to error messages. To do so, a two-dimentional array is defined, one member being the error number and the other member being a pointer to the corresponding error message. For example:

```
struct  error_struct
{
  int    error_code ;
  char  *error_message ;
} ;


struct error_struct   errors_array [ ] =
{
  { 1 , "invalid customer number" } ,
  { 5 , "account closed" } ,
  { 7 , "disk read error" }
} ;
```

```
display_error_message ( int  error_number )
{
int members , i ;

     members = (sizeof errors_array ) / (sizeof errors_array[0] ) ;

     for ( i = 0 ; i < members ; i++ )
     {
          if ( errors_array[i].error_code == error_number )
          {
               printf ( "%s" , errors_array[i].error_message );
               return ;
          }
     }
     printf ( "unknown error..." );
}
```

Note how general in purpose the example function is. It handles an array of any size, as the number of members in the array is determined in the function. It prints an error message of any length. If it cannot find the right error number, it displays a message indicating an unknown error. The code is also simple and easy to understand.

TYPICAL OPERATION

In this operation you enter, compile, and execute the program given in Example 10.1.

1. Begin at the DOS prompt, in your C source code directory. Invoke your text editor.
2. Type the C program given in Example 10.1, just like it is listed. Call the program ARRAYS21.C.
3. Compile and link the program with your C compiler.
4. Type **ARRAYS21** and press **Enter**. Notice the following output on your screen:

```
C:\C>ARRAYS21
row_column [2] [2]= 8
dim_3 [1][1][1]   = 6
title             =   Customer Inquiry
C:\C>_
```

5. Turn to Module 80 to continue the learning sequence.

Module 11

ATOI, ATOL, ATOF

```
NAME

     atoi      —    converts an ASCII string into an integer
     atol      —    converts an ASCII string into a long integer
     atof      —    converts an ASCII string into a float

USAGE

    int     atoi ( char *nptr );
    long    atol ( char *nptr );
    double  atof ( char *nptr );

PROTOTYPE in      stdlib.h  (atoi, atol, atof)
          in      math.h    (atof)

ANSI Synopsis

    #include <stdlib.h>
    int       atoi(const noalias char *nptr);
    long int  atol(const noalias char *nptr);
    double    atof(const noalias char *nptr);

RETURNS

    atoi returns the integer number found in the character string
    atol returns the long    number found in the character string
    atof returns the float   number found in the character string
```

DESCRIPTION

The *atoi* function analyzes the input string starting with the first character in the string until it finds a noninteger character (a character that is not either zero through nine, a minus sign, or a plus sign). The integer characters at the front of the string are converted to an integer value and returned to the calling function. The input string is not modified in any way.

Example 11.1, an example using the *atoi*, *atol*, and *atof* functions:

```
/*                              program name:     atoi1.c  */
#include <stdlib.h>
main()
{
    int      i , j ;
    long     l ;
    float    f ;
    char     string1 [ 9 ] ;
    char     string2 [ 9 ] ;

    strcpy ( string1 , "14A05    " );
    strcpy ( string2 , "-4005.7 " );

    i = atoi ( string1 );                                   /* line 1 */
    j = atoi ( string2 );                                   /* line 2 */

    printf ( "atoi of %s is:  %d\n", string1 , i );         /* line 3 */
    printf ( "atoi of %s is:  %d\n", string2 , j );         /* line 4 */

    l = atol ( string1 );                                   /* line 5 */
    f = atof ( string2 );                                   /* line 6 */

    printf ( "atol of %s is:  %dl\n", string1 , l );        /* line 7 */
    printf ( "atof of %s is:  %f\n" , string2 , f );        /* line 8 */

}   /* end of main */
```

Line 1 is an example of an *atoi* function call; it returns the value 14.

Line 2 is an example of an *atoi* function call; it returns the value – 4005.

Line 3 displays: atoi of 14A05 is: 14

Line 4 displays: atoi of – 4005.7 is: – 4005

Line 5 is an example of an *atol* function call; it returns the value 14.

Line 6 is an example of an *atof* function call; it returns the value – 4005.7

Line 7 displays: atol of 14A05 is: 14

Line 8 displays: atof of – 4005.7 is: – 4005.7000

Look at how the strings are stored in memory after line 2 executes:

string1										
char	1	4	A	0	5	0x20	0x20	0x20	\0	z
char#	0	1	2	3	4	5	6	7	8	9

string2										
char	-	4	0	0	5	.	7	0x20	\0	z
char#	0	1	2	3	4	5	6	7	8	9

The *atoi* function returns the integer value of + 14 for string1.
The *atoi* function returns the integer value of – 4005 for string2.
The *atol* function returns the long value of + 14 for string1.
The *atof* function returns the float value of – 4005.7 for string2.

Example 11.2, a programmed example using *atof*:

```
/* NAME:                       sqroot.c          */
/* PURPOSE:  calculate square root of a number */
#include <stdlib.h>
double double_abs ( double ) ;                              /* Line 1 */
double sqrt        ( double ) ;    /* square root by Newton's approximation */
main()
{
char     s0[512] ;
double  d ;

      puts ( "Enter a floating point number..." );
      gets ( s0 );
      d = atof ( s0 );                                       /* line 2 */
      d = sqrt( d );
      printf ( "Value = %s, square root = %f\n",s0,d );      /* line 3 */
} /* end main */

double double_abs ( double n )
{
      if ( n < 0 )
            return ( -n );
      else return (  n );
}                                     /* end double_abs */

double sqrt ( double n )              /* square root by Newton's approximation */
{
double  i , j ;

      j = n / 2 ;
      do
      {
            i = ( n / j ) - j ;
            i = double_abs ( i );
            j = (( n / j ) + j ) / 2 ;
      }     while ( i > ( j * .00001 ) );
      return ( j );
}                             /* end sqrt */
```

Line 1 shows the declaration of a noninteger standard library function outside of any other function.

Line 2 is the call to the atof function. The argument for this function is a double data type and it returns a value of double data type.

Line 3 displays the result of the square root function.

APPLICATIONS

A common use of the atoi function is in the coding of data input routines. A single input routine can be coded to input both alpha and numeric data. After the numeric data is input as a string of numbers, it can be converted to integer with the atoi function. Note that numbers must be converted to integer, long, or float to be added together, as numeric strings cannot be added together.

TYPICAL OPERATION

In this operation you enter, compile, and execute the programs given in Example 11.1 and Example 11.2.

1. Begin at the DOS prompt, in your C source code directory. Invoke your text editor.
2. Type the C program given in Example 11.1, just like it is listed. Call the program ATOI1.C.
3. Compile and link the program with your C compiler.
4. Type **ATOI1** and press **Enter**. Notice the following output on your screen:

```
C:\C>ATOI1
atoi of 14A05    is:  14
atoi of -4005.7  is: -4005
atol of 14A05    is:  14
atof of -4005.7  is: -4005.7000
C:\C>_
```

5. Type the C program given in Example 11.2, just like it is listed. Call the program SQROOT.C.
6. Compile and link the program with your C compiler.
7. Type **SQROOT** and press **Enter**. Type **36** and press **Enter**. Notice the following output on your screen:

```
C:\C>SQROOT
Enter a floating point number...36
Value = 36, square root = 6.0000
C:\C>_
```

8. Turn to Module 79 to continue the learning sequence.

Module 12

BREAK

```
NAME

    break  —  statement that causes an immediate exit from the
              do, for, switch, or while statement in which it
              appears.

USAGE

              break ;
```

DESCRIPTION

The break statement causes an immediate exit from the *do, for, switch*, or *while* statement in which it appears. The program continues executing with the next program statement following the *do, for, switch*, or *while* statement block.

If the break statement occurs in a nested statement, the exit is only from the innermost *do, for, switch*, or *while* statement which includes the break. The program continues executing with the next program statement following the *do, for, switch*, or *while* statement. The only way to exit from several nested statements with one instruction is to use the *goto* statement (see Module 45).

Example 12.1, example of *break* statement:

```
/*  Program name:   break1.c
        Purpose:        break  in a do loop:                */
main()
{

    int i = 0 , result = 1 ;

        do
        {
            i++ ;

            result = -result ;
```

```
            if ( result < 0 )
                break ;                                  /* line 1   */

            result = result + i ;

        }  while  ( i < 50) ;

        printf( "result = %d \n", result );              /* line 2   */

}     /* end of main  */
```

Line 1 is an example of a *break* statement within a *do* statement. If the *break* on line 1 executes, control transfers to line 2.

The output of Example 12.1 is:

```
result = -1
```

Example 12.2, another example of *break* statement:

```
/* Program name:   break2.c
   Purpose:        break in a for statement:        */
main()
{

    int i = 0 , result = 1 ;


        for ( i = 0 ; i < 20 ; i++ )
        {
              result = -result ;

              if ( result < 0 )
                  break ;                               /* line 1   */

              result = result + i ;
        }
        printf( "result = %d \n", result );             /* line 2   */

}      /* end of main */
```

Line 1 is an example of a *break* statement within a *for* statement. If the *break* on line 1 executes, control transfers to line 2.

The output of Example 12.2 is:

```
result = -1
```

Example 12.3, another example of *break* statement:

```
/* Program name:   break3.c
   Purpose:        break in a switch instruction:       */
main()
{

     int i = 3 , j = 1 , result ;

     switch ( i )
     {
          case 1:
                    j++ ;
                    break ;                              /* line 1 */
          case 3:
                    j = i * 2 ;
                    break     ;                          /* line 2 */

          case 2:
                    j-- ;
      }
      printf( "j = %d \n" , j );                         /* line 3 */
}    /* end of main */
```

Line 1 is an example of a *break* statement within a *switch* statement. If the *break* on line 1 or line 2 executes, control transfers to line 3. Control transfers to the instruction following the block of instructions that make up the *switch* statement.

The output of Example 12.3 is:

```
j = 6
```

Example 12.4, another example of *break* statement:

```
/* Program name:   break4.c
   Purpose:        break in a nested instruction:      */
main()
{

     int    i , j , result ;


       for ( i = 0 ;  i < 10 ; i++)
       {
            result = -result;

            if ( result == 0 )
                 break ;                                 /* line 1  */

            result = result + i ;

            for ( j = 0 ; j < 20 ; j++ )
            {
                 result = -result ;

                 if ( result < 0 )
                      break ;                            /* line 2 */
```

```
                result = result + j ;
            }
            printf( "Line 3  result = %d \n", result );     /* line 3 */
        }
        printf( "Line 4 result = %d \n", result );          /* line 4 */
}    /* end of main */
```

Line 1 is an example of a *break* statement within a *for* statement. If the *break* on line 1 executes, control transfers to line 4.

Line 2 is an example of a *break* statement within a nested *for* statement. If the *break* on line 2 executes, control transfers to line 3.

Line 3 receives control from a *break* instruction executed on line 2.

Line 4 receives control from a *break* instruction executed on line 1.

The output of Example 12.4 is:

```
Line 4 result = 0
```

APPLICATIONS

The normal usage for the break statement is to leave a loop when an error condition or an abnormal condition is encountered. One example is when a program is in a loop processing data that it expects to be numeric, and it encounters an alphabetic character. The break statement could be used in this example to go to the end of the loop and, at that place in the program, handle the error condition.

TYPICAL OPERATION

In this operation you enter, compile, and execute the programs in Example 12.1 amd Example 12.2.

1. Begin at the DOS prompt, in your C source code directory. Invoke your text editor.
2. Type the C program given in Example 12.1, just like it is listed. Call the program BREAK1.C.
3. Compile and link the program with your C compiler.
4. Type **BREAK1** and press **Enter**. Notice the following output on your screen:

```
C:\C>BREAK1
result = -1
C:\C>_
```

5. Type the C program given in Example 12.2, just like it is listed. Call the program BREAK2.C.
6. Compile and link the program with your C compiler.

7. Type **BREAK2** and press **Enter**. Notice the following output on your screen:

```
C:\C>BREAK2
result = -1
C:\C>_
```

8. Enter, compile, link, and execute the other examples in this module and verify the output screen with the output provided after each example.
9. Turn to Module 18 to continue the learning sequence.

Module 13
CALLOC

```
NAME

   calloc  --  allocates a group of blocks of memory for use

USAGE

   void    *calloc ( unsigned count , unsigned size ) ;

PROTOTYPE in       stdlib.h

ANSI Synopsis

    #include <stdlib.h>
    void *calloc(size_t nmemb, size_t size);

RETURNS
       returns a pointer to allocated memory, or a NULL
       pointer if not enough memory is available to allocate
       the requested amount
```

DESCRIPTION

The *calloc* function allocates a block of memory for an array with the number of elements specified by *count*, where the elements have the length specified by size. Each element is initialized to zero.

If not enough memory is available, a NULL pointer is returned. If the memory is allocated, a pointer to the memory is returned to the calling function.

If the memory allocated is of a type different from the pointer to char, then the memory allocation pointer can be *type cast* to the proper type. Many times the memory allocated is for a structure, and a *type cast* changes the definition of the returned pointer to that of the desired structure.

Example 13.1, an example using the *calloc* function:

```
/*                    program name:         calloc1.c       */
#include <stdio.h>          /* for NULL */
#include <stdlib.h>
main()
{
char      *mem_ptr ;

      mem_ptr = calloc ( 10 , 512 );                    /* line 1 */

      if ( mem_ptr == NULL )
           printf( "not enough memory for the allocation.\n");
      else printf( "memory allocated.\n");


}   /* end of main */
```

Line 1 allocates a block of memory that is 5120 bytes long. If this much memory isn't available, a NULL pointer is returned to the caller. If the memory is available, it is allocated and a pointer to the block is returned to the caller.

APPLICATIONS

The calloc function is often used to allocate memory for structures, when the number of structures is known. If the program determines that 10 structures are required and their length is 512, then the calloc call in Example 13.1 could be used to allocate the necessary memory of 5120 bytes.

TYPICAL OPERATION

In this operation you enter, compile, and execute the program given in Example 13.1.

1. Begin at the DOS prompt, in your C source code directory. Invoke your text editor.
2. Type the C program given in Example 13.1, just like it is listed. Call the program CALLOC1.C.
3. Compile and link the program with your C compiler.
4. Type **CALLOC1** and press **Enter**. Notice the following output on your screen:

```
C:\C>CALLOC1
memory allocated.
C:\C>_
```

5. Turn to Module 36 to continue the learning sequence.

Module 14

CLEARERR

```
NAME

  clearerr  --  sets errno for a stream file back to 0

USAGE

   void   clearerr ( FILE *stream ) ;

PROTOTYPE in      stdio.h

ANSI Synopsis

   #include <stdio.h>
   void clearerr(FILE *stream );

RETURNS
      returns no value
```

DESCRIPTION

The *clearerr* function resets the external variable errno associated with the stream file to 0. Once an error is encountered on a stream file, all functions return an error until the errno flag is reset.

Example 14.1, an example using the *clearerr* function:

```
/*                     program name:     clearer1.c        */
#include <stdio.h>
main()
{
    FILE     *stream ;
    int      c ;

    stream = fopen ("clearer1.c", "r" );    /* open for read */

    c = getc ( stream );

    if ( c == EOF )
    {
         perror ( "clearer1.c " );
         clearerr ( stream );                                /* line 1 */
    }
    else printf ( "file contains data....\n" );

    /* other file i/o can be placed here .....     */

}    /* end of main */
```

Line 1 is an example of the clearerr function call. In this example it is called when EOF is reached for the stream file and the error message is displayed. The *errno* system variable is reset to zero, and other file i/o can be performed on the stream file.

APPLICATIONS

The error flags in C are not automatically reset when read, so the clearerr function should be called to clear the error flags after an error is reported to the computer operator and the problem corrected.

TYPICAL OPERATION

In this operation you enter, compile, and execute the program given in Example 14.1.

1. Begin at the DOS prompt, in your C source code directory. Invoke your text editor.
2. Type the C program given in Example 14.1, just like it is listed. Call the program CLEARER1.C.
3. Compile and link the program with your C compiler.
4. Type **CLEARER1** and press **Enter**. Notice the following output on your screen:

```
C:\C>CLEARER1
file contains data....
C:\C>_
```

5. Turn to Module 30 to continue the learning sequence.

Module 15

CLOSE

```
NAME
    close  —  closes a low-level opened file
USAGE
    int    close ( int handle );
PROTOTYPE in     io.h
RETURNS
        returns -1 if error occurs during close, else 0
```

DESCRIPTION

The *close* function closes the file associated with the file descriptor passed to it. If an error occurs, the *close* function returns a − 1; otherwise, it returns 0. An error can occur if an unknown file descriptor is passed or the file is not available.

Note that this is not an ANSI function.

Example 15.1, an example using the *close* function:

```
/*                    program name:      close1.c          */
#include <io.h>
#include <fcntl.h>
main()
{
    int     status , fd , mode ;

    mode = O_RDWR ;                                     /* line 1 */

    fd = open ("filename", mode );

    status = close ( fd );                               /* line 2 */

    if ( status == -1 )
         printf( "file was not closed properly.\n" );
    else printf( "file closed properly.\n" );

}    /* end of main */
```

Line 1 sets the mode to both read and write access to the file.

Line 2 is an example of the close function call. It returns a −1 if an error occurs during the close, else a 0 is returned.

APPLICATIONS

It is a good programming practice to close opened files immediately after processing on the file is completed.

TYPICAL OPERATION

In this operation you enter, compile, and execute the program given in Example 15.1.

1. Begin at the DOS prompt, in your C source code directory. Invoke your text editor.
2. Type the C program given in Example 15.1, just like it is listed. Call the program CLOSE1.C.
3. Compile and link the program with your C compiler.
4. Type **CLOSE1** and press **Enter**. Notice the following output on your screen:

```
C:\C>CLOSE1
file closed properly.
C:\C>_
```

5. Turn to Module 65 to continue the learning sequence.

Module 16

COMMAND LINE ARGUMENTS

DESCRIPTION

This module describes command line arguments and command line redirection.

The main function, like any other function, can be passed arguments when it is called. These arguments are passed on the command line when you request the computer to run a program.

Example of command line arguments:

```
echo   hello from the echo program
```

In this example, *echo* is the program name requested to run, and the rest of the text on the line is command line arguments.

The argument, called *argc*, is the number of arguments entered on the command line. The second argument, called *argv*, is a pointer to an array of pointers to the arguments that are passed to main.

From the example,

- *argc* has a value of 6, since there are 6 arguments on the command line, including the program name.
- *argv* points to an array of 6 pointers, where each pointer is pointing to one of the words on the command line.

The first command line argument (argv[0]) is always the program name (the minimum value for *argc* is 1). Some operating systems do not place the name in the first command line argument. They leave it blank, but it is still the first argument. Before you try to use this argument, make sure your operating system places it in the first command line argument. If the program name is not present, argv[0] points to a null string.

The classic form for describing the main function is:

```
#include <stdio.h<>
main ( argc , argv )
int    argc ;                     /* argument count, 1 minimum */
char          *argv[] ;           /* pointers to arguments     */
{
     /* C code ....  */
}
```

The ANSI C form for describing the main function is:

```
#include <stdio.h>
main ( int argc , char *argv[] )
{
     /* C code ....  */
}
```

Example 16.1, an example of command line arguments:

```
/* program name:    echo.c
   purpose:         to echo the arguments back to the computer terminal
   author: ?
*/
#include <stdio.h>
main ( int argc , char *argv[] )
/* char                 *argv[]                          /* line 1 */
{

int     i ;

        for ( i = 1 ; i < argc ; i++ )                   /* line 2 */
        {
            printf( "%s ", argv[ i ] );                  /* line 3 */
        }

        printf ( "\n\n" );

}   /* end of main */
```

Line 1 describes argv, which is an array of pointers to *char* type. Some books declare this argument as:

```
char    **argv ;
```

This declaration points to a pointer that points to *char* type. The two definitions are the same. You can use either definition in your programs.

Line 2 shows that argc contains the number of arguments from the command line. When the variable i reaches the value of argc, the loop terminates.

Line 3 accesses the pointers to the arguments. This also says something about the arguments. It says that the arguments are kept in memory as strings, and can be manipulated as strings. All string functions work with the command line arguments.

***ARGV* AND ARGUMENTS IN MEMORY** Assume the following line is entered into the computer to execute the program *echo*:

```
echo My name is Emmett.
```

The program displays (starting with *argv[1]*):

```
My name is Emmett.
```

Memory for this example looks like this (addresses are arbitrary):

memory contents	memory address	variable name	comment
5	1000	argc	
900	1002	argv[0]	→ echo @ 900
905	1004	argv[1]	→ My @ 905
908	1006	argv[2]	→ name @ 908
90D	1008	argv[3]	→ is @ 90D
910	100A	argv[4]	→ Emmett. @ 910

•
•
•

memory contents	memory address	comment
echo\0	900 - 904	argument 0 - program name
My\0	905 - 907	argument 1
name\0	908 - 90C	argument 2
is\0	90D - 90F	argument 3
Emmett.\0	910 - 917	argument 4

The addresses show how the computer stores the command line arguments and the two variables, argc and argv. The addresses are in hex. The pointer length (2) was chosen to make the example simpler.

COMMAND LINE REDIRECTION Many operating systems allow stdin and stdout stream files to be redirected from the computer console to other devices or data files.

A program that accepts input from stdin can have its input redirected such that the input is from another computer device or from a data file. A program that outputs data to the stdout can have its output redirected to another device or to a data file.

The redirection is specified on the command line as the program is requested to be run. The redirection is only effective for this single time that the program is run. Refer to your operating system manual for full details.

Example of command line redirection:

```
sort   <infile   >outfile
```

This example assumes that the sort program has input functions that use stdin and output functions that use stdout.

The less-than sign specifies input redirection. In this example the input comes from the data file named *infile* instead of stdin, this one time the program runs.

The greater-than sign specifies output redirection. In this example the output is to the data file named *outfile* instead of to stdout, this one time the program runs.

APPLICATIONS

A typical application that uses command line options is your C compiler. On the command line you specify the C program to compile and compiler options. Most programs either accept their parameters from the command line or prompt for them. The reason for command line arguments is that programs can be placed into batch files and executed without further operator input after the batch file is begun.

TYPICAL OPERATION

In this operation you enter, compile, and execute the program given in Example 16.1.

1. Begin at the DOS prompt, in your C source code directory. Invoke your text editor.
2. Type the C program given in Example 16.1, just like it is listed. Call the program ECHO.C.
3. Compile and link the program with your C compiler.
4. Type **echo My name is Emmett.** and press **Enter**. Notice the following output on your screen:

```
C:\C>echo My name is Emmett.
My name is Emmett.
C:\C>_
```

5. Turn to Module 60 to continue the learning sequence.

Module 17
CONSTANTS

DESCRIPTION

This module describes the different types of constants available in C.

NAMED CONSTANTS *Constants* can be declared and named just like a variable. Once this constant is assigned its value, it would not be manipulated again, only referenced. These constants are usually placed in an *include* file since they don't change. The initialization of constants is usually done at compile time by most C compilers; others perform it at program run time.

Example of Named Constant:

```
int    number_of_months_in_year = 12 ;   /* declare and init to 12 */
```

SUBSTITUTION CONSTANT The C compiler can make substitutions at compile time. The compiler replaces an *identifier* with another group of identifiers, for example, it can replace one word with a phrase.

The syntax for a *substitution constant* is:

```
#define   identifier    this all replaces the identifier   /* comment */
```

Example:

```
#define   NUMBER_OF_MONTHS_IN_A_YEAR      12
```

The #define tells the C compiler a substitution constant is being defined.

The next word or identifier tells the compiler what identifier to find and replace during the compile.

The first non-whitespace character following the identifier starts the phrase that is going to replace the identifier. The phrase ends at the end of the line. Note that a *comment* can be part of the replacement phrase; however, the C compiler ignores all comments, so it would skip over it in this instance also. The replacement phrase is not always a constant, it can be anything allowed in C, like a calculation or a function call. This is discussed fully in Module 60 on Preprocessor Directives.

Usually a defined constant is entered in uppercase to make it stand out as a constant throughout the program. Place the *#define* statements at the beginning of the program, immediately following the *#include* for the *stdio.h* file and before the other *#include* files. The *#define* statements are placed in front of the *#include* statements because the *#include* statements often use the *#define* constants. The *#defines* are usually in an *include* file themselves.

UNNAMED CONSTANTS EMBEDDED IN THE SOURCE CODE Constants can be placed directly in C source code. Several different kinds of constants can be used:

1. Integer constants
2. Octal constants
3. Hex constants
4. Explicit long constants
5. Character constants
6. String constants
7. Floating point constants

Integer Constants When a number which does not start with 0 is used within a C program as a constant, it is assumed to be an *integer constant*. If the value is out of the range for a regular integer, it is assumed to be a *long* integer. Valid digits are 0 through 9.

Octal Constants When a number which does start with 0 is used within a C program as a constant, it is assumed to be an *octal constant*. Valid digits in octal numbers are only 0 through 7.

Hex Constants To enter a constant in hex just place a 0x or 0X in front of the number; it is then defined as a *hex constant*. Valid digits are 0 through 9 and A through F, in either upper or lower case. Hex constants are zero-filled to the left and are treated as unsigned numbers.

Explicit Long Constants If a constant number must be a long constant, then the number can be followed by an L, either upper or lower case, and the compiler forces it to be a long constant. The long constant can be applied to the integer constant, the octal constant, and the hex constant.

Examples of Integer, Octal, Hex, and Explicit long constants:

Decimal Integer	*Octal*	*Hex*	
12	014	0x0c or 0x0C or 0X0c or 0X0C	
255	0377	0xff or 0xFF or 0Xff or 0XFF	
65	0101	0x41	(character A)
12L	014L	0x0cL or 0x0Cl	(explicit long)
255L	0377L	0xffL or 0xFFl	(explicit long)

Character Constants A *character constant* is formed by enclosing any character in the C character set within single quotation marks. Only a single character is allowed within the quotation marks. The value of the constant is the value of the character.

The two exceptions to this are that the single quotation mark and the backslash cannot be used this way. To generate either the single quotation mark or the backslash as a character constant you must put a backslash character in front of it, all still within single quotation marks.

Example of character constants:

Formed Constant	*Character Used*
'Z'	upper case Z
'1'	one, a hex 31
'\\'	backslash
'\''	single quote mark

Special Character Constants Other special character constants defined in C also are enclosed within single quotation marks and preceded by a backslash.

The special character constants are:

Formed Constant	*Character Used*
'\'<	vertical tab character
'\a'	produce audible alert
'\n'	newline character
'\t'	horizontal tab character
'\b'	backspace character
'\r'	carriage return character
'\f'	form feed character
'\0'	null character, hex 00
'\ddd'	octal number, hex 00 to hex FF

String Constants A *string constant* is like a character constant except that many characters can be contained within double quotation marks.

For example, the form of a string constant is:

```
"This is a string constant."
```

The only characters that cannot be placed in the double quotation marks are the double quotation mark and the backslash. To include either of these characters as part of the string constant, put a backslash before it. The special character constants also can be used within a string constant just like within the character constant.

More examples of string constants are:

```
"This displays on one line, \n and this on the next"
"The newline character is \\n"
"She said \"I DO\" to the preacher's question."
```

The output from the above three examples with *printf* is:

```
This displays on one line,
 and this on the next.

The newline character is \n.

She said "I DO" to the preacher's question.
```

Floating Point Constants A *floating point constant* is used if the decimal number is presented in exponential form. Floating point constants receive the *double* type.

Examples of the different forms possible for expressing floating point numbers:

```
  1.234567
 3.14
 314e-2
-3.14
-314E-2
```

APPLICATIONS

Constants are usually declared in separate files from variables. This technique is extremely useful, as the file that contains the constants can be included in any program that uses them and you do not have to type them in again. This also prevents hard-to-find bugs such as a typing error in one of the constants for two separate programs that expect the constant to have the same value.

TYPICAL OPERATION

In this operation you enter, compile, and run a program using the constants described in this module.

1. Begin at the DOS prompt, in your C source code directory. Invoke your text editor.
2. Type the following C program, just like it is listed. Name the program CON1.C.

```
/* CONSTANTS example        CON1.c          */
main()
{
/* Example of Named Constant:    */
int   number_of_months_in_year = 12 ;          /* declare and init to  12  */

/* Example of Substitution Constant: */
#define  NUMBER_OF_MONTHS_IN_A_YEAR      12  /* declare as 12 */

/* Examples of Integer, Octal, Hex and Explicit long constants: */
int   x  =  12     ;              /* value of 12 */
int   y  =  \014   ;              /* value of 12 */
int   z1 =  \0x0c  ;              /* value of 12 */
int   z2 =  \0x0C  ;              /* value of 12 */
int   z3 =  \0X0c  ;              /* value of 12 */
int   z4 =  \0X0C  ;              /* value of 12 */
long  L1 =  12L    ;              /* value of 12 */
long  L2 =  \014L  ;              /* value of 12 */
long  L3 =  \0x0cL ;              /* value of 12 */
```

```
/* Examples  of Character Constants: */
char  c1 =   'Z'  ;                    /*  upper case Z          */
char  c2 =   '1'  ;                    /*  one, a hex 31         */
char  c3 =   '\\' ;                    /*  backslash             */
char  c4 =   '\'' ;                    /*  single quote mark     */

/* Examples of Special Character Constants are:
char  c5 =    '\v' ;                   /*  vertical tab character    */
char  c6 =    '\a'                     /*  produce audible alert     */
char  c7 =    '\n'                     /*  newline character         */
char  c8 =    '\t'                     /*  horizontal tab character  */
char  c9 =    '\b'                     /*  backspace character       */
char c10 =    '\r'                     /*  carriage return character */
char c11 =    '\f'                     /*  form feed character       */
char c12 =    '\0'                     /*  null character, hex 00    */
char c13 =    '\000'                   /*  octal number 0            */

/* Example of a string constant is: */
char c14[] = "This is a string constant." ;

/* Examples of floating point numbers: */

float  f1 =    1.234567 ;
float  f2 =    3.14     ;
float  f3 =    314e-2   ;
float  f4 =   -3.14     ;
float  f5 =   -314E-2   ;

}
```

3. Compile and link the program with your C compiler.
4. Type **CON1** and press **Enter** to execute the program. Note that there is no output from this program. You have accomplished the purpose of this operation when the example program compiles error free.
5. Turn to Module 53 to continue the learning sequence.

Module 18

CONTINUE

```
NAME

   continue -- Statement used with the loop instructions do, for,
               and while.  It transfers program control to the
               place in the program such that the next iteration of
               the loop will begin.

USAGE

               continue ;
```

DESCRIPTION

The *continue* statement is used with the loop instructions *do*, *for*, and *while*. It transfers program control to the place in the program where the next iteration of the loop in which it appears begins.

Continue IN *do* AND *while* STATEMENTS Execution of the *continue* statement in a *do* or *while* loop causes execution to resume with the test part of the loop statement. Execution then continues with the normal sequence of events for the statement.

***Continue* IN *for* STATEMENTS** Execution of the *continue* statement in a *for* loop causes execution to resume with the increment part of the *for* statement. Execution then continues with the normal sequence of events for the statement.

***Continue* IN *nested* STATEMENTS** If the *continue* statement occurs in a nested statement, execution transfers to the next iteration point of the innermost loop statement. The only way to leave the loop without going through this point is to use the *goto* statement. See Module 45, *goto*.

Example 18.1, example of *continue* statement:

```
/* Program name:   continu1.c
                                  continue in a do loop:    */
main()
{
    int     i = 0 , result = 1 ;

        do
        {
             i++ ;

             result = -result ;

             if ( result < 0 )
                 continue ;                            /* line 1   */

            result = result + i ;

         }
         while  ( i < 50 ) ;                           /* line 2   */

         printf( "result = %d \n", result );

}    /* end of main */
```

Line 1 is an example of a *continue* statement within a *do* statement. If the *continue* on line 1 executes, control transfers to line 2.

The output of Example 18.1 is:

```
result = 651
```

Example 18.2, example of *continue* statement:

```
/* Program name:   continu2.c
                                   continue in a for statement:  */
main()
{

    int i = 0 , result = 1 ;

        for ( i = 0 ; i < 20 ; i++ )
        {
             result = -result ;

             if ( result < 0 )
                 continue ;                            /* line 1   */

             result = result + i ;
        }
        printf( "result = %d \n", result );            /* line 2   */

}      /* end of main */
```

Line 1 is an example of a *continue* statement within a *for* statement. If the *continue* on line 1 executes, control transfers to line 2, the point where the next iteration of the *for* loop begins. At this point expression3 of the *for* (i + +) executes and then expression2 (the test_condition) executes.

The output of Example 18.2 is:

```
result = 101
```

Example 18.3, example of *continue* statement:

```
/* Program name:   continu3.c
                                      continue in a nested instruction:  */
main()
{
    int    i , j , result ;

      for ( i = 0 ;  i < 10 ; i++)
      {
           result = -result;

           if ( result == 0 )
                continue ;                                /* line 1  */

           result = result + i ;

           for ( j = 0 ; j < 20 ; j++ )
           {
                result = -result ;

                if ( result < 0 )
                    continue ;                            /* line 2 */

                result = result + j ;
           }

           printf( "Line 3  result = %d \n", result );    /* line 3 */

      }
      printf( "Line 4 result = %d \n", result );          /* line 4 */
}    /* end of main */
```

Line 1 is an example of a *continue* statement within a *for* statement. If the *continue* on line 1 executes, control transfers to line 4 so that the next iteration of the *for* begins.

Line 2 is an example of a *continue* statement within a nested *for* statement. If the *continue* on line 2 executes, control transfers to line 3 for the next iteration of the *for* in which the *continue* occurs.

The output of Example 18.3 is:

```
Line 4 result = 0
```

Example 18.4, example of *continue* statement:

```
/* Program name:   continu4.c  */
main()
{
     int  i ;

     for ( i = 0 ; i <= 10 ; i++ )
     {
         if ( i % 2 )                                        /* line 1  */
              continue ;                                     /* line 2  */
         printf ( "This number is even %d\n" , i );         /* line 3  */
     }                                                       /* line 4  */
} /* end main */
```

Line 1 evaluates the expression (i % 2). If the remainder is odd then line 3 is executed, transfering control to line 4.

Line 3 is executed when line 2 is not executed.

The output of Example 18.4 is:

```
This number is even 0
This number is even 2
This number is even 4
This number is even 6
This number is even 8
This number is even 10
```

APPLICATIONS

The continue statement is suited for processing in a loop when the processing for this particular interation of the loop is complete and you want to go on to the next iteration. For example, a program could be processing a list of numbers, using only the positive numbers for processing and ignoring the negative numbers. In this example, a test to see if the number is negative is made. If the number is negative, the continue statement takes the program execution to the bottom of the loop and starts the next iteration, which gets the next number. If the number is positive in the test, then the number is processed by the code in the loop.

TYPICAL OPERATION

In this operation you enter, compile, and execute the programs given in Example 18.1 and Example 18.2.

1. Begin at the DOS prompt, in your C source code directory. Invoke your text editor.
2. Type the C program given in Example 18.1, just like it is listed. Call the program CONTINU1.C.
3. Compile and link the program with your C compiler.

4. Type **CONTINU1** and press **Enter**. Notice the following output on your screen:

```
C:\C>CONTINU1
result = 651
C:\C>_
```

5. Type the C program given in Example 18.2, just like it is listed. Call the program CONTINU2.C.
6. Compile and link the program with your C compiler.
7. Type **CONTINU2** and press **Enter**. Notice the following output on your screen:

```
C:\C>CONTINU2
result = 101
C:\C>_
```

8. Enter, compile, link, and execute the other examples in this module and verify the output screen with the output provided after each example.
9. Turn to Module 45 to continue the learning sequence.

Module 19

CREAT

```
NAME

   creat   —  creates a new file, or opens and overwrites
              an old file

USAGE

   int   creat ( char *filename , int mode );

PROTOTYPE in      io.h

RETURNS
         returns a file descriptor or -1 if an error occurs
```

DESCRIPTION

The *creat* function is a low-level function that can either create and open a new file, or open and truncate an existing file. If the file named does not exist, it is created and opened for access. If the file already exists, it is truncated to a length of zero (which destroys the contents of the original file) and then it is opened for access. The *creat* function returns a file descriptor to the calling function. If an error occurs, a -1 is returned to the calling function.

The mode parameter is used to specify that the file is to be read, written, or both when opened. See your compiler manuals for the meaning of mode for your system.

Note that this function is not an ANSI function.

Example 19.1, an example using the *creat* function:

```
/*                      program name:          creat1.c             */
#include <io.h>
#include <fcntl.h>
main()
{
     int   status , mode ;

       mode = O_BINARY ;                                        /* line 1 */

       status = creat( "filename" , mode );                     /* line 2 */

       if( status == -1 )
            printf( "file could not be created...\n" );
       else printf( "file created...\n" );

}     /* end of main */
```

Line 1 sets the mode for the file as binary.

Line 2 is an example of the creat function call. It creates and opens the specified file in the specified mode. If the file is created and opened without error, a file descriptor is returned, else a -1 is returned.

APPLICATIONS

The creat function either creates a new file or opens and truncates an existing file. A program that copies files from one disk to another can use this function when it opens the destination file. If the destination file does not exist, it open a new destination file. If the destination file does exist, it is opened and truncated to a length of 0, such that the new destination file completely overwrites the old existing file. Be careful not to destroy a file that you wish to keep in programs when you use this function.

TYPICAL OPERATION

In this operation you enter, compile, and execute the program given in Example 19.1.

1. Begin at the DOS prompt, in your C source code directory. Invoke your text editor.
2. Type the C program given in Example 19.1, just like it is listed. Call the program CREAT1.C.
3. Compile and link the program with your C compiler.
4. Type **CREAT1** and press **Enter**. Notice the following output on your screen:

```
C:\C>CREAT1
file created...
C:\C>_
```

5. Turn to Module 52 to continue the learning sequence.

Module 20

DATA TYPES

DESCRIPTION

This module explains the different ways data can be described and used in C.

DATA STORAGE The typical computer accesses its memory in two ways. One way is a *byte* at a time and the other way is a *word* at a time. A byte is the amount of storage required for one character. A word is the amount of memory that a computer can naturally read and write with one access to memory. This is referred to as the word length of the computer. The *word length* of most computers is either two or four bytes.

A bit is the most fundamental element in computer memory. A bit can have two states, either turned on (a value of one), or turned off (a value of zero). A byte is composed of 8 bits. The different combinations that occur by the varying bit patterns (on and off in a byte) produce the alphabetic characters, the numeral digits, and the special characters used by the computer.

The most commonly used bit pattern character set is the ASCII code set. The ASCII code set is defined in Appendix B. The ASCII set only requires 7 bits per byte. The 8th bit is always off in the ASCII code set. The ASCII code set defines both printable characters and special control characters. The serious C programmer should become very familiar with the ASCII code set.

Some computers use a different code set than ASCII, but it makes no difference to C. It works fine with other character sets.

The data stored in a byte can also be a binary number, either signed or unsigned. One byte (8 bits) can contain an unsigned number ranging in value from 0 to 255. A byte can also contain a signed number ranging in value from − 127 to + 127. This is to say that the same bit pattern in memory can have different meanings. An ASCII character can be treated as a binary number and vice-versa. For example, the ASCII bit pattern for an A is 01000001. A byte with the value of 65 (decimal) also has the bit pattern 01000001.

The range for a signed binary number stored in a *word* on a computer with a word length of 2 bytes (16 bits) is from − 32767 to + 32767. The range for an unsigned number on the same computer is from 0 to 65535.

The range for a signed binary number stored in a *word* on a computer with a word length of 4 bytes (32 bits) is from − 2147483647 to + 2147483647. The range for an unsigned number on the same computer is from 0 to 4294967295.

VARIABLES Variables are data objects that are manipulated in a program. Information can be stored in a variable and later recalled.

When a variable is declared, it is also given a *data type*. The *data type* tells the program what kind of data the variable stores. You decide which data type is appropriate for each variable and assign that type to the variable when it is declared. Because some types (like *char* and *int*) process faster than others as the program executes, it is best to have the program maintain only as much precision as is necessary for each variable.

BASIC DATA TYPES The basic data types available in C are:

1. char — The *char* type holds one character of data. The *char* type can hold a one-byte binary number, a single alphanumeric or special character, or have each bit have its own individual value. The range for a binary number in *char* type is − 127 to + 127.
2. short — The *short* type is used to store integer numbers with a range of − 32767 to + 32767.
3. int — The *int* type stores integer number values. The size of an integer varies by the natural word length of the computer. See the table at the end of this module for a comparison of length of data types for some of the more popular computers. The length for *int* type is either two or four bytes on most computers.
4. long — The *long* type is used to store an integer value that has a range which is larger than a regular integer. The range for *long int* is − 2,147,483,647 to + 2,147,483,647.
5. float — The *float* type stores numbers that have a decimal place. The *float* type has at least 6 digits of precision. The decimal point can occur anywhere within the 6 digits.
6. double — The *double* type stores double-precision floating point numbers. *Double* type is like *float* type except that it has at least 10 digits of precision. These numbers are also stored in a standard format.

NOTE

The term "basic data types" is used throughout this book and refers to some of the above defined data types. The word *basic* is not to be confused with a programming language of the same name.

QUALIFIERS Data type qualifiers can be used with the *char*, *short*, *int*, *long*, and *double* data types.

The qualifier for *char* type is:

unsigned — The *unsigned char* type is designed for an extended character set, beyond the ASCII definition which only defines 7 of the 8 bits for a byte. The extended character set usually is used for graphics and for different character fonts. The range is from 0 to 255.

The qualifier for *short*, *int*, and *long* type is:

unsigned — The *unsigned* types are designed for integer values that are always positive. This allows for twice the normal range for the positive numbers of the corresponding signed type.

The qualifier for *double* type is:

long — The *long double* type may have more precision than as double.

If an *unsigned*, *short*, or *long* qualifier is not followed by one of the basic types, then the C compiler treats it as if *int* followed it.

The heirarchy of data types is:

`char` → `short` → `int` → `long` → `float` → `double` → `long double.`

TYPE DEFINITIONS Char type is large enough to hold any member of the basic character set.

There are four signed integer types: signed char, short int, int, and long int.

There are four unsigned integer types: char, unsigned short int, unsigned int, and unsigned long int. These occupy the same amount of storage as the four signed integer types.

There are three floating point types: float, double, long double.

The type char, the signed and unsigned integer types are collectively called the basic types.

There are three character types: char, signed char, and unsigned char.

An enumeration type comprises a set of named integer constant values.

The void type comprises an empty set of values.

Derived types are types constructed from the basic, void, and enumerated types. They are arrays, structures, unions, functions, and pointer types.

The type char, the signed and unsigned integer types, and the enumerated types are collectively called the *integral* types.

Integral and floating point types are collectively called *arithmetic* types.

Arithmetic and pointer types are collectively called *scalar* types.

Array and structure types are collectively called *aggregate* types.

Arrays, function, and pointer types are collectively called *derived declarator* types.

A type is characterized by its top type. An object that is declared as pointer to float, has a top type of pointer, not float.

A type is a qualified type if it has one of the following modifiers: const, noalias, or volatile.

A parameter type list specifies the types of and the parameters of a function.

TYPICAL DATA TYPE SUMMARY TABLE

Data Type	*Typical number of Bytes Used*	*Value Range*		
char	1	– 127	to	+ 127
unsigned char	1	0	to	+ 255
short	2	– 32767	to	+ 32767
unsigned short	2	0	to	+ 65535
int	2	– 32767	to	+ 32767
	and 4	– 2,147,483,647	to	+ 2,147,483,647
unsigned int	2	0	to	+ 65535
	and 4	0	to	+ 4,294,967,295
long	4	– 2,147,483,647	to	+ 2,147,483,647
unsigned long	4	0	to	+ 4,294,967,295
float	4	1e – 37 to 1e + 37 with 6 digits precision		
double	8	1e – 37 to 1e + 37 with 10 digits precision		

Since the types vary with each compiler, refer to your C include files for the exact precision of each type for your compiler. The include files < limits.h> and < float.h> describe the limits for your compiler. As an example, here are the limits from the Microsoft C Compiler, version 5.1:

```
CHAR_MAX         127                     /* maximum char value           */
CHAR_MIN        -127                     /* mimimum char value           */
SCHAR_MAX        127                     /* maximum signed char value    */
SCHAR_MIN       -127                     /* minimum signed char value    */
UCHAR_MAX        255                     /* maximum unsigned char value  */
CHAR_BIT         8                       /* number of bits in a char     */
USHRT_MAX        0xffff                  /* maximum unsigned short value */
SHRT_MAX         32767                   /* maximum (signed) short value */
SHRT_MIN        -32767                   /* minimum (signed) short value */
UINT_MAX         0xffff                  /* maximum unsigned int value   */
ULONG_MAX        0xffffffff              /* maximum unsigned long value  */
INT_MAX          32767                   /* maximum (signed) int value   */
INT_MIN         -32767                   /* minimum (signed) int value   */
LONG_MAX         2147483647              /* maximum (signed) long value  */
LONG_MIN        -2147483647              /* minimum (signed) long value  */

DBL_DIG          15                      /* # of decimal digits of precision */
DBL_EPSILON      2.2204460492503131e-016 /* smallest such that 1.0+DBL_EPSILON != 1.0 */
DBL_MANT_DIG     53                      /* # of bits in mantissa        */
DBL_MAX          1.7976931348623158e+308 /* max value                    */
DBL_MAX_10_EXP   308                     /* max decimal exponent         */
DBL_MAX_EXP      1024                    /* max binary exponent          */
DBL_MIN          2.2250738585072014e-308 /* min positive value           */
DBL_MIN_10_EXP  -307                     /* min decimal exponent         */
DBL_MIN_EXP     -1021                    /* min binary exponent          */
DBL_RADIX        2                       /* exponent radix               */
DBL_ROUNDS       0                       /* addition rounding: chops     */
```

```
FLT_DIG            6                   /* # of decimal digits of precision */
FLT_EPSILON        1.192092896e-07     /* smallest such that 1.0+FLT_EPSILON != 1.0 */
FLT_GUARD          0
FLT_MANT_DIG       24                  /* # of bits in mantissa         */
FLT_MAX            3.402823466e+38     /* max value                     */
FLT_MAX_10_EXP     38                  /* max decimal exponent          */
FLT_MAX_EXP        128                 /* max binary exponent           */
FLT_MIN            1.175494351e-38     /* min positive value            */
FLT_MIN_10_EXP     -37                 /* min decimal exponent          */
FLT_MIN_EXP        -125                /* min binary exponent           */
FLT_NORMALIZE      0
FLT_RADIX          2                   /* exponent radix                */
FLT_ROUNDS         0                   /* addition rounding: chops      */

LDBL_DIG           DBL_DIG             /* # of decimal digits of precision */
LDBL_EPSILON       DBL_EPSILON         /* smallest such that 1.0+LDBL_EPSILON != 1.0 */
LDBL_MANT_DIG      DBL_MANT_DIG        /* # of bits in mantissa         */
LDBL_MAX           DBL_MAX             /* max value                     */
LDBL_MAX_10_EXP    DBL_MAX_10_EXP      /* max decimal exponent          */
LDBL_MAX_EXP       DBL_MAX_EXP         /* max binary exponent           */
LDBL_MIN           DBL_MIN             /* min positive value            */
LDBL_MIN_10_EXP    DBL_MIN_10_EXP      /* min deimal exponent           */
LDBL_MIN_EXP       DBL_MIN_EXP         /* min binary exponent           */
LDBL_RADIX         DBL_RADIX           /* exponent radix                */
LDBL_ROUNDS        DBL_ROUNDS          /* addition rounding: chops      */
```

Turn to Module 86 to continue the learning sequence.

Module 21

DATA TYPES — PART 2

DESCRIPTION

This module explains how you can define your own data types and declare enumerated data types. This module also decribes how to determine the meaning of complex data definitions.

***TYPEDEF* DEFINITION** The *typedef* keyword allows you to define your own data types. The form of a *typedef* declaration is:

```
typedef     data_type        new_data_type_name ;
```

The keyword *typedef* begins the declaration. The C data_type appears next. Your name for the preceding data_type comes next and ends with a semicolon.

The C data_types allowed here are all basic data types, such as *int*, *short*, *unsigned*, *long*, *float*, and *double*. Also structures, pointers, and arrays are allowed as the data_type.

The *typedef* type is only a synonym for a C type. All the rules for regular variables apply to *typedef* variables. The *typedef* type creates a new keyword for the file in which it appears. It can be used any place a regular C type can be used.

Example 21.1, an example using *typedef*:

```
/*                    program name:    data2.c          */
#include <stdio.h>

typedef    int      index ;                                  /* line 1 */

typedef    struct   cust_rec                                 /* line 2 */
           {
             char        name [ 30 ] ;
             int         cust_number ;
           }
                    cust_rec_type  ;                         /* line 3 */

main()
{

   index            i ;                                      /* line 4 */

   cust_rec_type    customer_record ;                        /* line 5 */
   cust_rec_type    *customter_ptr  ;                        /* line 6 */
```

```
    customer_record.cust_number = 12056 ;                    /* line 7 */
    strcpy (customer_record.name , "Bob White") ;            /* line 8 */

    customer_ptr = &customer_record ;                        /* line 9 */

    printf ( "Name= %s, Nbr= %d\n" ,                         /* line 10 */
             customer_record->name ,
             customer_record->cust_number );

}   /* end of main */
```

Line 1 tells the C compiler that each time it finds the word index in the program, that word is just another word for int. The compiler substitutes int for index each time it finds the word index.

Lines 2 and 3 tell the C compiler that each time it finds the word cust_rec_type in the program it is to substitute the structure definition of cust_rec.

Line 4 declares a variable of *typedef* type for int. Index type is a synonym for int.

Line 5 declares a structure with the *typedef* type.

Line 6 declares a pointer to the *typedef* type.

Lines 7 and 8 access the members of a variable that are declared with the *typedef* type, just as if they were declared with the struct definition itself.

Line 9 is an example of taking the address of a structure that is declared with the *typedef* type.

Line 10 illustrates the use of members of a structure variable declared with the *typedef* type. Here again, the members of the variable are accessed just as if the variable is declared with the struct definition itself.

The output from this example is:

```
Name= Bob White, Nbr= 12056
```

ENUMERATED DATA TYPES In classic C, lists of values are defined using the *#define* preprocessor directive. For example,

```
#define  Sun 0
#define  Mon 1
#define  Tue 2
#define  Wed 3
#define  Thu 4
#define  Fri 5
#define  Sat 6
```

In ANSI C, you can use enumerated data types to describe the same data and have the same effect. For example,

```
typedef enum { Sun, Mon, Tue, Wed, Thu, Fri, Sat } days_of_week_type ;
```

Now you declare the variables that use these values with days_of_week_type. For example,

```
days_of_week_type    day_of_week ;    /* which day it occurred */
```

OTHER TYPE QUALIFIERS Three other type qualifiers are:

```
const
noalias
volatile
```

The qualifier const is used when you want to specify that the value of a variable is a constant and cannot be modified by the program. These objects are usually placed in read-only storage within the program.

The following are examples to clarify the use of the const qualifier. The first is an example of a variable pointer to a constant value. The second is a constant pointer to a variable value.

```
const int    *ptr_to_constant    ;          /* Example 1 */
int          *const constant_ptr ;          /* Example 2 */
```

In example 1 the pointer can be changed to point to a different integer object, but the integer object cannot be changed.

In example 2 the pointer cannot be changed to point to a different object, but the integer that the pointer is pointing to can be changed.

The qualifier volatile is used to specify that a variable may appear not to be changed within the program, but is actually being changed in a way not known to the compiler. An example of this use is date and time variables which are never changed by a C program but are updated through other means, usually a realtime clock within the computer.

The qualifier noalias is applied to indicate that an object is modifiable through its actual object only and not through a virtual object.

INCREASING SPIRAL RULE As you become more familiar with C, you will make more and more complex declarations. This rule helps to determine the meaning of a complex declaration.

First, find the identifier. It is usually near the middle of the declaration. Next, move to its right to the first C symbol, like an array bracket or a function parenthesis, and connect the two with a half circle. Then find the first C symbol to the left of the identifier and connect the symbol on the right to the symbol on the left with a half circle. Then find the next C symbol to the right. Connect it to the previous symbol with a half circle. Continue until the only remaining thing on the line is the data type, and connect it with an arc. The increasing arcs produce a spiral, hence the term "increasing spiral rule." The resulting diagram tells what the complex declaration means.

For example, a diagram of: char *argv[ ] ;

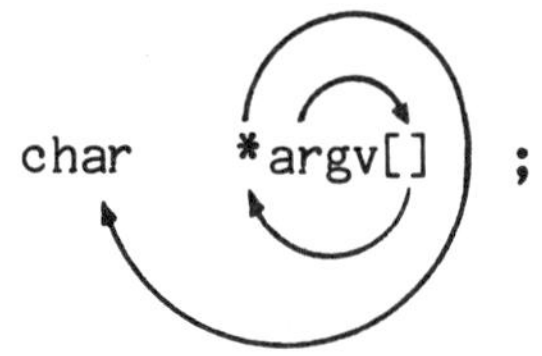

Meaning: The variable argv is an array of pointers to type *char*.

First, find the identifier argv near the middle. Next, move to the right and find the C symbols for arrays ([ ]). This tells you the identifer argv is an *array*. Then continue the spiral back to the left and find the C symbol for pointers (*). This tells you the variable *argv* is an *array* of *pointers*. Next, continue the spiral back to the right and find no symbol, so the definition does not change at this point. Finally, continue the spiral back to the left and find that the data type is the only symbol left, which terminates your quest for the meaning of the complex declaration. You now know the variable argv is an *array* of *pointers* to *char* type.

How would you diagram:

```
char  *(*fptr[])() ;
```

Answer: apply the increasing spiral rule:

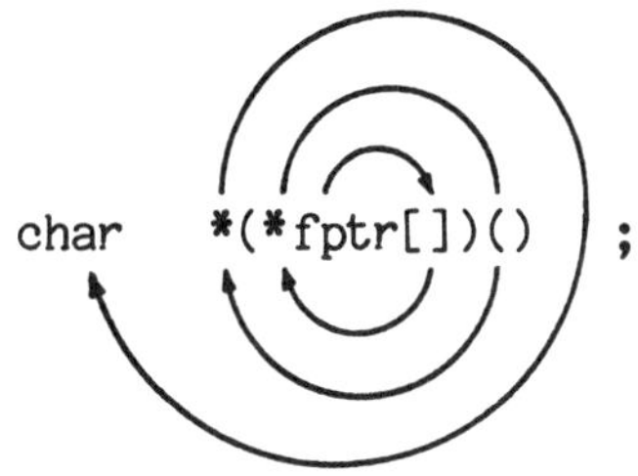

Meaning: The variable fptr is an *array* of *pointers* to functions that return a *pointer* to *char* type.

The increasing spiral rule, sometimes called the right-left rule, makes deciphering very complex declarations almost magically easy.

APPLICATIONS

The flexibility of C allows very complex statements to be created. Since more and more companies are selling the source code to their function libraries, it is very likely that you will eventually have to modify someone elses code written in C. Therefore, even if you do not personally use the more sophisticated constructs of C, you probably will have to unravel someone elses sophisticated code in the future. Understanding the right-left rule helps to unravel complex declarations.

TYPICAL OPERATION

In this operation you enter, compile, and execute the program given in Example 21.1.

1. Begin at the DOS prompt, in your C source code directory. Invoke your text editor.
2. Type the C program given in Example 21.1, just like it is listed. Call the program DATA21.C.
3. Compile and link the program with your C compiler.

4. Type **DATA21** and press **Enter**. Notice the following output on your screen:

```
C:\C>DATA21
Name= Bob White, Nbr= 12056
C:\C>_
```

5. Turn to Module 16 to continue the learning sequence.

Module 22

DO-WHILE

```
NAME

   do-while    -- executes a body of instructions at least one
                  time, and more if an expression remains true.

USAGE

    do
    {
          /* c code to execute once, and then repeat while
             expression remains true  */

     }    while ( expression ) ;

    /* next instruction here */
```

DESCRIPTION

The *do-while* statement is a loop statement that allows its body of instructions to be executed one or more times. The body of instructions in a *do-while* loop always executes at least once. The body of the *do* statement continues to execute as long as the result of the expression in the *while* statement remains true (non-zero).

Example 22.1, example of *do-while* statement:

```
/*                          program name:   do1.c             */
main()
{
  int      i , j ;

           i = 0 ;    j = 0 ;

           do                                                 /* line 1 */
           {                                                  /* line 2 */
                      j = j + 2*i ;
                      i++ ;
           }                                                  /* line 3 */
           while ( i < 10 );                                  /* line 4 */

           printf( "j = %d\n" , j );

}     /*   end of main   */
```

Line 1 through line 4 is an example of the *do-while* statement.

Line 2 through line 3 contain the body of statements that are conditionally executed for this *do-while* statement.

Line 4 contains the expression that is evaluated to determine if the body of statements executes again. The body of statements executes until the variable i equals or exceeds 10.

The output of Example 22.1 is:

```
j = 90
```

Example 22.2, another example of *do-while* statement:

```
/*                          program name:   do2.c               */
/* Purpose: sum the numbers from 1 to 10 */
main()
{
int sum    , number ;

     sum = 0 ;  number = 10 ;                          /* line 1 */
     do                                                /* line 2 */
     {
          sum += number ;                              /* line 3 */
          number-- ;                                   /* line 4 */
     }   while ( number > 0 );                         /* line 5 */

     printf ( "sum = %d \n" , sum );                   /* line 6 */

} /* end of main */
```

The output of DO1.C is:

```
sum = 55
```

The first time line 5 is reached the program has executed lines 3 and 4 (the body of the do-while) one time and number is equal to 9. Therefore control is transfered to line 3 for the body to be executed again. This continues until the body of the do-while has executed 10 times, and this time when line 5 is reached, number is equal to 0. Since 0 is not > than 0, control is passed to line 6 as the do-while is complete.

Sequence of events for *do-while* statement:

1) Encounter *do* statement and proceed to first instruction in body of *do-while* statement.
2) Execute all instructions in body of *do-while* statement.
3) Evaluate the expression in the *while* statement.
4) If the expression is true, control transfers to step #2 in this sequence.
5) If the expression is false, control transfers to the instruction following the *while* statement.

DO-WHILE STATEMENT FLOWCHART The following flowchart shows the sequence of events that occur in the execution of a *do-while* statement.

Form of do-while statement:

```
do
{
    body_of_do_while
}
    while  ( expression );
```

Flowchart:

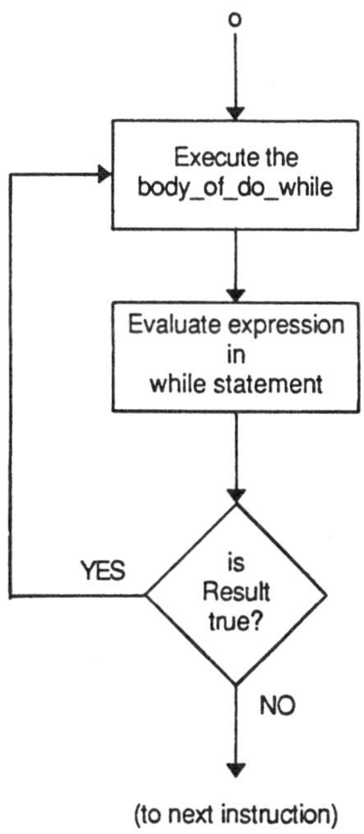

APPLICATIONS

The do-while loop is ideally suited for constructing a loop that must be executed at least one time, but it is impossible to determine in advance exactly how many executions are necessary.

One ideal application for the do-while loop is the construction of an input routine with error checking. The input operation must always be performed at least once, but there is no way of knowing in advance exactly how many tries it is going to take the user to input the data correctly. The user is repeatedly prompted for input until the input data passes the input validation test.

TYPICAL OPERATION

In this operation you enter, compile, and execute the program in Example 22.1.

1. Begin at the DOS prompt, in your C source code directory. Invoke your text editor.
2. Type the C program given in Example 22.1, just like it is listed. Call the program DO1.C.
3. Compile and link the program with your C compiler.
4. Type **DO1** and press **Enter**. Notice the following output on your screen:

```
C:\C>DO1
j = 90
C:\C>_
```

5. Type the C program given in Example 22.2, just like it is listed. Call the program DO2.C.
6. Compile and link the program with your C compiler.
7. Type **DO2** and press **Enter**. Notice the following output on your screen:

```
C:\C>DO2
sum = 55
C:\C>_
```

8. Calculate the values for DO1.C and DO2.C by hand to verify that these programs are calculating the correct values.
9. Turn to Module 31 to continue the learning sequence.

Module 23

EOF

```
NAME

    eof  -- tests whether end-of-file has been reached for a
            file opened as a low-level file.

USAGE

     int      eof ( int fd ) ;

PROTOTYPE in       io.h

RETURNS
       returns 1 if a file is at end-of-file, else returns 0
```

DESCRIPTION

The *eof* low-level function tests whether the file associated with the file descriptor is at end-of-file. If so, *eof* returns a value of 1; otherwise, it returns 0.

Example 23.1, an example using the *eof* function:

```
/*                    program name:        eof1.c          */
#include <io.h>
#include <fcntl.h>      /* defines O_RDWR                  line 1 */
main()
{
 int      fd , read_cnt , mode ;
 char     buffer [ 512 ];


         mode = O_RDWR  ;

         fd = open( "eof1.bok" , mode );

         read_cnt = read ( fd , buffer , 512 );

         if ( eof( fd )  == 1 )                          /* line 2 */
              printf( "file is at end-of-file.\n");
         else printf( "file is not at end-of-file.\n");

}      /* end of main */
```

Line 1 includes the file that define the file modes.

Line 2 is an example of the *eof* function call. It returns a value of 1 if at end-of-file, else it returns a value of 0.

APPLICATIONS

The eof function is normally called ahead of each read function to determine if end-of-file has been reached for a low-level file. When end-of-file is reached for a source file, then processing for the file terminates.

TYPICAL OPERATION

In this operation you enter, compile, and execute the program given in Example 23.1.

1. Begin at the DOS prompt, in your C source code directory. Invoke your text editor.
2. Type the C program given in Example 23.1, just like it is listed. Call the program EOF1.C.
3. Compile and link the program with your C compiler.
4. Type **EOF1** and press **Enter**. Notice the following output on your screen:

```
C:\C>EOF1
file is not at end-of-file.
C:\C>_
```

5. Turn to Module 49 to continue the learning sequence.

Module 24

EXIT

```
NAME

   exit  —  terminates a program normally

USAGE

    void    exit ( int status ) ;

PROTOTYPE in      stdlib.h

ANSI Synopsis

    #include <stdlib.h>
    void   exit (int status);

RETURNS
        no return value
```

DESCRIPTION

The *exit* function is the program termination call. This function call stops the execution of the program and returns control to the operating system. It writes all high-level input/output function buffers to disk and closes all open files.

The *exit* function is optional when it is the last statement in the main function. If C reaches the closing brace in the main function, it calls the *exit* function to end execution.

Some operating systems return the low byte of the *exit* function argument (status) to the operating system. Refer to your C compiler manual and operating system manual for more information.

Example 24.1, an example using *exit* function:

```
/*                         program name:    exit1.c        */
#include <stdlib.h>
main()
{
int error_flag ;

   error_flag = 1 ;

   /*  coding .... */

   if ( error_flag )
   {
        printf ( "error, program exiting....\n" );
        exit ( 0xff );                                    /* line 1 */
   }

}  /* end of main */
```

Line 1 is an example of returning a value to the operating system when the program performs the *exit* function call. The exit status is 255 (0xff) in this example, which normally indicates an error, as only an exit value of 0 indicates normal exit.

APPLICATIONS

The typical application of the exit function is to terminate the execution of a program for some error condition. For example, when the program encounters an error condition it prompts the user to enter yes if they want to end the execution of the program. If they enter yes, the program executes the exit function to immediately terminate the program.

TYPICAL OPERATION

In this operation you enter, compile, and execute the program given in Example 24.1.

1. Begin at the DOS prompt, in your C source code directory. Invoke your text editor.
2. Type the C program given in Example 24.1, just like it is listed. Call the program EXIT1.C.
3. Compile and link the program with your C compiler.
4. Type **EXIT1** and press **Enter**. Notice the following output on your screen:

```
C:\C>EXIT1
error, program exiting....
C:\C>_
```

5. Turn to Module 7 to continue the learning sequence.

Module 25

FCLOSE

```
NAME

   fclose --  closes a stream file

USAGE

  int     fclose ( FILE *fptr );

PROTOTYPE in      stdio.h

ANSI Synopsis

    #include <stdio.h>
    int   fclose(FILE *stream );

RETURNS
       returns 0 if closed properly, else -1 if an error
       occurs
```

DESCRIPTION

The *fclose* function writes the memory-buffered data to disk and then closes the stream file. A file must be opened again before it can be read from or written to. The *fclose* function returns a 0 if the file is closed properly. If an error occurs, a −1 is returned.

The actual error number can be retrieved from *errno* after an *fclose* error.

Example 25.1, an example using the *fclose* function:

```
/*                  program name:      fclose1.c        */
#include <stdio.h>
main()
{
    FILE    *stream ;
    int     status  ;

    stream = fopen ("fclose1.c", "r" );    /* open for reading */

    /* other file i/o goes here..... */
```

```
        status = fclose ( stream );                              /* line 1 */

        if ( status == -1 )
             printf( "file was not closed properly." );
        else printf( "file was closed properly." );

    }      /* end of main */
```

Line 1 is an example of the *fclose* function call. It is closing the stream file named "fclose1.c." The *fclose* function call is made after all reading or writing to a file is done.

APPLICATIONS

Most computer operating systems do not require the computer program to close the files that are open; the operating system does this automatically when a program terminates. One thing to remember is that there is a limit to the number of files that a program can have open at any one time, so it may be necessary to close some files that need not be open any longer in order to open other files that are needed. It is a good idea to always close a file as soon as it can be determined that the processing of a particular file is completed. If you do not close a file immediately after writing new data to it, it is possible the new data may be lost if the electricity goes off or the computer encounters a catastrophic error.

TYPICAL OPERATION

In this operation you enter, compile, and execute the program given in Example 25.1.

1. Begin at the DOS prompt, in your C source code directory. Invoke your text editor.
2. Type the C program given in Example 25.1, just like it is listed. Call the program FCLOSE1.C.
3. Compile and link the program with your C compiler.
4. Type **FCLOSE1** and press **Enter**. Notice the following output on your screen:

```
C:\C>FCLOSE1
file was closed properly.
C:\C>_
```

5. Turn to Module 27 to continue the learning sequence.

Module 26
FERROR

```
NAME

   ferror -- tests for an error on a stream file

USAGE

  int    ferror  ( FILE *stream ) ;

PROTOTYPE in      stdio.h

ANSI Synopsis

    #include <stdio.h>
    int   ferror(FILE *stream);

RETURNS
        returns nonzero value to indicate an error, else 0
```

DESCRIPTION

The *ferror* function tests for an error on a stream file. Testing for an error does not reset the error flag (*clearerr* resets the error flag). The error flag is also reset if the file is closed and then opened again, or if the rewind function is called to position the file pointer back to the front of the file.

The *ferror* function returns a non-zero value to indicate an error. If the error flag is not set for the stream, a value of 0 is returned.

Example 26.1, an example using the *ferror* function:

```
/*                program name:      ferror1.c        */
#include <stdio.h>
main()
{
    FILE    *stream ;
    int     crr ;


    stream = fopen ("filename", "w" );   /* open - write */

    /*  ...    other file i/o performed here...    */
```

```
        err = ferror ( stream ) ;                              /* line 1 */

        if ( err != 0 )
             printf ( "an error has occurred for file. " );
        else printf ( "no errors have occured for this file." );

    }    /* end of main */
```

Line 1 is an example of the ferror function call. If the value returned from the *ferror* function call is a non-zero value, then an error occurred in the file i/o.

APPLICATIONS

For a computer to be of value, it must be able to read and write data accurately. When a program cannot either read or write data accurately, the computer program must report this condition to the computer operator. The ferror function can be called after reading and writing of data to see if an error has occurred, and if so, either retry the operation or report it to the computer operator. The computer operator must then correct the problem before processing can continue.

TYPICAL OPERATION

In this operation you enter, compile, and execute the program given in Example 26.1.

1. Begin at the DOS prompt, in your C source code directory. Invoke your text editor.
2. Type the C program given in Example 26.1, just like it is listed. Call the program FERROR1.C.
3. Compile and link the program with your C compiler.
4. Type **FERROR1** and press **Enter**. Notice the following output on your screen:

```
C:\C>FERROR1
no errors have occured for this file.
C:\C>_
```

Note that this example, when executed as it is without any other file instructions, prints the message indicating no errors. However, this example does demonstrate to you that your C compiler recognizes the *ferror* function.

5. Turn to Module 55 to continue the learning sequence.

Module 27

FGETC

```
NAME

   fgetc  --  reads a single character from input stream

USAGE

   int      fgetc ( FILE *stream );

PROTOTYPE in       stdio.h

ANSI Synopsis

    #include <stdio.h>
    int    fgetc(FILE *stream);

RETURNS
         returns the character read, or EOF if end-of-file
         is reached
```

DESCRIPTION

The *fgetc* function reads a single character from the input stream file from the current position. It returns the character read or an EOF if the end-of-file is reached. The character is returned as an integer, without sign extended. Therefore the character value is always positive.

The actual error number can be retrieved from errno when an error occurs with the *fgetc* function.

Example 27.1, an example using the *fgetc* function:

```
/*                     program name:      fgetc1.c          */
#include <stdio.h>
main()
{
    FILE    *stream ;
    int      c ;

    stream = fopen ("fgetc1.c", "r" );    /* open for read */
```

```
    c = fgetc ( stream );                              /* line 1 */

    if ( c == EOF )
    {
        printf( "end of file has been reached." );
    }
    else printf ( "character read is: %c\n" , c );

    fclose ( stream );

}   /* end of main */
```

Line 1 is an example of the fgetc function call. Notice that the returned character is assigned to an *int* type variable because the EOF indicator is an integer minus one.

APPLICATIONS

The fgetc function is used to read data files when the files must be processed a byte at a time. Binary data files with variable length data records are often read with the fgetc function, unlike C source programs that are line-oriented text data that end with a newline character and can be processed a line at a time.

TYPICAL OPERATION

In this operation you enter, compile, and execute the program given in Example 27.1.

1. Begin at the DOS prompt, in your C source code directory. Invoke your text editor.
2. Type the C program given in Example 27.1, just like it is listed. Call the program FGETC1.C.
3. Compile and link the program with your C compiler.
4. Type **FGETC1** and press **Enter**. Notice the following output on your screen:

```
C:\C>FGETC1
character read is: /
C:\C>_
```

5. Turn to Module 28 to continue the learning sequence.

Module 28

FGETS

```
NAME

   fgets  --  reads a string from input stream

USAGE

  char    *fgets( char *cstring , int count , FILE *stream ) ;

PROTOTYPE in      stdio.h

ANSI Synopsis

    #include <stdio.h>
    char  *fgets(noalias char *s, int n , FILE *stream);

RETURNS
         returns the string read in cstring and a pointer to
         the string, or a NULL pointer if an error is
         encountered
```

DESCRIPTION

The *fgets* function reads a string from an input stream. It reads characters from the input stream until, either a '\n' character is found in the input stream, or the number of characters specified by count, minus one, has been read. A '\0' character is placed at the end of the string to indicate end-of-string.

Note that the '\n' character, when encountered in a string input with the *fgets* function, is retained in the string.

The actual error number can be retrieved from *errno* when an error occurs using the *fgets* function.

Example 28.1, an example using the *fgets* function:

```
/*                    program name:     fgets1.c              */
#include <stdio.h>
main()
{
    FILE    *stream ;
    char    name [ 81 ] , *status_ptr ;
```

```
        stream = fopen ("fgets1.c", "r" ) ;  /* open for read */

        status_ptr = fgets( name , 80 , stream );          /* line 1 */

        if ( status_ptr == NULL )
            printf( "attempted to read past end-of-file." );
        else printf ( "line = %s\n" , name );

    }    /* end of main */
```

Line 1 is an example of the fgets function call. This function call either reads 79 characters or reads until an '\n' character is found. A '\0' is placed onto the end of the string by the fgets function before it returns. In this example, there can be 80 characters of data plus the '\0' character; or there can be up to 79 characters of data plus the '\n' character plus the '\0' character.

Note that 61 characters are read in this example. There are sixty characters in the program name line plus the new-line character. The EOS character is stored to mark the end-of-string. Most users write a function to remove the new-line from the end of this line of input as it is not needed. Try doing that as an exercise.

The output from this example is:

```
    line = /*                   program name:      fgets1.c             */
```

APPLICATIONS

When performing input, use the fgets function to input text data that ends with the newline character. C programs are text files that end with the newline character, and therefore can be read with the fgets function.

TYPICAL OPERATION

In this operation you enter, compile, and execute the program given in Example 28.1.

1. Begin at the DOS prompt, in your C source code directory. Invoke your text editor.
2. Type the C program given in Example 28.1, just like it is listed. Call the program FGETS1.C.
3. Compile and link the program with your C compiler.
4. Type **FGETS1** and press **Enter**. Notice the following output on your screen:

```
C:\C>FGETS1
line = /*                   program name:      fgets1.c             */

C:\C>_
```

Explain the extra blank line in the output displayed by this example.

5. Turn to Module 42 to continue the learning sequence.

Module 29
FILE INPUT/OUTPUT

DESCRIPTION

This module introduces the disk filing system functions provided in the C standard library. This module describes how to manage information on disk. It describes the functions available to create a new file, to open an existing file, to read and write to files, and finally to close files. Other functions available are also described.

HIGH-LEVEL vs LOW-LEVEL FUNCTIONS The disk functions are divided into two categories:

- high-level functions
- low-level functions

High-level functions provide access to the data on disk in a more manageable way than the low-level functions. The high-level functions provide buffering of the data but allow access of the data a byte or a line at a time. The high-level functions call the low-level functions during execution. The high-level functions are preferred for their ease of use and portability. Files that are accessed with the high-level routines are called *streams*.

The low-level functions provide access usually in a way that is operating-system-dependent, typically a disk sector at a time. Low-level files are accessed with a number called a *file descriptor*.

Some of the high-level functions in the standard library are:

fopen	Open a file as a stream
fclose	Close a stream file
fgetc	Read a character from a stream
fgets	Read a string from a stream
getc	Read a character from a stream
fscanf	Read formatted input from a stream
fputc	Write a character to a stream
fputs	Write a string to a stream
putc	Write a character to a stream
fprintf	Write formatted output to a stream
fseek	Position a file to a desired location
ungetc	Write character back to a stream
ferror	See if an error occurred
perror	Display error message
clearerr	Clear error flag
feof	Check for end-of-file

Some of the low-level functions in the standard library are:

creat	Create a file
open	Open a file
close	Close a file
read	Read data from a file
write	Write data to a file
lseek	Position a file to a desired location
eof	Test for end of file
unlink	Remove a file from file system

One thing to remember is that you cannot mix the high- and low-level functions. The *open* statement for one level is not compatible with the *read* or *write* from the other level. As you study the following diagrams of the high- and low-level functions, this becomes more clear.

GENERALIZED PROGRAM FLOW These diagrams are provided to help you see the difference between *file descriptors* and *streams*. These diagrams are very general in nature but provide insight into the inner workings of the functions. Consult your compiler manual and your DOS manual for more details of your filing system functions.

The acronyms used in the following diagrams are:

fn	file name (pathname if applicable)
o	file operation desired — see your compiler manual
m	mode: read, write, read/write
fd	file descriptor
*fptr	pointer to a FILE for a stream
count	number of bytes to transfer
n	maximum number of bytes to transfer
c	a character
flag	result of operation flag
buf	memory buffer that holds the characters
x	operating-system-dependent arguments

HIGH-LEVEL DIAGRAMS Study the following diagrams of high-level functions.

fopen

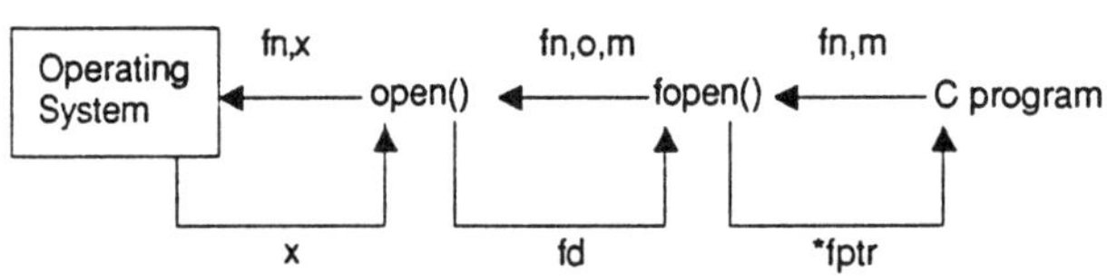

Explanation of *fopen* example:

- The C program calls the *fopen* function with a filename and an open mode.
- The *fopen* function allocates buffers for the file and then calls the *open* function with the filename, the mode, and a file operation.
- The *open* function calls the operating system with a filename and other operating-system-dependent arguments.
- The operating system attempts to open the appropriate disk file. It returns information to the *open* function to let it know if it opened the file.
- If the file opens successfully, the *open* function returns a file descriptor to the *fopen* function, else it returns a 0 value.
- The *fopen* function returns to the C statement a file pointer to the opened file if it opens, else it returns a NULL value.
- The file pointer is used by other high-level functions to read and/or write to the file just opened.

Descriptions comparable to the preceding one can be written for each of the following diagrams left as an exercise for you.

fclose

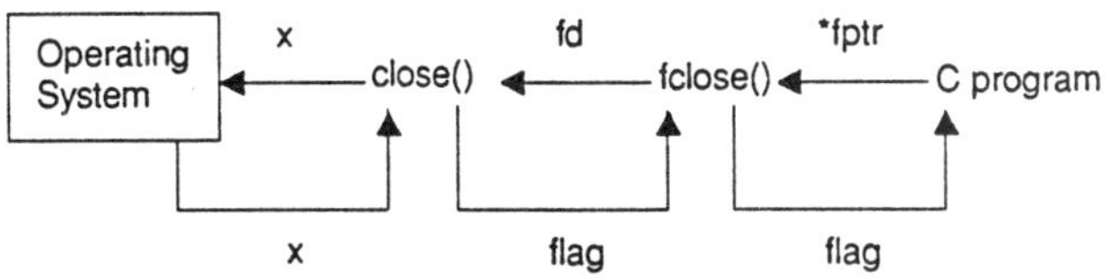

fgetc

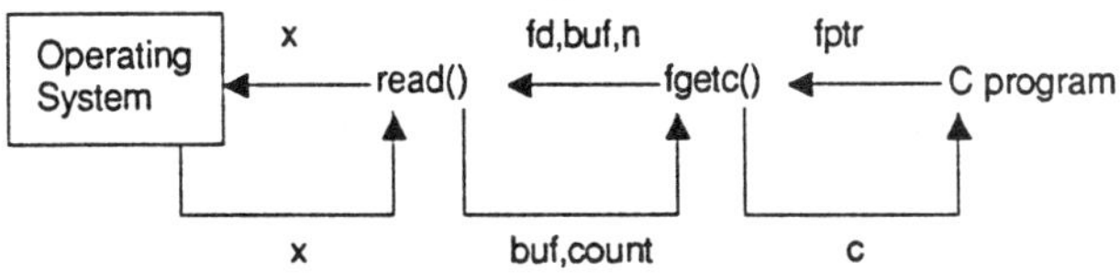

fputc

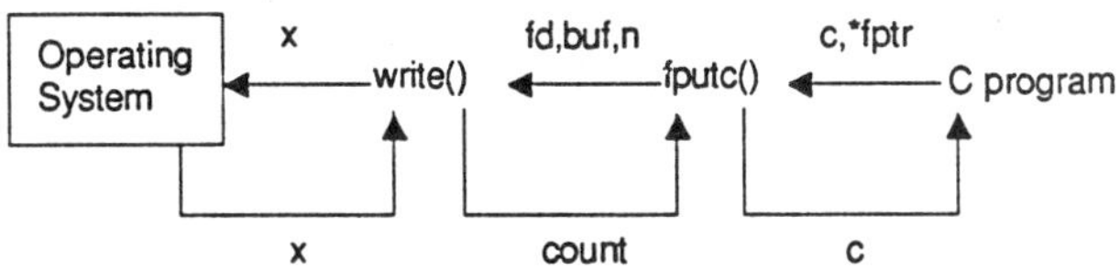

LOW-LEVEL DIAGRAMS Study and describe the following low-level function diagrams.

open

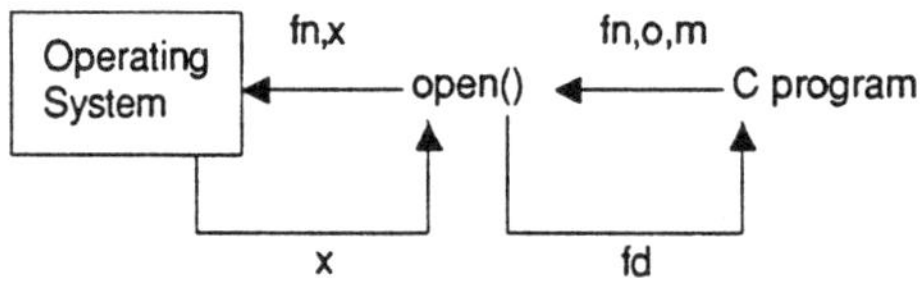

close

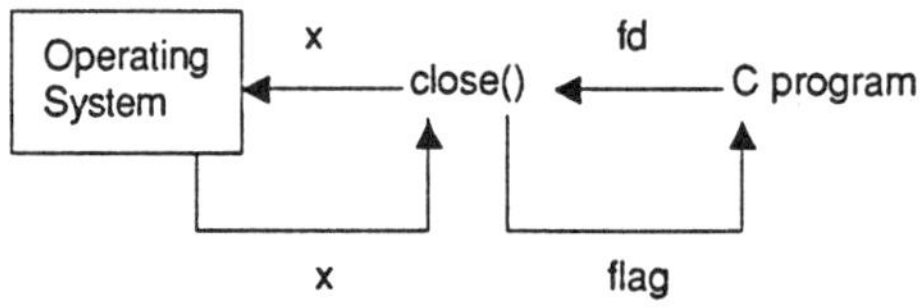

read

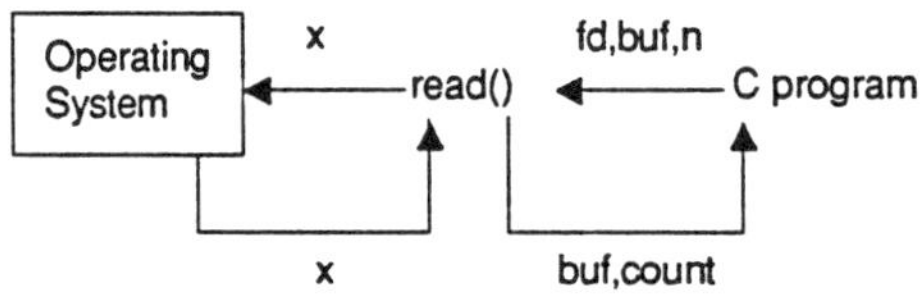

write

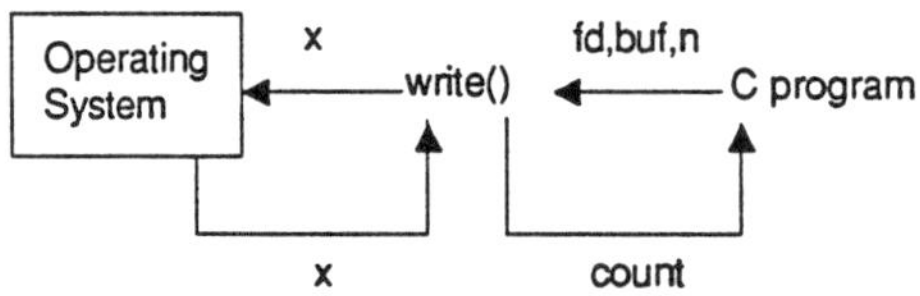

GENERAL INFORMATION CONCERNING I/O Before a file can be accessed in a program it must be opened. Before the program stops executing it must close all opened files.

When an error is encountered in the high-level routines, they return a flag value to indicate the error. You must refer to the variable *errno* to get the actual error number. The *perror* function can be called to display an error message based on *errno*. The function *clearerr* can be called to clear the error number. A few functions do not tell the caller of an error, but the function *ferror* can be called to see if an error occurred.

In all high-level functions, the *stdin*, *stdout*, and *stderr* stream files can be used instead of an actual data file. The *stdin* stream can be used with the input functions, and the *stdout* and the *stderr* streams can be used with the output functions. To use these streams, use the reference of *stdin*, *stdout*, or *stderr* for the stream argument. Using these streams causes the high-level function to get its input from, or output its data to, the computer console.

APPLICATIONS

Files are used to store computer information in a manner such that it can be recalled and used. C programs are stored as files on disk and are converted to executable object files on disk. Almost all computer programs either read or write data files so the C programmer must be able to use the C functions for opening, closing, reading, and writing files.

Turn to Module 26 to continue the learning sequence.

Module 30

FOPEN

```
NAME

   fopen  --  opens a file as a stream file

USAGE

   FILE  *fopen (char *filename , char *access ) ;

PROTOTYPE in      stdio.h

ANSI Synopsis

    #include <stdio.h>
    FILE  *fopen(const noalias char *filename,
                 const noalias char *mode );

RETURNS
        returns a pointer to the file, a NULL pointer if an
        error
```

DESCRIPTION

The *fopen* function opens a file as a stream for a specific type of access. A file must be opened before it can be accessed. Files can be opened for reading, writing, reading/writing, and appending. The access mode is given when the file is opened.

The access mode is one of the following:

"r"	open to read from the file as a stream which exists else the fopen fails
"w"	open to write to the file as a stream and if it exists its contents are destroyed
"a"	open to write to the end of a file (append) as a stream
"r + "	open to both read and write to the file as a stream which exists else the fopen fails
"w + "	open to both read and write to the file as a stream and if the file exists its contents are destroyed
"a + "	write to end of a file (append) as a stream, if the file does not exist it is created

The above access modes are for text files. To make the modes applicable for binary files, append a 'b:' "rb," "wb," "ab," "r + b," "w + b," and "a + b."

The *fopen* function returns a *stream pointer* to the file. If an error occurs, a NULL pointer is returned. When the file is *fopened*, the pointer is positioned at the beginning of the file for "r" and "w" access, or at the end of the file for "a" access.

The actual error number can be retrieved from *errno*.

The following high-level functions can be used with the *fopen* function:

> *fclose, fprintf, fgetc, fgets, getc, fscanf, fputc, fputs, putc, fseek, ungetc, ferror, perror,* and *clearerr*.

Example 30.1, an example using the *fopen* function:

```
/*                      program name:       fopen1.c        */
#include <stdio.h>
#include <errno.h>
main()
{
    FILE     *stream ;

    stream = fopen ("fopen1.c", "r" );    /* open for read */    /* line 1 */

    if ( stream == NULL )                                         /* line 2 */
        printf( "ERROR: %d, file can not be opened.", errno );
    else printf ( "file opened properly...\n" );

}   /* end of main */
```

Line 1 is an example of the *fopen* statement. If the file is available for read access, then a pointer to the file is returned. If the file is not available, then a NULL pointer is returned to the calling function and stored here in the variable named stream.

Line 2 checks the results of the *fopen* function and here displays a message indicating the results. The results of all *fopen* functions should be checked and the appropriate action taken for each specific error condition.

APPLICATIONS

Before a file can be accessed, the file must be opened successfully. The file must also be opened in the correct mode, because if a file is opened in the write mode and the file contains data, the data in that file is lost. Be sure a file is opened successfully before performing any reading or writing to the file. The fopen function returns a NULL pointer when the file is not opened successfully.

TYPICAL OPERATION

In this operation you enter, compile, and execute the program given in Example 30.1.

1. Begin at the DOS prompt, in your C source code directory. Invoke your text editor.
2. Type the C program given in Example 30.1, just like it is listed. Call the program FOPEN1.C.

3. Compile and link the program with your C compiler.
4. Type **FOPEN1** and press **Enter**. Notice the following output on your screen:

```
C:\C>FOPEN1
file opened properly...
C:\C>_
```

5. Turn to Module 25 to continue the learning sequence.

Module 31
FOR

```
NAME

    for — loop statement that executes a body of
          instructions as long as expression 2 (as
          impacted by expression 2 or the body of the
          for) remains true.

USAGE

    for ( expression1 ; expression2 ; expression3 )
    {
          /*  C code to execute during for  */
    }
```

DESCRIPTION

The *for* statement is a loop instruction that provides an initialization part, an expression evaluation for terminating the loop, and a part to prepare for the next iteration of the loop. All three expressions are required, but a null statement is valid for one of the expressions. The semicolons separating the expressions are required.

Using the *for* statement greatly simplifies loops and makes the intent of the loop obvious because all of the control expressions concerning the loop are together.

The expressions in the *for* statement are:

- Expression1 is the initialization part. It always executes just once, as the first step in the execution process.
- Expression2 is the test_expression_condition for terminating the loop. The test_expression_condition is evaluated each time to see if the body should execute. The body executes when the result of the expression is true.
- Expression3 is the part which prepares for the next iteration of the loop. It also executes once for each time the body of instructions executes. This expression usually manipulates a variable that is used in expression2.

Example 31.1, example of *for* statement:

```
 *                          program name:    for1.c            */
main()
{
        int   i , j = 0 ;
/*
Example to display the numbers from 1 to 8 and their sum on
the standard output device (terminal).
*/

           for ( i = 1  ;                               /* line 1 */
                           i <= 8   ;                   /* line 2 */
                                    i++ )              /* line 3 */
           {
                  printf( "%d ", i ) ;                  /* line 4 */

                  j += i ;                              /* line 5 */
           }
           printf( "  summed = %d \n", j );             /* line 6 */

}   /* end of main  */
```

The output of Example 31.1 is:

```
1 2 3 4 5 6 7 8   summed = 36
```

Line 1 contains expression1, the i = 1 statement. This line is the initialization line and executes just once. Usually the lines 1 to 3 are on the same line; they were separated only for reference purposes in this example.

Line 2 contains expression2, the i < = 8 statement. This line is evaluated and the result of the evaluation determines whether or not the body of the *for* statement executes. The body executes as long as the result of this expression remains true (non-zero).

Line 3 contains expression3, the i + + statement. In this example, this line executes and modifies the variable that is used in expression2 for determining whether to stop executing the body of instructions.

Line 4 and line 5 are the instructions that make up the *for* body. They execute as long as the result of expression2 remains true.

Line 6 receives control and executes as soon as the result of expression2 is false.

Example 31.2, another example of *for* statement:

```
/*                       program name:    for2.c            */
/* Purpose: sum the numbers from 1 to 10 */
main()
{
int sum    , number ;

     for ( sum = 0 , number = 1 ; number <= 10 ; number++ )  /* line 1 */
          sum += number ;                                    /* line 2 */

     printf ( "sum = %d \n" , sum );                         /* line 3 */

} /* end of main */
```

The output of Example 31.2 is:

```
sum = 55
```

The first time the for statment executes it initializes the value of sum to 0 and the value of number to 1. C then tests to see if it has to execute the body of the for by evaluating the expression number < = 10. Since the value of number is 1, it executes the body of the for, which is line 2. C then evaluates the third expression which increments number by one to prepare for the next iteration of the loop. C again tests to see if it has to execute the body of the for by evaluating expression 2, number < = 10. Since the value of number is now 2, C executes the body of the for again. When it has executed the body of the for ten times and prepared for the next iteration, the value of number is 11. This time the test in expression 2 is false and control is passed to line 3.

Sequence of events in a *for* statement:

1) Expression1 executes. (It only executes this one time.)
2) Expression2 is evaluated for a resulting value.
3) If result of expression2 is not zero (true), execution continues with step 4 in this sequence of events. If the result is false, control transfers to the statement following the *for* statement, step 7.
4) The body of C code in the *for* statement executes.
5) Expression3 executes.
6) Control transfers back to step 2 in this sequence of events.
7) Control transfers to the statement following the body of the *for* statement when the result of step 2 is false; execution resumes with this instruction.

FOR STATEMENT FLOWCHART

The following flowchart shows the sequence of events that occur in the execution of a *for* statement.

Form of *for* statement:

```
for ( expression1 ; expression2 ; expression3 )
{
    body_of_C_code_in_for_statement
}
```

Flowchart:

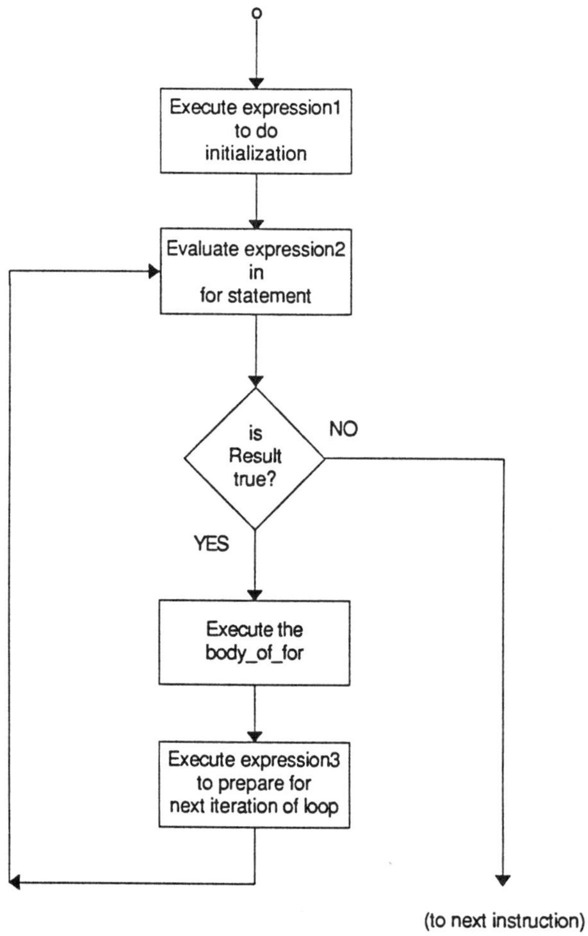

APPLICATIONS

The *for* loop is ideally suited for constructing a loop that executes one or more times, until a specific condition is met.

One application of the *for* loop is in a program where the first and last name is kept in one field, separated by a comma, with the last name first. The *for* loop works ideally because last names vary in length and the *for* loop continues to execute until the comma is reached or until the last character in the field is reached. In this example the loop is executed until either of the two terminating conditions is met.

TYPICAL OPERATION

In this operation you enter, compile, and execute the programs in Example 32.1 and Example 32.2.

1. Begin at the DOS prompt, in your C source code directory. Invoke your text editor.
2. Type the C program given in Example 31.1, just like it is listed. Call the program FOR1.C.
3. Compile and link the program with your C compiler.
4. Type **FOR1** and press **Enter**. Notice the following output on your screen:

```
C:\C>FOR1
1 2 3 4 5 6 7 8     summed = 36
C:\C>_
```

5. Type the C program given in Example 32.2, just like it is listed. Call the program FOR2.C.
6. Compile and link the program with your C compiler.
7. Type **FOR2** and press **Enter**. Notice the following output on your screen:

```
C:\C>FOR2
sum = 55
C:\C>_
```

8. Turn to Module 81 to continue the learning sequence.

Module 32

FPRINTF, VFPRINTF

```
NAME

   fprintf   --  displays formatted output to an output stream
  vfprintf   --  displays formatted output to an output stream

USAGE

   int      fprintf ( FILE *stream , char *output-string , ... ) ;
   int     vfprintf ( FILE *stream , char *output-string ,
                                                   va_list arg_ptr ) ;

PROTOTYPE in      stdio.h

ANSI Synopsis

    #include <stdio.h>
    int  fprintf(FILE *stream, const noalias char *format, ...);

    #include <stdio.h>
    #include <stdarg.h>
    int  vfprintf(FILE *stream, const noalias char *format,
                                                   va_list  arg_ptr );

RETURNS
       returns the number of characters output to the stream.
```

DESCRIPTION

The *fprintf* function is used to format output to the specified stream. Formatted output means that the data to be displayed can be of one data type, but that it can be output in the same or a different data type. It also means the number of decimal places can be specified and that the minus sign or plus sign can be affixed to signed numbers.

Besides containing the codes describing the output format of the data, the output string can also contain a series of characters that are directly output to the stream. Any characters that are not part of an output specification string are directly output.

The input data types of the arguments include all integers, floating point, character, and character strings. The output data types include signed and unsigned decimal, octal, hex, exponential, character, and character strings.

OUTPUT-STRING The output-string contains two types of information:

- It contains an *output format specification* field.
- It contains a series of characters that are directly output to the standard output device.

The output-string is read from left to right. When the first format specification is encountered, the first argument is output in the appropriate output format. If there are more arguments than output format specifications, the extra arguments are ignored, but the output may not be as desired. If there are too few arguments, the output is unpredictable.

OUTPUT FORMAT SPECIFICATION FIELD The % character is used to specify that formatting is to begin in the output character string. The character(s) following % specify the output data format. Following the output format specifier, either another formatted output field or characters to be output directly can begin.

No arguments are necessary if there are no format specification fields in the output format string.

The general form of an output format specification field is:

```
%[flag][width][.precision][L]type
```

The format specification begins with the % and ends with the desired output data type. It can contain four other optional fields. A description of the optional fields is followed here by a table describing the output data type:

flag	The *flag* controls the justification of the data. The five flags are explained in the next table.
width	The *width* controls the minimum number of characters that are to be output for this argument. If the output width is less than this specifier, the output is padded with blanks. An asterisk is a valid entry, meaning that the width is contained in an argument to this function.
precision	The *precision* controls the number of digits output. For strings, this specifies the maximum number of characters to output. For floating point E and F, this specifies how many digits are to appear after the decimal point. For floating point G, this specifies the maximum number of significiant digits. For the other types, it specifies the minimum number of digits to output. An asterisk is a valid entry, meaning that the width is contained in an argument to this function.
L	The L character (uppercase or lowercase is acceptable) is used if a long integer or long double argument is expected.

NOTE

All of the above optional flags can be used together which gives you complete control over the formatted output.

Flags for Data Output Table

Character	*Flag*	*Output Format*
–	justification flag	The data is left-justified when the minus sign is present.
+	sign flag	The data value is always to be displayed with plus or minus sign.
0	zero padded on left side flag	The data is zero-padded on left and not space-padded.
space	sign conversion	If signed data field and a positive number, use space for sign character.
#	alternate form	Don't remove trailing zeroes from G type. Include decimal on E, F, G types. Place 0x on hexadecimal type. Put 0 in front of octal numbers.
*	minimum field width	The asterisk specifies that the next argument to the fprintf function indicates the minimum number of positions to be used to output data value.
L	argument is long type flag	The input argument is a long data type.
.	next field is precision field	The next field in the specifier is the precision field.
1 to n	precision field	The precision field specifies the maximum number of characters to output for *d,u,o,x* type. This is exact number of characters to output for float and double.
*	precision field	The asterisk specifies that the next argument to the fprintf function indicates the number of decimal places after decimal point.

Output Data Type Table

Character	*Input Type*	*Output Format*
d	integer	The argument is output in signed decimal notation.
u	integer	The argument is output in unsigned decimal notation.
o	integer	The argument is output in unsigned octal notation with a leading zero.
x	integer	The argument is output in unsigned hexadecimal notation with the 0x.
c	character	Output is a single character.
p	pointer	Output is a pointer.
s	string of characters	The argument is output until either the \0 character is reached in the string or the precision is reached.
e	floating point	Output is in exponential format of the form [–]m.nnnnnnE[+ –]xx, where n is the precision; default is 6.
f	floating point	Output is in signed decimal notation of the form [–]mmm.nnnnnn, where n is the precision; default is 6.
g	floating point	Output uses either the %e or %f notation, whichever is shorter. Insignificant zeros are not shown.

Example 32.1, an example using the fprintf function:

```
/*                     program name:       fprintf1.c           */
#include <stdio.h>
main()
{
  int    dollars = 12 , cents = 5 ;
  float  f = 456.789 ;

    stream = fopen( "test.fpf" , "w" );

    if ( stream == NULL )
    {
         printf( "could not open file test.fpf\n" );
         exit ( 0 );
    }
                              /*  examples of formatted output to stream file */
                                                    /* output is:             */
    fprintf( stream , "\n'%d'" ,  23456  );    /* '23456'                  */
    fprintf( stream , "\n'%8d'",  23456  );    /* '   23456'               */
    fprintf( stream , "\n'%08d'", 23456  );    /* '00023456'               */
    fprintf( stream , "\n'%-8d'", 23456  );    /* '23456   '               */

    fprintf( stream , "\n'%x'",   255    );    /* 'ff'                     */
    fprintf( stream , "\n'%4x'",  254    );    /* '  fe'                   */
    fprintf( stream , "\n'%04x'", 100    );    /* '0064'                   */
    fprintf( stream , "\n'%-4x'", 101    );    /* '65  '                   */
    fprintf( stream , "\n'%c%c'", '9', '$' );  /* '9$'                     */
    fprintf( stream , "\n'%s'"  , "testing");  /* 'testing'                */
    fprintf( stream , "\n'%10s'", "testing");  /* '   testing'             */
    fprintf( stream , "\n'%-10s'","testing");  /* 'testing   '             */
    fprintf( stream , "\n'%3.4s'","testing");  /* 'test'                   */
    fprintf( stream , "\n'%.4s'", "testing");  /* 'test'                   */

    fprintf( stream , "\n'Amount $%05u.%02u'",
                      dollars, cents );        /* 'Amount $00012.05'       */
    fprintf( stream , "\n'Amount $%u.%02u'",
                      dollars, cents );        /* 'Amount $12.05'          */
    fprintf( stream , "\n'Amount $%u.%u'",
                      dollars, cents );        /* 'Amount $12.5'           */

    fprintf( stream , "\n'%.3f'" , f      );   /* '456.789'                */

    fprintf( stream , "\n'%e'"   , f      );   /* '4.567890e+002'          */
    fprintf( stream , "\n'%.0f'" , f      );   /* '457'                    */
    fprintf( stream , "\n'%.2f'" , f      );   /* '456.79'                 */
    fprintf( stream , "\n'%.*f'" , 2 , f  );   /* '456.79'                 */

    fclose ( stream );

}   /* end of main */
```

The comment to the right of each fprintf statement shows the associated output.

vfprintf The *vfprintf* function is functionally equivalent to *fprintf*, except that the argument list is replaced by a pointer to a list of arguments. See Module 40 for more information on functions using a variable number of arguments.

APPLICATIONS

The applications for the fprintf function are the same as for the printf function, except the output is directed to a file pointer. See Module 61 to review the typical applications for the printf function.

TYPICAL OPERATION

In this operation you enter, compile, and execute the program given in Example 32.1.

1. Begin at the DOS prompt, in your C source code directory. Invoke your text editor.
2. Type the C program given in Example 32.1, just like it is listed. Call the program FPRINTF1.C.
3. Compile and link the program with your C compiler.
4. Type **FPRINTF1** and press **Enter**. Notice the following output on your screen:

```
C:\C>FPRINTF1
C:\C>_
```

5. Type **COPY TEST.FPF CON** and press **Enter**. Notice the following output on your screen:

```
C:\C>COPY TEST.FPF CON
'23456'
'   23456'
'00023456'
'23456   '
'ff'
'  fe'
'0064'
'65  '
'9$'
'testing'
'   testing'
'testing   '
'test'
'test'
'Amount $00012.05'
'Amount $12.05'
'Amount $12.5'
'456.789'
'4.567890e+002'
'457'
'456.79'
'456.79'
C:\C>_
```

6. Turn to Module 37 to continue the learning sequence.

Module 33

FPUTC

```
NAME

  fputc  --  writes a single character to a stream file

USAGE

   int   fputc ( int c , FILE *stream ) ;

PROTOTYPE in      stdio.h

ANSI Synopsis

    #include <stdio.h>
    int    fputc(int c, FILE *stream);

RETURNS

   returns the character that was output to the stream file
          or end-of-file if an error is detected
```

DESCRIPTION

The *fputc* function writes a single character to the stream file. It returns the character output unless an error is detected, in which case EOF (end-of-file) is returned.

The actual error number can be retrieved from *errno* when an error occurs using the *fputc* function.

Example 33.1, an example using the *fputc* function:

```
/*                  program name:        fputc1.c         */
#include <stdio.h>
main()
{
    FILE    *stream ;
    int     status  ;
    char    c = 'a' ;

    stream = fopen ("filename", "w" );    /* open for write */
```

```
    status = fputc ( c , stream );                          /* line 1 */

    if ( status == EOF )
         printf ( "write to file not completed successfully...\n" );
    else printf ( "write to file completed successfully...\n" );

}    /* end of main */
```

Line 1 is an example of the fputc function call. It returns the character output unless an error is detected and then EOF is returned.

Example 33.2, a program that copies a file using high-level functions:

```
/*                            program name:       hcopy.c
Purpose:    copy a file

Usage:      hcopy   source-file-name   destination-file-name
*/
#include <stdio.h>
main ( argc , argv )                                          /* line 1 */
int     argc ;
char           *argv[] ;
{
    FILE    *stream   ;        /* source file */
    FILE    *stream2  ;        /* destination file */
    int     in_char   ;        /* read char  */
    int     out_char  ;        /* write char */


    if ( argc < 3  || argc > 3 )                             /* line 2 */
    {
         fprintf( stderr , "Usage:\n" );
         fprintf( stderr ,        hcopy  source-file  destination-file\n\n" );
         exit(0);
    }

    stream = fopen ( argv[1] , "rb" );                        /* line 3 */

    if( stream == NULL )                                      /* line 4 */
    {
         fprintf( stderr , "Source file missing\n\n" );
         exit(0);
    }

    stream2 = fopen ( argv[2] , "wb" );                       /* line 5 */

    if( stream2 == NULL )                                     /* line 6 */
    {
         fprintf( stderr , "Can not open Destination file\n\n" );
         fclose( stream );
         exit(0);
    }

    do                                                        /* line 7 */
    {
```

```
        in_char = fgetc ( stream );                    /* line 8 */

        if ( in_char != EOF )                          /* line 9 */
        {
            out_char = fputc ( in_char , stream2 );    /* line 10 */

            if ( out_char == EOF )                     /* line 11 */
            {
                fprintf( stderr, "file write error -- run stopped.\n\n" );
                fclose ( stream  );
                fclose ( stream2 );
                exit(0);
            }
        }

    } while ( in_char != EOF ) ;                       /* line 12 */

    fclose ( stream );                                 /* line 13 */
    fclose ( stream2 );                                /* line 14 */

    printf( "file copy complete.\n\n" );               /* line 15 */

}   /* end of hcopy */
```

Line 1 is the *main* function name and includes the parameters for command line arguments since this program receives the name of the file to copy on the command line when the program is run.

Line 2 tests to make sure only 2 arguments plus the program name are on the command line when the program is run. If there are more or less than 2 arguments the program displays the proper command usage to run this program, and then stops executing and returns to the operating system.

Line 3 opens the file specified in the first command line argument, the source file. This file is opened in the read mode. The result of the *fopen* is assigned to a variable.

Line 4 tests the result of the open statement on the source file. If the resulting pointer is NULL then the file was not on the disk or could not be opened, therefore an error message is displayed and the program stops executing.

Line 5 opens the file specified in the second command line argument in the write mode. Any data in an existing file by the same name is lost as this open sets the file length to 0. The result of the *fopen* is assigned to a variable.

Line 6 tests the result of the open statement on the destination file. If the resulting pointer is NULL then the file was not opened, therefore an error message is displayed, the source file is closed, and the program stops executing.

Line 7 through line 12 contain the code that actually copies the file.

Line 8 gets a character from the source file and stores it into a variable. An EOF (– 1) is stored if end-of-file is reached in the source file.

Line 9 tests the variable storing the character read for EOF. If EOF is not reached, the body of the *if* is performed.

Line 10 writes the character just read to the destination file. The status of the write is stored into a variable.

Line 11 tests the status of the *fputc* write. If the status is EOF, then an output error occurred, an error message is displayed, both the source and the destination files are closed, and the program stops executing.

Line 12 tests to see if the input character is EOF. If it is then end-of-file is reached and the file is copied and the program can leave the *do-while* loop.

Line 13 closes the source file.

Line 14 closes the destination file.

Line 15 displays a message that the copy is complete.

APPLICATIONS

When performing output, use the fputc function when writing to a binary file and the output is being made a character at a time. This function is often used to output an array of binary characters to a data file.

TYPICAL OPERATION

In this operation you enter, compile, and execute the program given in Example 33.2.

1. Begin at the DOS prompt, in your C source code directory. Invoke your text editor.
2. Type the C program given in Example 33.2, just like it is listed. Call the program HCOPY.C.
3. Compile and link the program with your C compiler.
4. Type **HCOPY HCOPY.C HCOPY2.C** and press **Enter**. Notice the following output on your screen:

```
C:\C>HCOPY HCOPY.C HCOPY2.C
file copy complete.

C:\C>_
```

Note that the program *HCOPY* copies files. This program is a good starting point for writing a program that reads, modifies, and writes the modified copy of the file back to disk. Programs like this are called data conversion programs.

5. Turn to Module 34 to continue the learning sequence.

Module 34

FPUTS

```
NAME

   fputs  --  writes a string to a stream file

USAGE

   int fputs ( char *string , FILE *stream ) ;

PROTOTYPE in      stdio.h

ANSI Synopsis

    #include <stdio.h>
    int    fputs(const noalias char *s, file *stream);

RETURNS

   returns the last character output, if no error.  If an
   error is detected, EOF is returned
```

DESCRIPTION

The *fputs* function writes a string to a stream file and returns the last character output. The function sends and returns the *newline* character as the last character. The '\0' end of string character is not output. If an error occurs, an EOF is returned instead of the last output character.

The actual error number can be retrieved from *errno* if an error occurs using the *fputs* function.

Example 34.1, an example using the *fputs* function:

```
/*                  program name:      fputs1.c        */
#include <stdio.h>
main()
{
   int     err ;
   FILE    *stream ;
```

```
            stream = fopen ("filename", "w" );    /* open for write */

            err = fputs( "string" , stream );              /* line 1 */

            if ( err == EOF )
               printf( "an error occurred on output" );

    }       /* end of main */
```

Line 1 is an example of the *fputs* function call. It writes a string variable or constant to a stream file. It returns an EOF if anerror occurs. In this example, the "string" plus the '\n' newline character is output to the stream.

Example 34.2, an example using the both the *fgets* and *fputs* functions:

```
/* NAME    : fgetput.c   */
/* PURPOSE: program to display itself on the stdout device */
#include <stdio.h>
main()
{
FILE    *stream ;
int     status ;
char    buffer [ 513 ] ;

     stream = fopen ( "fgetput.c", "r" );
     if ( stream == NULL )
     {
          printf ( "fgetput.c could not be found...." );
          exit ( -1 );
     }
     do
     {
          status = fgets ( buf , 512 , stream );         /* line 1 */
          if ( status != 0 )
               fputs ( buffer , stdout );               /* line 2 */
     } while ( status != 0 );                           /* line 3 */
     status = fclose ( stream );
     if ( status == -1 )
          printf ( "fgetput.c not closed properly..." );
}
```

Line 1 uses the fgets function to read data into the variable named buffer, for a maximum length of 512 bytes. The buffer is defined as 513. The input data is read from the input file_ptr named stream.

Line 2 uses the fputs function to write data from the variable named buffer to the stream stdout. Output data continues until the end-of-string character is found.

Line 3 is the line that terminates the loop when the variable status equals the value zero. Note that status can be assigned the value zero in two places, one in the input statement and the other in the output statement. If end-of-file is reached for the input, then status is assigned zero; or if an error occurs in output to the standard output device, then status is assigned the value of zero.

APPLICATIONS

When performing output, use the fputs function to output text data that are strings. A good example of reading and writing text files is Example 34.2 in this module. This example uses the fgets function to read itself from disk and the fputs function to write itself on the computer console.

TYPICAL OPERATION

In this operation you enter, compile, and execute the program given in Example 34.2.

1. Begin at the DOS prompt, in your C source code directory. Invoke your text editor.
2. Type the C program given in Example 34.2, just like it is listed. Call the program FGETPUT.C.
3. Compile and link the program with your C compiler.
4. Type **FGETPUT** and press **Enter**. Notice the following output on your screen:

```
C:\C>
/* NAME    : fgetput.c    */
/* PURPOSE: program to display itself on the stdout device */
#include <stdio.h>
main()
{
FILE   *stream ;
int    status ;
char   buffer [ 513 ] ;

     stream = fopen ( "fgetput.c", "r" );
     if ( stream == NULL )
     {
          printf ( "fgetput.c could not be found...." );
          exit ( -1 );
     }
     do
     {
          status = fgets ( buf , 512 , stream );      /* line 1 */
          if ( status != 0 )
               fputs ( buffer , stdout );             /* line 2 */
     }  while ( status != 0 );                        /* line 3 */
     status = fclose ( stream );
     if ( status == -1 )
          printf ( "fgetput.c not closed properly..." );
}
C:\C>_
```

5. Turn to Module 46 to continue the learning sequence.

Module 35

FREAD

```
NAME

   fread  —  reads data from an opened stream file into
             a memory buffer

USAGE

 unsigned  fread ( void *buffer, int size, int count, FILE *stream ) ;

PROTOTYPE in      stdio.h

ANSI Synopsis

    #include <stdio.h>
    size_t fread(noalias void *ptr, size_t size, size_t nmemb,
                 FILE *stream);

RETURNS
      returns number of items read
```

DESCRIPTION

The *fread* function reads into the buffer from the associated stream a specific number (count) of items of the specified size. Reading begins with the current file position. The file position is updated after the *fread*. The *fread* function returns the number of items successfully read, not the number of bytes read. The buffer may or may not be an array. The buffer associated with the file is usually declared as a structure with a count to read of 1. In data processing the buffer associated with a file for input and output is often referred to as a record. The fields in the structure can be any of the normal data types like integer, string, long, and float.

The form of the *fread* function is:

```
number_items = fread ( buffer , size , number_to_read , stream ) ;
```

where:

1) Buffer specifies where to read the data into. The buffer length must be equal to or greater than size times number_to_read.
2) Size specifies the size of one of the records to be read.
3) Number_to_read specifies the number of records to read.
4) Stream specifies which stream to read the data from.
5) The number_items equals the number of records read.

Example 35.1, an example using the *fread* function:

```
/*                  program name:        fread1.c              */
#include <stdio.h>
main()
{
FILE   *stream ;
int     status ,
char    buffer [ 512 ] ;

    stream = fopen ( "fread1.c" , "rb" );                  /* line 1 */

    status = fread ( buffer , 1 , 60 , stream );           /* line 2 */

    if ( status !=  60 )                                   /* line 3 */
         printf( "read error occurred." );

    buffer[60] = 0x00 ;

    printf ( "line = %s\n" , buffer );

}    /* end of main */
```

Line 1 sets the mode to allow read access to the binary file when it is opened.

Line 2 is an example of the *fread* function call. It returns the number of items read, which should be 60 in this example.

Line 3 tests to see if all 60 items are read. If not all 60 items are read then an error is reported.

See Module 41, *fwrite*, for a complete working program using the *fread* function.

APPLICATIONS

Two types of data that the fread function is useful for reading are structures and arrays. For structures, the length of the structure is known, so any number of data structures can be read into memory with one call to the fread function. For arrays, any number of array elements can be read into memory for any size of array element. The fread function also is useful for reading in binary data bytes when you know how many data bytes to read, as you set the length of the data to one for this type of read.

TYPICAL OPERATION

In this operation you enter, compile, and execute the program given in Example 35.1.

1. Begin at the DOS prompt, in your C source code directory. Invoke your text editor.
2. Type the C program given in Example 35.1, just like it is listed. Call the program FREAD1.C.
3. Compile and link the program with your C compiler.
4. Type **FREAD1** and press **Enter**. Notice the following output on your screen:

```
C:\C>FREAD1
line = /*                    program name:        fread1.c          */
C:\C>_
```

5. Turn to Module 41 to continue the learning sequence.

Module 36

FREE

```
NAME

   free  —  returns allocated memory for reuse

USAGE

    void   free ( void *memptr ) ;

PROTOTYPE in      stdlib.h

ANSI Synopsis

    #include <stdlib.h>
    void    free(noalias void *ptr);

RETURNS
       nothing returned
```

DESCRIPTION

The *free* function returns previously allocated memory to the heap to be reused. The argument must be a previously allocated pointer. After the call, the memory is available to be allocated again.

There is no return value.

Example 36.1, an example using the *free* function:

```
/*                   program name:            free1.c           */
#include <stdlib.h>
main()
{
char       *mem_ptr ;

       mem_ptr = calloc ( 10 , 512 );                        /* line 1 */

        /* coding ... */

       free ( mem_ptr );                                     /* line 2 */
       printf ( "memory freed.\n" );

 }    /* end of main  */
```

Line 1 allocates a 5120-byte block of memory.

Line 2 returns the block of memory back to the heap, so that the memory is available to be allocated again by another allocation function call.

APPLICATIONS

After memory is allocated it must be freed before it can be allocated again. In programs that do a lot of allocating and freeing of memory, it is imperative that each segment of memory that is allocated be freed. If each segment of memory allocated is not freed, sooner or later the program runs out of available memory to allocate from and therefore cannot continue to operate. The use of common functions in a program to allocate and free memory helps to gurantee that each segment allocated is freed.

TYPICAL OPERATION

In this operation you enter, compile, and execute the program given in Example 36.1.

1. Begin at the DOS prompt, in your C source code directory. Invoke your text editor.
2. Type the C program given in Example 36.1, just like it is listed. Call the program FREE1.C.
3. Compile and link the program with your C compiler.
4. Type **FREE1** and press **Enter**. Notice the following output on your screen:

```
C:\C>FREE1
memory freed.
C:\C>_
```

5. Turn to Module 58 to continue the learning sequence.

Module 37

FSCANF

```
NAME

   fscanf   —   reads data from a file into arguments as specified by
                the format string.

USAGE

     int      fscanf ( FILE *stream , char *format-string  , ...  );

PROTOTYPE in      stdio.h

ANSI Synopsis

    #include <stdio.h>
    int   fscanf(FILE *stream, const noalias char *format, ...);

RETURNS
       fscanf returns the number of successfully assigned input
       fields.  EOF is returned if end-of-file is encountered.
```

DESCRIPTION

The *fscanf* function is used to accept input data from a stream. The *fscanf* function takes a variable number of parameters. The format-string parameter describes how the data is to be input from the stream and what type of data it is. The argument parameters describe where to place the data when it is input.

Form for *fscanf*:

```
fscanf ( stream , format-string , arguments ) ;
           ↑            ↑             ↑
           |            |             └──── Describes where to place
           |            |                   the data when input.
           |            |
           |            └──── Describes the input data from the stream,
           |                  its length and its conversion type.
           |
           └──── Specifies the data file from which input data comes.
```

STREAM The stream specifies the data file from which the input data comes. The stream specified must be an opened data file.

FORMAT-STRING The format-string contains one or more of each of the following three types of fields:

1) Whitespace characters that are skipped.
2) An input format specification field which describes the input data from the stream file. This describes the maximum length of the data for each data field in the input file and the data type of the corresponding argument where the data is stored. All input format specification fields begin with a percent-sign, '%.' The input format specification field is described in detail later in this module.
3) A non-input format specifications field which causes *fscanf* to skip over (read, but not store) characters in the input data file. These characters are expected to match the next non-whitespace character input from the data file.

ARGUMENTS The arguments specify where the input data fields are to be stored in memory as the fields are input from the data file. There must be an argument for each input format specification field in the *format-string*. If there are more arguments than input specification fields, the extra arguments are ignored. If there are too few arguments, then the results are unpredictable and undefined. The arguments to the *fscanf* function are pointers. The most common programming error in the use of the fscanf function is to not make the arguments pointers.

The format-string is read from left to right, and the data is also stored in the arguments left to right, one field per argument.

FORMAT SPECIFICATION FIELD The general form of an input format specification field is:

```
%[sup-flag][max-width][size]data-type
```

The format specification begins with the % and ends with the desired input data type and can contain three other optional fields. A description of the optional fields is followed here by a table describing the input data type:

sup-flag	This flag is a *suppression flag* and is an *. If it is present, the input field is skipped and no output is made to the corresponding output argument.
max-width	The width controls the maximum number of characters that are to be input for this argument. An input field is completed when it reaches either the maximum field width or a whitespace character in the input data.
size	The L character specifies that the input field is a long double for type E, F, and G. The l character specifies that the input field is a double for types E, F, and G. The L character for the other types indicate a long integer. The h character indicates that it is also a short type.

Data Type Input Table

Character	*Input Type*	*Type Ouput Argument-Pointer*
d	decimal integer	The argument is a pointer to a decimal integer.
o	octal integer	The argument is a pointer to a decimal integer.
x	hexadecimal integer	The argument is a pointer to a decimal integer.
p	pointer	The argument is a pointer to a pointer.
c	single character	The argument is a pointer to a character. The whitespace rule is not in effect for this type.
s	string of characters	The argument is a pointer to an array of characters large enough to hold input string and \0 character.
e, f, g	floating point (exponential)	The argument is a pointer to a floating point number.
h	short integer	The argument is a pointer to a short integer.

DATA FIELDS An input data field is a string of non-whitespace characters that are contained in the input file. An input data field ends when one of the following occurs as the data is input:

1) The maximum width as defined in the input format specification field is reached.
2) A whitespace character (tab, space, or newline) is reached.
3) A character that cannot be converted according to the field definition in the input format specification field is reached.

Example 37.1, an example using the *fscanf* function:

```
/*                    program name:    fscanf1.c              */
#include <stdio.h>
main()
{
    int         empno ;
    int         ssn1 , ssn2   , ssn3 ;
    int         hireday   , hiremonth , hireyear  ;
    char        firstname [ 31 ] , middleinitial ;
    char        lastname  [ 31 ] , city [ 31 ] ,
                    state [ 3  ] , zip  [ 10 ] ;
    float       payrate ;

    FILE        *stream ;


    if ( (stream = fopen( "payroll" , "r" )) == NULL)
    {
         printf("payroll file error --- run aborted.");
         exit ( 0 );
    }
```

```
    fscanf ( stream , "%4d" , &empno );                    /* line 1 */

    fscanf ( stream , "%3d-%2d-%4d", &ssn1 ,               /* line 2 */
                      &ssn2 , &ssn3 );

    fscanf ( stream , "%2d%2d%2d", &hiremonth ,            /* line 3 */
                      &hireday   , &hireyear );

    fscanf ( stream , "%*lf" , &payrate );                 /* line 4 */

    fscanf ( stream , "%30s %1c %30s",                     /* line 5 */
          firstname , &middleinitial  , lastname  );

    fscanf ( stream , "%30s %2s %9s",                      /* line 6 */
                    city , state , zip );

    fclose ( stream );

}   /* end of main */
```

Line 1 is an example of the input of a number with a maximum length of 4 characters, that is to be stored in an *int* type variable. Notice that the variable has an ampersand leading it so that a pointer to the variable is passed as the parameter, as required.

Line 2 is an example of the input of three numbers which are separated in the input file with minus signs. The three numbers are stored into three variables and the minus signs are read from the input file but not stored.

Line 3 is an example of the input of three numbers which are not separated in the input file, but are separated by the *fscanf* function and stored into three different variables.

Line 4 is an example of the reading of an input data field where the data is not stored into the variable because of the asterisk in the input specification field.

Line 5 is an example of the input of two 30-character strings and the input of a 1-character data field. Notice first that the definition of the character string variables is one character longer than the input. This is because the *fscanf* function places the EOS character at the end of the string when it is input. Notice that the 1-character length variable is defined with a length of one as it is just a character, not a string. Also notice that the strings do not need an ampersand, as strings are automatically passed as pointers, but the character variable must be passed with the leading ampersand since *char* type is passed by value.

Line 6 is another example of string input. This example of valid data demonstrates how the data is stored in the respective variables for the above example:

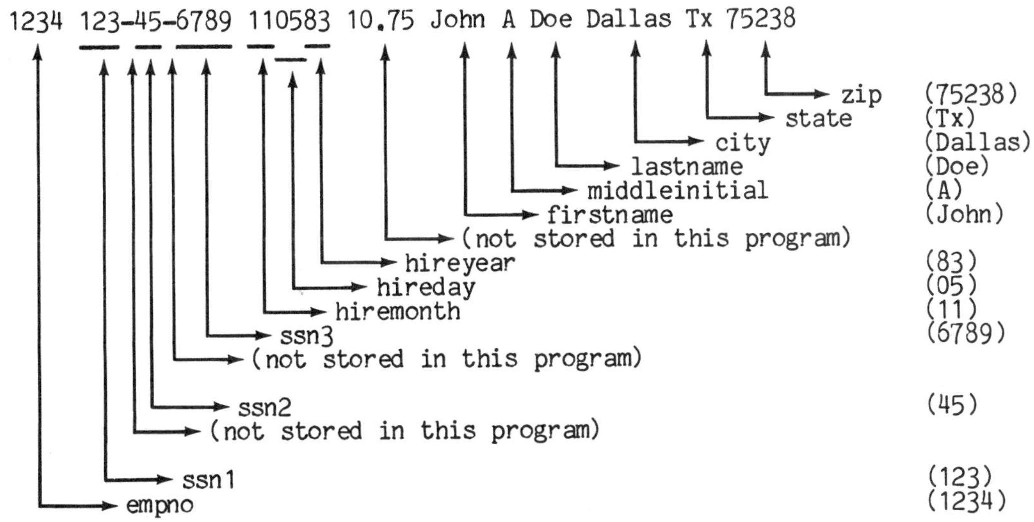

APPLICATIONS

The applications for the fscanf function are the same as for the scanf function except the output is directed to a file pointer. (Refer to Module 68, scanf.)

Turn to Module 19 to continue the learning sequence.

Module 38

FSEEK

```
NAME
   fseek —  moves to a new location within a file
USAGE
   int    fseek ( FILE *stream , long offset , int start_position ) ;
PROTOTYPE in     stdio.h
ANSI Synopsis
    #include <stdio.h>
    int    fseek(FILE *stream, long int offset, int whence);
RETURNS
      returns 0 if moved properly, else -1 if an error
```

DESCRIPTION

The *fseek* function moves the file pointer to a new location in a file. With this function you can move to any location in the file at any time. You can move in either direction, forward or backward, in any combination or sequence. This function is used to set the file pointer to any location within the file. The *fread* function reads data and moves the file pointer to the byte after the last byte read. The *fseek* function can be used to position the pointer at a record already read so that it can be read again with the next *fread* function call.

The form for the fseek function is:

```
status = fseek ( stream , offset , origin ) ;
```

where:

1) Stream specifies in which stream to perform the seek.
2) Offset is how far to move from the starting point. Offset must be a long value.
3) Origin is the starting point for moving the file pointer.
4) Status is 0 if the move was ok, − 1 if there is an error.

The origin can have three values:

Origin	Starting Position
0	beginning of file
1	current position
2	end of file

Therefore, the position to move to is calculated by adding the offset to the origin location. Offset is a signed long value so the move can be a positive move (forward in the file) or a negative move (backward in the file).

For example, to move to the beginning of the file:

```
status = fseek ( stream , 0L , 0 );
```

Note that the fseek here moves the file pointer to the beginning of the file like the rewind function; however, the fseek does not reset the ferror flag or the end-of-file flag. (The EOF and ferror flags are reset by the rewind() and clearerr() functions or closing and reopening the file.)

To move to the end of file:

```
status = fseek ( stream , 0L , 2 );
```

To move to the 10th record in a file where the records are declared to be a structure of rec_struct_type:

```
status = fseek ( stream , (long)(10 * sizeof ( rec_struct_type )) , 0 );
```

The location is combined with the indicated start position to calculate the new file pointer location. The *fseek* returns 0 if the move executes properly or −1 if an error occurs. The pointer can be moved past the end of the file but cannot be moved ahead of the beginning of the file.

The actual error number can be retrieved from *errno* if an error occurs while using the *fseek* function.

Example 38.1, an example using the *fseek* function:

```
/*                    program name:       fseek1.c          */
#include <stdio.h>
main()
{
    int     status ,  mode ;
    long    location = 0 ;
    FILE    *stream ;
    char    buffer[81] ;

    stream = fopen ("fseek1.c", "r" );

    fgets ( buffer , 80 , stream );

    location = fseek ( stream , location , 0 ) ;          /* line 1 */
```

```
        if ( location == -1 )                                    /* line 2 */
            printf( "file pointer was not located properly." );
        else printf( "file pointer was located properly." );

    }   /* end of main */
```

Line 1 is an example of the *fseek* instruction that requests to move to location 0 from the beginning of the stream file. If an error occurs − 1 is returned, else a 0 value is returned. The file pointer is moved back to the beginning of the file in this example.

Line 2 tests the returned value from the *fseek* function call for an error condition. If an error exists, an error message is displayed.

Example 38.2, example using the fread, fwrite, and fseek functions:

```
/* NAME:   readwrit.c   */
#include <stdio.h>
main()
{
FILE    *stream ;
int     seek_status , status ;
int     number, origin ;
long    offset ;

struct data_struct
{
char     name[50] ;
float    balance  ;
} ;

struct data_struct   data_rec_out ;
struct data_struct   data_rec_in ;

    stream = fopen ( "readwrit.dat", "w+b" );
    if ( stream == NULL )
    {
        printf ( "readwrit.dat could not be found...." );
        exit ( -1 );
    }
    data_rec_out.balance = 125.83 ;
    strcpy ( data_rec_out.name , "Mr. and Mrs. John Smith" );
    number = fwrite ( &data_rec_out ,
             sizeof ( struct data_struct ) ,1, stream ) ;   /* line 1 */
    if ( number != 1 )                                       /* line 2 */
    {
        printf ( "readwrit.dat could not be written to ..." );
        fclose ( stream );
        exit ( -1 );
    }
    offset   = 0 ;                                           /* line 3 */
    origin   = 0 ;                                           /* line 4 */
    seek_status = fseek ( stream , offset , origin );        /* line 5 */
    if ( seek_status == -1 )                                 /* line 6 */
    {
        printf ( "readwrit.dat could not be written to ..." );
        fclose ( stream );
        exit ( -1 );
    }
```

```
        number = fread ( &data_rec_in ,
                 sizeof ( struct data_struct ) ,1, stream ) ;     /* line 7 */

        if ( number != 1 )                                        /* line 8 */
        {
            printf ( "readwrit.dat could not be read from ..." );
            fclose ( stream );
            exit ( -1 );
        }
        printf ( "name = %s , balance = %.2f\n" ,                 /* line 9 */
                 data_rec_in.name , data_rec_in.balance );
        status = fclose ( stream );
        if ( status == -1 )
            printf ( "readwrit.dat not closed properly..." );
    }
```

The output from the above program is:

```
name = Mr. and Mrs. John Smith , balance = 125.83
```

Line 1 writes one data record to the data file. The record written is named data_out_rec which is a structure with 2 fields defined. After the write, the internal file pointer is positioned to the second record location, ready to write another record.

Line 2 checks to see if the fwrite executed successfully. If not, it displays an error message and terminates the program.

Line 3 assigns the variable named offset the value 0, which specifies the number of characters to offset the file pointer relative to the origin. Offset of 0 means move 0 bytes from the origin location.

Line 4 assigns the variable named origin the value 0, which specifies the offset relative to the beginning of the file.

Line 5 uses the fseek command to position the file pointer as specified in the parameters, which specifies 0 characters from the beginning of the file, which is the beginning of the file.

Line 6 checks to see if the fseek command executed as specified. If not, an error message is displayed, the file is closed, and the program terminates.

Line 7 uses the fread command to read the record pointed to by the file pointer, which is the first and only record written to the file. It reads one record into the buffer named data_in_rec for a length of the structure named data_struct. The number of records read in is stored in the variable named number, which is 1 if executed properly, else 0.

Line 8 checks to see if the number of records read is correct. If it is not equal to one then the read did not execute properly, so the program displays an error message, closes the file, and terminates.

Line 9 displays the variables of the record so that you will know that it actually did read the record that was previously written.

APPLICATIONS

The fseek function is most often used in the processing of random data files. For the processing of these data files, an index is made. In the index is contained the offset of the record and the key to the record. A key is the thing that uniquely identifies this record. In accounting applications the key is usually the customer account number. Therefore for accounting applications the index contains the record offset and the customer account number. The index contains one of these records for each customer in the data file. To access the data file, the program searches the index till it matches the customer account number it is looking for. When found, it then fseeks to the location in the file using the corresponding offset in the index. The data at that location is then read with one of the C read functions.

An example is as follows, for a data file with a length of 100 bytes for each customer record, and with only records 1,3,5,7, and 11 in the data file:

index:

1 , 000
3 , 100
5 , 200
7 , 300
11, 400

data_file:

1 , name , address, balance, ...
3 , name , ...
5 , name , ...
7 , name , ...
11, name , ...

TYPICAL OPERATION

In this operation you enter, compile, and execute the program given in Example 38.1.

1. Begin at the DOS prompt, in your C source code directory. Invoke your text editor.
2. Type the C program given in Example 38.1, just like it is listed. Call the program FSEEK1.C.
3. Compile and link the program with your C compiler.
4. Type **FSEEK1** and press **Enter**. Notice the following output on your screen:

```
C:\C>FSEEK1
file pointer was located properly.
C:\C>_
```

5. Turn to Module 84 to continue the learning sequence.

Module 39
FUNCTIONS

DESCRIPTION

This module introduces the use of functions and describes the exchange of data between functions. It decribes how to indicate the data types of the information or arguments passed to a function and how to indicate the data type of the argument passed back from a function. This module also shows how to return from a function and how to terminate a program.

A function is a complete unit of executable code that can be called and executed from another function. Control transfers to the called function, it executes, and then it transfers control back to the calling function to the statement following the function call.

C programs are composed of a set of one or more functions. The functions are used to divide large programs into smaller, easier to handle pieces. Each function normally performs one specific task. The functions work together to accomplish the goal of the whole program.

Every program must contain one function named main where the program always begins execution. The main function may call other functions, which in turn may call still other functions. When a function is called, program execution is transferred to the first statement in the called function. The function is completed when it executes the last statement in the function or it executes a return statement. After a function returns to the calling function, execution continues with the evaluation of the expression in which the call was made. A value can be returned when a function completes, and that returned value can be used as an operand in an expression. If the returned value is not assigned or used, then it is simply discarded.

Functions can communicate data between themselves in two ways. One through global variables and the other through an argument or parameter list. The argument list of a function defines variables that are used to contain values passed from the calling functions.

FUNCTION DEFINITION A function definition has two forms. Form 1 is the new ANSI form with type error checking. Form 2 is the classical style definition with little error checking. Form 1 is recommended as it takes advantage of all the error checking the compiler can do for you, which can save you hours and hours of debugging subtle and hard-to-trace bugs. The first form forces conversion of the arguments of subsequent calls to the function, whereas the second form does not.

Function definition Form 1, ANSI error checking:

```
return_data_type   function_name ( type1 arg1 , type2 arg2 , ... ,
                                   typeN argN )
{
    /* function body */
}
```

Function definition Form 2, classical with little error checking:

```
return_data_type   function_name ( arg1 , arg2 , ... , argN )
          type1                    arg1 ;
          type2                           arg2 ;
          typeN                                       argN;
{
    /* function body */
}
```

where:

return_data_type	The data type of the variable that is the argument in the return statement within the body of the function.
function_name	The name given to this function. Other functions use this name to identify this particular function.
arg1, arg2, argN	The names of the arguments that this function uses to access the variables passed to it.
type1, type2, typeN	The data types of argument number 1, etc.

NOTE

Every variable has a data type amd every function that has arguments must specify what data types it is expecting for each argument. If a data type is not declared, it is assumed to be int.

Sample of both forms of function definitions:

```
int    swap_values ( int *a, int *b )      /* ANSI, modern form */
{
     /* body of function goes here  */
}

int    swap_values ( a,  b )               /* classical form */
int                 *a, *b ;
{
     /* body of function goes here  */
}
```

PROTOTYPES The other half of the error checking that corresponds to the ANSI form of function definition is prototypes. In C it is has always been required that you declare a function for the compiler if it returned a data type other than integer, but the parameter did not have to be described. In ANSI C, to maximize error checking by the compiler, prototypes were developed. Prototypes are placed at the front of your programs to describe the functions you are calling with their parameters.

The prototype for the *swap*_values function in ANSI form is:

```
int    swap_values ( int *a, int *b );      /* ANSI, modern form */
```

The classical declaration is to leave it out, since it returns int type, or to declare it as follows:

```
int    swap_values ( );                    /* classical declaration */
```

The prototype for the printf function is as follows:

```
int   printf ( const = char *format, ...);
```

The ellipsis (...) means that this function can have a variable number of arguments and that no type checking is performed on these arguments.

Note that all C compilers that conform to the ANSI specification include the prototypes in their include files for all the functions in the standard library.

FUNCTION ARGUMENTS Functions are effective in C because they provide good two-way communications between the calling function and the called function. When a function is called in C, data arguments pass to the called function. The data arguments passed are a copy of the data in the calling function so the called function can change it and not destroy the original data in the calling function. When the called function completes, it may return a value to the calling function. The default data type that a function returns is *int* type, but any of the basic data types can be returned.

In Module 40, Functions — Part 2, a method is explained for returning more than one value to a function.

For instance, the parameters passed to the *printf* function name the data to be displayed and control how it is displayed. However, *printf* does not return anything. Most functions do. Typically, the return value is the completion status of the called function or the results of the function.

If no arguments are needed by a function, the function name is followed by an empty argument list, (). Otherwise, the argument list specifies a name for each argument, which the function uses to reference the particular argument. All the data types of the arguments are declared immediately following the function list. If a data type is not declared, then the data type is assumed to be int (integer). A good programming practice is to always specify the argument's data type.

If no value is to be returned by the function, then the word void is used in front of the function name when defined to specify that there is no return value.

Example of the generalized form of using functions:

```
/*                    program name:    function.c     */
/* prototypes  of internal functions */
void      funct1 ( int  arg1 , int arg2 ) ;      /* show how called    line 1 */
int       funct2 ( int argument ) ;  /* show call, return data type    line 2 */

#include <stdio.h>                               /* include file       line 3 */
main( )                                          /* main function      line 4 */
{                                                /* start of main      line 5 */
int  arg1 , arg2 ;
int  value ;
   funct1( arg1 , arg2 ) ;                       /* call function 1    line 6 */

   value = funct2( arg1 ) ;                      /* call function 2    line 7 */

}                                                /* end of main        line 8 */

void funct1 ( int  arg1 , int arg2 )             /* show how called    line 9 */
{                                                /* start function 1   line10 */
int    value ;

    value = funct2 ( arg1 );                     /* call function 2    line11 */

}                                                /* end of function 1  line12 */

int       funct2( int argument )     /* show call, return data type    line13 */
{                                                /* start function 2   line14 */
int    value ;

   /*  code within this function goes here   */

   return ( value ) ;     /* leave function, return value to caller    line15 */

}                                                /* end function 2     line16 */
```

Line 1 is the prototype for function funct1. It has two arguments, both integer type, and does not return a value.

Line 2 is the prototype for function funct2. It has one integer argument and returns an integer value.

Line 3 *includes* the stdio.h file.

Line 4 *names* the main function.

Line 5 (opening brace) marks the beginning of the function.

Line 6 calls another function from within a function. Here, funct1 is called and two parameters, or arguments, pass to funct1. Note that the function name is given, then followed by the open parenthesis, an argument, a comma, another argument, a close parenthesis, and then the semicolon.

Line 7 is an example of a call to another function, which in this case returns some data that it placed in the variable named *value*. The equal sign instructed the compiler to place the returned data into the variable.

Line 8 (closing brace) marks the end of the main function.

Line 9 marks the beginning of funct1. The name of the function is given, an open parenthesis, arg1, a comma to separate the arguments, arg2, and a close parenthesis. Note that no semicolon is required here.

Line 10 (open brace) marks the beginning of the function.

Line 11 calls a function. The data returned by the function is assigned to a variable.

Line 12 (close brace) marks the end of the function.

Line 13 is the beginning of funct2. In this instance, in front of the function name is the keyword *int*. *Int* is placed here to tell the C compiler this function returns data of the *int* type. After *int* comes the name of the function, an open parenthesis, the argument passed to this function, and a close parenthesis.

Line 14 (open brace) marks the beginning of the function.

Line 15 shows how data is returned to the calling function. The return statement is given, then an open parenthesis, the value being returned, a close parenthesis, and a semicolon. Value returns as an integer as instructed in line 12.

Line 16 (close brace) marks the end of the function.

Example of function arguments and return value:

```
/* NAME:                    func2.c */
/* prototypes  */
int   f1 ( int j , float f ) ;                    /* line 1 */
int   f2 ( float fx )  ;                          /* line 2 */

main()
{
int   i , r ;
float f ;

    r = f1 ( i , f ) ;                            /* line 3 */
    r = f2 ( f ) ;                                /* line 4 */
}

int  f1 ( int j , float f )                       /* line 5 */
{
int  k ;
     /* body of function here */
     return ( k ) ;                               /* line 6 */
}

int   f2 ( float fx )                             /* line 7 */
{
int k ;
     /* body of function here */
     return ( k ) ;                               /* line 8 */
}
```

Line 1 is the prototype for function f1. It has two parameters and returns a value that has int type.

Line 2 is the prototype for function f2. It has one parameter of float type and returns a value that has int type.

Line 3 is an example of a call to a function named f1. The function f1 has two parameters, an integer parameter first, and second a float parameter. The returned value is of integer type.

Line 4 is an example of a call to a function named f2. The function f2 has one parameter, a float parameter. The return value is of integer type.

Line 5 is the declaration for function f1. There are two parameters. Since the return data type is not specified, it returns an integer value to the place in the program where the function is used.

Line 6 is the return statement for this function. This is consistent with the declaration, which was integer type since it is not declared.

Line 7 is the declaration for function f2. There is one parameter. The return data type is declared to be integer type.

Line 8 is the return statement for this function. This is consistent with the declaration, as the data type of the return value is integer just like the function declaration in line 7.

FUNCTION SOURCE FORM Functions in C have the same general form as a regular C program except that the function name replaces the word *main*. Functions can exist in several forms. They can be included in the main module and be compiled with it. They can be in a module alone and be compiled separately. Several functions can be placed within a module together and compiled. After the functions are compiled, they can be kept separate. Or, if you have a *librarian*, they can be combined into a library, just like the standard library that came with your C compiler.

FUNCTION ADVANTAGES Functions provide many advantages. They allow a larger task to be subdivided into several smaller tasks. Smaller functions with a smaller purpose are usually easier to understand, code, debug, and modify.

Once a function is coded and debugged, it is normally placed into a library so that it can be used over and over again by many programs. As your library of functions grows, it makes for easier and faster coding and less debugging. It also makes each program smaller because all that is required in a program that uses the function is a one-line statement (rather than a whole section of code). And, you already know the function works.

Functions also allow multiple programmers on a large project to work separately on portions of a program and then combine the functions into the final program. It also allows for the sharing of function libraries among programmers.

FUNCTION BODY The statements enclosed within the outermost left and right braces ({}) form the body of the function. The body of a function can contain variable declarations along with coding statements. The variables must be declared before any coding statements. The variables declared within a function can only be accessed by the coding statements within this function.

A function terminates when it executes the last statement within the function or it executes a return statement. The return value of the function is the argument in the return statement. The value in the return statement is converted to the data type specified in the function declaration before it is returned to the calling function. If a function is supposed to return a value but does not execute a return statement, then the return value is undefined.

Example 39.1, an example function that has one parameter of int type and returns a value of int type:

```
/* Purpose:   return the number of days in a year (for year > 1751) */

int  calc_days_in_year ( year )          /* calcdays.c     */
int                      year ;          /* input argument */
{
        if ( year == 1752 )     /* Gregorian to Julian conversion year */
              return ( 355 ) ;
        if ( year  < 1800 )     /* Julian calendar */
        {
              if ( year % 4 == 0 )
                    return ( 366 );        /* leap year     */
              else return ( 365 );         /* non-leap year */
        }
        if (      ( year % 400 == 0 )
              || ( year % 4    == 0  && year % 100 != 0 ) )
              return ( 366 ) ;         /* leap year */
        return ( 365 ) ;               /* non-leap year */
}

main()
{
   int    year ;
   int    days ;

   printf ( "enter year ..." );
   scanf ( "%d" , &year ) ;
   days = calc_days_in_year( year );
   printf ( "\nyear %d has %d days.\n" , year , days );
}
```

NOTE

The function name is calc_days_in_year. The function returns a data type of int. The function has one argument and the data type of the argument is int.

RECURSION (Note: Advanced programming concept) Each time a function is called, memory is reserved for the variables declared within the function. When the function completes and returns to the calling function, then the memory is freed. This is explained in Module 71. This is only mentioned here because of the topic being covered.

When a function calls itself, this is referred to as recursion. There is no practical limit to the number of times a function may call itself. However, each time in the recursion of a function memory is reserved, so if a program gets into an infinite loop doing recursive calls it will eventually run out of memory and stop executing. Each time the function calls itself is called an activation. At some point in the recursive process, the function must quit calling itself, otherwise the endless loop. When one activation completes, it returns to the calling function which happens to be itself. Finally the first activation will complete and control will be returned to the original calling function.

This example is a program that does recursion. The purpose of the program is to calculate the factorial of a number (e.g., 5! = 5 * 4 * 3 * 2 * 1). This program computes the factorial by calling a recursive function.

Example 39.2, example of a recursive function call:

```
/* purpose:  calculate  n! (n factorial)   */
float   factorial( n )                /* factoral.c */
int               n ;
{
  float f ;

  if ( n == 1 ) return ( 1 );
  f = n * factorial ( n - 1 );
  return ( f ) ;
}

main()
{
  int    n ;
  float  f ;

  printf ( "Enter number to compute factorial..." );
  scanf ( "%d" , &n ) ;
  f = factorial ( n );
  printf ( "\nfactorial of %d is %f\n" , n , f );
}
```

Notice that when the factorial function is called with the argument n, it calls itself n – 1 times. Each time it calls itself, it reduces the value of the argument n by 1. When the value is equal to 1, it returns rather than calling itself again. There will be n activations of the factorial function.

Also notice that the factorial function is declared before the main function. The reason is that the compiler must know that the function returns a value of type other than integer type. For the time being, declare and code all functions that have a return type other than integer before the main function.

APPLICATIONS

Functions provide the basis for good structured programming style. A function is a type of subprogram. The function's parameters specify its interface with the outside world, which may be your main function or another function. The function calling another function has no knowledge of how the function performs its work. It is totally insulated by the function heading.

Use functions to clarify your programs and make them easily maintainable, or you can use them to confuse, obfuscate, and confound anyone trying to understand what you have written—including yourself after even a remarkably short break.

Some guidelines for writing good functions:

- Use global variables with extreme caution. It is always preferable to pass the address of a variable instead of using a global variable.
- Make each function less than one page in length. The mind has a difficult time understanding functions longer than a single page.
- Document your function when you write it. Think about the next person who may try to understand your function.
- Only have a function perform a single task. Name the function something that is representative of its task.

These are only guidelines, not absolute rules. However, experienced programmers find that by following these guidelines their programs are easier to develop, debug, document, and maintain.

TYPICAL OPERATION

In this operation you enter, compile, and execute the programs given in Example 39.1 and Example 39.2.

1. Begin at the DOS prompt, in your C source code directory. Invoke your text editor.
2. Type the C program given in Example 39.1, just like it is listed. Call the program DAYS1.C.
3. Compile and link the program with your C compiler.
4. Type **DAYS1** and press **Enter**. Type **1988** and press **Enter**. Notice the following output on your screen:

```
C:\C>DAYS1
enter year ...1988
year 1988 has 366 days.
C:\C>_
```

5. Type the C program given in Example 39.2, just like it is listed. Call the program FACTOR.C.
6. Compile and link the program with your C compiler.
7. Type **FACTOR** and press **Enter**. Type **6** and press **Enter**. Notice the following output on your screen:

```
C:\C>FACTOR
Enter number to compute factorial...6
factorial of 6 is 720
C:\C>_
```

8. Turn to Module 67 to continue the learning sequence.

Module 40

FUNCTIONS — PART 2

DESCRIPTION

This module explains how to declare functions that return a value other than *int* type. It explains the difference between passing an argument to a function by value and passing an argument by reference. A description of functions that take a variable number of arguments is also included.

FUNCTION DECLARATION The C compiler assumes that if a function returns a value, it is an integer value. If it returns any other type, the function must be declared before it is referenced so the compiler is informed what kind of data to expect. The declaration of functions returning a data type other than *int* is usually made after the #include statements and before the function name.

***VOID* Return Type** If a function does not return a value, then the function is said to return a null, or void value. To make this obvious, the word void is used as the return data type in the function source code and in documentation describing it. This lets the user know that the function does not return a value.

Example 40.1, an example of function return types:

```
/*                    program name:    funct21.c         */
#include <stdio.h>

/* prototypes */
long    long_math_function ( int , int );              /* line 1 */
extern  double   sqrt( long ) ;                        /* line 2 */
extern  void     sum_routine( ) ;                      /* line 3 */

main()
{
long    value , value2;
int     i , j ;

  struct
  {
     int     xyz [ 12 ] ;
     int     xyz_sum    ;
  }       xyz_struct     ;
```

```
        i = local_math_function ( j );                          /* line 4 */
        value = long_math_function ( i , j );                   /* line 5 */
        value2 = sqrt( value );                                 /* line 6 */
        sum_routine ( &xyz_struct );                            /* line 7 */
    }   /* end of main */

    long    long_math_function ( int x , int y )               /* line 8 */
    {
          return ( x * x * x * y * y ) ;                        /* line 9 */
    }  /* end of long_math_function */

    static   int   local_math_function( int x )                /* line 10 */
    {
             return ( x * x ) ;
    }   /* end of local_math_function */
```

Line 1 shows the syntax of a function definition.

Line 2 defines a function returning a value other than an integer.

Line 3 defines a function that returns no value and specifies the void type.

Line 4 calls a local function (one that can only be accessed within this module).

Line 5 calls a function that returns a value which is not *int* type.

Line 6 calls an external function that returns a value which is not *int* type.

Line 7 calls a function that does not return a value.

Line 8 declares a function that returns a value which is not *int* type.

Line 9 is a return statement for a function that returns a value which is not *int* type.

Line 10 declares a *static* function. This function can only be accessed from within this file.

PASSING ARGUMENTS BY VALUE AND BY REFERENCE As described earlier, when C passes an argument of a data type other than a structure or an array, the argument is passed by value. This is to say that the called function gets a copy of the value of the variable argument. The called function can manipulate the value of the variable without disturbing the original variable. When the called function returns the original variable, it is the same value as before the function call. The original variable has its privacy and is protected.

C allows you to pass a variable such that the called function can change the original value of the variable in the calling function. This is called *passing by reference*. To do this, you pass the address of the variable instead of its value. Yes, you pass a pointer to the variable. The called function manipulates the real variable. When this called function returns, the copy of the pointer is destroyed and the original variable is changed. Functions that pass arguments are usually not *recursive*, since copies of the variable are not made each time another function call is made.

Example 40.2, an example passing arguements by reference:

```
/*                   program name:     funct22.c           */
#include <stdio.h>
main()
{
    int i = 2 ;
    int j = 5 ;

     function1( &i , j ) ;                              /* line 1 */

     printf( "i = %d,  j = %d \n", i , j );             /* line 2 */

}  /* end of main */

function1( x , y )
int       *x ;                                          /* line 3 */
int         y ;
{
       y += 10 ;

      *x  = 10  + y ;                                   /* line 4 */

}  /* end of function1 */
```

Line 1 passes an *int* type by value and by reference. The variable i is passed by reference, since its address is what gets passed. The variable j is passed by value, because its value is passed.

Line 2 displays the value of both variables. What is displayed?

Line 3 declares an argument that is passed by reference. It is declared as a pointer to the data type as declared in the calling function.

Line 4 shows both the variable passed by reference and the variable passed by value. Line 2 displays: i = 25, j = 5. The value of i was changed in the called function and the value of j was not changed in the called function.

VARIABLE NUMBER OF ARGUMENTS The most common example of a function that take a variable number of arguments is the *printf* function. The following is a general method for creating functions that take a variable number of arguments, using *va*_start, va_end, and va_arg.

First, before any of the variable arguments can be accessed, *va*_start is called to initialize the argument pointer. Next the arguments are returned by calling the *va*_arg function. Finally, after all the arguments are processed, a call to *va*_end is made.

Example 40.3, an example passing a variable number of arguments, using *va_arg*:

```
/*                  program name:     funct23.c        */
#include <stdio.h>
#include <stdarg.h>
main()
{
double  average ( );                                        /* line 1 */
double   avg ;

     avg = average ( 6 , 92. , 84. , 97. , 91. , 83. , 99. ); /* line 2 */

     printf ( "average is %f\n" , avg );
}

double average ( int count )
{

     va_list   Vptr ;
     float     sum  ;
     int i ;

     va_start ( Vptr , count );                             /* line 3 */

     for ( sum = i = 0 ; i < count ; i++ )
     {
          sum  += va_arg ( Vptr , double );                 /* line 4 */
     }
     va_end ( Vptr );                                       /* line 5 */

     return ( sum / count );
}
```

Line 1 defines the function that takes a variable number of arguments.

Line 2 is the function call to the function that takes a variable number of arguments.

Line 3 initializes the variable named *Vptr* to begin processing the variable number of arguments.

Line 4 reads the next variable argument off the stack. The argument value is then added to the variable named *sum*.

Line 5 terminates the variable arguments processing for this function.

APPLICATIONS

The most common application of passing variables by reference is the passing of arrays and structures, although structures can be passed by value. The other reason for passing by reference is when two values must be returned by the function. Since a function can only return one value, the function must change the other function via a pointer to the variable, i.e., passing by reference.

TYPICAL OPERATION

In this operation you enter, compile, and execute the program given in Example 40.2.

1. Begin at the DOS prompt, in your C source code directory. Invoke your text editor.
2. Type the C program given in Example 40.2, just like it is listed. Call the program FUNCT22.C.
3. Compile and link the program with your C compiler.
4. Type **FUNCT22** and press **Enter**. Notice the following output on your screen:

```
C:\C>FUNCT22
i = 25, j = 5
C:\C>_
```

5. Turn to Module 21 to continue the learning sequence.

Module 41

FWRITE

```
NAME

   fwrite  -- writes data to an opened stream file

USAGE

 unsigned fwrite ( void *buffer, int size, int count, FILE *stream ) ;

PROTOTYPE in      stdio.h

ANSI Synopsis

    #include <stdio.h>
    size_t fwrite(const noalias void *ptr, size_t size,
                  size_t nmemb, FILE *stream );

RETURNS
      returns number of items written
```

DESCRIPTION

The *fwrite* function writes from the buffer from the associated stream a specified number (count) of items of the specified size. Writing begins with the current file position. The file position is updated after the *fwrite*. The *fwrite* function returns the number of items successfully written, not the number of bytes written. The buffer may or may not be an array. The buffer associated with the file is usually declared as a structure with a count to read of 1. In data processing the buffer associated with a file for input and output is often referred to as a record. The fields in the structure can be any of the normal data types such as integer, string, long, and float.

The form for the fwrite function is:

```
number_items = fwrite ( buffer , size , number_to_write , stream ) ;
```

where:

1) Buffer specifies from where to write the data. The buffer length must be equal to or greater than size times number_to_write.
2) Size specifies the size of one of the records to be written.
3) Number_to_write specifies the number of records to write.

4) Stream specifies which stream to write the data to.
5) Number_items equals the number of items written.

Example 41.1, an example using the *fwrite* function:

```
/*                    program name:       fwrite1.c          */
#include <stdio.h>
main()
{
FILE    *stream ;
int      status , i ;
char     buffer [ 512 ] ;

    stream = fopen ( "filename" , "wb" );                       /* line 1 */

    for ( i = 0 ; i < 512 ; i++ )
       buffer[i] = i ;

    status = fwrite ( buffer , 1 , 512 , stream );              /* line 2 */

    if ( status !=  512 )                                       /* line 3 */
         printf( "write error occurred." );

}     /* end of main */
```

Line 1 sets the mode to allow write access to the binary file when it is opened. Any existing file with name "filename" is destroyed.

Line 2 is an example of the *fwrite* function call. It returns the number of items written.

Line 3 tests to see if all 512 items are written. If not, an error is reported.

Example 41.2, a program that copies a file using high-level functions:

```
/*                             program name:       fcopy.c
Purpose:   copy a file

Usage:      fcopy   source-file-name    destination-file-name
*/
#include <stdio.h>                                          /* line 1 */
#define COUNT  512                                          /* line 2 */
main ( argc , argv )                                        /* line 3 */
int     argc ;
char          *argv[] ;
{
    FILE     *sin  ;            /* source file */
    FILE     *sout ;            /* destination file */
    int      read_cnt  ;
    int      write_cnt ;
    char     buffer [ COUNT ] ;


    if ( argc < 3  || argc > 3 )                            /* line 4 */
    {
         fprintf( stderr , "Usage:\n" );
         fprintf( stderr , "      fcopy  source-file  destination-file\n\n" );
         exit(0);
    }
```

```
    sin = fopen ( argv[1] , "rb" );                         /* line 5 */

    if ( sin == NULL )                                      /* line 6 */
    {
        fprintf ( stderr , "Source file missing\n\n" );
        exit(0);
    }

    sout = fopen ( argv[2] , "wb" );                        /* line 7 */

    if ( sout == NULL )                                     /* line 8 */
    {
        fprintf( stderr , "Can not create Destination File\n\n" );
        close( fd );
        exit(0);
    }

    do                                                      /* line 9 */
    {
         read_cnt = fread ( buffer , 1 , COUNT , sin ) ; /* line 10 */

         if ( read_cnt > 0 )                                /* line 11 */
         {
            write_cnt = fwrite ( buffer, 1 ,
                                  read_cnt , sout );        /* line 12 */

            if ( write_cnt != read_cnt )                    /* line 13 */
            {
                fprintf( stderr, "file write error -- run stopped.\n\n" );
                close( fd );
                close( fd2 );
                exit(0);
            }
         }

    } while ( read_cnt == COUNT ) ;                         /* line 14 */

    fclose ( sin  );                                        /* line 15 */
    fclose ( sout );                                        /* line 16 */

    printf( "file copy complete.\n\n" );                    /* line 17 */

}   /* end of fcopy */
```

Line 1 includes the stdio.h file.

Line 2 defines the length of each data read, which is 512 for this example.

Line 3 is the *main* function name and includes the parameters for command line arguments since this program receives the name of the file to copy on the command line when the program is run.

Line 4 tests to make sure 2 arguments plus the program name are on the command line when the program is run. If there are more or less than 2 arguments, the program displays the proper command usage to run this program and then stops executing.

Line 5 opens the file specified in the first command line argument, the source file. This file is opened in the read only mode for a binary file. The result of the *fopen* is assigned to variable sin.

Line 6 tests the result of the open statement on the source file. If the resulting file pointer is NULL then the file was not on the disk or could not be opened, therefore an error message is displayed and the program stops executing.

Line 7 creates the file specified in the second command line argument and opens it in the write mode of a binary file. Any data in an existing file by the same name is lost, as this open sets the file length to 0. The result of the *fopen* is assigned to variable sout.

Line 8 tests the result of the open statement on the destination file. If the resulting file pointer is NULL then the file was not opened; therefore an error message is displayed, the source file is closed, and the program stops executing.

Line 9 through line 14 contain the code that actually copies the file.

Line 10 reads a block of data from the source file, stores it into the buffer, and stores the number of characters read into a variable. A value of 0 is stored in the number of characters read if end-of-file is reached in the source file.

Line 11 tests the variable storing the characters read for EOF. If EOF is not reached, the body of the *if* is performed.

Line 12 writes the block of data just read to the destination file. The number of characters actually written is stored into a variable.

Line 13 tests to see if the whole buffer is written. If not, then an output error occurred, an error message is displayed, both the source and the destination files are closed, and the program stops executing.

Line 14 tests to see if the source file is at end-of-file. If the number of characters read is less than the number requested, then end-of-file is reached. If end-of-file is reached,the file is copied and the program can leave the *do-while* loop.

Line 15 closes the source file.

Line 16 closes the destination file.

Line 17 displays a message that the copy is complete.

APPLICATIONS

The fwrite function is useful to write structures, arrays, and character-oriented data files to disk. Use the fread function to read the data written by the fwrite function. See the fread function for more information.

TYPICAL OPERATION

In this operation you enter, compile, and execute the program given in Example 41.1.

1. Begin at the DOS prompt, in your C source code directory. Invoke your text editor.
2. Type the C program given in Example 41.1, just like it is listed. Call the program FCOPY.C.
3. Compile and link the program with your C compiler.
4. Type **FCOPY FCOPY.C FCOPY1.C** and press **Enter**. Notice the following output on your screen:

```
C:\C>FCOPY FCOPY.C FCOPY1.C
file copy complete.
C:\C>_
```

5. Turn to Module 38 to continue the learning sequence.

Module 42

GETC

```
NAME

   getc  —  reads a single character from stream file

USAGE

   int   getc ( FILE *stream ) ;

PROTOTYPE in      stdio.h

ANSI Synopsis

    #include <stdio.h>
    int     getc(FILE *stream);

RETURNS

   returns the next character entered from a stream file,
           or EOF if end of file or an error is detected
```

DESCRIPTION

The *getc* function reads and returns a single character from a stream file. If an error occurs or end-of-file is encountered, (EOF) is returned instead of the character. The return data type is *int*. The character is converted to *int* type without sign extension.

The actual error number can be retrieved from *errno* if an error occurs.

The *getc* function is often implemented as a macro instead of a function in the standard library. Do not be concerned about the term macro here as it is part of the preprocessor, is handled by the preprocessor, and is transparent to you.

Example 42.1, an example using the *getc* function:

```
/*                    program name:        getc1.c       */
#include <stdio.h>
main()
{
    FILE    *stream ;
    int     c ;

    stream = fopen ("getc1.c", "r" );    /* open for read */

    c = getc ( stream );                              /* line 1 */

    if ( c == EOF )                                   /* line 2 */
         printf( "error occurred on file read." );
    else printf ( "first character input is: %c\n" , c );

}   /* end of main */
```

Line 1 is an example of a *getc* function call. This function returns the next character in the stream file, or EOF when the end-of-file in the stream file is reached. Notice that the variable receiving the returned character is *int* type and not *char* type. It is this way because EOF is an integer value.

Line 2 tests the returned value from line 1 for EOF.

The output of this example is:

```
first character input is: /
```

APPLICATIONS

The getc function is the same as the fgetc function. Look back at Module 27 to review its typical applications.

TYPICAL OPERATION

In this operation you enter, compile, and execute the program given in Example 42.1.

1. Begin at the DOS prompt, in your C source code directory. Invoke your text editor.
2. Type the C program given in Example 42.1, just like it is listed. Call the program GETC1.C.
3. Compile and link the program with your C compiler.
4. Type **GETC1** and press **Enter**. Notice the following output on your screen:

```
C:\C>GETC1
first character input is: /
C:\C>_
```

5. Turn to Module 33 to continue the learning sequence.

Module 43

GETCHAR

```
NAME

   getchar  —  read a single character from stdin

USAGE

   int getchar ( void ) ;

PROTOTYPE in      stdio.h

ANSI Synopsis

    #include <stdio.h>
    int  getchar(void);

RETURNS

   returns the next character entered from stdin,
           or EOF if end of file or if an error is detected
```

DESCRIPTION

The *getchar* function reads and returns a single character from stdin. If an error occurs or the end of the file is encountered, *getchar* returns *end-of-file*. The return data type of the character is *int*. The character is returned as an integer, without sign extended.

The *getchar* function can be expressed alternately as:

```
getc ( stdin ) ;
```

The *getchar* function is often expressed as a macro as getc(stdin) in most C compilers.

Example 43.1, example using *getchar*:

```
/*                          program name:    getchar1.c          */
#include <stdio.h>
main()
{
    int   c ;

        c = getchar();                              /* line 1 */

        printf( "\ncharacter input is:  %c\n" , c );

}  /* end of main */
```

Line 1 assigns the character returned by *getchar* to the *int* type variable c.

The getchar function has a few side effects you should be aware of:

a. Execution does not continue until <ENTER> is pressed.
b. If a single character is entered followed by <ENTER>, the program will act on the first character; then when getchar is invoked again, the carriage return character (from the <ENTER> key, hex 0D) is returned.
c. If getchar is invoked again after the EOF character is input, getchar returns EOF (– 1) forever.

TYPICAL OPERATION

In this operation you enter, compile, and execute the program given in Example 43.1.

1. Begin at the DOS prompt, in your C source code directory. Invoke your text editor.
2. Type the C program given in Example 43.1, just like it is listed. Call the program GETCHAR1.C.
3. Compile and link the program with your C compiler.
4. Type **GETCHAR1** and press **Enter**. Type an **A** and press **Enter**. Notice the following output on your screen:

```
C:\C>GETCHAR1

character input is:  A
C:\C>_
```

5. Turn to Module 63 to continue the learning sequence.

Module 44

GETS

```
NAME

   gets  —  reads a line from stdin and stores the input in
            a memory buffer.

USAGE

   addr = gets ( char *buffer ) ;

PROTOTYPE in      stdio.h

ANSI Synopsis

    #include <stdio.h>
    char   *gets(noalias char *s);

RETURNS

   returns the address of the buffer, or a NULL pointer if an
   end-of-file or an error is detected
```

DESCRIPTION

The *gets* function reads a line from *stdin*, stores the input in a buffer, and returns the address of the buffer. If an error occurs or the end of the file is encountered, a NULL pointer is returned instead of the buffer address. The *gets* function stores input from stdin into the buffer until a *newline* character is entered. The *newline* is not placed in the buffer. However, *gets* does place a '\0' at the end to mark the end of the input string.

The *gets* returns the address of the buffer if the input is entered without an error. If an error is encountered, a NULL pointer is returned.

Example 44.1, an example of the gets function:

```
/*                  program name:    gets1.c       */
/* Purpose: to demonstrate one way to get operator input into the computer,
and then to print what the operator has input.                         */
#include <stdio.h>
main()
{
```

```
        char      *buff_ptr ;
        char      buffer[ 512 ] ;

          buff_ptr = gets ( buffer );                           /* line 1 */

          printf( "Buffer= %s\n", buffer );                     /* line 2 */

          printf( "Buffer= %s\n", buff_ptr );                   /* line 3 */

    }   /* end of main */
```

Line 1 This *gets* function call places the keyboard input into the variable named buffer and then returns the address of the buffer to the caller. If an error is encountered, a NULL pointer is returned.

Lines 2 and 3 both display the contents of the buffer variable, which is the operator input from the keyboard.

APPLICATIONS

The gets function is one method for getting operator input into the computer. It places all characters that are typed on the keyboard into the specified string. The input ends when the Enter key is pressed.

An example of using the gets function is the mailing list application which can be programmed to accept input of the name, address, city, state, and zip, all with the gets function.

```
#include <stdio.h>
struct
{
  char name      [ 30 ] ;
  char addr      [ 30 ] ;
  char CityStZip [ 40 ] ;
}  mail ;

main()
{
      gets ( mail.name );
      gets ( mail.addr );
      gets ( mail.CityStZip );
}
```

Notice that the danger in using the gets function is that the length of the input data is not checked. If too many characters are input, then memory after the field is destroyed or the program will abort due to a memory fault. Either case is not acceptable. Either use a large buffer to guarante that the operator will not enter too many characters, or input the characters one at a time and count them in your own function.

TYPICAL OPERATION

In this operation you enter, compile, and execute the program given in Example 44.1.

1. Begin at the DOS prompt, in your C source code directory. Invoke your text editor.
2. Type the C program given in Example 44.1, just like it is listed. Call the program GETS1.C.
3. Compile and link the program with your C compiler.
4. Type **GETS1** and press **Enter**. Type **My name is Emmett.** and press **Enter**. Notice the following output on your screen:

```
C:\C>GETS1
My name is Emmett.
Buffer= My name is Emmett.
Buffer= My name is Emmett.
C:\C>_
```

5. Turn to Module 64 to continue the learning sequence.

Module 45

GOTO

```
NAME

    goto —   transfer control to a specified C statement

USAGE

     goto  LABEL ;
     /*  ....   more C statements would follow here */

LABEL:
     /* C statement  */    /* goto transfers control here */
```

DESCRIPTION

The C *goto* statement has a label as its object. When the goto statement executes, control transfers to the C statement that follows the label where it is defined. The label definition must reside in the function that references it and must be defined only once. A label name follows the standard naming rules of C and has a colon attached to its right side. When a *goto* statement refers to a label the colon is not used.

NOTE

Good programming practice usually avoids the use of the *goto* statement. A section of code normally can be restructured to avoid using *goto*.

Two common sense rules about using the *goto* statement are:

1. Do not *goto* a label in the middle of the body of one of the looping instructions. The result is undefined.
2. Do not *goto* a label in the middle of a *switch* statement. The result is undefined.

Example 45.1, example of *goto* statement:

```
/*                      program name:    goto1.c           */
main()
{
    int  age = 12 ;                                   /* line 0 */
```

```
        if ( age > 125 )
            goto  INPUT_ERROR ;                              /* line 1 */

        printf( "Age value is within range! \n" );

        exit( 0 );    /* end program */

INPUT_ERROR:                                                 /* line 2 */
        printf( "Age value is out of range! \n" );           /* line 3 */

}     /* end of main */
```

Line 1 is an example of a *goto* statement. If this *goto* statement executes, then control transfers to the C statement in this module that follows the definition of the label used in the *goto* statement. In this example, if age is greater than 125, control transfers to line 3.

Line 2 is an example of the definition of a label that can be the object of a goto statement.

Line 3 is the instruction that follows the label defined in line 2. This line executes next if the *goto* in line 1 executes.

The output of Example 45.1 is:

```
Age value is within range!
```

TYPICAL OPERATION

In this operation you enter, compile, and execute the program given in Example 45.1.

1. Begin at the DOS prompt, in your C source code directory. Invoke your text editor.
2. Type the C program given in Example 45.1, just like it is listed. Call the program GOTO1.C.
3. Compile and link the program with your C compiler.
4. Type **GOTO1** and press **Enter**. Notice the following output on your screen:

```
C:\C>GOTO1
Age value is within range!
C:\C>_
```

5. Edit the C program GOTO1.C. In Line 0 set age equal to 150. Call the program GOTO2.C.
6. Compile and link the program with your C compiler.
7. Type **GOTO2** and press **Enter**. Notice the following output on your screen:

```
C:\C>GOTO2
Age value is out of range!
C:\C>_
```

8. Turn to Module 72 to continue the learning sequence.

Module 46

IF-ELSE

```
NAME

   if - else   --  Conditionally executes the body of statements
             that follow either the if or the else, depending
             on the result of an expression or condition.

USAGE 1

       if ( test-expression-condition )   /* evaluate to true or false */
       {
            /* c code to execute if evaluation is true */
       }

USAGE 2

       if ( test-expression-condition )   /* evaluate to true or false */
       {
            /* c code to execute if evaluation is true */
       }
       else
       {
            /* c code to execute if evaluation is false */
       }
```

CONTROL STATEMENTS IN C

Control statements allow decision making within programs. The control statements direct the program to perform alternative actions based upon the tested conditions. The program acts upon the conditions which tell it what statement to execute next. Control statements add to the efficiency and readability of programs.

Control statements come in several different forms to provide flexibility in the controlling of program execution. One form is to optionally execute C statements. Another form is to form a loop, where all the statements in a loop are executed repeatedly until the exit condition is satisfied. Another form is to branch to a certain statement and continue execution.

The simplest C statement that demonstrates the ability to optionally execute statements is the *if* statement. The format of the *if* statement is:

```
if ( expression )                   /* if the expression is true */
     statement ;                    /* execute this statement.   */
else
     statement ;                    /* false then this statement */

if ( expression )                   /* if the expression is true */
{
     statement1 ;                   /* execute this statement    */
     statement2 ;                   /* and this statement.       */
}
else
{
     statement3 ;                   /* false then this statement */
     statement4 ;                   /* and   then this statement */
}
```

Braces are used for grouping of statements. When a single statement is to be executed after the if statement, note that braces are not required. When more that one statement is going to be executed after the if statement, then the statements must be grouped by enclosing them within braces. Statements within braces are treated as one statement by the compiler. The statements within braces following the if statement are referred to as a *body* of statements. This rule for the grouping of statements with braces applies to all the C control statements.

The following is a summary of the C control statements:

1. if-else — The if-else statement can be used to select one of two mutually exclusive courses of action in a program. The body of statements following the if statement is executed when the expression is true. When the expression is false and an else is included with the if, the body of statements following the else is executed.

2. while — The body of statements following the while loop statement is executed until the conditional expression becomes false (zero). The body does not execute when the expression is false in its first evaluation.

3. do-while — The statements following the do statement are executed and then the expression in the while statement is evaluated. The body of statements following the do is executed until the conditional expression becomes false (zero). The body of statements following the do will always execute at least once.

4. for — The body of statements following the for loop statement is executed until the conditional expression becomes false (zero). The body of statements does not execute when the expression is false in its first evaluation.

5. switch — The switch statement controls the selection of one body of statements to be executed based upon the value of a case selector expression whose value equals the evaluated expression in the switch statement.

6. break — The break statement causes an immediate exit from the control statement in which it appears.

7. continue — The continue statement transfers program control to the place in the program such that the next iteration of the loop begins.

8. goto — The goto statement transfers control to the C statement that follows the label designated in the goto statement.

DESCRIPTION OF *if* STATEMENT

The *if* C statement conditionally executes the body of statements that follows *if*, depending on the result of an expression/condition.

The *if* statement first evaluates the test-expression/condition. If the result is true (a non-zero value) then the body of C statements that immediately follow the *if* statement executes. If the result is false then the body of C statements immediately following is not executed. The *if* statement is used to either execute C statements or not execute C statements, depending on some condition tested.

An optional *else* statement is available for the *if* statement. If the result is false and an *else* statement is included, the statements immediately following the *else* execute.

NESTING OF *if-else* STATEMENTS The statement following an *if* or *else* statement can be another *if-else* series of statements. When this occurs, it is called *nested ifs*. Since the else statement is optional, there does not have to be an equal number of *if* and *else* statements. C resolves any ambiguities by pairing an *else* statement with the most recent *if* statement which lacks an *else*. To prevent ambiguities (and unexpected results), braces can be used to group statements together. This can clarify or simplify the code.

Example 46.1, example of *if-else* statement:

```
/*                    program name:   if1.c            */
#include <stdio.h>
main()
{
    int  i , j , k ;

    i = 3 ;
    j = 10 ;

    printf ( "i = %d, j = %d\n" , i , j );

    if ( i > 4 )
         printf(  "i is greater than 4\n" );         /* line 1 */
    else printf ( "i is not greater than 4\n" );

    if ( i >= 0 )
    {
        k = i ;
        printf( " k  set equal to i \n" );           /* line 2 */
    }
```

```
        if ( i >0 )                                          /* line 3 */
        {
             if  ( j < 100 )                                 /* line 4 */
             {
                   printf( "i is > 0 and J is < 100 \n" );
             }
             else k = 0 ;                                    /* line 5 */
        }                                                    /* line 6 */
    }      /* end of main */
```

Line 1 is an example of a statement that executes only when the result of the expression in the *if* statement is true. Since there is only one statement dependent on the condition of the test, it does not have to be placed in braces.

Line 2 is an example of two statements that executes conditionally so they must be enclosed in braces.

Lines 3 through 6 are an example of *nested if* statements. If the test on line 3 is true then the block of statements in the braces following line 3 executes. The first statement in the braces is an *if* statement. If the result of this statement is true then the statement following it will be executed. Note it is ok to place the one statement in braces if you like. The *else* statement on line 5 goes with the inside *if* statement on line 4. The statements following the *else* statement would execute when the result of the test in line 4 is false.

An *if-else* statement is considered one statement in C; therefore the braces from the *if* on line 3 can be left out and the program still executes properly, as the *else* statement is given to the closest *if* statement when it must choose what it thinks you want it to do.

The output of Example 46.1 is:

```
i = 3, j = 10
i is not greater than 4
i is > 0 and J is < 100
```

Example 46.2, another example of an if statement:

```
/* Purpose: calculate number of days in any month (since 1752) */
/* program name                      if2.c                     */
main()
{
int month , year   , days ;

     month = 4 ;
     year  = 1988 ;

     if ( month == 2 )     /* Feb */                             /* line 1 */
     {                                                            /* line 2 */
          if (     ( year % 4   == 0 && year % 100 != 0 )         /* line 3 */
                || ( year % 400 == 0 ) )                          /* line 3 */
                days = 29 ; /* leap year */                       /* line 4 */
          else days = 28 ; /* reg. year */                        /* line 5 */
     }                                                            /* line 6 */
```

```
   else   if (    ( month == 4 ) || ( month == 6 )                   /* line 7 */
                || ( month == 9 ) || ( month == 11 ) )               /* line 8 */
                  days = 30 ;       /* Apr  , Jun  , Sept, Nov        line 9 */
           else   days = 31 ;       /* Jan,Mar,May,Jul,Aug,Oct,Dec    line 10 */
   printf ( "number of days in month %d of year %d is %d" ,
                                       month ,      year , days   );
} /* end of main */
```

The output of Example 46.2 is:

```
number of days in month 4 of year 1988 is 30
```

Line 1 compares for the month 2 (February) since it is a special case. If the month is February then line 3 executes next, else control is transfered to line 7 to execute next. If the month is February then line 3 is executed to see if the year is a leap year. If it is true that it is leap year then line 4 executes else line 5 executes. If the month is not February then in line 7 a test is made to see if the month is April, June, September, or November. If the month is one of the ones tested then line 9 executes, otherwise line 10 executes. Note that the if-else C statement is considered to be a single statement to C and that there are not braces around the if-else statement in line 7 thru line 10. Also the braces on lines 2 and 6 are not necessary in this case, but are placed there by the authors to prevent programming errors occuring like the following:

Example 46.3, example of if-else statement that contains an ERROR **********.

```
/* Purpose: calculate number of days in any month (since 1752) */
main()
{
int month , year   , day   , days ;

    month = 4 ;              /* April */
    year  = 1988 ;
    days = 28 ;              /* Feb. in non-leap year */
    if ( month == 2 )        /* Feb */                               /* line 1 */
        if (    ( year % 4   == 0 && year % 100 != 0 )              /* line 2 */
              || ( year % 400 == 0 ) )                               /* line 2 */
             days = 29 ; /* leap year */                             /* line 3 */
    else if (    ( mmmonth == 4 ) || ( month == 6 )                  /* line 4 */
              || ( month == 9 ) || ( month == 11 ) )                 /* line 5 */
                days = 30 ;       /* Apr  , Jun  , Sept, Nov          line 6 */
         else   days = 31 ;       /* Jan,Mar,May,Jul,Aug,Oct,Dec      line 7 */
    printf ( "number of days in month %d of year %d is %d" ,
                                       month ,      year , days   );
} /* end of main */
```

See if you can find the error in the above program. What would this program calculate as the number of days in April?

The error occurs because of the nested if rule that says that an else statement is always associated with the closest if statement. Therefore, the else statement in line 4 is matched with the if in line 2 and not line 1. At the end of this program, the variable days would always be equal to 31 unless the year was a leap year, in which case it would be equal to 29, because the only time the program would execute the else in line 4 would be when month = = 2 and, therefore, the else in line 7 executes.

WARNING

Indenting the way it appears the program will execute does not cause the program to execute in that sequence.

if STATEMENT FLOWCHART The following flowchart shows the sequence of events that occur in the execution of an *if* statement.

Form of if statement:

```
if ( expression )
{
      if_body_of_instructions
}
else
{
      else_body_of_instructions
}
```

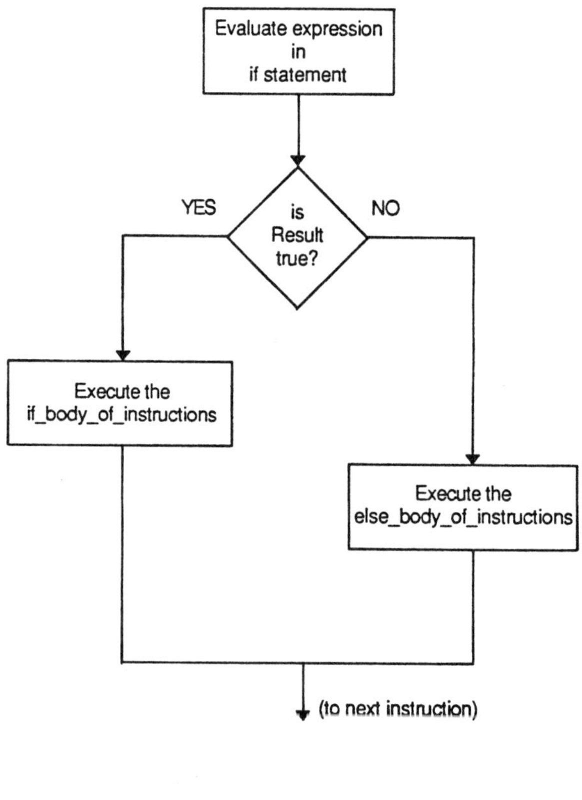

APPLICATIONS

The *if* statement is useful for allowing a C program to select between two possible courses of action. Through the use of nested if statements, a C program can choose among several possible actions.

For example, a payroll program might have a function to calculate regular wages as Payrate * Hours for the first 40 hours per week and overtime wages for hours worked over 40 hours per week as Payrate * hours * 1.5. Assuming all variables are properly declared and have appropriate values, the following code segment performs the computation of wages:

```
if ( Hours <= 40 )
     wages = Payrate * Hours ;
else wages = [Payrate * 40) + ([Hours - 40) * Payrate * 1.5 ) ;
```

TYPICAL OPERATION

In this operation you enter, compile, and execute the program in Example 46.1.

1. Begin at the DOS prompt, in your C source code directory. Invoke your text editor.
2. Type the C program in Example 46.1, just like it is listed. Call the program IF1.C.
3. Compile and link the program with your C compiler.
4. Type **IF1** and press **Enter**. Notice the following output on your screen:

```
C:\C>IF1
i = 3, j = 10
i is not greater than 4
i is > 0 and J is < 100
C:\C>_
```

5. Type the C program in Example 46.2, just like it is listed. Call the program IF2.C.
6. Compile and link the program with your C compiler.
7. Type **IF2** and press **Enter**. Notice the following output on your screen:

```
C:\C>IF2
number of days in month 4 of year 1988 is 30
C:\C>_
```

8. Turn to Module 88 to continue the learning sequence.

Module 47

IS______

```
NAME

   is______ — group of functions that tests a characters
              class

USAGE

   int  is____ ( int  c ) ;

PROTOTYPE in      ctype.h

ANSI Synopsis

    #include <ctype.h>
    int   is___(int c);

RETURNS
      returns 1 if character in test class, else returns a 0
```

DESCRIPTION

These are the character class test functions:

```
isalnum( c )        /*  alphanumeric test          */
isalpha( c )        /*  alphabetic test            */
isascii( c )        /*  defined ASCII test         */
iscntrl( c )        /*  ASCII control character    */
isdigit( c )        /*  digit test                 */
islower( c )        /*  lower-case alpha test      */
isprint( c )        /*  printable character        */
ispunct( c )        /*  punctuation character      */
isspace( c )        /*  a whitespace character     */
isupper( c )        /*  upper-case alpha test      */
isxdigit(c )        /*  valid hexidecimal char     */
```

These functions test whether the character argument is a member of the class being tested. If the character is a member of the class being tested, the function returns 1 for true. Otherwise, it returns 0 for false.

The characters in each class are:

```
isalnum( c )        'a' thru 'z', 'A' thru 'Z', '0' thru '9'
isalpha( c )        'a' thru 'z', 'A' thru 'Z'
isascii( c )        0x00 thru 0x7F
iscntrl( c )        0x00 thru 0x1F, 0x7F
isdigit( c )        '0' thru '9'
islower( c )        'a' thru 'z'
isprint( c )        0x20 thru 0x7E
ispunct( c )        ! " # $ % & ' ( ) * + , - . /
                    : ; < = > ? [ \ ] ^ _ { | } ~  space
isspace( c )        space, '\t', '\n'
isupper( c )        'A' thru 'Z'
isxdigit(c )        'a' thru 'f', 'A' thru 'F', '0' thru '9'
```

Example 47.1, an example of a program using the character class test functions:

```
/*                          name:  is1.c     */
main()
{
char    c ;

  do
  {
    printf ( "\n\ninput character ('x' to end): " );
    scanf ( "%c" , &c );

    if ( isprint ( c ) )
         printf ( "\nThe character '%c' is in the following classes:\n",c );
    else printf ( "\nThe character is in the following classes:\n" );

    if ( isalnum ( c ) )  printf ( " alphanumeric\n" );
    if ( isalpha ( c ) )  printf ( " alpha\n" );
    if ( isascii ( c ) )  printf ( " ascii\n" );
    if ( iscntrl ( c ) )  printf ( " control character\n" );
    if ( isdigit ( c ) )  printf ( " digit\n" );
    if ( islower ( c ) )  printf ( " lowercase alphabetic\n" );
    if ( isprint ( c ) )  printf ( " printable character\n" );
    if ( ispunct ( c ) )  printf ( " punctuation\n" );
    if ( isspace ( c ) )  printf ( " white space character\n" );
    if ( isupper ( c ) )  printf ( " uppercase alphabetic\n" );

  }     while ( c != 'x' );
}
```

APPLICATIONS

The is_______ functions are well suited for editing functions. They provide an easy way for testing a character to see if it is a number, if it is lowercase or uppercase, if it is printable, or if it is a punctuation character. Using these functions makes the program easily understood and maintainable.

TYPICAL OPERATION

In this operation you enter, compile, and execute the program given in Example 47.1.

1. Begin at the DOS prompt, in your C source code directory. Invoke your text editor.
2. Type the C program given in Example 47.1, just like it is listed. Call the program IS1.C.
3. Compile and link the program with your C compiler.
4. Type **IS1** and press **Enter**. Type **5** and press **Enter**. Type **x** and press **Enter**. Notice the following output on your screen:

```
C:\C>IS1

input character ('x' to end): 5
The character '5' is in the following classes:
 alphanumeric
 ascii
 digit
 printable character

input character ('x' to end): x
The character 'x' is in the following classes:
 alphanumeric
 alpha
 ascii
 lowercase alphabetic
 printable character
C:\C>_
```

5. Execute the program with other values and check its output. Enter all kinds of keys on the keyboard, including function keys, arrow keys, and keyboard combinations, like Ctrl + W. Enter x to terminate the program.
6. Turn to Module 8 to continue the learning sequence.

Module 48

LSEEK

```
NAME

   lseek --  moves to a new location within a low-level opened
             file

USAGE

   long  lseek ( int fd , long location , int start_position ) ;

PROTOTYPE in       io.h

RETURNS
        returns the new offset within the file
```

DESCRIPTION

The *lseek* function moves the file pointer to a new location in a file. The start_position from which to calculate the new location is one of three values:

0 — beginning of file
1 — current position in file
2 — end of file

The location is added to the proper start location to calculate the new file pointer location. The *lseek* returns the new file pointer location, or −1 if an error occurs.

Example 48.1, an example using the *lseek* function:

```
/*                   program name:       lseek1.c          */
#include <io.h>
#include <fcntl.h>
main()
{
    int     status , fd , mode ;
    long    location = 512 ;

    mode = O_RDWR ;                                 /* line 1 */

    fd = open ("filename", mode );
```

```
        location = lseek ( fd , location , 0 ) ;             /* line 2 */

        if ( location == -1 )
             printf( "file was not lseeked properly.\n" );
        else printf( "file was lseeked properly.\n" );

   }    /* end of main */
```

Line 1 sets the file access mode to read and write.

Line 2 is an example of an *lseek* function call requesting that the file location pointer be moved to byte 512 from the beginning of the file. This function returns a −1 value if an error occurs, else the new offset is returned. It is moved to 512 from the beginning of the file since the start_position has the value of 0.

APPLICATIONS

The lseek function allows a program to access a file randomly. One application that sometimes requires processing files randomly is accounts receivable. In the master data file the data is kept in account number sequence. However, statements need to be printed in zip code sequence to get the lowest postage rate. To accomplish this task an index is created for the master data file. In the index is the zip code and the offset of the master data record. After the index is created, it is sorted into zip code sequence. The index is then read sequentially, and as each record in the index is read, the corresponding master data record is accessed randomly by using the lseek function followed by the read function. In this manner, the statements are printed in zip code sequence.

TYPICAL OPERATION

In this operation you enter, compile, and execute the program given in Example 48.1.

1. Begin at the DOS prompt, in your C source code directory. Invoke your text editor.
2. Type the C program given in Example 48.1, just like it is listed. Call the program LSEEK1.C.
3. Compile and link the program with your C compiler.
4. Type **LSEEK1** and press **Enter**. Notice the following output on your screen:

```
C:\C>LSEEK1
file was lseeked properly.
C:\C>_
```

5. Turn to Module 66 to continue the learning sequence.

Module 49

MALLOC

```
NAME

   malloc  —  allocates a block of memory for use

USAGE

   void    *malloc ( unsigned size ) ;

PROTOTYPE in      stdlib.h

ANSI Synopsis

    #include <stdlib.h>
    void  *malloc(size_t size);

RETURNS
       returns a pointer to allocated memory, or NULL
       pointer if not enough memory is available to
       allocate this block
```

DESCRIPTION

The *malloc* function allocates a block of memory as large as required by size.

If less memory than size is available, it returns a NULL pointer. If the memory is allocated, it returns a memory pointer to the calling function.

If the memory allocated is not the same type as required by the pointer to char, then the memory allocation pointer can be *type cast* to the proper type. Many times the memory allocated is for a structure. A type cast changes the definition of the returned pointer to that of the desired structure.

Example 49.1, an example using the *malloc* function:

```
/*                    program name:       malloc1.c       */
#include <stdio.h>
#include <stdlib.h>
main()
{
char       *mem_ptr ;
```

```
struct     cust_type
{
 char        name [ 30 ] ;
 char        addr [ 30 ] ;
 char        city [ 20 ] ;
 char        state[ 20 ] ;
 float       balance     ;
} ;

struct     cust_type     *cust_ptr ;

      mem_ptr = malloc ( 512 );                              /* LINE 1 */

      if ( mem_ptr == NULL )
          printf( "not enough memory for the array.");
                                                             /* LINE 2, below */
      cust_ptr = (struct cust_type   *)malloc( sizeof( struct cust_type ));

      cust_ptr->balance = 0 ;                                /* LINE 3 */

      printf ( "balance = %d\n" , cust_ptr->balance );

}    /* end of main */
```

Line 1 allocates 512 bytes of memory.

Line 2 allocates enough memory for a structure of the calculated length. A *type cast* is performed on the pointer returned by malloc, changing it to a pointer of the desired structure type. Remember, the *type cast* is placed in parentheses in front of the expression to be converted. The asterisk indicates the *type cast* is a pointer and the struct cust_type indicates the pointer type.

Line 3 uses the allocated memory. Remember, the pointer definition only allots memory for the pointer, not what it is pointing to. Also, the pointer must be initialized before it can be used.

DYNAMIC MEMORY MANAGEMENT C programs are usually loaded in lower memory, the stack in upper memory, and the memory between them is called the *heap*. The heap is available for temporary storage during program execution. After the memory is used, it is freed to the heap where it can be allocated again as necessary during execution. When the program stops, all of memory is freed to the operating system. This includes the program memory, the stack, and the heap. The memory allocations discussed here are only active during program execution. They need not be freed when the program stops executing, but must be freed if you need to reuse the memory during program execution.

This *dynamic memory allocation* scheme is a powerful tool for the C programmmer.

The three dynamic memory allocation functions covered in this text are:

malloc	—	allocate a block of memory
calloc	—	allocate an array of blocks of memory
free	—	free allocated memory for reuse

APPLICATIONS

When the amount of memory required for data storage in a program varies, the malloc function is often used to meet the necessary requirements. One such application is in banking where each month the number of checks written varies with each customer. In a program where all the data for all checks written by one customer is required to be in memory at the same time, the malloc function can be called multiple times to continue to allocate space until all the check data is read into memory. The allocated blocks are also usually chained together. After each customer is processed, all of the allocated blocks are freed, allowing this memory to be allocated for use again.

TYPICAL OPERATION

In this operation you enter, compile, and execute the program given in Example 49.1.

1. Begin at the DOS prompt, in your C source code directory. Invoke your text editor.
2. Type the C program given in Example 49.1, just like it is listed. Call the program MALLOC1.C.
3. Compile and link the program with your C compiler.
4. Type **MALLOC1** and press **Enter**. Notice the following output on your screen:

```
C:\C>MALLOC1
balance = 0
C:\C>_
```

5. Turn to Module 13 to continue the learning sequence.

Module 50

MEMSET

```
NAME

   memset  --  sets memory to a byte value

USAGE

 void  *memset ( void *mem_ptr , int value , int count ) ;

PROTOTYPE in      string.h

ANSI Synopsis

    #include <string.h>
    void  *memset(noalias void *s, int c, size_t n);

RETURNS
       returns the pointer to the block of memory
```

DESCRIPTION

The *memset* function sets a block of memory to the specified value (a byte value). This function is often used to zero a block of memory.

The function returns the pointer to the block of memory.

Example 50.1, an example using the *memset* function:

```
/*                      program name:       memset1.c       */
#include <string.h>
main()
{
        int      i ;
        char     work_area [ 512 ] ;

        memset( work_area , 0 , 512 );                       /* line 1 */

        for ( i = 0 ; i < 10 ; i++ )
            printf ( "%02x" , work_area[i] );

}    /* end of main */
```

Line 1 is an example of the *memset* function call. It fills the entire work_area with zeros.

APPLICATIONS

The most common use of the memset function is to set each byte in a structure to 0x00. You can set each field within the structure to 0x00 or use a loop to set each byte to 0x00, but the processing time takes longer and does not benefit you at all. One thing to remember is to always use the sizeof operator to determine the size of a structure within your programs; in this way, if you change a structure, then your code continues to perform correctly.

TYPICAL OPERATION

In this operation you enter, compile, and execute the program given in Example 50.1.

1. Begin at the DOS prompt, in your C source code directory. Invoke your text editor.
2. Type the C program given in Example 50.1, just like it is listed. Call the program MEMSET1.C.
3. Compile and link the program with your C compiler.
4. Type **MEMSET1** and press **Enter**. Notice the following output on your screen:

```
C:\C>MEMSET1
00 00 00 00 00 00 00 00 00 00
C:\C>_
```

5. Turn to Module 87 to continue the learning sequence.

Module 51

NUMBERING SYSTEMS

DESCRIPTION

This module introduces the binary number system, the octal number system, the hexadecimal (hex) number system, and their relationships to the decimal number system. It also explains floating-point numbers and binary addition and subtraction.

When you finish this module, you should be able to convert between *number system bases* in the following ways:

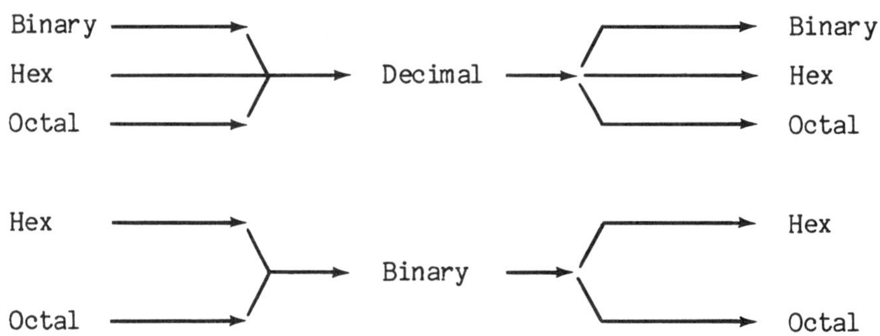

Numbering systems are for counting. We use the decimal number system (base 10) for our everyday numbering system. If people only had 8 fingers, we might be using the base 8 (octal) system for counting, instead of base 10 (decimal).

The different numbering systems are simple, once you understand the basics. All numbering systems can be placed into an algebraic notation which associates "place" with "value." This is to say that the decimal numbers 1234 and 4321 have a different total value, even though both numbers consist of the very same digits — they are just in a different place within the numbers.

The value of a number in any base can be calculated by multiplying each digit in a number by the value of the digit position, and then adding the results together to get the value. The value of each digit position (place) is found by raising the number of the base to the power of the place number. The place numbers begin on the right side of a number with zero and move from right to left.

Example of general form for numbering systems:

number is XYZ, with Z in place0 of the number in base B
Y in place1 of the number in base B
X in place2 of the number in base B

$X \cdot B^2 + Y \cdot B^1 + Z \cdot B^0 = \text{number value}$

Any number raised to the power of 0 has the value of 1.

For example: $1^0 = 1.$ $10^0 = 1.$ $12938476^0 = 1.$

Any number raised to the power of 1 has the value of the base.

For example: $1^1 = 1.$ $10^1 = 10.$ $12938476^1 = 12938476.$

Example showing the value of decimal number 1234 in base 10:

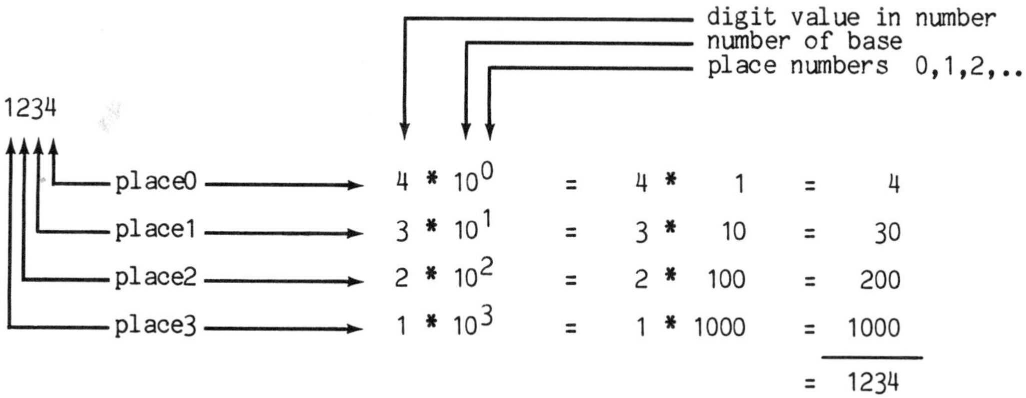

BINARY NUMBERING SYSTEM The binary numbering system is the one used by digital computers. The binary numbering system can have only two possible digit values for each place, 0 and 1. The binary numbering system values of 0 and 1 are used to represent the on and off states of binary data in a digital computer.

The values for each place, according to our formula, are:

$2^0, 2^1, 2^2, 2^3, 2^4, 2^5, 2^6, 2^7, 2^8, 2^9, 2^{10}, \ldots, 2^N$ ← place number / base

and the place value for each place is:

1, 2, 4, 8, 16, 32, 64, 128, 256, 512, 1024, ... ← place values

Convert Binary To Decimal To convert the binary number 10010011 to decimal:

```
             number   place
10010011     value    value

              1    *    1  =    1
              1    *    2  =    2
              0    *    4  =    0
              0    *    8  =    0
              1    *   16  =   16
              0    *   32  =    0
              0    *   64  =    0
              1    *  128  =  128
                              ---
   10010011 in base 2      =  147 in base 10
```

Learn the place values for the binary number system. It is not hard, as the *place0* starts with the value 1, and the next place is always twice the value of the previous place. So, to multiply a binary number by two, simply shift the bits one place to the left and put a zero in *place0*.

OCTAL NUMBERING SYSTEM The octal numbering system (base 8) has eight possible digit values for each place (0 through 7).

The values for each place, according to our formula:

```
0   1   2   3   4   5   6   7   8   9   10        N  <---- place number
8,  8,  8,  8,  8,  8,  8,  8,  8,  8,  8,  ... , 8  <---- base
```

give the place value for each place to be:

```
1,  8, 64, 512, 4096, 32768, 262144, ...             <---- place values
```

Convert Octal To Decimal To convert the octal number 137 to decimal:

```
         number   place
137      value    value

          7    *    1  =   7
          3    *    8  =  24
          1    *   64  =  64
                          --
   137 in base 8       =  95 in base 10
```

Convert Octal To Binary Because octal is a multiple of the base 2, it is easy to convert octal to binary. Each place in octal requires three binary places for the conversion. To verify this, add the place values for the first three places in binary. Yes, 1 + 2 + 4 does equal 7.

To convert the octal number 1137 to binary:

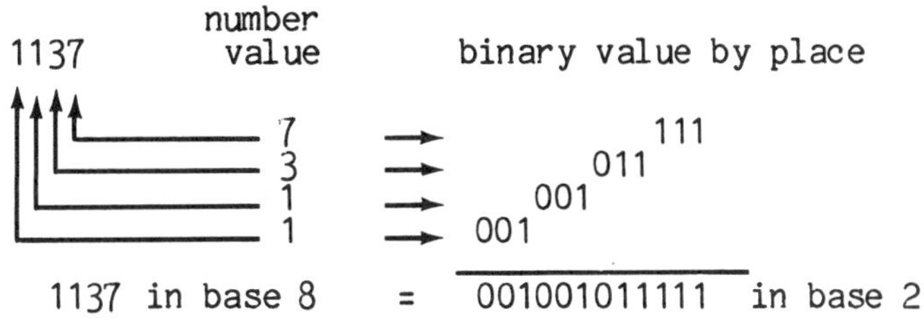

Binary Back To Octal To convert a binary number back to octal, group the binary places into groups of three and take the value for each place.

To convert the answer from the previous example back to octal:

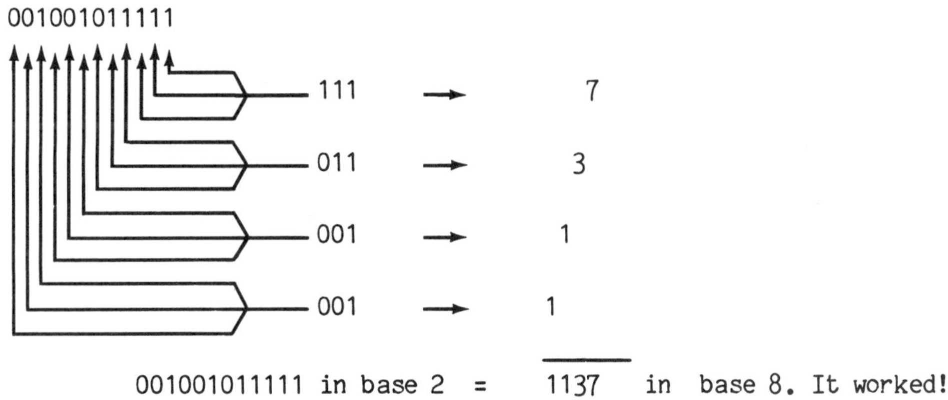

HEX NUMBERING SYSTEM The hex numbering system (base 16) has 16 possible digit values for each place, 0 through F, with A through F being used to represent the values 10 through 15 respectively. *A* has the value of 10, *B* has the value of 11, *C* has the value of 12, *D* has the value of 13, *E* has the value of 14, and *F* has the value of 15.

The values for each place, according to our formula:

```
  0    1    2    3    4    5    6    7    8          N ←— place number
16,  16,  16,  16,  16,  16,  16,  16,  16,  ... , 16 ←— base
```

give the place value for each place to be:

```
1, 16, 256, 4096, 65535, 1048576, ...              ←— place values
```

Convert Hex To Decimal To convert the hex number 1B3F to decimal:

```
          number    place
1B3F      value     value

          15    *      1  =    15
           3    *     16  =    48
          11    *    256  =  2816
           1    *   4096  =  4096
                             ----
    1B3F in base 16       =  6975 in base 10
```

Convert Hex To Binary Because hex is a multiple of the base 2, it is easy to convert to binary. Each place in hex requires four binary places for the conversion. To check this, add the values in the first four places in binary. The sum is 15, which is the maximum value in place0 in hex.

To convert the hex number 1B3F to binary:

```
          number
1B3F      value       binary value by place

          15    -->                     1111
           3    -->                0011
          11    -->           1011
           1    -->      0001
                     -------------------
    1B3F in base 16  =   0001 1011 0011 1111   in base 2
```

Binary Back To Hex To convert a binary number to hex, group the binary places into groups of four and take the value for each place.

To convert the answer from the previous example back to hex:

```
1101100111111

            1111   -->    F

            0011   -->    3

            1011   -->    B

            0001   -->    1
                        ----
1101100111111 in base 2  =   1B3F   in  base 16. It worked!
```

DECIMAL NUMBERING SYSTEM The decimal numbering system (base 10) is the one you are probably most familiar with.

Converting from decimal to another base is a straightforward division process. Divide the decimal number by the base (it's called the *radix*). Note the quotient and the remainder. Continue to divide the new quotient and to note the remainder until the quotient is zero. The remainders are combined to form the converted number. A few examples will make this clear.

Decimal To Binary Conversion To convert the decimal number 147 to binary:

	radix	quotient	remainder	(calculation)
147:	2	147		
		73	1	(147 - 2 * 73)
		36	1	(73 - 2 * 36)
		18	0	(36 - 2 * 18)
		9	0	(18 - 2 * 9)
		4	1	(9 - 2 * 4)
		2	0	(4 - 2 * 2)
		1	0	(2 - 1 * 1)
		0	1	(1 - 2 * 0)

147 in base 10 = 10010011 in base 2

Decimal To Octal Conversion To convert the decimal number 95 to octal:

	radix	quotient	remainder	(calculation)
95:	8	95		
		11	7	(95 - 8 * 11)
		1	3	(11 - 8 * 1)
		0	1	(1 - 8 * 0)

95 in base 10 = 137 in base 8

Decimal To Hexadecimal Conversion To convert the decimal number 6975 to hexadecimal:

	radix	quotient	remainder	(calculation)
6975:	16	6975		
		435	15	(6975 - 16 * 435)
		27	3	(435 - 16 * 27)
		1	11	(27 - 16 * 1)
		0	1	(1 - 16 * 0)

95 in base 10 = 1B3F in base 8

FLOATING POINT NUMBERING SYSTEM The data types for numbers with decimal points in C are *float* and *double*. Floating point numbers are stored in the computer in *scientific notation*. This means that any number can be expressed as a decimal fraction multiplied by a power of ten.

Floating point numbers are stored in three parts:

1. the decimal fraction, a number less than one
2. the power of ten exponent
3. the sign of the number, either positive or negative

Floating point numbers in C are stored in two precisions:

1. six decimal digits of precision, called *float*
2. at least 15 decimal digits of precision, called *double*

BINARY ARITHMETIC Numbers can be added in any base number system. In binary, just like in other numbering system, when adding if there is a carry from a place, it is added to the ext place.

Binary Addition The following chart contains the rules for binary addition:

Addition Facts for Binary:

+	0	1
0	0	1
1	1	10

In binary:

```
0 + 0 ──▶ 0
0 + 1 ──▶ 1
1 + 1 ──▶ 10     where "10" in base 2 is two in base 10
```

For example:

```
add:         01001001 in base 2     (a decimal 73)
         +   00100001 in base 2     (a decimal 33)
             ________
         =   01101010 in base 2     (a decimal 106)
```

Binary Subtraction Subtraction is performed by taking the *two's complement* of the number being subtracted, adding the numbers together, and ignoring the carry bit.

The *two's complement* is calculated by reversing all the bit values in a number and adding 1.

For example:

The *two's complement* of decimal 201 (which is binary 11001001) is:

```
11001001 ──▶  00110110
            + 00000001
            ──────────
              00110111
```

Therefore, to subtract decimal 201 from 250:

```
             decimal  250 ──▶    11111010
two's complement of 201 ──▶  +   00110111
                                ──────────
               result =       1 00110001 (ignore carry)

                      =         00110001  which is decimal 49.
```

Appendixes C, D, E, F, and G include numbering systems tables that can be useful when dealing with computers. Use them to increase the speed of your number conversions by developing shortcuts.

Turn to Module 20 to continue the learning sequence.

Module 52

OPEN

```
NAME
    open  —  opens a file for low-level access
USAGE
    int  open ( char *filename , int mode, [int permission] );
PROTOTYPE in      io.h
RETURNS
          returns a file descriptor, or -1 to indicate an error
```

DESCRIPTION

The *open* function is a low-level function that opens a file. The file is opened for access according to the mode argument, which indicates type of access: read, write, or both. The *open* function returns a file descriptor if the file opens satisfactorily, else a −1 is returned.

C maintains the current file location for the user. When a file opens, the file location is set to the beginning of the file. After doing reads, writes, and seeks, the file location updates to the new file location.

The following low-level functions can be used with files opened with the *open* function:

read, write, close, and *lseek*.

Note that this is not an ANSI function.

Example 52.1, an example using the *open* function:

```
/*                    program name:        open1.c           */
#include <io.h>
#include <fcntl.h>      /* defines O_RDWR                    line 1 */
main()
{
 int      status , mode ;

          mode = O_RDWR  ;

          status = open( "filename" , mode );               /* line 2 */
```

```
        if ( status == -1 )
             printf( "file could not be opened.\n");
        else printf( "file opened.\n");

}     /* end of main */
```

Line 1 includes the file that defines O_RDWR, read/write access to the file.

Line 2 is an example of the low-level open function call. If it opens the file without an error it returns a file descriptor, else it returns a −1.

APPLICATIONS

Before files can be read or written with low-level functions they must be opened with the open function. Just like high-level functions, before files can be read or written to they must be opened successfully. Do not do reads or writes to low-level files unless they are opened successfully.

TYPICAL OPERATION

In this operation you enter, compile, and execute the program given in Example 52.1.

1. Begin at the DOS prompt, in your C source code directory. Invoke your text editor.
2. Type the C program given in Example 52.1, just like it is listed. Call the program OPEN1.C.
3. Compile and link the program with your C compiler.
4. Type **OPEN1** and press **Enter**. Notice the following output on your screen:

```
C:\C>OPEN1
file opened.
C:\C>_
```

5. Turn to Module 15 to continue the learning sequence.

Module 53
OPERATORS

DESCRIPTION

The C language offers a rich set of operators to specify action on data. *Operator* is the term used to describe the action to be taken between two data operands. An identifier (or a constant) used with an operator is called an *operand*. For example, the arithmetic multiply operator is used to multiply two identifiers together, and the assignment operator is used to set an identifier equal to a value.

Expressions are made by combining *operators* between operands. Expressions are evaluated by applying the *operator* to the operands involved. An expression consists of an operator and an identifier or a sequence of identifiers. When several operators are in one expression, some of the operators are acted on before others. Some parts of the expression are also acted on before other parts. The rules concerning precedence are covered in Module 54, Operators — Part 2.

The general form for operators:

```
operand1    operator    operand2
```

The value of operand2 is applied to operand1 as directed by the operator. For example, the multiply operator is used to multiply 2 variables (operands) and the assignment operator assigns the value of one operand to another operand.

In this example:

```
operand3 = operand1 * operand2 ;
         ↑          ↑
         |          └──────── operator 1
         |
         └──── operator 2
```

Operator 1 is the multiply operator and operator 2 is an assignment operator. First operator 1 multiplies operand1 times operand2. Next, the assignment operator 2 assigns the value of the result of the multiply to operand3.

The operators available in C include:

1. Assignment (to set equal to)
2. Arithmetic (add, subtract, multiply, divide, modulus)
3. Relational (equal to, less than, greater than, not equal to, less than or equal to, greater than or equal to)

4. Increment & decrement (add one, subtract one)
5. Bit (and, or, xor, shift, one's complement)
6. Logical or Boolean (and, or, not)
7. Compound assignment (plus equals, minus equals, times equals, divide equals, modulus equals, shift equals, bit-wise AND equals, bit-wise OR equals, bit-wise XOR equals)
8. Condition expression (condensed if-then-else)

ASSIGNMENT OPERATOR The *assignment operator* is to "set equal to." The variable on the left side of the equal sign is set equal to the value of the operand on the right side of the equal sign. The operand on the right side may be an expression that contains other operands and operators. The special character used for the *assignment operator* is the equal sign.

FORM: `operand1 = operand2 ;`

The assignment operator specifies that the first *operand* is assigned the value of the second operand. Operand2 is evaluated and the result is assigned to operand1.

Operator	*Usage*
=	to set equal to

EXAMPLE:

```
x = y ;    /*   x   is set equal to the value of y  */
```

ARITHMETIC OPERATORS The *arithmetic operators* are: add, subtract, multiply, divide, and modulus for integer and floating-point numbers.

FORM for arithmetic operators:

```
operand1  arithmetic_operator  operand2
```

The *add operator* specifies that the first operand is added to the second operand.

The *subtract operator* specifies that the second operand is subtracted from the first operand.

The *multiplication operator* specifies that the first operand is multiplied by the second operand.

The *division operator* specifies that the first operand is divided by the second operand. If the two operands are integers, then the result is an integer and any remainder is truncated.

The *modulus operator* specifies that the first operand is divided by the second operand and that the remainder is the resulting value. The *modulus operator* is sometimes called the *remainder operator*.

Operator	*Usage*
+	add
–	subtract
*	multiply
/	divide
%	modulus

Example 53.1, example of arithmetic operators:

```
/*                          program name:    oper1.c               */
#include <stdio.h>
main()
{
  int    x , y , z ;

      z = 2 ;
      y = 3 ;

      x = y + z ;       /* the value of y and the value of z are
                           added together and the result assigned to x */

     printf ( "%d + %d = %d\n" , y , z , x )

      x = y - z ;       /* the value of z is subtracted from the value
                           of y and the result assigned to  x          */

     printf ( "%d - %d = %d\n" , y , z , x )


      x = y / z ;       /* the value of y is divided by the value of z
                           and the result assigned to x, any remainder
                           is truncated                                */

     printf ( "%d / %d = %d\n" , y , z , x )

      x = y % z ;       /* the value of y is divided by the value of z
                           and the remainder is assigned to  x         */

     printf ( "%d modulus %d = %d\n" , y , z , x )

}    /* end of main */
```

The output of Example 53.1 is:

```
3 + 2 = 5
3 - 2 = 1
3 / 2 = 1
3 modulus 2 = 1
```

RELATIONAL OPERATORS The relational and equality operators are used to test or compare the value between two operands. The relational and equality operators produce an integer result to express the condition of the comparison. If the condition is false then the integer result is 0 (zero). If the condition is true then the integer result is non-zero. The logical operators also produce the same results, 0 for false and a non-zero value for true.

The most common usage of the relational and logical operators is in a C control statement. The if-else C statement uses the value result from the relational and logical operators to optionally execute C statements. The conditional expression operator is a shortcut form for the if-else statement.

The form of the if-else C control statement looks like this:

```
if ( expression )           /* expression to evaluate     */
     statement ;            /* execute if result is true  */
else
     statement ;            /* execute if result is false */
```

Note that if the expression evaluates to either a true (non-zero) or false (zero) value, then the control statement executes the proper body of statements following the control statement.

The *relational operators* are: equal to, less than, greater than, not equal to, less than or equal to, and greater than or equal to. The relational operators are normally used with C's *flow control* statements, like *if*, *do-while*, *while*, and *for*.

FORM for relational operators:

```
operand1  relational_operator  operand2
```

The first operand is compared, according to the operator, to the second operand. If the operands are not equal then the test is false and the result is zero. Otherwise, if the operands are equal then the test is true and the result is one. Note that these tests do not change the value of any variables, they are only compared. The result of a test always has either the value of 0 or the value of 1 (0 for false and 1 for true).

Operator	*Usage*
= =	to compare if equal to (double equal signs)
<	to compare if less than
>	to compare if greater than
! =	to compare if not equal to
< =	to compare if less than or equal to
> =	to compare if greater than or equal to

Example 53.2, example of relational operators:

```
/*                        program name:    oper2.c          */
#include <stdio.h>
main()
{
  int    x , y ;

    x = 2 ;
    y = 3 ;

    printf ( "x = %d, y = %d\n" );          /* display value of variables */

    if ( x == y )                           /*  if x is equal to y then   */
       printf( "x and y are equal\n" );     /*  do the printf statement   */
```

```
    if ( x < y )                          /*  if x is less than y then    */
       printf( "x IS LESS THAN y\n");     /*  do the printf statement     */

    if ( x > y )                          /*  if x is greater than y then */
       printf( "x IS GREATHER THAN y\n"); /*  do the printf statement     */

    if ( x != y )                         /*  if x is not equal to y      */
       printf( "x is not equal to y\n" ); /*  then do the printf          */

    if ( x <= y )                         /*  if x is less than or equal  */
       printf( "x IS LESS THAN OR EQUAL y\n"); /*  y then do the printf   */

    if ( x >= y )                              /* if x is greater than or */
       printf( "x IS GREATER THAN OR EQUAL y\n"); /* equal y do the printf */

}      /* end of main  */
```

The output of Example 53.2 is:

```
x = 2, y = 3
x IS LESS THAN y
x is not equal to y
x IS LESS THAN OR EQUAL y
```

INCREMENT AND DECREMENT OPERATORS The *increment* and *decrement operators* are: "add one" and "subtract one." *Increment* and *decrement* have a very special property — they can increment or decrement the value either before or after the value of the variable is used. If the operator appears in front of the variable, it is called a *prefix operator*. The value used is the value before it is updated. If, however, the operator appears on the right hand side of the variable, it is called a *postfix operator* and the value used is the updated value.

FORM for increment and decrement operators:

```
(operand)operator          /* postfix operator */
operator(operand)          /* prefix  operator */
```

Note that the parentheses are added only in this form to separate the words and are not required in actual usage.

These operators specify that the operand is either incremented or decremented, either before or after the value of the operand is used, in the context of the C statement.

Operator	*Usage*
+ +	increment the variable
− −	decrement the variable

Example 53.3, example of increment and decrement operators:

```
/*                            program name:   oper3.c          */
#include <stdio.h>
main()
{
  int    x , y ;

      x = 2 ;
      y = 3 ;

      x++ ;    /* add 1 to the variable x.  Same as x = x + 1 ;    */

      y-- ;    /* subtract 1 from y.        Same as y = y - 1 ;    */

      x = 6   ;
      y = ++x ;   /* add 1 to x and assign the result to y.  The value
                     x is 7, and the value of y is 7 when completed. */

      x = 6   ;
      y = x++ ;   /* get value of x and assign to y. Then increment the
                     value of x. The value of x is 7, and value of y is 6   */

      printf( "x = %d, y = %d\n", x , y );

}    /*  end of main  */
```

The output of Example 53.3 is:

```
x = 7, y = 6
```

BIT OPERATORS The *bit operators* are:

`and, or, xor, right shift, left shift, and one's complement.`

The bit operators change the value of a result at the bit level. Note that these operators do not change the value of the operands. They only use the value of the operands to calculate a resulting value. The value must be assigned with the assignment operator to affect the value of a variable.

FORM of bit operators:

```
operand1  bit_operator  operand2
```

Shift The *shift operators* specify that the first operand is shifted left or right the number of bit positions according to the value of the second operand.

Left Shift The left shift move starts with the leftmost bit. The bits shifted off the left hand side are truncated and lost. All vacated bits on the right side are set to zero.

Right Shift The shift to the right is not as simple as the shift to the left. If the shift is to the right and the variable is unsigned, then the vacated bits are also set to zero. If, however, the variable is a signed data type, the sign bit (the leftmost bit) is placed into each vacated bit. The bits shifted off the right hand side are truncated and lost.

AND The *AND operator* specifies that the corresponding bits of both the first and second operands are ANDed together. The corresponding bit of both operands must be *on* for the resulting bit to be *on*, otherwise the resulting bit is *off*. See the following truth table.

OR The *OR operator* specifies that the corresponding bits of both the first and second operands are OR'd together. If either corresponding bit of either operand is *on* then the resulting bit is *on*, else the resulting bit is *off*. See the following truth table.

XOR The bit-wise *XOR operator* specifies that the corresponding bits of both the first and second operands are XOR'd together. Only one of the corresponding bits can be *on* for the resulting bit to be *on*, otherwise the resulting bit is *off*. See the following truth table.

Logical Truth Table for AND, OR, XOR

AND			*OR*			*XOR*		
a	b	a & b	a	b	a ¦ b	a	b	a ^ b
0	0	0	0	0	0	0	0	0
0	1	0	0	1	1	0	1	1
1	0	0	1	0	1	1	0	1
1	1	1	1	1	1	1	1	0

ONES COMPLEMENT The *ones complement operator* specifies that each bit of an operand reverses its value. All bits *on* are turned *off*, all bits *off* are turned *on*.

Operator	*Usage*
<<	left shift of bits
>>	right shift of bits
&	AND of bits
¦	OR of bits
^	XOR (exclusive or) of the bits
~	Ones Complement (NOT operator)

Example 53.4, example of bit operators:

```
/*                          program name:   oper4.c            */
#include <stdio.h>
main()
{
  int    x , y , z ;

      x = 2 ;
      y = 3 ;

      z = x << 2 ;      /* shift bits in x left 2 places.  Value of z is  8
                           and the value of x remains 2; it's not changed!
                           x =  00000010
                           z =    00001000      after assignment          */
```

```
    printf( "2 << 2 = %d \n", z );

    z = y >> 1 ;     /* shift bits in y right 1 place.  Value of z is 1
                        and the value of y remains 3; it's not changed.
                        y =  00000011
                        z = 00000001          after assignment          */

    printf( "3 >> 1 = %d \n", z );

    z = x << y ;     /* shift bits in x left 3 places.  Value of x remains
                        2, value of y remains 3, and z becomes  16
                        x =  00000010
                        z =      00010000     after assignment          */

    printf( "2 << 3 = %d \n", z );

    z = x &  y ;     /* and bits of x and y,  2 & 3 gives 2.
                                x = 2 =  00000010
                                y = 3 =  00000011
                                         --------
                                x & y =  00000010   which is 2.         */

    printf( "2 & 3 = %d \n", z );

    z = x ¦  y ;     /* or bits of x and y,   2 ¦ 3  gives 3.
                                x = 2 =  00000010
                                y = 3 =  00000011
                                         --------
                                x ¦ y =  00000011   which is 3.         */

    printf( "2 ¦ 3 = %d \n", z );

    z = x ^  y ;     /* xor bit of x and y,   2 ^ 3  gives 1.
                                x = 2 =  00000010
                                y = 3 =  00000011
                                         --------
                                x ^ y =  00000001   which is 1.         */

    printf( "2 ^ 3 = %d \n", z );

}   /* end of main */
```

The output of Example 53.4 is:

```
2 < 2 = 8
3 > 1 = 1
2 << 3 = 16
2 & 3 = 2
2 | 3 = 3
2 ^ 3 = 1
```

LOGICAL OPERATORS (Boolean expressions) The *logical operators* are AND, NOT and OR.

The logical operators are called *Boolean operators* because the tests between values are reduced to either true or false, with zero being false and one being true. Note that these operators do not change the value of the operands. They only use the value of the operands to calculate a resulting value. The value must be assigned with the assignment operator to affect the value of a variable.

FORM for logical operators:

```
operand1 boolean_operator operand2
```

The *logical AND operator* evaluates the first operand, and if the result is true (a non-zero value), it evaluates the second operand. If the second operand's value also is true, the result of the operator is true (= one). However, if the first operand evaluates false, the second operand is not evaluated and the result of the operator is false (= zero).

The *logical OR operator* evaluates both operands and if the result of both operands is zero, then the result of the operator is zero; otherwise, the result is one.

Operator	*Usage*
&&	logical/boolean AND
||	logical/boolean OR
!	logical/boolean NOT

Example 53.5, example of logical operators:

```
/*                         program name:   oper5.c              */
#include <stdio.h>
main()
{
  int    x , y , z ;

      x = 2 ;
      y = 3 ;

      printf ( "x = %d, y = %d\n" , x , y );

      if ( x == 2 && y == 3 )
         printf( "both values matched as expected!\n");

/*  In the above example, the program checks to see if
x is equal to 2; if it is, it then checks to see if y is
equal to 3; if it is, it then executes the printf statement.
With the && operator both expressions must be true for the
body of the if to execute.                                  */


      if ( x == y && y >= 3 )
          printf( "both conditions were true.\n");
      else printf( "one of the conditions was not true.\n");

/*  In the above example, the program checks to see if
x is equal to the value of y; if it is, it then checks to see if y
is greater than or equal to 3; if it is, it then executes the body
of the if.  If the check for x equal to y is false, it immediately
executes the body of the else associated with the if statement.

With the && operator if the first expression is false, then the
second expression is not checked or evaluated, IT IS IGNORED.
This is a very IMPORTANT FACT to remember.                      */
```

```
    if ( x == 5 || y >= x )
            printf( "one of the expressions is true.....\n");
    else    printf( "neither expression is true, both false.\n");

/* In the above example, the program checks to see if x is equal to
5; if it is it does the body of the if.  If the value is not equal to 5,
the program checks to see if y is greater than or equal to value of x; if
it is, it executes the body of the if.  Otherwise it executes the body of
the else associated with the if.                                          */

}    /*  end of main  */
```

The output of Example 53.5 is:

```
x = 2 , y = 3
both values matched as expected!
one of the conditions was not true.
neither expression is true, both false.
```

COMPOUND ASSIGNMENT OPERATORS The *compound assignment* statements are: plus equals, minus equals, times equals, divide equals, modulus equals, shift equals, bit-wise AND equals, bit-wise OR equals, and bit-wise XOR equals.

FORM of compound assignment operators:

```
operand1    compound_assignment_operator    operand2
```

The rules given for the noncompound types hold true for the *compound assignment statements*, where the operand of the left side of the operator is used as operand one, the operand to the right of the operator is operand two, and the assignment is made to the operand on the left side of the operator. These operators do affect the value of the left operand.

Operator	*Usage*
+=	add assignment operator
−=	minus assignment operator
*=	times assignment operator
/=	divide assignment operator
%=	modulus assignment operator
<<=	left shift assignment operator
>>=	right shift assignment operator
&=	bit-wise AND assignment operator
¦=	bit-wise OR assignment operator
^=	bit-wise XOR assignment operator
~=	ones complement assignment operator

Example 53.6, example of compound assignment operators:

```
/*                          program name:   oper6.c          */
#include <stdio.h>
main()
{
  int    x , y , z ;

      x = 2 ;
      y = 3 ;

      x <<= 2 ;     /* shift bits in x left 2 places.  Value of x is 8  */

      x >>= 1 ;     /* shift bits in x right 1 place.  Value of x now 4 */

      x <<= y ;     /* shift bits in x left 3 places.  Value of x now 32 */

      x = 2 ;

      x &=  y ;     /* value of x is now 2 */

      x |=  y ;     /* value of x is becomes 3 */

      x ^=  y ;     /* value of x is now 0 */

}   /* end of main  */
```

The values of x during the execution of Example 53.6 are provided in the comments.

CONDITIONAL EXPRESSION OPERATOR The *conditional expression operator* is a condensed form of an if-then-else C statement. The question mark and the colon are the special characters used to form the *conditional expression operator*.

FORM for conditional operator:

```
operand1 ? operand2 : operand3
```

The *conditional expression* specifies that the operand1 is evaluated and, if the result is true (non-zero value), then operand2 is evaluated. The result, then, of the *conditional expression* is the value of operand1. If, however, the result of operand1 is false, then operand3 is evaluated and its result is the value returned by the *conditional expression*.

Operator	*Usage*
? :	conditional expression

Example 53.7, example of conditional operator:

```
/*                         program name:    oper7.c           */
#include <stdio.h>
main()
{
  int   passing , failing , grade_average ;

     passing = 0 ;  failing = 0 ;
     grade_average = 75 ;

    ( grade_average >= 70 ) ?  passing++ : failing++ ;    /*  line  1     */

     printf( "number passing  = %d\n" , passing );        /*  = 1         */

     printf( "number failing  = %d\n" , failing );        /*  = 0         */

}    /*  end of  main  */
```

Line 1 The conditional statement above is evaluated and the result is true. Therefore the first operand is evaluated and not the second. The result of the first operand evaluation increments the variable passing from 0 to 1; therefore the result of this expression is 1.

The output from Example 53.7 is:

```
number passing  = 1
number failing  = 0
```

MIXED MODE ARITHMETIC Mixed mode arithmetic is the use of more than one data type in an expression. C performs type conversions before the evaluating of an expression. The type conversions are always upward, giving a more precise result. Therefore, the application of the following rules increases the accuracy of the calculated results. The rules are applied to all expressions in the order listed:

1. First, if either operand has type long double, the other operand is converted to long double.
2. Otherwise, if either operand has type double, the other operand is converted to double.
3. Otherwise, if either operand has type float, the other operand is converted to float.
4. Otherwise, if either operand has type unsigned long int, the other operand is converted to unsigned long int.
5. Otherwise, if one operand has type long int and the other has type unsigned int, if a long int can represent all values of an unsigned int, the operand of type unsigned int is converted to long int; otherwise, both operands are converted to unsigned long int.
6. Otherwise, if either operand has type long int, the other operand is converted to long int.
7. Otherwise, if either operand has type unsigned int, the other operand is converted to unsigned int.
8. Otherwise, if the operand is not int, the operand is converted to int type.

There are also implicit downward type conversions in C. These type conversions take place when the result of an expression is assigned to a variable that is less precise that the result. Downward type conversions can result in loss of accuracy because the value is truncated to fit the type of its destination.

Mixed mode arithmetic is covered in more detail in Module 87, but is presented here to make you aware of the fact that the compiler helps when it can but will round and truncate when values are assigned to less precise variables.

APPLICATIONS

Operators are used constantly in C programs. Operators are used to perform arithmetic functions on data. Operators are also used to manipulate data in C, even down to the bit level.

Mastering the use of operators is one way of improving your programming skills. One way to optimize your code for speed is to use tricks with operators. For instance, dividing is relativly slow in computers. When you need to divide an integer value by two, you can simply shift the data one bit to the right and it divides the value by two. This is many times faster than dividing the value by two.

TYPICAL OPERATION

In this operation you enter, compile and run the program in Example 53.1. You are also invited to do the same thing for the other examples in this module.

1. Begin at the DOS prompt, in your C source code directory. Invoke your text editor.
2. Type the C program given in Example 53.1, just like it is listed. Call the program OPER1.C.
3. Compile and link the program with your C compiler.
4. Type **OPER1** and press **Enter**. Notice the following output on your screen:

```
C:\C>OPER1
 3 + 2 = 5
 3 - 2 = 1
 3 / 2 = 1
 3 modulo 2 = 1
C:\C>_
```

5. Type the C program given in Example 53.2, just like it is listed. Call the program OPER2.C.
6. Compile and link the program with your C compiler.
7. Type **OPER2** and press **Enter**. Notice the following output on your screen:

```
C:\C>OPER2
x = 2, y = 3
x IS LESS THAN y
x is not equal to y
x IS LESS THAN OR EQUAL y
C:\C>_
```

8. Enter, compile, link, and execute the other examples in this module and verify your output on the screen with the output provided in the text after each example.
9. Turn to Module 46 to continue the learning sequence.

Module 54

OPERATORS — PART 2

DESCRIPTION

This module further explains: *sizeof* operators, the *address* operator, *lvalue*, and *rvalue*.

***SIZEOF* OPERATOR** The *sizeof* operator determines the size in bytes of a data object. The *sizeof* operator can determine the size in bytes of a variable declared to be any of the basic types, or the size in bytes of an array, a structure, or an array of structures.

The *sizeof* operator is not a function; it's an *operator*. The actual calculation of the size of an object is done at compile time, not when the program is actually running. The size of an object is a constant; therefore, the result of the *sizeof* operator is a constant.

Example 54.1, an example using *sizeof* operators:

```
/*                    program name:     oper21.c        */
#include <stdio.h>
main()
{
    char         letter_grade ;
    int          length ;
    double       balance ;

    struct    customer_record_type
    {
      char       cust_name   [ 30 ] ;
      char       cust_number [  5 ] ;
    } ;

    struct    customer_record_type       cust_records [ 12 ] ;

     length  =  sizeof ( length );                     /* line 1  */
     printf( "the size of an integer is %d\n" , length );

     length  =  sizeof ( letter_grade );               /* line 2  */

     length  =  sizeof ( balance );                    /* line 3  */

     length  =  sizeof ( cust_records );               /* line 4  */

     length  =  sizeof ( cust_records[0].cust_name ) ;  /* line 5  */

}   /* end of main */
```

Line 1 shows the size of an *int* type being determined. The size of an integer varies by computer. Run this program to determine your *int* type size.

Line 2 shows the size of a *char* type being determined. The size of char is one byte.

Line 3 shows the size of a *float* type being determined. The *float* size can vary from computer to computer.

Line 4 shows the size of an array of structures being determined. In this case, the program makes the calculation of 12 elements at a structure length of 35 bytes (420 bytes).

Line 5 shows the size of an array of char being determined. It is good programming practice to take the size of an object rather than using a constant value for the size. If the length of the variable is changed later, your program still executes properly.

ADDRESS OPERATOR The *address operator* (&) is closely associated with pointers, since a pointer uses an address as its value. The *address operator* determines the starting memory address of a variable, an array, or a structure. Once the starting address has been determined, it can be used in an expression or assigned to a pointer.

Example 54.2, an example using the *address operator*:

```
/*                  program name:          oper22.c         */
#include <stdio.h>
main()
{
     int        i ;
     int        *int_ptr ;

      int_ptr = &i ;                                        /* line 1 */

     *int_ptr = 5 ;                                         /* line 2 */

     printf( "i = %d\n", i );

}    /* end of main */
```

Line 1 takes the address of a variable and the address of the variable i is then placed into a pointer variable int_ptr.

Line 2 uses a pointer to place a value into an *int* variable. When this instruction has completed, the *int* variable i has a value of 5.

LVALUE and RVALUE An assignment statement has an equal sign between two operands. The term for the operand on the right is *rvalue*. The term for the operand on the left is *lvalue*.

Rvalue can be the value of a variable, the result of an expression, or the address of a variable. *Lvalue* refers to an address, a memory location. The assignment operator, after determining the data value on the right and the destination memory address on the left, can place the data value into the destination memory address.

In the example,

```
pay = rate * hours ;
```

rvalue is the result of multiplying the value of rate by the value of hours. *Lvalue* is the address in memory assigned to pay.

The term *lvalue* is used in many C language syntax charts. Remember that *lvalue* is an operand that refers to a memory location.

INCREMENT AND DECREMENT OPERATORS The *increment* and *decrement* operators, described in the module "Operators, Part 1," require an *lvalue* operand.

One powerful feature of the increment and decrement operators is not obvious.

When they are applied to pointers, the increment and decrement to the address is the length of the destination's *type*. For example, if the pointer is to a structure 512 bytes long, when the increment or decrement operator is applied, it either adds or subtracts 512 from the address in the pointer.

Example 54.3, an example of increment and decrement operators:

```
/*                  program name:       oper23.c        */
#include <stdio.h>
main()
{
        char            name [ 30 ] ;
        int             counts [ 10 ] ;
        int             i ;

        char            *name_ptr ;                         /* line 1  */
        int             *counts_ptr ;                       /* line 2  */

        name_ptr    = &name  [ 0 ] ;

        counts_ptr = &counts[ 0 ] ;

        *name_ptr   = 'B' ;

        name_ptr++        ;                                 /* line 3  */

        *name_ptr   = 'J' ;

        for ( i = 0 ; i < 10 ; i++ )
        {
                *counts_ptr = 0 ;
                 counts_ptr++   ;                           /* line 4  */
        }

}      /* end of main */
```

Line 1 declares a pointer that points to a *char* type.

Line 2 declares a pointer that points to an *int* type.

Line 3 *post-increments* the pointer to *char* type. Since the length of a *char* type is 1, this increment adds 1 to the address in the pointer.

Line 4 increments the pointer to *int* type. The increment adds the length of an *int* to this pointer when it increments the address in it. This points to the next *int* variable in the array, not the next byte in the first *int* variable.

APPLICATIONS

A typical application using the address operator is in the designing of data structures that are likely to change in the future, and you want the program you are writing now to work with no changes when the data structure has new fields added to it in the future. For instance, consider a data structure that has three sections to it, a header section, a detail section, and a summary section. You want to write your program such that if any section has new fields added to it, your existing program executes properly. One way to accomplish this is to put two fields in the header section that contain the offset from the start of the header to each of the other two sections. The following is an example of a definition that illustrates this structure.

```
struct header_data
{
  int      offset_detail ;
  int      offset_summary ;
  char     name[30] ;
  /* place new data here */
} ;

struct detail_data
{
  char    detail[5] ;
  /* place new data here */
}

struct summary_data
{
  float    balance ;
  /* place new data here */
} ;

/* data structure in memory is:   header_data, detail_data, summary_data
   but defined as an array of 1000 characters, named  our_data              */
char            our_data[1000] ;

struct header_data  *header_ptr ;
struct detail_data  *detail_ptr ;
struct summary_data *summary_ptr ;
char                *work ;


show_data()
{

     work = (char *)&our_data[0] ;
     header_ptr  = (struct header_data *) work ;
     detail_ptr  = (struct detail_data *)  ( work + header_ptr->offset_detail );
     summary_ptr = (struct summary_data *) ( work + header_ptr->offset_summary );
```

```
        printf ( "%s %s %f\n" , header_ptr->name , detail_ptr->detail ,
                                summary_ptr->balance );
    }
```

More fields can be added to the end of all three data sections, yet the show_data function will continue to execute properly. Of course, the offsets in the new data will reflect the changes in the data structures.

TYPICAL OPERATION

In this operation you enter, compile, and execute the program given in Example 54.1.

1. Begin at the DOS prompt, in your C source code directory. Invoke your text editor.
2. Type the C program given in Example 54.1, just like it is listed. Call the program OPER21.C.
3. Compile and link the program with your C compiler.
4. Type **OPER21** and press **Enter**. Notice the following output on your screen:

```
C:\C>OPER21
the size of an integer is 2
C:\C>_
```

Note that the answer to the above example may be 4 on your computer, since some computers have a 32-bit word length.

5. Enter, compile, link, and execute the other examples in this module. When you enter these examples, liberally place printf function calls throughout the programs. This will help you understand the execution of the programs.
6. Turn to Module 59 to continue the learning sequence.

Module 55

PERROR

```
NAME

   perror -- prints to stderr a description of last
             function error

USAGE

  void   perror  ( char *string ) ;

PROTOTYPE in      stdio.h

ANSI Synopsis

    #include <stdio.h>
    void  perror(const noalias char *s);

RETURNS
          no return value, VOID
```

DESCRIPTION

The perror function prints to *stderr* the string argument and a description of the last function error that occurred. The perror function uses the external variable errno to determine which error description to print.

The perror function returns no value. Its data type is void.

Example 55.1, an example using the perror function:

```
/*                   program name:       perror1.c         */
#include <stdio.h>
main()
{
    FILE    *stream ;

    stream = fopen ("filename", "w" );         /* open - write */

    if ( stream == NULL )
```

```
        perror ( "perror1.c: " ) ;                      /* line 1 */
    else printf ( "no file errors have occurred.\n" );

}    /* end of main */
```

Line 1 is an example of the perror function call. If an error occurs during the fopen then a NULL pointer is returned and placed into stream. Then when stream is tested for NULL, the perror function is called and the error description is displayed.

APPLICATIONS

When an error occurs using a C filing system function, the perror function can be called to display the appropriate, specific error message to the computer operator, so the computer operator can take the appropriate action for this specific error condition.

TYPICAL OPERATION

In this operation you enter, compile, and execute the program given in Example 55.1.

1. Begin at the DOS prompt, in your C source code directory. Invoke your text editor.
2. Type the C program given in Example 55.1, just like it is listed. Call the program PERROR1.C.
3. Compile and link the program with your C compiler.
4. Type **PERROR1** and press **Enter**. Notice the following output on your screen:

```
C:\C>PERROR1
no file errors have occurred.
C:\C>_
```

Note that if the file open in *PERROR1* fails, an error message displays on your screen instead of the above message.

5. Turn to Module 14 to continue the learning sequence.

Module 56

POINTERS

DESCRIPTION

This module explains the definition, declaration, and usage of *pointers*.

A *pointer* is a variable that contains the address of another variable. A pointer can contain the address of a variable of any basic data type, of arrays, structures, functions, and unions. Pointers contain addresses, not values.

One important quality of C that stands out is the ease of use and power that pointers provide. Pointers are sophisticated and sometimes a little harder to master than other programming concepts. However, if you study this module carefully and run the examples, you can feel comfortable with pointers and be able to use pointers effectively.

Up to now, you have worked only with a value that is stored or retrieved from a variable. With pointers, you have a variable that points to another variable. This is called *indirection*. You still do not have to be concerned with memory addresses, even though physically this is how pointers work. The compiler and operating system will keep up with and manage the addresses of data for you.

The two fundamental operators used with pointers are:

1) the address operator &
2) the indirection operator *

The *address operator* returns the address of a variable. The *indirection operator* returns the value of the variable that the pointer is pointing to.

POINTER DECLARATIONS The form for declaring a *pointer* is:

```
data_type       *pointer_name ;
```

The declaration of a pointer defines a *data*_type to which the pointer points. It has a *name*, and the name is preceded by an asterisk. The asterisk is the operator that tells the C compiler that this is a *pointer variable*.

The following are valid pointer declarations:

```
char                    *name_pointer ;          /* pointer to char   */
int                     *pointer_to_counter ;    /* pointer to int    */
float                   *balance_pointer ;       /* pointer to float  */
struct customer_record  *record_pointer ;        /* pointer to struct */
char                    *errors_pointers[ 5 ] ;  /* array of pointers */
```

The use of pointers is often called *indirection* because of the indirect path required to manipulate the variable's value.

WHY POINTERS? Two reasons for using pointers are:

1. Sometimes it is *more convenient* or flexible to work with the address of a variable than the actual variable.
2. Sometimes in C you *must* work with the address, and not the value, of a variable. This is covered shortly in Module 40. It is not as difficult as it sounds.

POINTERS' MEMORY REQUIREMENTS The amount of memory the compiler uses for a pointer to store an address of another variable varies from computer to computer. The amount of memory required for pointers on most microcomputers is either two or four bytes.

NOTE

When a pointer to any type is declared, the compiler allots memory only for *the pointer*, not for *the type* to which it points. The variable to which the pointer points must be declared independently of the pointer. Both the pointer and the variable must be declared, and the pointer must be assigned the address of the declared variable before the pointer can be used.

For instance, although a pointer is declared to point to a structure 512 bytes long, only two or four bytes (on a microcomputer) are allotted to the pointer because it can contain *only the address of a structure*. The structure is declared separately, and the 512 bytes are allotted for the structure when the structure is declared. The address of the structure must be placed into the pointer before the pointer can be used to access the members of the structure.

POINTER ASSIGNMENT Before a pointer can be used, it must contain the address of a variable. The method of assigning a pointer the address of a variable is with the *ampersand operator*. This symbol & instructs the C compiler to get the address of a variable, instead of its value. When the address in a pointer is zero, it is called a *null pointer*.

Example 56.1, an example using pointers:

```
/*                     program name:    pointer1.c         */
#include <stdio.h>
main()
{
   int         count ;
   int         i ;
   char        alphabet [ 26 + 1 ] ;
   char        letter ;

   int         *int_pointer ;                          /* line 1 */
   char        *char_pointer ;                         /* line 2 */
```

```
    letter = 'A' ;

    int_pointer   = &count ;                          /* line 3 */

    char_pointer  = &alphabet[ 0 ] ;                  /* line 4 */

    *int_pointer = 26 ;                               /* line 5 */
    count        = 26 ;                               /* line 6 */


    for( i = 0 ; i < *int_pointer ; i++ )             /* line 7 */
    {
         *char_pointer = letter ;                     /* line 8 */
         char_pointer++ ;                             /* line 9 */
         letter++ ;
     }

     *char_pointer = '\0' ;                           /* line 10 */

     printf( "%d %d\n" , *int_pointer , count );      /* line 11 */
     printf( "%s\n" , alphabet );                     /* line 12 */

}    /* end of main */
```

The output of this example is:

```
26 26

ABCDEFGHIJKLMNOPQRSTUVWXYZ
```

Line 1 declares a pointer variable that points to int type.

Line 2 declares a pointer variable that points to char type.

Line 3 uses the *ampersand operator* to place the address of a variable (instead of its value) into the pointer.

Line 4 uses the *ampersand operator* to place the address of the first character of a string into a pointer.

Line 5 assigns a constant to a variable whose address is in a pointer. The mechanics of this statement are:

1. The program finds the address where the pointer is kept in memory.
2. The program puts the value of the constant into memory at that address.

Line 6 does the same thing that line 5 does. Here, 26 is moved into the variable count; whereas, in line 5 the 26 was moved into the pointer's address (which was *the address* of count).

Line 7 uses a pointer in a *for* statement.

Line 8 uses a pointer to a string and places the value of letter into the string according to the element of the string where the pointer points. Every time this statement executes, one character in the string changes.

Line 9 increments the pointer to the next element in the string. This *for* loop indexes its way through the string variable.

Line 10 assigns a constant to the address stored within a pointer. This time it places the end-of-string marker at the end of the string just built.

Line 11 uses a pointer within a *printf* statement. The same value (26) prints for both variables.

Line 12 displays the value of a variable that was never directly assigned a value. The string is manipulated indirectly via the pointer.

Example 56.2, a programmed example to illustrate address and indirection operators:

```
/*                      program name:    pointer2.c          */
main()
{
    int     number ;                                  /* line 1 */
    int    *number_ptr ;                              /* line 2 */

    number_ptr = &number ;                            /* line 3 */
    number = 12 ;                                     /* line 4 */
    *number_ptr = 666 ;                               /* line 5 */
    printf ( "number      = %d\n" , number );         /* line 6 */
    printf ( "*number_ptr = %d\n" , *number_ptr );    /* line 7 */
}
```

The output of this program is:

```
number      = 666
*number_ptr = 666
```

Line 1 is the declaration of an integer variable.

Line 2 is the declaration of a pointer to an integer variable.

Line 3 is an address operator. The way this instruction executes is as follows:

1. The program gets the address in memory where the value for number is stored.
2. The address determined in step 1 is stored into the pointer variable number_ptr.

Line 4 assigns a value to a variable. Here 12 is assigned to the variable number. The program takes the value 12 and places it into the address of where it knows that the variable number is located.

Line 5 is the new way you are learning, and that is to use a pointer to assign a value to a variable. Here 666 is assigned to the variable number. The way this instruction executes is as follows:

1. The value on the right side of the equal sign is determined to be 666.
2. The program knows that on the left side of the equal sign is a pointer to a variable instead of a variable. The program gets the address of where it will store the value 666 from the variable number_ptr.
3. The program takes the value 666 and stores it into the address determined in step 2, which is the address of the variable number. The value 666 is written over the value 12 which was placed into the same variable in line 4.

Line 6 prints the value of number. Output is:

```
number      = 666
```

Line 7 prints the value of the variable pointed to by number_ptr. Number_ptr is pointing to the variable number. Output is:

```
*number_ptr = 666
```

CAUTION

Pointers must be initialized with the address of a variable before they are used. The data stored in a pointer is always an address of another variable. If a pointer is not initialized, then the results are predictable — YOUR SYSTEM WILL CRASH sooner or later. The results of the crash are unpredicable.

ACCESSING STRUCTURE MEMBERS WITH POINTERS A pointer uses the *right-arrow operator* to access the members of a structure. There is a way to use the dot operator to access structure members via a pointer, but the form is generally not used. The right-arrow operator is a minus sign followed immediately by a greater than sign (– >).

Example 56.3, an example of using pointers to access structure members:

```
/*                      program name:     pointer3.c          */
#include <stdio.h>
main()
{
   struct   customer_record_type
   {
     char      name [ 30 ] ;
     float     balance ;
   } ;

   struct customer_record_type        *record ;            /* line 1 */

   struct customer_record_type        customer_record ;    /* line 2 */

    record = &customer_record ;                            /* line 3 */

    record->balance = 100.00 ;                             /* line 4 */
    (*record).balance = 100.00 ;                           /* line 5 */

    printf( "balance = %f\n", customer_record.balance );

}   /* end of main */
```

Line 1 is the declaration of a pointer that points to a structure. The pointer at this stage contains no known address, not even a *null address*.

Line 2 is the declaration of the structure type to which the pointer points. A structure must be declared before a pointer can be assigned the structure's address.

Line 3 places the address of a declared structure into a pointer. The variable's *type* must match that of the data at the pointer's destination (see Line 1).

Line 4 assigns a value to a member of the structure at the pointer's destination.

Line 5 is another method for accessing a structure member. The other way is more clear but both work equally well.

NOTE

A pointer must be initialized with the address of a variable before the pointer can be used. A pointer only contains an address; it contains no data. A pointer can point to different variables of the same type at different times within a module.

Example 56.4, another example of accessing structure members with a pointer:

```
/*                      program name:    pointer4.c          */
main()
{
struct    data_struct
{
    int     count ;
    long      total ;
} ;

struct data_struct   men ;
struct data_struct   women ;
struct data_struct  *data_ptr ;                          /* line 1 */
char      gender ;
long      grade ;

    men.count = women.count = 0 ;                        /* line 2 */
    men.total = women.total = 0 ;                        /* line 3 */
    gender = 'M' ;
    grade  = 93 ;
    if ( gender == 'M' )
        data_ptr = &men ;                                /* line 4 */
    else data_ptr = &women ;                             /* line 5 */
    update_score ( data_ptr , grade );                   /* line 6 */
    show_score ( &men , "MEN" ) ;                        /* line 7 */
    show_score ( &women , "WOMEN" ) ;                    /* line 8 */
}   /* end main */

update_score (       data_ptr , grade )                  /* line 9 */
struct data_struct *data_ptr ;                           /* line 10 */
long                          grade ;
{
    data_ptr->count++ ;                                  /* line 11 */
    data_ptr->total += grade ;                           /* line 12 */
}   /* end update_score */


show_score (         data_ptr , type )                   /* line 13 */
struct data_struct *data_ptr ;                           /* line 14 */
char                          type[] ;
{
    printf ( "%s count is %d\n",type,data_ptr->count);   /* line 15 */
    printf ( "%s total is %ld\n",type,data_ptr->total); /* line 16 */
}   /* end show_score */
```

Line 1 declares a pointer to a structure.

Line 2-3 accesses the members of a structure directly with the dot operator.

Line 4-5 assignes the address of a structure to a pointer. Depending on the value of gender, either the address of the men or the women structure is assigned to the data_ptr. In this example line 4 executes, so data_ptr points to men.

Line 6 passes a pointer as a parameter to a function.

Line 7-8 passes the address of a structure as a parameter, which is passing a pointer as a parameter, like line 6.

Line 9 declares the function and its parameters.

Line 10 declares that the data_ptr is a pointer to the structure data_struct. It is probably just like you expected.

Line 11-12 updates a member of a structure with a pointer. In this example, the members men.count and men.total are updated.

Line 13 declares the function and its parameters, like line 9.

Line 14 declares that the data_ptr is a pointer to the structure data_struct. Again, it is probably just like you expected.

Line 15-16 shows how structure members are accessed with pointers.

POINTERS WITH INCREMENT AND DECREMENT OPERATORS The purpose of the increment and decrement operators is, like their names imply, to increment and decrement data objects. The data objects can be variables of any of the basic data types or a pointer.

When the increment or decrement operator is applied to one of the basic data types, it increments or decrements the value by 1.

When the increment or decrement operator is applied to a pointer, it increments or decrements the value by the length of the data object. If the pointer is pointing to a structure of length 100, when the pointer is incremented or decremented, it is by the value of 100.

Example 56.5, a programmed example of pointers with increment and decrement operators:

```
/*                        program name:    pointer5.c          */
main()
{
    int      months [ 12 ] ;
    struct   cust_struct
    {
       char     name[30] ;
       float    balance ;
    } ;
    struct cust_struct      cust_rec [ 10 ] ;
    char                   *name_ptr ;
    int                    *month_ptr ;
    struct cust_struct     *cust_ptr ;
```

```
/* initialize pointers */
     month_ptr  = &months[0] ;                           /* line 1 */
     cust_ptr   = &cust_rec[0] ;                          /* line 2 */
     name_ptr   = &cust_ptr->name[0] ;                    /* line 3 */
/* increment examples */
     name_ptr++ ;                                         /* line 4 */
     month_ptr++ ;                                        /* line 5 */
     cust_ptr++ ;                                         /* line 6 */
}  /* end of main */
```

Line 1 initializes a pointer to first element of an array of integers.

Line 2 initializes a pointer to the first element of an array of structures.

Line 3 initializes a pointer by taking where another pointer is pointing to a character that is a member of a structure in an array. This is powerful — see how much work the compiler is doing for you.

Line 4 increments a pointer to a character. Since the length of a character is one byte, 1 is added to the pointer. Now the pointer points to the second character in the name.

Line 5 increments a pointer to an integer. If the length of an integer is 2, 2 is added to the pointer. Now the pointer points to the second element in the array.

Line 6 increments a pointer to a structure. Since the length of the structure is 34, 34 is added to the pointer. Now the pointer points to the second structure in the array.

APPLICATIONS

Pointers are extremely useful in maintaining linked lists, i.e., lists that are linked together. One item in the list points to the next item in the list, and the next item points to the item that follows it, etc., with the last item in the list having a NULL or empty pointer. The items in a linked list are typically in a structure definition, with one member of the structure being a pointer to the same structure definition. This appears contradictory, to use a definition that you are in the process of defining. Don't give it a second thought; C handles it painlessly for you. An example of a structure that contains a pointer to a structure of the same type is shown below.

```
struct   data_struct
{
     struct data_struct    *next_data_ptr ;
     char                   data1[100] ;
     int                    data2      ;
} ;
```

In linked list processing there are normally two other pointers used to maintain the linked list, a head pointer and a tail pointer. The head pointer points to the first item in the list, and the tail pointer points to the last item in the list. Each item in the list points to the next item, except the last which has a NULL pointer. A linked list can be illustrated as follows:

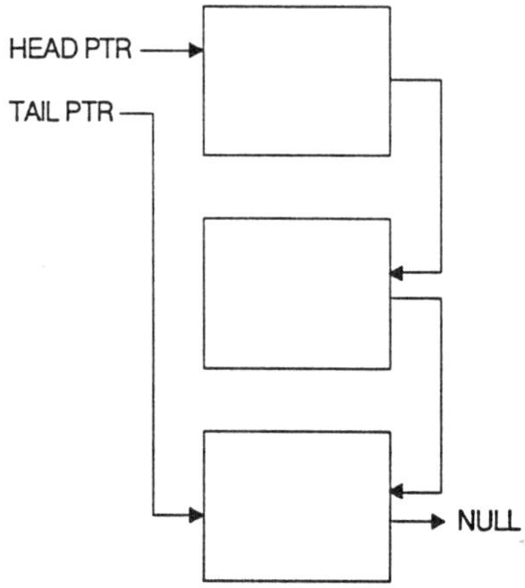

The major coding advantage of using a linked list is that the coding in the program remains the same, no matter how many items are contained in the list. Lists like this are easily maintained in C. Items can be added to the list at any point and any item in the list can be deleted. Of course when these operations take place, the pointers are updated accordingly. Note that items are very easily added to and removed from both the head and tail of the list.

A common application for a linked list is maintaining a *fifo* list (first in, first out). An example of this is a teller line at the bank where you go to the end of the line as you arrive and the next available bank teller assists the first person in line. The following code segment illustrates this principle of adding a new item to the end of the linked list and removing the first item from the linked list:

```
#include <stdio.h>
struct   data_struct
{
    struct data_struct     *next_data_ptr ;
    char                    data1[100] ;
    int                     data2      ;
} ;

struct data_struct   *head_ptr , *tail_ptr ;


 add_to_tail ( struct data_struct  *new )
 {
      tail_ptr->next_data_ptr = new  ;
      new->next_data_ptr      = NULL ;
      tail_ptr                = new  ;
 }

 struct data_struct *remove_from_head()
 {
 struct data_struct   *hold_ptr ;

      hold_ptr = head_ptr ;
      head_ptr = hold_ptr->next_data_ptr ;

      return ( hold_ptr );
 }
```

Adding or removing items in the middle of the lists is more complicated and, again, is left as an exercise for you to develop.

A *double-linked* list is a linked list where an item points both to the next item and to the previous item. An example of a structure that contains two pointers to structures of the same type for a double-linked list is as follows:

```
struct   data_struct
{
    struct data_struct      *next_data_ptr ;
    struct data_struct      *previous_data_ptr ;
    char                     data1[100] ;
    int                      data2      ;
} ;
```

In a double-linked list you can begin accessing the linked list at the head or at the tail, and you can access items on either side of an item. In single linked lists you must start at the head and process towards the tail only.

TYPICAL OPERATION

In this operation you enter, compile, and execute the program given in Example 56.1.

1. Begin at the DOS prompt, in your C source code directory. Invoke your text editor.
2. Type the C program given in Example 56.1, just like it is listed. Call the program POINTER1.C.
3. Compile and link the program with your C compiler.
4. Type **POINTER1** and press **Enter**. Notice the following output on your screen:

```
C:\C>POINTER
26 26
ABCDEFGHIJKLMNOPQRSTUVWXYZ
C:\C>_
```

5. Enter, compile, link, and execute the other examples in this module and verify the output screen with the output provided after each example.
6. Turn to Module 73 to continue the learning sequence.

Module 57

POINTERS — PART 2

DESCRIPTION

This module explains initializing pointers, pointer arithmetic, and passing pointers as function arguments.

POINTER INITIALIZATION The form for initializing a pointer when declared is:

```
data_type      •pointer_name  =  expression ;
```

For *auto* type pointers, the expression can be any expression where the result is an address. For *global* type pointers, the expression must be a constant expression where the result is an address. Pointers defined as *extern* may not be initialized, as pointers can only be initialized when declared.

NULL Value A pointer can be declared and assigned an initial value of NULL, which is a constant (zero). The NULL value can be assigned to a pointer that points to any type. A pointer is usually assigned a NULL value if the programmer needs to check whether the pointer has been used.

Example 57.1, an example of a pointer with a NULL value:

```
/*                     program name:    pointr21.c       */
#include <stdio.h>
main()
{
       char      *pointer_to_name  = NULL ;                  /* line 1 */

       if ( pointer_to_name == NULL )                        /* line 2 */

             printf( "The name has not been enter yet ....\n" );
                                   ******  entered ?  ******
}      /* end of main */
```

Line 1 is an example of the initialization of a pointer to a null value. In ANSI C the value of NULL is no longer 0, so be sure and use the #define constant NULL in your code.

Line 2 is an example of testing a pointer for a null value.

Address of Extern or Static Variable, Structure, and Array An *auto* pointer can be declared and assigned an initial value that is the address of an *extern* or *static* variable.

Example 57.2, an example of a pointer with extern variables:

```
/*                     program name:      pointr22.c       */
#include <stdio.h>

struct  x_type
{
   char    name [ 30 ] ;
   int     loan_nbr    ;
} ;

extern     int              hours_used [ 31 ] ;
extern     float            amount_collected ;

static     int              count ;
extern     struct x_type    customer_record ;

main()
{
       float    *pointer_to_amount = &amount_collected ;    /* line 1 */

       int      *ptr_count         = &count ;               /* line 2 */
       int      *ptr_hours         = hours_used ;           /* line 3 */
       int      *ptr_first         = &hours_used [ 0 ] ;    /* line 4 */

       struct x_type   *my_record  = &customer_record ;     /* line 5 */


        /* coding .... */

}          /* end of main */
```

Line 1 through line 5 are examples of the initialization of pointers to extern and static variables.

Line 3 is an example of how the ampersand is not used to get the address of an array when the array is accessed by its name, as it gets the address of the first member.

Line 4 is an example of how the ampersand is required to get the address of an array member.

String Constants A pointer to *char* type can be declared and assigned an initial value that is the address of a string constant.

Example 57.3, an example of a pointer to a string constant:

```
/*                      program name:      pointr23.c       */
#include <stdio.h>

        char     *report_title    =  "CUSTOMER LIST" ;       /* line 1 */

        char     *error_description [ ]  =                   /* line 2 */
        {
                 "fatal error"             ,
                 "printer off-line"        ,
                 "printer out of paper"    ,
                 "Lost carrier ... "       ,
                 "directory full"
         } ;                                                 /* line 3 */
```

```
main()
{
int err ;

        err = 2 ;

        printf( "error = %s\n", error_description[err] );   /* line 4 */

}   /* end of main */
```

Line 1 is an example of initialization of a pointer to a string constant.

Line 2 thru line 3 is an example of an array of pointers initialized to the address of each string. Because the strings are of different lengths, this is called a *ragged array*. Notice that the number of elements is missing, but is filled in automatically by the C compiler. The *printf* statement shows how to reference a member of the array of pointers to ragged string arrays.

Line 4 displays the error message, which is the third error message in this example.

The output from this example is:

```
error = printer out of paper
```

Function Address A pointer to a function can be declared and assigned a function's address as an initial value. When this pointer is used, the function whose address is in the pointer is called. You can think of this as calling a function by first getting the address of the function and then calling the address where the function is located to execute.

Example 57.4, an example of a pointer to a function:

```
/*                program name:       pointr24.c          */
#include <stdio.h>

extern   int   sort_ascending () ;
extern   int   sort_descending() ;

static   int   (*function_pointer)() = sort_ascending ;    /* line 1 */

main()
{
       sort_ascending() ;                                  /* line 2 */

       (*function_pointer)() ;                             /* line 3 */

}     /* end of main */
```

Line 1 is an example of the initialization of a pointer to the address of a function. Notice that the two sort functions are external to this program. The address of the sort_ascending function is stored in the function_pointer variable.

Line 2 is a function call to the sort_ascending function.

Line 3 is an example of using a pointer to call a function. Here the sort_ascending function is called. This accomplishes the same thing as line 2 does.

POINTER ARITHMETIC Pointer arithmetic includes the following operations:

- Initialize a pointer to NULL or to the address of an array, structure, variable, or function.
- Increment and decrement a pointer.
- Add and subtract an integer value from a pointer.
- Compare two pointers for either equal or not equal.

C knows the length of all data types, arrays, and structures in a program and uses the defined length in all pointer operations. For instance, when a pointer to an array or a structure is incremented or decremented, the pointer is adjusted by the length of an element in the array or structure, and not by the value of 1 byte.

Example 57.5, an example of a pointer to an array of integers:

```
/*                  program name:     pointr25.c         */
#include <stdio.h>

   int      i [ 5 ]  =
   {
       500 , 100 , 5 , 256 , 30
   } ;

main()
{
   int      *ptr ;

            ptr = &i[ 0 ] ;                           /* line 1 */

            printf ( "value at ptr is: &d\n" , *ptr );

            ptr++ ;                                   /* line 2 */

            printf ( "value at ptr is: &d\n" , *ptr );    /* line 3 */

}   /* end of main */
```

Line 1 is an example of initializing a pointer to the address of the first element in an array of integers. The pointer is pointing to the first byte of the first integer element.

Line 2 is an example of incrementing a pointer pointing to an array of integers. When incremented, the pointer is adjusted to point to the first byte of the second integer element in the array, and not to the second byte of the first integer element.

Line 3 prints the value that the pointer is pointing to.

The output of this example is:

```
value at ptr is: 500
value at ptr is: 100
```

POINTERS AS FUNCTION ARGUMENTS Pointers can be function arguments. Pointer are passed as function arguments by value, which means that the address that the pointer contains is passed as the argument value. A pointer to a pointer is also a valid function argument.

Example 57.6, an example of passing a pointer as a function argument:

```
/*                    program name:      pointr26.c        */
#include <stdio.h>
function1 ( pointer_to_int )
int         *pointer_to_int ;
{
      *pointer_to_int  = 12 ;                              /* line 1 */

}   /* end of function1 */
main()
{
            int       i ;
            int       *pointer_to_int ;

            pointer_to_int = &i ;

            function1 ( pointer_to_int ) ;                 /* line 2 */

            printf ( "i = %d\n" , i );                     /* line 3 */

}    /* end of main */
```

Line 1 is an example of changing the value of a variable whose address was passed as a function argument. The variable *i* in the *main* function is assigned the value of 12 when this statement is executed.

Line 2 is an example of passing a pointer as a function argument. Here the pointer to the variable *i* is passed to the called function. The address of *i* is the argument value.

Line 3 displays the value assigned to the variable *i*.

The output of this example is:

```
i = 12
```

Example 57.7, an example of pointer initialization, arithmetic, and function arguments:

```
/*                    program name:      pointr27.c        */
#include <stdio.h>
  struct  cust_struct
  {
     int   cust_no ;
     char  cust_name[30] ;
  } ;

  struct cust_struct   customer ;
  struct cust_struct  *customer_ptr = &customer ;        /* line 1 */

main()
{
int    i[5] , *i_ptr ;

     i_ptr = &i[0] ;                                     /* line 2 */
     zero ( i_ptr );                                     /* line 3 */
     i_ptr++ ;                                           /* line 4 */
```

```
} /* end main */

zero ( x )
int   *x ;                                   /* line 5 */
{
      *x = 0 ;                               /* line 6 */
       x = 0 ;                               /* line 7 */
} /* end zero */
```

Line 1 shows an initialization of a pointer where the address of the structure is placed within the pointer.

Line 2 shows the placing of the address of the first element of the array variable i into the pointer i_ptr.

Line 3 shows the passing of the pointer i_ptr as a function parameter.

Line 4 is an example of pointer arithmetic. Before the increment, i_ptr is pointing to i[0]. After the increment, i_ptr is pointing to the i[1] element. If an integer in your compiler is a length of 2 bytes, then the pointer is increment by 2.

Line 5 shows how to declare a pointer that is being passed as a function argument. Since it is a pointer, the pointer identifier (asterisk) is present. Here x is declared to be a pointer to an integer.

Line 6 shows the proper syntax for using a pointer when passed as a function argument. The way to read line 6 is: set the integer variable that x is pointing to a value of 0.

Line 7 is an example of moving a 0 (NULL) value to the pointer x.

NOTE

1) An address must be placed again within x before it can be used to access a variable.

2) Since function parameters are treated as automatic variables, this assignment does not change the value of i_ptr in line 3.

Passing Arguments by Value and by Reference The term used to describe an argument where the value of the variable is passed is "passed by value." The term used to describe an argument where the address of the variable is passed is "passed by reference." Passing a pointer to a variable is passing it by reference and passing the value of a variable is passing by value.

Example 57.8, an example of a function declaration, a void return data type, and passing variables by value and by reference:

```
/*                   program name:     pointr28.c       */
void update();                                          /* line 1 */
main()
{
  int  i , j ;

     i = j = 0 ;
     update ( &i );                                     /* line 2 */
     xchg_values ( &i , &j );                           /* line 3 */
} /* end main */
```

```
void update ( x )
int          *x ;
{
     *x += 10 ;                                      /* line 4 */
} /* end update */

xchg_values ( m ,  n )                               /* line 5 */
int          *m , *n ;
{
int    hold ;

     hold = *m   ;                                   /* line 6 */
     *m   = *n   ;                                   /* line 7 */
     *n   = hold ;                                   /* line 8 */
}
```

Line 1 is an example of a function declaration that does not return a value, therefore void is specified as the return data type.

Line 2 is an example of passing a variable by reference since the address of the variable is passed as the parameter and not the value of the variable.

Line 3 passes two variables by reference. The addresses of both i and j are passed to the xchg_values function.

Line 4 is an example of changing a variable that is passed by reference. Here the variable i in Line 2 has 10 added to its value.

Line 5 is the declaration of the xchg_values function. The purpose of this function is to exchange the values of the two parameters. The value of m is assigned to n, and the value of n is assigned to m.

Line 6 accesses the value of the variable i via the pointer passed to this function and named m. Note that m contains the address of i, and *m contains the value of the variable i.

Line 7 accesses the value of the variable j and places it into the variable i.

Line 8 places the value in the variable named hold and places it into the variable j. Now, the variables i and j from Line 3 have their values exchanged.

POINTERS AND ARRAYS SUMMARY Here are some examples using pointers and arrays, summarizing what you have learned about pointers and arrays.

Example 57.9, an example summary of arrays and pointers:

```
/*                     Name:    pointr29.c    */
main()
{

int     i , x ,  a [ 10 ] , *pa ;

int     a2 [ 10 ] [ 10 ] ;


     for ( i = 0 ; i < 10 ; i++ )        /* assign array element a value   */
          a [i] = i ;                    /* equal to its element number    */
```

```
for ( i = 0 ; i < 10 ; i++ )
{                                   /* assign array element a value  */
     for ( x = 0 ; x < 10 ; x++ )   /* equal to the sum of its two   */
          a2 [i][x] = x + i ;       /* element numbers               */
}

pa = &a[0] ;          /* pa points to a[0]                           */
pa =  a    ;          /* pa points to a[0]                           */

x  =  *pa  ;          /* x assigned 0,  value in a[0]                */
x  =  *pa + 1 ;       /* x assigned 1,  value in a[0] + 1            */

x  =  *(pa + 1 ) ;    /* x assigned 1,  value in a[1]                */

pa++ ;                /* pa incremented at points at a[1]            */

x =   *( pa++ ) ;     /* x assigned 1,  value in a[1];
                         pa incremented and points to a[2]           */

x =   *( ++pa ) ;     /* pa incremented and points to a[3];
                         x assigned 3,  value in a[3]                */

(*pa)++ ;             /* a[3] incremented, assigned value of  4      */

x = function ( a[0] );    /* parameter is 0, value of a[0]           */

x = function ( a );       /* parameter is address of a[0]            */

x = function ( &a[0] );   /* parameter is address of a[0]            */

x = function ( a[1] );    /* parameter is 1, value of a[1]           */

x = function ( a + 1 );   /* parameter is address of a[1]            */

x = function ( &a[1] );   /* parameter is address of a[1]            */

pa = a2 ;                 /* pa points to a2[0][0]                   */
pa = &a2[0][0] ;          /* pa points to a2[0][0]                   */

pa = &a2[0]    ;         /* pa points to a2[0], first row of the array */

 x = *a2[0]    ;         /* x assigned 0, value at a[0][0]           */

 x = a2[0][0]  ;         /* x assigned 0, value at a[0][0]           */

 x = a2[5][6]  ;         /* x assigned 11, value at a[5][6]          */

}
```

Example 57.10, another summary example of arrays and pointers:

```
/*                   Name:    pointr30.c     */
main()
{

int      i , x ,  a [ 10 ] , *pa ;

int      a2 [ 10 ] [ 10 ] ;
```

```
        for ( i = 0 ; i < 10 ; i++ )              /* assign array element a value  */
             a [i] = i ;                          /* equal to its element number   */

        for ( i = 0 ; i < 10 ; i++ )
        {                                         /* assign array element a value  */
             for ( x = 0 ; x < 10 ; x++ )         /* equal to the sum of its two   */
                   a2 [i][x] = x + i ;            /* element numbers               */
        }

        pa = &a[0] ;          /* pa points to a[0]                                 */
        pa =  a    ;          /* pa points to a[0]                                 */

         x  = 5    ;          /* x assigned 5                                      */
        *pa = x    ;          /* a[0] assigned the value of 5                      */
        *(pa + 1 ) = x ;      /* a[1] assigned the value of 5                      */

        *pa++      = x ;     /* a[0] assigned the value of 5;
                                pa incremented and points to a[1]                  */

        *( pa++ )  = x ;      /* pa incremented and points to a[2] ;
                                 a[2] assigned the value of 5                      */


        *( ++pa )  = x ;        /* pa incremented and points to a[3];
                                   a[3] assigned the value of 5                    */
   }
```

APPLICATIONS

A typical example for pointers is, again, the common input routine for all menu answers in a program. One function accepts the keyboard input to answer all menu prompts in an application and also contains a pointer to a function to validate the input data. The structure that contains the data for this input routine follows:

```
   struct  menu_answer_struct
   {
      int     row, column   ;   /* screen row and column location for input   */
      int     length        ;   /* length of input                            */
      char    type          ;   /* input type: 0=numbers, 1=alpha, 2=any keys */
      char   *ans           ;   /* location to place keyboard input           */
      int    (*validate)()  ;   /* pointer to function to validate input      */
   } ;
```

The function to call to validate the input is placed in the menu_answer_struct. After the operator inputs the data and presses Enter, the validation routine is called. Notice that the validation routine returns an integer value back to the menu input routine to indicate success or failure.

TYPICAL OPERATION

In this operation you enter, compile, and execute the programs given in Example 57.3.

1. Begin at the DOS prompt, in your C source code directory. Invoke your text editor.
2. Type the C program given in Example 57.3, just like it is listed. Call the program POINTR23.C.
3. Compile and link the program with your C compiler.
4. Type **POINTR23** and press **Enter**. Notice the following output on your screen:

```
C:\C>POINTR23
error = printer out-of_paper
C:\C>_
```

5. Enter, compile, link, and execute the other examples in this module. Then verify the output of each example with the output provided in the text.
6. Turn to Module 40 to continue the learning sequence.

Module 58
PORTABILITY

DESCRIPTION

This module defines some of the problems of portability with C programs. This module discusses portability for C coding and C data.

C CODING To create portable C code, consider the following guidelines.

Function Arguments When constants are used as function arguments they are passed as integers. If a constant is used for a function argument that is not an integer, then the constant must be type cast to the proper data type.

One constant that may need to be type cast is the null pointer. The null pointer type cast is: (char *)0

If a pointer is the same length as a long, some compiler manuals suggest using the following for a null pointer: 0L

Sizeof Structures Always use the *sizeof* operator to determine the length of structures instead of calculating the length manually. This will produce portable code when data types vary in length.

Shift Operations Shift operations to the right on signed values fill the vacated bits with sign bits, sometimes yielding an unexpected result. To avoid sign extension, mask out the undesired bits after the shift.

Functions Returning A Non-integer Type Functions that return a type other than integer must be defined in the module before the function is used. Some of the functions overlooked in this respect are the *strcpy*, *strcat*, *upper*, and *lower* string functions, which return pointers. Others are the file system functions that return values other than integer.

C DATA The problems associated with data portability are more associated with the actual computer hardware than with the C language.

Strings Since strings are stored in memory in the same sequence, they are portable.

Example of a String in Memory:

```
string:    "abcde"  at address 100

            100  101  102  103  104  105  106      <- Memory
                                                      Address
memory:    | a  | b  | c  | d  | e  | \0 |    |    <- data
```

Data Storage Byte Order The main portability problem is that different computers store the bytes of integers in memory in different sequences. Some computers store the least significant byte first, followed by the most significant byte, but some use the opposite sequence. When data is written to disk, it is written just like it is stored in memory. Therefore the data for one computer probably is not in the proper sequence for another computer. The bytes that store increasingly larger parts of numbers are said to be more significant.

Example of a short integer stored in an 8086-based computer:

```
decimal number 258, (0x0102  in hex)  at address 100:

            100  101  102  103  104  105  106      <- Memory
                                                      Address
memory:    | 02 | 01 |    |    |    |    |    |    <- data
             ^    ^
             |    |____ Byte 1, most significant, stored last
             |_________ Byte 0, least significant, stored first
```

Example of a short integer stored in an M68000-based computer:

```
decimal number 258, (0x0102  in hex)  at address 100:

            100  101  102  103  104  105  106      <- Memory
                                                      Address
memory:    | 01 | 02 |    |    |    |    |    |    <- data
             ^    ^
             |    |____ Byte 0, least significant, stored last
             |_________ Byte 1, most significant, stored first
```

From these examples you can see how different computers store integer numbers. One way to move numeric data from one computer to another is to convert it to string data, move it to the new computer, and there convert it back to numeric data.

Table of storage sequence for a few computer processors:

Short Integer Type, usually 16 bits wide

Processor	Storage sequence
Z80	byte 0, byte 1
8086	byte 0, byte 1
M68000	byte 1, byte 0
Z8000	byte 1, byte 0
80286	byte 0, byte 1
DEC VAX	byte 0, byte 1

Long Integer Type, usually 32 bits wide

Processor	Storage sequence
Z80	byte 0, byte 1, byte 2, byte 3
8086	byte 0, byte 1, byte 2, byte 3
M68000	byte 3, byte 2, byte 1, byte 0
Z8000	byte 3, byte 2, byte 1, byte 0
80286	byte 0, byte 1, byte 2, byte 3
DEC VAX	byte 0, byte 1, byte 2, byte 3

APPLICATIONS

When portability is important, write your programs only with the standard functions of C. Avoid tricks and quirks of a particular C compiler. However, when data is moved between computers with different kinds of processors then you may need to know how data is stored for each particular processor in order to access the data accurately.

You have completed the learning sequence.

Module 59

PRECEDENCE IN EXPRESSIONS

DESCRIPTION

This module explains the forming of expressions in C and defines the sequence in which complex expressions are solved (called *precedence*).

EXPRESSIONS The expressions in C perform the operation or purpose of a program. The expression is a combination of *operands* and *operators* that are evaluated and produce a value.

When an expression contains more than one assignment or comparison, it is called a complex expression. In complex expressions an expression acts like an operand where the values of expressions are combined with operators that finally produce a value. Even a complex expression can be an operand to another expression.

The understanding that an expression can become an operand to another expression is a key concept involved in mastering the C language. Reusing a value in a statement is a powerful concept which allows for very concise (but sometimes complicated and cryptic) code.

The use of *complex expressions* is not required but advanced programmers use them frequently. If you purchase C source code, you may encounter *complex expressions*; therefore, you must be able to read and understand them, whether you actually write them or not. C is the only programming language that allows a skilled programmer to write the equivalent of a proverb in literature. The ability to solve a common but complex programming problem in a short, simple, straightforward way is one of the rewards and joys of programming in C.

PRECEDENCE To achieve the desired result in an expression, you must understand the order in which operands in an expression are evaluated. This defined order is called the *precedence* of operators. The C precedence table is shown in this chapter and also in Appendix H for easy reference.

The *precedence* of an operator is only meaningful when there are multiple operators and operands in an expression. The expression with the operator of *highest precedence is evaluated first*. Level 1 (at the top of the table) has the highest precedence. Level 15 (at the bottom of the table) has the *lowest precedence* and *is performed last*.

Example 59.1, an example of precedence:

```
/*                      function name:    lowbyte.c        */
#include <stdio.h>
lowbyte( z )               /* The purpose of this function is to return */
int      z ;               /* the low byte of the integer parameter.    */
{
   int    y ;

   y = z & 0xff ;          /* The statement that does the work  */

   return ( y );

}   /* end of lowbyte */
main()
{
int i ;

    i = 0x1234 ;

    printf ( "i = %x, lowbyte(i)= %x\n" , i , lowbyte( i ) ;   /* Line 1 */

}   /* end of main */
```

In this example, there are two operators in the same C statement. They are the *bit-wise AND operator* (&) and the *assignment operator* (=). If you look up the precedence of each you find that the bit-wise AND operator has a precedence level of 8, which is higher than the precedence level (14) of the assignment operator.

Therefore, the expression (z & 0xff) involving the bit-wise AND is evaluated first. Operand1 is the variable z; operand2 is the constant *0xff*. The value of operand2 is 255. Applying the bit-wise AND operator to operand1, the value of this expression is the low byte of the parameter z, because the bit-wise AND turns off the high bits in calculating the value of this expression. Note that the value of z does not change. Its value is only read and used to calculate the value of this expression.

Now the next expression is to be evaluated. This expression is y = (value of first expression). For this expression, operand1 is y and operand2 is the value of the first expression. The value of operand2 is calculated in the above expression. So, applying the *assignment operator*, the value from the first expression is assigned to the variable y.

The output of this example is:

```
i = 1234, lowbyte(i) = 34
```

ASSOCIATIVITY When operators with the same precedence are in an expression, the *associativity* of the operators controls the evaluation, either right to left or left to right. The *associativity* is also defined for you on the precedence chart.

For example:

```
x = y = z = 0 ;
```

Look at the precedence chart. You see that the equal sign is in the 14th level of precedence and its associativity is right to left. Therefore, since each operator has the same precedence, use the associativity rule. Going right to left, this example is evaluated like this:

1. The first expression evaluated is the rightmost expression, z = 0.
   Operand2 which is a constant of zero, is evaluated and has a value of 0, which is assigned to the variable z.
2. The next expression to evaluate is the second one (going from right to left, according to the rule), which is y = *(value of expression1)*. The value for operand2 of this expression is the value of expression1. So, from the above evaluation, its value is 0. This is the value assigned to operand1, the variable y.
3. The next expression to evaluate is the leftmost one, z = *(value of expression2)*. The value for operand2 of this expression is the value of expression2 (or, 0). So this value is assigned to operand1, the variable x.

NOTE

When the same operator appears more than once in an expression, there are no guarantees which one is evaluated first. When you must guarantee that one operation is performed first, break up the complex expression into a series of less complex ones and store intermediate results in temporary variables. Divide and conquer.

Sometimes the multiple use of a variable (where one of the uses is an *assignment*) causes a problem if the order of evaluation is not guaranteed.

Example of a problem in evaluation:

```
i = ( j++ ) + j * 16 ;
```

The order of evaluation is not guaranteed. You cannot predict whether the j + + operand is evaluated before the j * 16 operand. The order of evaluation definitely affects the value of the result of the expression.

Precedence and Associativity of the Operators in C

	Operator	*Description*	*Associativity*
1.	( )	Function call	left to right
	[ ]	Array element	
	– >	pointer to structure member	
	.	structure member	
2.	!	Logical negation operator	right to left
	~	One's complement	
	+ +	Increment	
	– –	Decrement	
	–	Unary minus (negate)	
	(type)	Cast (forced type conversion)	
	*	Indirection	
	&	Address	
	sizeof	Size of an object	
3.	*	Multiplication	left to right
	/	Division	
	%	Modulo (remainder)	
4.	+	Addition	left to right
	–	Subtraction	
5.	< <	Left shift	left to right
	> >	Right shift	
6.	<	Less than	left to right
	< =	Less than or equal to	
	>	Greater than	
	> =	Greater than or equal to	
7.	= =	Equality	left to right
	! =	Inequality	
8.	&	Bitwise AND	left to right
9.	^	Bitwise exclusive OR (XOR)	left to right
10.	¦	Bitwise inclusive OR	left to right
11.	&&	Logical AND	left to right
12.	¦ ¦	Logical OR	left to right
13.	?:	Conditional expression	right to left
14.	=	Assignment	right to left
	* = / = % = + =	Assignment (compound form)	
	& = ¦ = ^ = – =		
	< < = > > =		
15.	,	Comma separator	left to right

APPLICATIONS

The knowledge of precedence in C is important since you want your programs to execute just like you think they are going to. However, the precedence of operations is logical and, therefore, you do not have to be overly concerned about it when you code simple C statements. In complex C statements be careful. As a general rule, always try to avoid complex C statements.

TYPICAL OPERATION

In this operation you enter, compile, and execute the programs given in Example 59.1.

1. Begin at the DOS prompt, in your C source code directory. Invoke your text editor.
2. Type the C program given in Example 59.1, just like it is listed. Call the program LOWBYTE.C.
3. Compile and link the program with your C compiler.
4. Type **LOWBYTE** and press **Enter**. Notice the following output on your screen:

```
C:\C>LOWBYTE
i = 1234, lowbyte(i) = 34
C:\C>_
```

5. Turn to Module 10 to continue the learning sequence.

Module 60

PREPROCESSOR DIRECTIVES

DESCRIPTION

This module describes the C preprocessor directives.

PREPROCESSOR DEFINITION The *preprocessor* program is the first program to run in the series of programs necessary to compile a C program. It reads the C source code looking for preprocessor directives. These directives are marked by a pound sign (#) in the first character position of the source code line.

These directives control how the preprocessor modifies the source code before it goes to the compiler.

One common use of preprocessor directives is to specify which computer and operating system to use to run the program. Other directives in the C source code can then include or delete other statements so that the resulting statements match the target computer and operating system. The same source code then can run on many computers and operating systems. Only the short directive file included in the C source code need be different.

Preprocessor directive syntax is different from the strict syntax of the C language. This is allowed because the preprocessor directives are discarded after they are executed. However, the statements the directive creates must follow C syntax. The directives are designed to make this easy.

You must run the preprocessor even if you do not use preprocessor directives, because the STDIO.H file provided by the compiler writers more than likely includes preprocessor directives.

The preprocessor directives are:

#include	Inserts another file into this file
#define	Defines a preprocessor macro
#undef	Removes a preprocessor macro definition
#if	Tests a constant expression to include text
#elif	Else if clause (for #if, #ifdef, #ifndef) to include text
#else	Else clause (for #if, #ifdef, #ifndef) to include text
#endif	Terminates if directive
#ifdef	Tests for definition of a macro name to include text
#ifndef	Tests for non-definition of a macro name to include text
#line	Supplies line numbers for compiler messages

#error	Produces a diagnostic message
#pragma	Gives instructions to the C compiler
#	This directive has no effect, it is null.

A "preprocessor operator" is an operator that is only recognized as an operator within the context of preprocessor directives. The preprocessor operators are discussed later in this module. They are the following:

#	"stringizing" operator
##	"token-pasting" operator
defined	evaluates to 1 if identifier defined, else 0

Predefined Macro Names The following macro names are predefined:

__LINE__	The line number of the current source line during the compilation phase.
__FILE__	The name of the source file during the compilation phase.
__DATE__	The date of the compilation.
__TIME__	The time of the compilation.
__STDC__	The decimal constant 1.

#include Directive The form for *#include* is:

```
#include "filename"
        or

#include <filename>
```

The *#include* directive causes another file to be included in place of the *#include* line. The file included can contain other preprocessor directives, even *#include*.

The filename that follows *#include* is enclosed in either quote marks " " or angle brackets < >. They determine where the compiler searches for the file to be included. The compiler usually searches the "current" directory for files included in quote marks. This book uses quote marks so that all files are to be in the same directory. Normally, on larger computers, the files provided with the C compiler are placed in "standard places." These are computer dependent. Therefore, programs including them use angle brackets and place all user-defined programs in quote marks.

Examples of #include directives:

```
#include <stdio.h>          /* line 1 */
#include "stdio.h"          /* line 2 */
#include "portable.h"       /* line 3 */
```

Line 1 shows how to include the stdio.h file if it is kept in the standard place on your computer. On a large computer this is desirable because many people can share the same file. And, if you get a new version of the compiler, you only have to put the stdio.h file one place for everyone to have access to it. This filename is in angle brackets.

Line 2 shows hows to include the stdio.h file if it is kept in the same directory as your C source code, indicated by quotes.

Line 3 shows how to reference a user file. It is usually kept in the same directory as the source code, indicated by quotes.

#define Directive Form 1 for *#define* is:

```
#define identifier  replacement text goes here to end of line
```

Form 2 for *#define* is:

```
#define identifier( argument1, ... , argumentN)  replacement text goes here
```

The #define form 1 is used to define a word that is replaced throughout the C program with the text that follows the identifier. Everything that follows the identifier (up to the end of the line) replaces the identifier in the C program.

Example of #define:

```
#define   TRUE       1            /* line 1 */
```

Line 1 is an example of the word TRUE that is to be replaced throughout the C program with the following:

```
                     1       /* line 1 */
```

Did you wonder why there is a comment when the example is only one line long? The comment is ignored when the replace line is looked at by the preprocessor program. This is valid.

The #define form 2 is used to replace a word that is associated in text with arguments in parentheses. The substitution is done in the C program, but the arguments can be copied in the replacement text as desired. An argument can be used in multiple places in the replacement text or not at all.

Example of #define (form 2):

```
#define PERCENT(x,y)  printf(" = %d, %d pct",x,100*x/y)   /* line 1 */
amount = 20 ;  total_amount = 50 ;
PERCENT( amount , total_amount );                          /* line 2 */
```

Line 1 shows the word and parameters to use to replace text in a C source line.

Line 2 is the code you would write. The C processor changes that line into:

```
printf( " = %d, %d pct", amount , 100*amount/total_amount);
```

When the program executes, the output is:

```
= 20, 40 pct
```

#undef Directive The form for *#undef* is:

```
#undef identifier
```

The *#undef* directive tells the preprocessor program to stop making replacements for the identifier that follows *#undef*. When the preprocessor encounters this directive, it "forgets" the original directive and no more replacements are done in this program. Some C compilers act differently; refer to your manual for the exact way your compiler works.

Example of #undef:

```
#define   X  x
 C text ...
#undef X
 More C text ....
```

In the C text between the *#define* of X and the *#undef* X, the preprocessor replaces the letter X with the letter x. After the *#undef* X directive, the letter X is not replaced by anything unless specified by another directive.

#if, #else, and #endif Directives The form for *#if*, *#else*, and *#endif*:

```
#if      constant_expression
         lines of text to include
#else
         lines of text to include
#endif
```

The *#if* statement evaluates the constant expression that follows it. If the result of the evaluation is true (non-zero), the preprocessor includes the next group of lines until it reaches either *#else* or *#endif*. If the value is false (zero), the preprocessor searches for *#else* or *#endif*. If it finds *#endif*, it terminates the *#if* directive. If it finds *#else*, it starts including text until it reaches a line that begins with *#endif*.

The *#if*/#else statement can be "nested;" that is, within the body of a *#if* another directive can occur.

Example 60.1, an example of *#if, #else, #endif* preprocessor commands:

```
#include <stdio.h>

#define TRUE  1
#define FALSE 0
#define DEBUG TRUE

main()
{

#if (DEBUG)                                              /* line 1 */
    printf("in debug mode....\n");
#else
    printf( "COPYRIGHT (c)1985 by MY-COMPANY INC." );
#endif
```

```
        /*   coding  ...  */
    }   /* end of main */
```

Line 1 #if evaluates the expression that follows. In this case, the result of the expression is a non-zero value, so the result is true.

Since the result is true, the preprocessor program includes the following lines of text into the program until it finds either *#else* or *#endif*. In this case, it includes one line of text and then finds *#else*. The *#else* terminates the *#if* directive so the preprocessor program ignores all text until it finds the *#endif* and then starts searching for another directive.

If the result had been false, the preprocessor would have searched for either *#else* or *#endif*. If it had found *#endif*, it would have terminated that *#if* and started searching for another directive. In this case if the result had been false, the preprocessor would have found *#else* then started including text until it found *#endif* (to terminate the *#if*).

#ifdef Directive The form for *#ifdef*:

```
#ifdef    identifier
```

The *#ifdef* preprocessor command checks to see if the identifier has a replacement defined. If it does, then the preprocessor starts including the line(s) of text that follow until it reaches *#endif* or *#else*. If it has no replacement, the preprocessor searches for either *#endif* or *#else*. If it finds *#endif* it terminates the *#ifdef* directive. If it finds *#else* it starts including text until it reaches *#endif* (which instructs it to stop including text).

Example of #ifdef:

```
#define  DEBUG

#ifdef   DEBUG
       printf( "values are %d %d %d \n", x , y , z );
#endif
```

The *#ifdef* directive causes the preprocessor to check to see if it currently has the word DEBUG defined. Since it does, it includes the next line of the program. That would be the only line it included, since *#endif* is found on the next line.

#ifndef Directive The *#ifndef* preprocessor command checks to see if the identifier has a replacement defined. If it does not, then the preprocessor starts including the line(s) of text that follow until it reaches *#endif* or *#else*. If it has a replacement, the preprocessor searches for either *#endif* or *#else*. If it finds *#endif* it terminates the *#ifdef* directive. If it finds *#else* it starts including text until it reaches *#endif* (which instructs it to stop including text).

Example of #ifndef:

```
#define  FINAL_VERSION

#ifndef  FINAL_VERSION
       printf( "values are %d %d %d \n", x , y , z );
#endif
```

The *#ifndef* directive causes the preprocessor to check to see if it currently has the word FINAL_VERSION defined. Since it does, it does not include the next line of the program. The preprocessor program then searches for either *#endif* or *#else*. Since it finds *#endif*, it terminates the *#ifndef* directive.

#line Directive The form for *#line*:

```
#line      integer-constant      "filename"
```

The *#line* directive advises the compiler that the next line in this program is *#included* from another file, and that the line number in the other file is the integer-constant. The filename follows the integer-constant line number.

This allows the C compiler to print the filename and line number where an error occurs.

If the filename is missing, the preprocessor program displays the last name used in a *#line* directive.

Example of #line:

```
#line     21       "filename"
/* C line of text */                          /* line 1 */
```

If a C syntax or coding error exists in line 1, then when the C compiler displays the error message, it shows:

```
filename  21    error-message.
```

You would then correct the error, not in the file being compiled, but on line 21 of the file named "filename."

#define Using Arguments The syntax when using arguments with #define is:

```
#define identifier(arg1, arg2,...) substitution_text
```

This form of the #define preprocessor directive, that allows arguments, can be thought of as a function-like macro since it takes arguments. Each occurence of the arguments in the substitution_text is replaced by the formal arguments found in the #define directive. All the arguments can occur any number of times in the substitution_text. The preprocessor is not sensitive to string constants and will replace occurrences of the arguments within string constants.

Note that no white-space character can occur between the identifier and the opening parenthesis.

Beware that some types of arguments produce unexpected results (side effects). Sometimes parentheses can control side effects because they control the interpretation of a statement, where precedence could produce the wrong result.

Example 60.2, an example of preprocessor commands:

```
#define SCREEN_WIDTH  80
#define GRAPH_WIDTH  (SCREEN_WIDTH - 8)
#define ERR_WIDTH     SCREEN_WIDTH - 8

#define LESS(x,y)  ((x) < (y)) ? (x) : (y)

int v[12] =
    { 1 , -2 , 3 , -4 , 5 , -6 , -7 , -8 , 9 , 10 , 11 , -12 } ;

main()
{
int   i , graph_height ;

      graph_height = GRAPH_WIDTH / 2 ;                    /* line 1 */

      graph_height = ERR_WIDTH / 2 ;                      /* line 2 */

      for ( i = 0 ; i < 11 ; i++ )
         printf("of %d %d, %d is less \n",v[i],v[i+1],
                               LESS(v[i],v[i+1]) );      /* line 3 */

      for ( i = 0 ; i < 11 ; )
         printf("of %d %d, %d is less \n",v[i],v[i+1],
                              LESS(v[i],v[++i]) );       /* line 4 */

}
```

In line 1 first the substitution is made to produce:

```
graph_height = ( SCREEN_WIDTH - 8 ) / 2 ;
```

Next the substitution is made to produce:

```
graph_height = ( 80 - 8 ) / 2 ;
```

which results in the value (72) / 2, or 36.

In line 2 first the substitution is made to produce:

```
graph_height =  SCREEN_WIDTH - 8  / 2 ;
```

Next the substitution is made to produce:

```
graph_height =  80 - 8 / 2 ;
```

which results in the value 80 - 4, or 76.

Note that the divide is performed first because the divide operator (/) has a higher precedence than the addition operator (+). Always use parentheses when there is any doubt as to the evaluation sequence.

In line 3 the expression LESS(v[i],v[i + 1]) is replaced by:

```
( (v[i]) < (v[i+1]) ) ? (v[i]) : (v[i+1]) ;
```

which on the first iteration becomes:

```
((1) < (-2)) ? (1) : (-2), or -2.
```

In line 4 the expression LESS(v[i],v[++i]) is replaced by:

```
( (v[i]) < (v[++i]) ) ? (v[i]) : (v[++i]) ;
```

CAUTION

NOTICE that the expression v[++i] may be executed twice, causing an error, as the desired result is to have it evaluated once on each iteration.

Example 60.3, an example using preprocessor argument substitution:

```
/* NAME: echoarg.c */
#define PRINT(x)        printf ( "i = %d, x = %s\n" ,i, x );

main( argc , argv )
int   argc ;
char        *argv[] ;
{
int         i ;
char     *ptr ;

     for ( i = 1 ; i < argc ; i++ )
          PRINT(argv[i]) ;                                /* line 1 */
}                              /* end main */
```

In line 1 PRINT(argv[i]); produces:

```
printf ( "i = %d, argv[i] = %s\n" ,i, argv[i] );
```

Notice that argv[i] replaced the x both places that it occurred in the substitution string. The C preprocessor simply replaces each occurence of the x argument with the formal argument.

For example, if the following is entered from the DOS prompt:

```
C:\>echoarg MY name is EMMETT
```

then the output of the program is:

```
i = 1, argv[i] = MY
i = 2, argv[i] = name
i = 3, argv[i] = is
i = 4, argv[i] = EMMETT
```

#error Directive The #error directive has the following form:

```
#error diagnostic_message
```

This directive displays the diagnostic_message during the compilation phase.

#pragma Directive The #pragma directive has the following form:

```
#pragma message
```

This directive behaves uniquely to each C compiler.

PREPROCESSOR OPERATORS The preprocessor operators are:

#	"stringizing" operator
##	"token-pasting" operator
defined	evaluates to 1 if identifier defined, else 0

"Stringizing" Operator The stringizing operator preceding a macro formal parameter name in the body of a preprocessor macro causes the corresponding actual argument to be enclosed in string quotation marks.

An example of a stringizing operator:

```
#define  P(x) printf( #x )

main()
{
    P(this is a string);
}
```

After the preprocessor has completed, the following code is produced:

```
main()
{
    printf("this is a string");
}
```

"Token-pasting" Operator The token-pasting operator allows tokens used as actual arguments to be concatenated to form other tokens.

An example of a token-pasting operator:

```
#define  P(x) printf( "value = %d", value##x )

main()
{
    P(4);
}
```

After the preprocessor has completed, the following code is produced:

```
main()
{
    printf("value = %d", value4 );
}
```

Defined Operator The defined operator is of the form:

```
defined(identifier)
```

The constant expression is considered true (non-zero) if the identifier is currently defined. Otherwise, the expression is considered false (zero). Even if the identifier is defined as void, it is considered defined. The defined operator is used with the #if, #elif, #else, and #endif directives.

APPLICATIONS

A good programming habit to develop is to place all constants for an application in one module that is shared by all programmers working on the project. Meaningful names are assigned to the constants with the #define statement. This provides several benefits. First, all programs developed for the application share the common definitions and are therefore all using the same values. When a value changes, it is propigated throughout the whole system automatically. Next, all programs use the same name throughout the whole system. And having a meaningful name, the program is easier to write, as the programmers can remember the names of the variables easier. Also, the programs are understood by someone else easier, as the names are meaningful.

TYPICAL OPERATION

In this operation you enter, compile, and execute the program given in Example 60.3.

1. Begin at the DOS prompt, in your C source code directory. Invoke your text editor.
2. Type the C program given in Example 60.3, just like it is listed. Call the program ECHOARG.C.
3. Compile and link the program with your C compiler.
4. Type **echoarg MY name is EMMETT** and press **Enter**. Notice the following output on your screen:

```
C:\C>echoarg MY name is EMMETT
i = 1, argv[i] = MY
i = 2, argv[i] = name
i = 3, argv[i] = is
i = 4, argv[i] = EMMETT
C:\C>_
```

5. Turn to Module 44 to continue the learning sequence.

Module 61

PRINTF
VPRINTF

```
NAME

    printf   —  displays formatted output to the standard output device
    vprintf  --  displays formatted output to the standard output device

USAGE

    int      printf ( char *output-string , ...  ) ;
    int     vprintf ( char *output-string , va_list arg_ptr ) ;

PROTOTYPE in      stdio.h

ANSI Synopsis

    #include <stdio.h>
    int   printf(const noalias char *format, ...);

    #include <stdio.h>
    #include <stdarg.h>
    int  vprintf(const noalias char *format, va_list  arg_ptr );

RETURNS
        Returns the number of characters displayed on the
        standard output device.
```

DESCRIPTION

The *printf* function writes formated output to the standard output device. Formatted output means that the data to be displayed can be of one data type but that it can be output in the same or a different data type. It also means the number of decimal places can be specified and that the minus sign or plus sign can be output on signed numbers.

The input data types of the arguments include all integers, floating point, characters, and character strings. The output data types include signed and unsigned decimal, octal, hex, exponential, character, and character strings.

OUTPUT-STRING DESCRIPTION The output-string contains two types of information:

- It contains an *output format specification* field.
- It contains a series of characters that are directly output to the standard output device.

The output string is read from left to right. When the first format specification is encountered, the first argument is output in the appropriate output format. If there are more arguments than output format specifications, the extra arguments are ignored, but the output may not be as desired. If there are too few arguments, the output is unpredictable.

OUTPUT FORMAT SPECIFICATION FIELD The % character is used to specify that formatting is to begin in the output character string. The character(s) following % specify the output data format. Following the output format specifier, either another formatted output field or characters to be output directly can begin.

No arguments are necessary if there are no format specification fields in the output format string.

The general form of an output format specification field is:

```
%[flag][width][.precision][L]type
```

The format specification begins with the % and ends with the desired output data type. It can contain four other optional fields. A description of the optional fields is followed by tables describing the flags for output and output data types:

flag — The *flag* controls the justification of the data. The five flags are explained in the next table.

width — The *width* controls the minimum number of characters that are to be output for this argument. If the output width is less than this specifier, the output is padded with blanks. An asterisk is a valid entry, meaning that the width is contained in an argument to this function.

precision — The *precision* controls the number of digits output. For strings, this specifies the maximum number of characters to output. For floating point e and f, this specifies how many digits are to appear after the decimal point. For floating point g, this specifies the maximum number of significant digits. For the other types, it specifies the minimum number of digits to output. An asterisk is a valid entry, meaning that the width is contained in an argument to this function.

L — The L character (uppercase or lowercase is acceptable) is used if a long integer or long double argument is expected.

NOTE

All of the above optional fields can be used together, giving complete control over how the data is output.

FLAGS for DATA OUTPUT TABLE

Character	Flag	Output Format
–	justification flag	The data is left-justified when the minus sign is present.
+	sign flag	The data value is always to be displayed with plus or minus sign.
0	zero padded on left side flag	The data is zero-padded on left and not space-padded.
space	sign conversion	If signed data field and a positive number, use space for sign character.
#	alternate form	Don't remove trailing zeroes from G type. Include decimal on E, F, G types. Place 0x on hexidecimal type. Put 0 in front of octal numbers.
*	minimum field width	The asterisk specifies that the next argument to the printf function indicates the minimum number of positions to be used to output data value.
L	argument is long type flag	The input argument is a long data type.
.	next field is precision field	The next field in the specifier is the precision field.
1 to n	precision field	The precision field specifies the maximum number of characters to output for *d,u,o,x* type. This is exact number of characters to output for float and double.
*	precision field	The asterisk specifies that the next argument to the printf function indicates the number of decimal places after decimal point.

DATA TYPE OUTPUT TABLE

Character	Input type	Output Format
d	integer	The argument is output in signed decimal notation.
u	integer	The argument is output in unsigned decimal notation.
o	integer	The argument is output in unsigned octal notation with a leading zero.
x	integer	The argument is output in unsigned hexadecimal notation with the 0x.
c	character	Output is a single character.
p	pointer	Output is a pointer.
s	string of characters	The argument is output until either the \0 character is reached in the string or the precision is reached.
e	floating point	Output is in exponential format of the form [–]m.nnnnnnE[+ –]xx, where n is the precision; default is 6.
f	floating point	Output is in signed decimal notation of the form [–]mmm.nnnnnn, where n is the precision; default is 6.
g	floating point	Output uses either the %e or %f notation, whichever is shorter. Insignificant zeros are not shown.

Example 61.1, example of *printf* function:

```
/*                          program name:    printf1.c          */
#include <stdio.h>
main()
{
  int    dollars = 12 , cents = 5 ;
  float  f = 456.789 ;

/*  examples of formatted output to standard output */

                                            /* output is:                */
    printf( "\n'%d'" ,  23456  );           /* '23456'                   */
    printf( "\n'%8d'",  23456  );           /* '   23456'                */
    printf( "\n'%08d'", 23456  );           /* '00023456'                */
    printf( "\n'%-8d'", 23456  );           /* '23456   '                */

    printf( "\n'%x'",   255    );           /* 'ff'                      */
    printf( "\n'%4x'",  254    );           /* '  fe'                    */
    printf( "\n'%04x'", 100    );           /* '0064'                    */
    printf( "\n'%-4x'", 101    );           /* '65  '                    */

    printf( "\n'%c%c'", '9', '$' );         /* '9$'                      */
    printf( "\n'%s'"  , "testing");         /* 'testing'                 */
    printf( "\n'%10s'", "testing");         /* '   testing'              */
    printf( "\n'%-10s'","testing");         /* 'testing   '              */
    printf( "\n'%3.4s'","testing");         /* 'test'                    */
    printf( "\n'%.4s'", "testing");         /* 'test'                    */

    printf( "\n'Amount $%05u.%02u'",
                      dollars, cents );     /* 'Amount $00012.05'        */
    printf( "\n'Amount $%u.%02u'",
                      dollars, cents );     /* 'Amount $12.05'           */
    printf( "\n'Amount $%u.%u'",
                      dollars, cents );     /* 'Amount $12.5'            */

    printf( "\n'%.3f'" , f      );          /* '456.789'                 */
    printf( "\n'%e'"   , f      );          /* '4.567890e+002'           */
    printf( "\n'%.0f'" , f      );          /* '457'                     */
    printf( "\n'%.2f'" , f      );          /* '456.79'                  */
    printf( "\n'%.*f'" , 2 , f  );          /* '456.79'                  */

}    /* end of main */
```

The comment to the right of each printf statement shows the output of the associated printf function call.

vprintf The *vprintf* function is functionally equivalent to *printf*, except that the argument list is replaced by a pointer to a list of arguments. See Module 40 for more information on functions using a variable number of arguments.

APPLICATIONS

The printf function is one of the most powerful and useful functions in C. It is the most commonly used function to output data to the console, especially formatted data.

One common example is a memory dump program. On the left side of the memory dump is the hex representation of the byte in memory. On the right-hand side is the displayable character if it is printable, else a period is displayed. The programmer does not have to convert the character to hex to display it, the printf function does it for the programmer. The program does have to check to see if the character is displayable or not and to then display the appropriate character.

TYPICAL OPERATION

In this operation you enter, compile, and execute the program given in Example 61.1.

1. Begin at the DOS prompt, in your C source code directory. Invoke your text editor.
2. Type the C program given in Example 61.1, just like it is listed. Call the program PRINTF1.C.
3. Compile and link the program with your C compiler.
4. Type **PRINTF1** and press **Enter**. Notice the following output on your screen:

```
C:\C>PRINTF1
'23456'
'   23456'
'00023456'
'23456   '

'ff'
'  fe'
'0064'
'65  '
'9$'
'testing'
'    testing'
'testing    '
'test'
'test'

'Amount $00012.05'
'Amount $12.05'
'Amount $12.5'

'456.789'
'4.567890e+002'
'457'
'456.79'
'456.79'
C:\C>_
```

5. Turn to Module 39 to continue the learning sequence.

Module 62

PUTC

```
NAME

  putc  --  writes a single character to a stream file

USAGE

   int   putc ( int c , FILE *stream ) ;

PROTOTYPE in      stdio.h

ANSI Synopsis

    #include <stdio.h>
    int      putc(int c, FILE *stream );

RETURNS

   returns the character that was output to the stream file
           or end-of-file if an error detected
```

DESCRIPTION

The *putc* function writes a single character to the stream file. It returns the character output unless an error is detected, in which case EOF (end-of-file) is returned. The character is returned without sign extended.

The actual error number can be retrieved from *errno* if an error occurs using the *putc* function.

Example 62.1, an example using the *putc* function:

```
/*                    program name:      putc1.c        */
#include <stdio.h>
main()
{
   FILE    *stream ;
   int     status  ;
   char    c = 'a' ;

   stream = fopen ("filename", "w" );    /* open for write */

   status = putc ( c , stream );                      /* line 1 */
```

```
    if ( status == EOF )
        printf( "write to stream was not completed." );

}   /* end of main */
```

Line 1 is an example of the putc function call. It writes a single character to the stream file. It returns the character output unless an error occurs and then an EOF is returned.

Example 62.2, another example using both the *getc* and *putc* functions:

```
/* NAME    : getput.c    */
/* PURPOSE: program to display its source code on the stdout device */
#include <stdio.h>
main()
{
FILE    *stream ;
int     status , done ;
char    c ;

     done = 0 ;
     stream = fopen ( "getput.c", "r" );
     if ( stream == NULL )
     {
          printf ( "getput.c could not be found...." );
          exit ( -1 );
     }
     do
     {
          c = getc ( stream );                                /* line 1 */
          if ( c == EOF )                                     /* line 2 */
          {
               done = 1 ;
               status = ferror ( stream );
               if ( status != 0 )
                    printf ( "ERROR %d on stream\n" , status );
               status = feof ( stream );
               if ( status != 0 )
                    printf ( "END-OF-FILE reached.\n" );
          }                                                    /* line 3 */
          else  status = putc ( c , stdout );                  /* line 4 */
          if ( status == EOF )                                 /* line 5 */
          {
               done = 1 ;
               if ( (status = ferror ( stdout )) != 0 )
                    printf ( "ERROR %d on stdout\n" , status );
          }                                                    /* line 6 */
     }  while ( done == 0 );
     clearerr ( stream );                                      /* line 7 */
     if ( fclose ( stream )  == -1 )                           /* line 8 */
          printf ( "getput.c not closed properly..." );
}
```

The output from the above program is the above program.

Line 1 reads one character from the file named getput.c and the character read is assigned to the variable c. If end-of-file is reached, the value of EOF is assigned to the variable c.

Lines 2 thru 3 check the error condition. Since the error condition can either be an error or end-of-file, both are tested. If it is an error then the error number is displayed in the error message. If it is the end-of-file condition then an end-of-file message is displayed.

Line 4 outputs to the standard output device the character read, and the status of the write is stored in the variable status.

Lines 5 and 6 tests the status of the write and displays an error number if an error occurs.

Line 7 is an example of the use of the clearerr function.

Line 8 closes the stream and compares the return status to – 1. If an error is encountered while closing the file, an error message is displayed.

APPLICATIONS

The putc function is the same as the fputc function. Refer to Module 33 to review the typical application of the fputc function.

TYPICAL OPERATION

In this operation you enter, compile, and execute the program given in Example 62.1.

1. Begin at the DOS prompt, in your C source code directory. Invoke your text editor.
2. Type the C program given in Example 62.1, just like it is listed. Call the program GETPUT.C.
3. Compile and link the program with your C compiler.
4. Type **GETPUT** and press **Enter**. Notice the following output on your screen:

```
C:\C>GETPUT
/* NAME    : getput.c    */
/* PURPOSE: program to display its source code on the stdout device */
#include <stdio.h>
main()
{
FILE    *stream ;
int     status , done ;
char    c ;

     done = 0 ;
     stream = fopen ( "getput.c", "r" );
     if ( stream == NULL )
     {
          printf ( "getput.c could not be found...." );
          exit ( -1 );
     }
     do
     {
          c = getc ( stream );                              /* line 1 */
          if ( c == EOF )                                   /* line 2 */
          {
               done = 1 ;
               status = ferror ( stream );
               if ( status != 0 )
```

```
                    printf ( "ERROR %d on stream\n" , status );
               status = feof ( stream );
               if ( status != 0 )
                    printf ( "END-OF-FILE reached.\n" );
          }                                                  /* line 3 */
          else  status = putc ( c , stdout );                /* line 4 */
          if ( status == EOF )                               /* line 5 */
          {
               done = 1 ;
               if ( (status = ferror ( stdout )) != 0 )
                    printf ( "ERROR %d on stdout\n" , status );
          }                                                  /* line 6 */
     }  while ( done == 0 );
     clearerr ( stream );                                    /* line 7 */
     if ( fclose ( stream )  == -1 )                         /* line 8 */
          printf ( "getput.c not closed properly..." );
}
C:\C>_
```

5. Turn to Module 35 to continue the learning sequence.

Module 63

PUTCHAR

```
NAME

  putchar  --  writes a single character to stdout

USAGE

   int  putchar ( int c ) ;

PROTOTYPE in      stdio.h

ANSI Synopsis

    #include <stdio.h>
    int  putchar(int c );

RETURNS

   returns the character that was output to stdout
           or EOF if an error is detected
```

DESCRIPTION

The *putchar* function writes a single character to the stdout device. It returns the character output unless an error is detected, in which case it returns EOF (end-of-file). The character is converted to an integer without sign extended and returned.

The *putchar* function can be expressed alternately as:

```
putc ( c , stdout ) ;
```

Many compilers use putc(c,stdout) as a macro for putchar(c).

Example 63.1, example using *putchar*:

```
/*                      program name:    putchar1.c          */
#include <stdio.h>
main()
{
    int     c   =   'x' ;

     putchar(c);                                     /* line 1 */
     putchar('\n');                                  /* line 2 */

}    /* end of main */
```

Line 1 outputs the current value of c to stdout. The value returned is assigned to the *int* type variable err. The value returned is either the character output or EOF if an error occurred in trying to output the character.

Line 2 outputs a newline character to stdout.

The output of Example 63.1 is:

```
x
```

Here is a program called echo1.c which illustrates the use of getchar, putchar, stdin, and stdout. This program accepts input from the computer keyboard and displays it on the computer screen until EOF is entered.

Example 63.2, example using *putchar*:

```
/* program name:    ECHO1.C    */
#include <stdio.h>                                        /* line 1 */
main()
{
int    c ;                                                /* line 2 */

      printf ( "Enter your name (Ctrl+Z to end) ..." );   /* line 3 */
      do
      {
            c = getchar( ) ;                              /* line 4 */

            if ( c != EOF )                               /* line 5 */
                  putchar ( c );                          /* line 6 */

      }  while ( c != EOF ) ;                             /* line 7 */

      printf ( "\ninput complete.\n" );                   /* line 8 */

} /* end of main */
```

Line 1 illustrates how to include a file into a program. In this case the compiler finds the file stdio.h and reads it and makes it part of this program. The lines within that file are treated just as if they were typed into this program. (Appendixes K and L show typical listings of this file.)

Line 2 is the declaration of the variable c which is used to hold the integer value returned from the getchar function.

Line 3 is used to request operator input (name). It also prompts the operator to enter a Ctrl + Z to end the entry. (Ctrl + Z is entered by holding down the Ctrl key, then pressing and releasing the Z key, and then releasing the Ctrl key.) The getchar function recognizes this key combination as end of input and returns the EOF value to the program.

Line 4 is the getchar function call. Either the character typed by the operator or EOF will be returned and assigned to the variable c.

Line 5 is used to test whether the valued returned was a typed character or the EOF status. If it is not the EOF status, then Line 6 is executed.

Line 6 is used to output the character in the variable c to stdout (actually the console).

Line 7 is a loop instruction used to see if all input is complete. If the EOF character was not the last character input then control is passed back to line 4 to be executed next. Note that this loop is performed once for each character input.

Line 8 displays a message when the input is complete.

APPLICATIONS

The typical application for using the putchar function is simply to write a character to the console.

TYPICAL OPERATION

In this operation you enter, compile, and execute the programs given in Example 63.1 and Example 63.2.

1. Begin at the DOS prompt, in your C source code directory. Invoke your text editor.
2. Type the C program given in Example 63.1, just like it is listed. Call the program PUTCHAR1.C.
3. Compile and link the program with your C compiler.
4. Type **PUTCHAR1** and press **Enter**. Notice the following output on your screen:

```
C:\C>PUTCHAR1
x
C:\C>_
```

5. Type the C program given in Example 63.2, just like it is listed. Call the program ECHO1.C.
6. Compile and link the program with your C compiler.
7. Type **ECHO1** and press **Enter**. Type **YOUR_NAME** and press **CTRL + Z**. Notice the following output on your screen:

```
C:\C>ECHO1
YOUR_NAME
input complete.
C:\C>_
```

8. Turn to Module 61 to continue the learning sequence.

Module 64

PUTS

```
NAME

   puts  --  writes a string to stdout

USAGE

   int  puts ( char *string ) ;

PROTOTYPE in      stdio.h

ANSI Synopsis

    #include <stdio.h>
    int     puts(noalias char *s);

RETURNS

   If an error is detected, EOF is returned; otherwise
   a newline character is returned
```

DESCRIPTION

The *puts* function writes the string to *stdout* and returns the last character output. The function appends a *newline* character to the output. The '\0' end of string character is not output. If an error occurs, an EOF is returned, otherwise the last character output is returned, which is the new-line character.

Example 64.1, an example using the puts function.

```
/*                    program name:       puts1.c            */
#include <stdio.h>
main()
{
   int  err ;


       err = puts( "Insert backup disk and press Enter." );     /* line 1 */

}    /* end of main */
```

Line 1 writes the string to *stdout*. If an error is encountered, EOF is returned. Otherwise, the newline character is returned.

APPLICATIONS

The puts function is a good function for writing string text to the screen. A typical application example using the puts function is outputing help screens to the user.

TYPICAL OPERATION

In this operation you enter, compile, and execute the program given in Example 64.1.

1. Begin at the DOS prompt, in your C source code directory. Invoke your text editor.
2. Type the C program given in Example 64.1, just like it is listed. Call the program PUTS1.C.
3. Compile and link the program with your C compiler.
4. Type **PUTS1** and press **Enter**. Press **Enter**. Notice the following output on your screen:

```
C:\C>PUTS1
Insert backup disk and press Enter.
C:\C>_
```

5. Turn to Module 68 to continue the learning sequence.

Module 65

READ

```
NAME

   read  --  reads data from a low-level opened file into
             a memory buffer

USAGE

   int     read ( int fd , void *buffer , int count ) ;

PROTOTYPE in       io.h

RETURNS
        returns number of bytes read, or -1 if an error occurs
```

DESCRIPTION

The *read* low-level function attempts to count the number of bytes read into the buffer from the associated file descriptor. Reading begins with the current file position. The file position is updated after the *read*. *Read* returns the number of bytes between the two positions. If an error occurs, *read* returns a −1.

Note that this is not an ANSI function.

Example 65.1, an example using the *read* function:

```
/*                    program name:       read1.c            */
#include <io.h>
#include <fcntl.h>         /* defines O_RDWR                    line 1 */
main()
{
    int      status , fd , mode ;
    char     buffer [ 512 ] ;

    mode = O_RDWR ;

    fd = open ("read1.c", mode );

    status = read ( fd , buffer , 512 );                     /* line 2 */
```

```
    if ( status == -1 )
         printf( "read error occurred.\n" );
    else printf( "no read error occurred.\n" );

}     /* end of main */
```

Line 1 sets the mode to allow both read and write access to the file.

Line 2 is an example of the *read* function call. It returns the number of bytes read unless an error occurs in which case it returns a −1.

APPLICATIONS

Use the read function to read data from files opened with the low-level open function. Refer to the C library reference manual of your compiler if you are trying to use the number of bytes read in text mode, since the count returned may not actually be the number of bytes read.

TYPICAL OPERATION

In this operation you enter, compile, and execute the program given in Example 65.1.

1. Begin at the DOS prompt, in your C source code directory. Invoke your text editor.
2. Type the C program given in Example 65.1, just like it is listed. Call the program READ1.C.
3. Compile and link the program with your C compiler.
4. Type **READ1** and press **Enter**. Notice the following output on your screen:

```
C:\C>READ1
no read error occurred.
C:\C>_
```

5. Turn to Module 89 to continue the learning sequence.

Module 66
REMOVE

```
NAME

   remove  --  removes a file from the filing system

USAGE

   int        remove ( char *filename );

PROTOTYPE in       stdio.h

ANSI Synopsis

    #include <stdio.h>
    int   remove(const noalias char *filename );

RETURNS
       returns 0 if file deleted successfully, else nonzero
```

DESCRIPTION

The *remove* function deletes closed files from the filing system of the computer. The file is permanently removed.

The *remove* function returns a 0 if the file is deleted successfully. If an error occurs, a non-zero value is returned.

The actual error number can be retrieved from *errno*.

Example 66.1, an example using the *remove* function:

```
/*                program name:       remove1.c              */
#include <stdio.h>
main()
{
     int    status ;

     status = remove ("filename" );                         /* line 1 */
```

```
        if ( status == -1 )
            printf( "file was not deleted properly.\n" );
        else printf( "file was deleted properly.\n" );

    }   /* end of main */
```

Line 1 is an example of the *remove* function call. It removes the specified file from the disk.

APPLICATIONS

Use the remove function to delete a file from disk. Once a file is deleted it cannot be recovered under normal operating procedures. Programs normally verify that the proper disk is inserted before deleting files.

TYPICAL OPERATION

In this operation you enter, compile, and execute the program given in Example 66.1.

1. Begin at the DOS prompt, in your C source code directory. Invoke your text editor.
2. Type the C program given in Example 66.1, just like it is listed. Call the program REMOVE1.C.
3. Compile and link the program with your C compiler.
4. Type **REMOVE1** and press **Enter**. Notice the following output on your screen:

```
C:\C>REMOVE1
file was deleted properly.
C:\C>_
```

5. Turn to Module 23 to continue the learning sequence.

Module 67

RETURN

```
NAME

   return --   terminates a function and optionally passes
               a value to the caller.

USAGE

   return ( expression );
```

DESCRIPTION

The *return* statement passes execution to the function which called the function containing the *return*. If the expression is present, it is evaluated and the value, after being converted to the type returned by the function, is returned to the calling function.

The *return* is not required if no value is returned to the calling function, because when the end of a function is reached, return is automatic.

Example 67.1, example of *return* statement:

```
/*                       program name:    return1.c            */
#include <stdio.h>
void function1 ( int j )
{
     if ( j < 0 )
         return ;                                       /* line 1 */

}     /* end of function1 */


long   function2 ( int j )
{
     if ( j < 0 )
         return ( -1 ) ;                                /* line 2 */

     return ( j ) ;                                     /* line 3 */

}   /* end of function2 */
main()
{
  int i = 12 ;
```

```
    long   k ;
           function1 ( i );
           k = function2 ( i );                         /* line 4 */
           function2 ( i + 1 );                         /* line 5 */
           printf ( "k = %d\n" , k );
}   /* end of main */
```

Line 1 is an example of a return from a function which does not return a value. Notice on functions that do not return a value that you do not need a return statement.

Line 2 is an example of a return that returns a – 1 in *long integer data type* to the calling function.

Line 3 converts j to *long data type* and then returns j in *long data type* to the calling function.

Line 4 calls function2 and stores the value returned in the variable k.

Line 5 calls function2 but does not use the value returned. When the return value is not used, the value is discarded.

The output of RETURN1.C is:

```
k = 12
```

APPLICATIONS

The normal use of the return statement is to stop the execution of a function and continue the execution of the calling function at the statement following the function call. A value is normally returned to the calling function. The value returned is normally either the result of a calculation in the function containing the return, or the success or failure of the function to accomplish its task.

TYPICAL OPERATION

In this operation you enter, compile, and execute the program given in Example 67.1.

1. Begin at the DOS prompt, in your C source code directory. Invoke your text editor.
2. Type the C program given in Example 67.1, just like it is listed. Call the program RETURN1.C.
3. Compile and link the program with your C compiler.
4. Type **RETURN1** and press **Enter**. Notice the following output on your screen:

```
C:\C>RETURN1
k = 12
C:\C>_
```

5. Turn to Module 47 to continue the learning sequence.

Module 68

SCANF

```
NAME

   scanf   --  reads data from stdin into arguments specified
               by the format string.

USAGE

      int      scanf (  char *format-string  , ...  ) ;

PROTOTYPE in      stdio.h

ANSI Synopsis

    #include <stdio.h>
    int    scanf(const noalias char *format, ...);

RETURNS
       returns the number of successfully assigned input
       fields.  EOF is returned if end of file is encountered.
```

DESCRIPTION

The *scanf* function is used to accept input data from the standard input device. The format-string describes how the data is to be input from the standard input device and the arguments describe where to place the data field as it is input.

The form for *scanf* is:

```
scanf (  format-string , arguments ) ;
                |              |
                |              L_____ Describes where to place
                |                     the data when input.
                |
                L_____ Describes the input data from the
                       standard input device, its length and
                       its conversion type.
```

FORMAT-STRING DESCRIPTION The format-string contains one or more of each of the following three types of fields:

1) Whitespace characters that are skipped.
2) An input format specification field describes the input data from stdin. The input format specification field describes the maximum length of the data for each data field in the input and the data type of the corresponding argument where the data is stored.
3) A non-input format specifications field which causes *scanf* to skip over (read, but not store) characters from stdin. These characters are expected to match the next non-whitespace character input from stdin.

ARGUMENTS DESCRIPTION The arguments specify where the input data fields are to be stored as they are input from the standard input device. There must be an argument for each input format specification field in the *format-string*. If there are more arguments than input specification fields, the extra arguments are ignored. If there are too few arguments, then the results are unpredictable and undefined. The arguments to the *scanf* function are pointers. The most common programming error in the use of the scanf function is to not make the arguments pointers.

The format-string is read from left to right, and the data is also stored in the arguments left to right, one field per argument.

FORMAT SPECIFICATION FIELD The general form of an input format specification field is:

```
%[sup-flag][max-width][size]data-type
```

The format specification begins with the % and ends with the desired input data type and can contain three other optional fields. A description of the optional fields is followed here by a table describing the input data type:

sup-flag	—	This flag (*) is a *suppression flag*. If it is present, the input field is skipped and no output is made to the corresponding output argument.
max-width	—	The width controls the maximum number of characters that are to be input for this argument. An input field is completed when it reaches either the maximum field width or a whitespace character in the input data.
size	—	The L character specifies that the input field is a long double for type E, F, and G. The l character specifies that the input field is a double for types E, F, and G. The L character for the other types indicate a long integer. The h character indicates that it is also a short type.

INPUT DATA TYPE TABLE

Character	*Input type*	*type output argument-pointer*
d	decimal integer	The argument is a pointer to a decimal integer.
o	octal integer	The argument is a pointer to a decimal integer.
x	hexadecimal integer	The argument is a pointer to a decimal integer.
p	pointer	The argument is a pointer to a pointer.
c	single character	The argument is a pointer to a character. The whitespace rule is not in effect for this type.
s	string of characters	The argument is a pointer to an array of characters large enough to hold input string and \0 character.
e, f, g	floating point (exponential)	The argument is a pointer to a floating point number.
h	short integer	The argument is a pointer to a short integer.

DATA FIELDS An input data field is a string of non-whitespace characters that are contained in the input file. An input data field ends when one of the following occurs as the data is input:

1) The maximum width as defined in the input format specification field is reached.
2) A whitespace character (tab, space, or newline) is reached.
3) A character that cannot be converted according to the field definition in the input format specification field is reached.

Example 68.1, an example using the scanf function:

```
/*                  program name:       scanf1.c         */
#include <stdio.h>
main()
{
float     miles , gallons ;

     printf ( "Enter number of miles traveled .... " );        /* line 1 */
     scanf  ( "%f" , &miles );                                 /* line 2 */
     printf ( "Enter number of gallons used ...... " );        /* line 3 */
     scanf  ( "%f" , &gallons );                               /* line 4 */
     printf("Your car gets %.1f miles per gallon\n" ,
                                     miles/gallons );          /* line 5 */
}
```

Line 1 prompts the operator to input the number of miles traveled.

Line 2 is the input instruction that gets the number of miles from the computer operator.

Line 3 prompts the operator to input the number of gallons used.

Line 4 is the input instruction that gets the number of gallons from the computer operator.

Line 5 is the output instruction that displays how many miles per gallon the car gets.

Example 68.2, another example using the scanf function:

```
/*                   program name:      scanf2.c          */
#include <stdio.h>
main()
{
    int         empno ;
    int         ssn1 , ssn2  , ssn3 ;
    int         hireday  , hiremonth , hireyear  ;
    char        firstname [ 31 ] , middleinitial ;
    char        lastname  [ 31 ] , city [ 31 ] ,
                    state [ 3  ] , zip  [ 10 ] ;

    float       payrate ;


    scanf (  "%4d" , &empno );                                 /* line 1 */

    scanf (  "%3d-%2d-%4d", &ssn1 ,                            /* line 2 */
                      &ssn2 , &ssn3 );

    scanf (  "%2d%2d%2d", &hiremonth ,                         /* line 3 */
                      &hireday    , &hireyear );

    scanf (  "%*lf" , &payrate );                              /* line 4 */

    scanf (  "%30s %1c %30s",                                  /* line 5 */
        firstname , &middleinitial    , lastname   );

    scanf (  "%30s %2s %9s",                                   /* line 6 */
                    city , state , zip );
}   /* end of main */
```

Line 1 is an example of the input of a number, with a maximum length of 4 characters, that is to be stored in an *int* type variable. Notice that the variable has an ampersand leading it, indicating that a pointer to the variable is passed as the parameter.

Line 2 is an example of the input of three numbers which are separated in the input file with minus signs. The three numbers are stored into three variables and the minus signs are read from the standard input device but not stored.

Line 3 is an example of the input of three numbers which are not separated in the standard input device input, but are separated by the *scanf* function and stored into three different variables.

Line 4 is an example of the reading of an input data field, but the data is not stored into the variable because of the asterisk in the input specification field.

Line 5 is an example of the input of two 30-character strings and the input of a 1-character data field. Notice first that the definition of the character string variables is one character longer than the input. This is because the *scanf* function places the EOS character at the end of the string when it is input. Notice that the 1-character variable is defined with a length of one as it is just a character, not a string. Also notice that the strings do not need an ampersand, as strings are automatically passed as pointers, but the character variable must be passed with the leading ampersand since *char* type is passed by value.

Line 6 is another example of string input.

The following chart is an example of data that can be entered through the standard input device and how this data is stored in the respective variables at the end of the program:

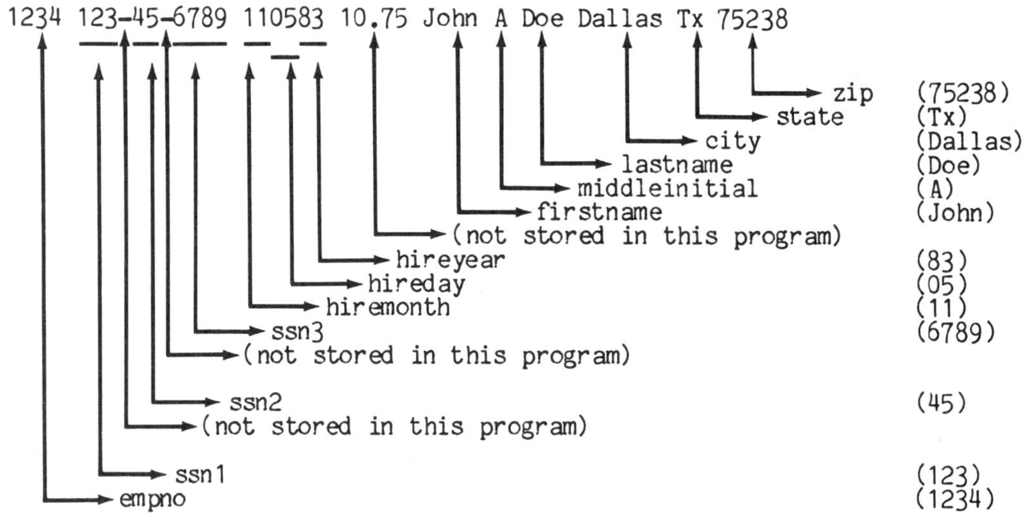

APPLICATIONS

The scanf function is the built-in function for console input of all types of data into the computer. The scanf function accepts multiple arguments but usually, in a program input, is made one field at a time.

TYPICAL OPERATION

In this operation you enter, compile, and execute the program given in Example 68.1.

1. Begin at the DOS prompt, in your C source code directory. Invoke your text editor.
2. Type the C program given in Example 68.1 just like it is listed. Call the program SCANF1.C.
3. Compile and link the program with your C compiler.
4. Type **SCANF1** and press **Enter**. Type **235.0** and press **Enter**. Type **10.0** and press **Enter**. Notice the following output on your screen:

```
C:\C>SCANF1
Enter number of miles traveled ....235.0
Enter number of gallons used ......10.0
Your car gets 23.5 miles per gallon
C:\C>_
```

5. Turn to Module 70 to continue the learning sequence.

Module 69

SPRINTF
VSPRINTF

```
NAME

   sprintf   --  displays formatted output to an output buffer
  vsprintf   --  displays formatted output to an output buffer

USAGE

    int      sprintf ( char *buffer , char *output-string , ...  ) ;
    int     vsprintf ( char *buffer , char *output-string ,
                                                  va_list arg_ptr ) ;

PROTOTYPE in       stdio.h

ANSI Synopsis

    #include <stdio.h>
    int  sprintf(noalias char *s, const noalias char *format, ...);

    #include <stdio.h>
    #include <stdarg.h>
    int  vsprintf(const noalias char *format, va_list  arg_ptr );

RETURNS
     returns the number of characters output to the buffer.
```

DESCRIPTION

The *sprintf* function is used to format output to the specified buffer. Formatted output means that the data to be output can be of one data type and that it can be output in the same or a different data type. It also means the number of decimal places can be specified and that the minus sign or plus sign can be output on signed numbers.

The input data types of the arguments include all integers, floating points, characters, and character strings. The output data types include signed and unsigned decimal, octal, hex, exponential, character, and character strings.

OUTPUT-STRING DESCRIPTION The output-string contains two types of information:

- It contains an *output format specification* field.
- It contains a series of characters that are directly output to the standard output device.

The output-string is read from left to right. When the first format specification is encountered, the first argument is output in the appropriate output format. If there are more arguments than output format specifications, the extra arguments are ignored, but the output may not be as desired. If there are too few arguments, the output is unpredictable.

OUTPUT FORMAT SPECIFICATION FIELD The % character is used to specify that formatting is to begin in the output character string. The character(s) following % specify the output data format. Following the output format specifier, either another formatted output field or characters to be output directly can begin.

No arguments are necessary if there are no format specification fields in the output format string.

The general form of an output format specification field is:

```
%[flag][width][.precision][L]type
```

The format specification begins with the % and ends with the desired output data type. It can contain four other optional fields. A description of the optional fields and a table describing the output data type is:

flag — The *flag* controls the justification of the data. The five flags are explained in the next table.

width — The *width* controls the minimum number of characters that are to be output for this argument. If the output width is less than this specifier, the output is padded with blanks. An asterisk is a valid entry, meaning that the width is contained in an argument to this function.

precision — The *precision* controls the number of digits output. For strings, this specifies the maximum number of characters to output. For floating point E and F, this specifies how many digits are to appear after the decimal point. For floating point G, this specifies the maximum number of significant digits. For the other types, it specifies the minimum number of digits to output. An asterisk is a valid entry, meaning that the width is contained in an argument to this function.

L — The L character (uppercase or lowercase is acceptable) is used if a long integer or long double argument is expected.

NOTE

All of the above optional fields can be used together which gives you complete control over the formatted output.

FIELDS for DATA OUTPUT TABLE

Character	*Field*	*Output Format*
–	justification flag	The data is left-justified when the minus sign is present.
+	sign flag	The data value is always to be displayed with plus or minus sign.
0	zero padded on left side flag	The data is zero-padded on left and not space-padded.
space	sign conversion	If signed data field and a positive number, use space for sign character.
#	alternate form	Don't remove trailing zeroes from G type. Include decimal on E, F, G types. Place 0x on hexadecimal type. Put 0 in front of octal numbers.
*	minimum field width	The asterisk specifies that the next argument to the sprintf function indicates the minimum number of positions to be used to output data value.
L	argument is long type flag	The input argument is a long data type.
.	next field is precision field	The next field in the specifier is the precision field.
1 to n	precision field	The precision field specifies the maximum number of characters to output for *d,u,o,x* type. This is exact number of characters to output for float and double.
*	precision field	The asterisk specifies that the next argument to the sprintf function indicates the number of decimal places after decimal point.

OUTPUT DATA TYPE TABLE

Character	*Input type*	*Output Format*
d	integer	The argument is output in signed decimal notation.
u	integer	The argument is output in unsigned decimal notation.
o	integer	The argument is output in unsigned octal notation with a leading zero.
x	integer	The argument is output in unsigned hexadecimal notation with the 0x.
c	character	Output is a single character.
p	pointer	Output is a pointer.
s	string of characters	The argument is output until either the \0 character is reached in the string or the precision is reached.
e	floating point	Output is in exponential format of the form [–]m.nnnnnnE[+ –]xx, where n is the precision; default is 6.
f	floating point	Output is in signed decimal notation of the form [–]mmm.nnnnnn, where n is the precision; default is 6.
g	floating point	Output uses either the %e or %f notation, whichever is shorter. Insignificant zeros are not shown.

Example 69.1, an example using the sprintf function:

```
/*                          program name:     sprintf1.c            */
#include <stdio.h>
main()
{
  int    dollars = 12 , cents = 5 ;
  float  f = 456.789  ;
  char   buffer[ 50 ] ;

/*  examples of formatted output to a buffer */

                                                /* output is:            */
    sprintf( buffer , "\n'%d'" ,  23456  );    /* '23456'               */
    sprintf( buffer , "\n'%8d'",  23456  );    /* '   23456'            */
    sprintf( buffer , "\n'%08d'", 23456  );    /* '00023456'            */
    sprintf( buffer , "\n'%-8d'", 23456  );    /* '23456   '            */

    sprintf( buffer , "\n'%x'",   255    );    /* 'ff'                  */
    sprintf( buffer , "\n'%4x'",  254    );    /* '  fe'                */
    sprintf( buffer , "\n'%04x'", 100    );    /* '0064'                */
    sprintf( buffer , "\n'%-4x'", 101    );    /* '65  '                */

    sprintf( buffer , "\n'%c%c'", '9', '$' ); /* '9$'                  */
    sprintf( buffer , "\n'%s'" , "testing"); /* 'testing'             */
    sprintf( buffer , "\n'%10s'", "testing"); /* '   testing'          */
    sprintf( buffer , "\n'%-10s'","testing"); /* 'testing   '          */
    sprintf( buffer , "\n'%3.4s'","testing"); /* 'test'                */
    sprintf( buffer , "\n'%.4s'", "testing"); /* 'test'                */

    sprintf( buffer , "\n'Amount $%05u.%02u'",
                   dollars, cents );           /* 'Amount $00012.05'     */
    sprintf( buffer , "\n'Amount $%u.%02u'",
                   dollars, cents );           /* 'Amount $12.05'        */
    sprintf( buffer , "\n'Amount $%u.%u'",
                   dollars, cents );           /* 'Amount $12.5'         */

    sprintf( buffer , "\n'%.3f'" , f       );  /* '456.789'              */
    sprintf( buffer , "\n'%e'"   , f       );  /* '4.567890e+002'        */
    sprintf( buffer , "\n'%.0f'" , f       );  /* '457'                  */
    sprintf( buffer , "\n'%.2f'" , f       );  /* '456.79'               */
    sprintf( buffer , "\n'%.*f'" , 2 , f   );  /* '456.79'               */

}    /* end of main */
```

The comment to the right of each sprintf statement shows the associated output.

vsprintf The *vsprintf* function is functionally equivalent to *sprintf*, except that the argument list is replaced by a pointer to a list of arguments. See Module 40 for more information on functions using a variable number of arguments.

APPLICATIONS

The sprintf function builds a single output string of formatted data from many data fields. A common application of this function is when the output of a program can be displayed on the computer screen, printed on the printer, or written to disk. The program builds the output in memory, using the sprintf function, and then outputs the single output string to the appropriate device.

TYPICAL OPERATION

In this operation you enter, compile, and execute the program given in Example 69.1.

1. Begin at the DOS prompt, in your C source code directory. Invoke your text editor.
2. Type the C program given in Example 69.1; however, modify the program to include the following statement after each sprintf statement:

   ```
   printf ( "%s", buffer );
   ```

   Call the program SPRINTF1.C.
3. Compile and link the program with your C compiler.
4. Type **SPRINTF1** and press **Enter**. Notice the following output on your screen:

```
C:\C>SPRINTF1

'23456'
'   23456'
'00023456'
'23456   '
'ff'
'  fe'
'0064'
'65  '
'9$'
'testing'
'    testing'
'testing     '
'test'
'test'
'Amount $00012.05'
'Amount $12.05'
'Amount $12.5'
'456.789'
'4.567890e+002'
'457'
'456.79'
'456.79'
C:\C>_
```

5. Turn to Module 69 to continue the learning sequence.

Module 70

SSCANF

```
NAME

   sscanf   —  reads data from a buffer into arguments as specified by
               the format string.

USAGE

     int     sscanf ( char *buffer , char *format-string  , ...  );

PROTOTYPE in      stdio.h

ANSI Synopsis

    #include <stdio.h>
    int   sscanf(const noalias char *s,
                 const noalias char *format, ...);

RETURNS
      returns the number of successfully assigned input
      fields.  EOF is returned if end of file is encountered.
```

DESCRIPTION

The *sscanf* function is used to accept input data from a buffer. The format-string describes how the data is to be input from the buffer and the arguments describe where to place the data field as it is input.

The form for *sscanf* is:

```
sscanf ( buffer , format-string , arguments ) ;
           ↑            ↑              ↑
           |            |              └── Describes where to place
           |            |                  the data when input.
           |            |
           |            └── Describes the input data from the buffer,
           |                its length, and its conversion type.
           |
           └── Specifies the buffer to input the data from.
```

BUFFER The buffer specifies the location in memory from which to input the data.

FORMAT-STRING DESCRIPTION The format-string contains one or more of each of the following three types of fields:

1) Whitespace characters that are skipped.
2) An input format specification field which describes the input data in the buffer. This describes the maximum length of the data for each data field in the input buffer and the data type of the corresponding argument where the data is stored.
3) A non-input format specification field which causes *sscanf* to skip over (read, but not store) characters in the input buffer. These characters are expected to match the next non-whitespace character input from the buffer.

ARGUMENTS DESCRIPTION The arguments specify where the input data fields are to be stored in memory as the fields are input from the buffer. There must be an argument for each input format specification field in the *format-string*. If there are more arguments than input specification fields, the extra arguments are ignored. If there are too few arguments, then the results are unpredictable and undefined. The arguments to the *sscanf* function are pointers. The most common programming error in the use of the sscanf function is to not make the arguments pointers.

The format-string is read from left to right, and the data is also stored in the arguments left to right, one field per argument.

FORMAT SPECIFICATION FIELD The general form of an input format specification field is:

```
%[sup-flag][max-width][size]data-type
```

The format specification begins with the % and ends with the desired input data type and can contain three other optional fields. A description of the optional fields is followed here by a table describing the input data type:

sup-flag	—	This flag (*) is a *suppression flag*. If it is present, the input field is skipped and no output is made to the corresponding output argument.
max-width	—	The width controls the maximum number of characters that are to be input for this argument. An input field is completed when it reaches either the maximum field width or a whitespace character in the input data.
size	—	The L character specifies that the input field is a long double for type E, F, and G. The l character specifies that the input field is a double for types E, F, and G. The L character for the other types indicate a long integer. The h character indicates that it is also a short type.

INPUT DATA TYPE TABLE

Character	*Input type*	*type output argument-pointer*
d	decimal integer	The argument is a pointer to a decimal integer.
o	octal integer	The argument is a pointer to a decimal integer.
x	hexadecimal integer	The argument is a pointer to a decimal integer.
p	pointer	The argument is a pointer to a pointer.
c	single character	The argument is a pointer to a character. The whitespace rule is not in effect for this type.
s	string of characters	The argument is a pointer to an array of characters large enough to hold input string and \0 character.
e, f, g	floating point (exponential)	The argument is a pointer to a floating point number.
h	short integer	The argument is a pointer to a short integer.

DATA FIELDS An input data field is a string of non-whitespace characters that are contained in the input file. An input data field ends when one of the following occurs as the data is input:

1) The maximum width as defined in the input format specification field is reached.
2) A whitespace character (tab, space, or newline) is reached.
3) A character that cannot be converted according to the field definition in the input format specification field is reached.

Example 70.1, an example using the sscanf function. This example demonstrates how to do formatted input from a buffer into variables:

```
/*                 program name:      sscanf1.c        */
#include <stdio.h>
main()
{
    int       empno ;
    int       ssn1 , ssn2  , ssn3 ;
    int       hireday  , hiremonth , hireyear  ;
    char      firstname [ 31 ] , middleinitial ;
    char      lastname  [ 31 ] , city [ 31 ] ,
                  state [ 3  ] , zip  [ 10 ] ;

    float     payrate ;
    char      buffer [ 200 ] ;


    strcpy ( buffer ,
          "1234 123-45-6789 110583 10.75 John A Doe Dallas Tx 75238 " );

    sscanf ( buffer , "%4d" , &empno );                     /* line 1 */
```

```
    sscanf ( buffer , "%3d-%2d-%4d", &ssn1 ,              /* line 2 */
                      &ssn2 , &ssn3 );

    sscanf ( buffer , "%2d%2d%2d", &hiremonth ,          /* line 3 */
                      &hireday   , &hireyear );

    sscanf ( buffer , "%*lf" , &payrate );                /* line 4 */

    sscanf ( buffer , "%30s %1c %30s",                    /* line 5 */
         firstname , &middleinitial  , lastname  );

    sscanf ( buffer , "%30s %2s %9s",                     /* line 6 */
                    city , state , zip );

    printf ( "Name: %s %s,  Zip: %s\n" ,                  /* line 7 */
                          firstname , lastname , zip );

}    /* end of main */
```

Line 1 is an example of the input of a number, with a maximum length of 4 characters, that is to be stored in an *int* type variable. Notice that the variable has an ampersand leading it so that a pointer to the variable is passed as the parameter.

Line 2 is an example of the input of three numbers which are separated in the input file with minus signs. The three numbers are stored into three variables and the minus signs are read from the input file but not stored.

Line 3 is an example of the input of three numbers which are not separated in the input file, but are separated by the *sscanf* function and stored into three different variables.

Line 4 is an example of the reading of an input data field, but the data is not stored into the variable because of the asterisk (suppression flag) in the input specification field.

Line 5 is an example of the input of two 30-character strings and the input of a 1-character data field. Notice first that the definition of the character string variables is one character longer than the input. This is because the *sscanf* function places the EOS character at the end of the string when it is input. Notice that the 1-character length variable is defined with a length of one as it is just a character, not a string. Also notice that the strings do not need an ampersand, as strings are automatically passed as pointers, but the character variable must be passed with the leading ampersand since *char* type is passed by value.

Line 6 is another example of string input, filling 3 variables with values from the buffer.

Line 7 displays some of the input values on the screen.

The output from this example is:

```
Name: John Doe, Zip: 75238
```

The following chart describes how the data in this example is stored in the respective variables at the end of the program:

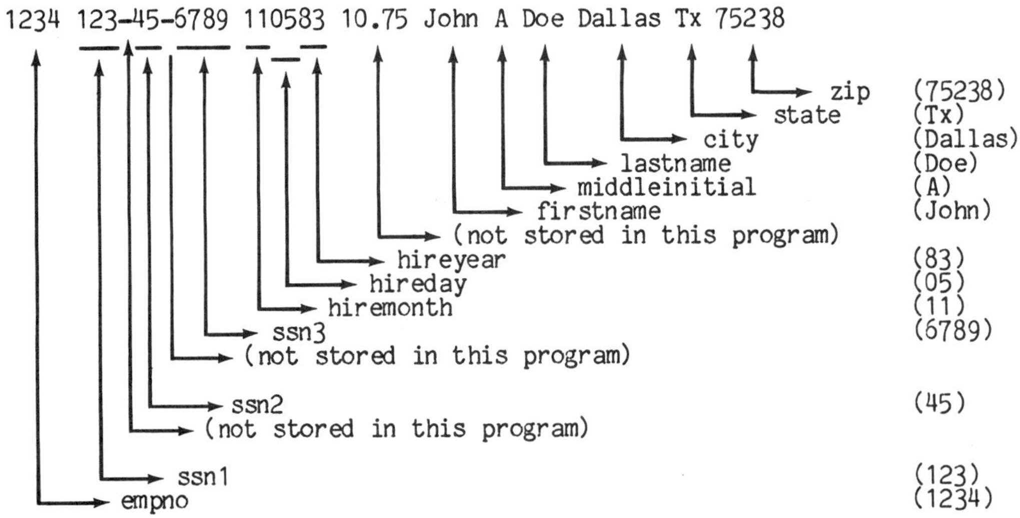

APPLICATIONS

The sscanf function is a powerful function that moves data from a single input string in memory to many data fields of all data types in memory. This one function can replace many lines of regular C code moving or converting data in a string to separate data fields of all data types. Most disk files are maintained in a fixed format, and once a data record is read from disk into memory, the sscanf function is one method of separating the data into individual data fields.

TYPICAL OPERATION

In this operation you enter, compile, and execute the program given in Example 70.1.

1. Begin at the DOS prompt, in your C source code directory. Invoke your text editor.
2. Type the C program given in Example 70.1, just like it is listed. Call the program SSCANF1.C.
3. Compile and link the program with your C compiler.
4. Type **SSCANF1** and press **Enter**. Notice the following output on your screen:

```
C:\C>SSCANF1
Name: John Doe,  Zip: 75238
C:\C>_
```

5. Turn to Module 69 to continue the learning sequence.

Module 71
STACK

DESCRIPTION

This module explains the concept of a stack and how C uses it.

The *stack* is an area of memory set aside during program execution for the temporary storage of variables. A *stack* acts like a stack of physical objects, just like a stack of books. Two operations are allowed to manipulate the *stack*: we can add an item to the top of the *stack*, or we can take the top item off the *stack*. Thus, the Last item In is the First item Off. This is called a LIFO operation — a LIFO *stack*.

STACK IN MEMORY A *stack* can be pictured in memory as an array of variables with a pointer pointing to the last item placed on the *stack*. As items are placed on and removed from the *stack*, the pointer to the last item is adjusted to always point to the last item on the *stack*.

The address of the start of the stack is also maintained.

Example 71.1, an example of a stack that contains four variables:

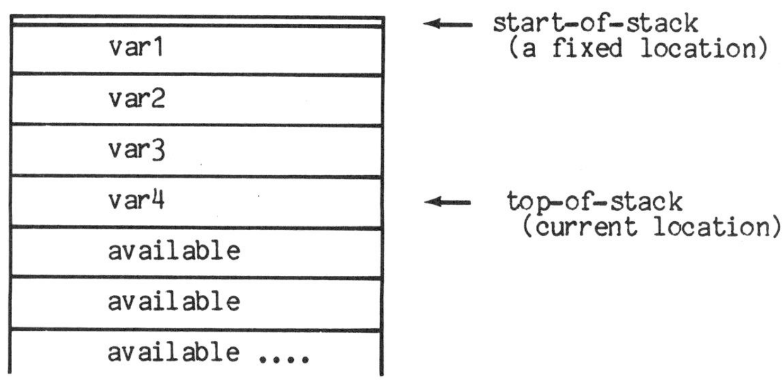

In this example, var1 was the first item to be placed on the stack and, therefore, the last item to be removed. Var4 was the last item to be placed onto the stack and, therefore, the next one which can be removed.

The start of the stack for a program has a fixed address. Once the start of the stack is established, it does not change. The top-of-stack is a pointer variable. As items are placed onto the stack or removed from the stack, the address in the pointer changes. The stack is maintained by the C program automatically and requires no attention by the programmer.

HOW C USES THE STACK When a function is called and executes, several things occur:

The arguments being passed to the called function are placed on the stack.

- The return address to the calling function is placed on the stack.
- The automatic variables declared in the called function are placed on the stack.
- The called function executes, manipulating the arguments and the automatic variables placed on the stack.
- When the called function completes its operation, it removes the automatic variables from the stack.
- The called function returns to the calling function by using the return address which is now on top of the stack.
- The calling function removes the parameters from the stack, and now the stack is at the same location as before the call occurred.

EXAMPLE OF STACK USAGE Example 71.2, a program that uses the stack:

```
/*                         program name:     stack.c          */
#include <stdio.h>
main()
{
 int          var1 ;
 char         var2 ;
 short        var3 ;
 long         var4 ;


        var1 = 10  ;                                  /* line 1  */
        var2 = 'z' ;                                  /* line 2  */
        var3 = 5   ;                                  /* line 3  */
        var4 = var1 + var3 ;                          /* line 4  */

        funct1( var1 , var3 );                        /* line 5  */

        funct2( var2 , var3 , var1 );                 /* line 6  */

}    /* end of main */


funct1 ( arg1 , arg2 )
int      arg1 ;
short           arg2 ;
{
int      f1_var1 ;

    /* coding for this function */

}    /* end of function1 */


funct2 ( arg1 , arg2 , arg3 )
char     arg1 ;
short           arg2 ;
int                    arg3 ;
```

```
{
    /* coding for this function */
}   /* end of function2 */
/* end of program */
```

This is what the stack looks like in memory while this program runs:

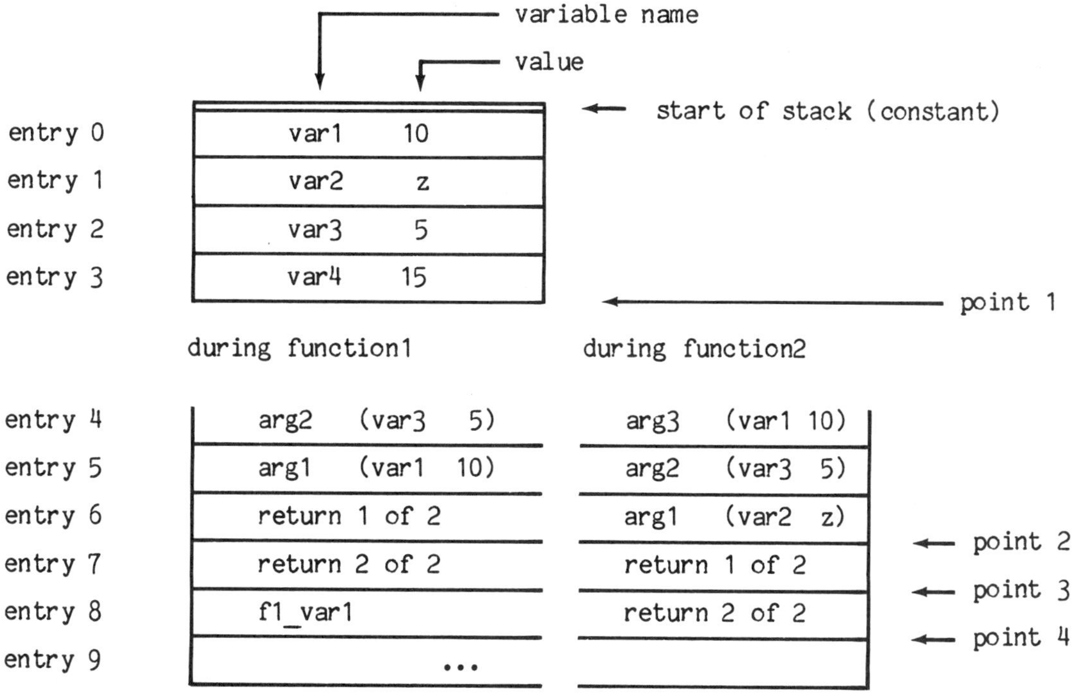

This is what this program does when it executes:

- When this program starts executing, it determines the start address of the stack (which is constant).
- It then allots stack space for the four automatic variables which are stored on the stack.
- It executes Line 1 of the main() and this statement moves 10 into the memory location on the stack assigned to var1.
- When the program executes line 2, it moves a 'z' to var2.
- When the program executes line 3, it moves 5 to var3.
- When the program executes line 4, it retrieves the values for var1 and var3 from their memory locations on the stack, adds them, and then places the result into the memory location on the stack assigned to var4. The stack pointer is at *point 1* on the stack.
- The program executes line 5. It first retrieves the values of var1 and var3 from their locations on the stack.
- It then places the rightmost argument, arg2, on the stack first.

- It then gets the next argument to the left of the last one placed on the stack. This is arg1, a second copy of var1.
- The program then places the call address on the stack so the function will know where to return. The amount of room on the stack required for the return_address varies from computer to computer. This example assumes two stack entries. The stack pointer is now at *point3*.
- Next, the program calls function1, which allots stack space for its automatic variable and then executes.
- When it reaches the closing brace, it frees the memory assigned to the automatic variable. It then uses the return address to return to the calling function, which takes the return address off the stack.
- The program takes the arguments from the stack and the stack pointer is back at *point1*.
- When the program executes line 6, it goes through the same procedure. When it completes and returns, the stack pointer is back at *point1*.

ADVANTAGES OF STACK USE An important point to learn here is that when a function is called, the arguments passed to the called function are only copies of the original variables, not the real variables in the calling function.

Two good reasons for using a stack are:

- It conserves memory.
- It allows a function to be called many times in a long series of function calls, since each new call assigns new automatic variables. The new call does not disturb the values of the same or other functions whose automatic variables are still on the stack. This allows a function to call itself (which is called recursion).

Turn to Module 50 to continue the learning sequence.

Module 72

STDIN, STDOUT, STDERR

DESCRIPTION

This module introduces the method used for console input, console output, and error message output.

When a C program begins execution, three stream files automatically open for use by the program. They are the standard input file (stdin), the standard output file (stdout), and the standard error file (stderr). All three files by default use the computer console. These files are defined in the standard input/output library, and many library functions use them for their input and output automatically.

The main purpose of these three stream files is to provide:

- console input from the user (stdin)
- message output to the user (stdout)
- system error message output to the user (stderr)

Since C does not provide for input/output, the input/output is in the standard library file as functions.

When a program expects input from the standard input file, the input comes from the console. Likewise, when a program writes to the standard output file the output is displayed on the console. Yes, when the functions in the standard library display their error messages, they appear on the console through the standard error file.

These three files are also available for the program's use. The normal conversation with the user should be through the *stdin* and *stdout* files, and the serious error messages to the user should be displayed through the *stderr* file.

These files default to the console. In Module 16, Command Line Arguments, there is a discussion of how to redirect the standard input or the standard output somewhere besides the console *at run time*. Notice the distinction "at run time." This means the redirection is temporary and is only active for that single execution of the program. Another time when the program is run, they could be redirected somewhere else, or not redirected. The stderr file cannot be redirected; the system errors are always displayed on the console so the user can see them.

APPLICATIONS

One typical application of the redirection is to write the output of a program to the printer when the output is normally displayed on the console. If you want output of the program on paper, simply redirect the output of the program to your printer.

An example of redirected input and output is the *sort* program in both UNIX and MS/PC-DOS. The sort program accepts data input from the keyboard, sorts the data, and then outputs the sorted data to the console. Both the input and the output can be redirected by the *sort* program. For example,

```
sort  <infile  >sortfile
```

the input to *sort* is from a file named *infile*, and the output of *sort* is output to a file named *sortfile*.

In this MS/PC-DOS example,

```
sort  <infile  >lpt1
```

the input to *sort* is from a file named *infile*, and the output of *sort* is output to the *lpt1* printer.

Turn to Module 43 to continue the learning sequence.

Module 73

STORAGE CLASSES

DESCRIPTION

This module describes the different places within a C program where variables can be declared, which functions have access to the variables declared/defined in a specific location, and how long the value in the variable is valid.

SCOPE When a variable is declared, it is only accessible to a certain specific area of the program. The specific area where a variable can be accessed is called the *scope* of the variable. The *scope* of a variable depends on where and how it is declared. Where a variable is declared is called its *storage class*. When an identifier is within its scope it is called *visible*. There are four kinds of scopes: function, file, block, and function prototypes.

A label name is the only kind of identifier that has function scope. The label can be used in a goto statement only within the function in which the label is defined.

Every other identifier has scope determined by the placement of its declaration. If an identifier is declared within a block, then the identifier has block scope. If an identifier is declared outside of a block or list of parameters then it has file scope.

If within a block an identifier is declared with the same name as an identifier declared with file scope, then the identifier with file scope is hidden within that block and the locally declared identifier within the block is visible.

The scope of a structure, union, and enumeration identifier begins as soon as they are declared.

The different storage classes to be discussed are:

1. Auto (automatic)
2. Register (fast)
3. Static (local)
4. Global (common)
5. Extern (external)
6. Arguments (local)

STORAGE CLASS DECLARATION Variables can be declared at several different places within a C program. Where and how a variable is declared determines which function(s) have access to the variable and which do not.

Auto (Automatic) *Automatic variables* are stored on the stack. The only function that has access to this class of variable is the module in which the variable has been declared. Since it is using the stack (which is temporary storage), the data is only valid while the function executes. Once the function in which it is declared does a RETURN, the stack space allotted to the variable is freed and the variable and its data no longer exist. The next time this function is called, new stack space is allotted for the variable so it can be manipulated. If the function in which the variable is declared calls another function, which does a RETURN, the variable is still valid because the function in which the variable is declared has not, itself, done a RETURN.

Auto variables are declared within a function, after the opening brace and before the first line of coding. Some compilers even allow variables to be declared in the coding block in the middle of a function. These variables are still *auto* variables and are placed on the stack. They can only be accessed while in that particular block of coding. For instance, if a variable is declared within a *do-while* statement, as long as the *do-while* is executing the variable can be accessed. As soon as the program leaves the *do-while* loop, the variable can no longer be referenced, as it no longer exists.

Register The *register* class is a variation of the *auto* class. By specifing that the variable is in the register class, the C program is telling the C compiler that this variable is heavily accessed in the program and should be placed within one of the computer's fast-access registers, instead of on the stack. Some C compilers do not support the register class and, therefore, ignore this class-specifier, storing the variable on the stack.

Static The *static* storage class specifies that the variable is to be kept in permanent memory, not on the temporary stack. The value of this variable is maintained throughout the life of the program. Performing a RETURN statement does not destroy the value of these variables. Unless otherwise modified, the value is the same for a variable when a function is called as it was when the same function finished executing last time it was called.

Static variables can be declared both inside and outside a function. Static variables declared inside a function are called *internal*, while those outside a function are called *external*. External static variables are known only within the module from which they are declared. Internal static variables are known only within the function from which they are declared.

All objects in static storage are initialized before program startup. If an object is not assigned a value, then zero is automaticlly assigned as a value to the object.

Global The *global* storage class specifies that this variable is to be kept in permanent memory, not on the stack. This variable can be accessed by all functions in the program. Any function in the program can manipulate or use the value of this variable. See external storage class definition.

This class of variable is declared outside all function definitions.

External The *external* storage class tells the C compiler to reference a variable declared in another module. The compiler does not allot memory for a variable defined as external because memory is allotted for it in another module where it is declared as a global variable.

This class of variable is declared outside all function definitions. It should *not* be confused with *external static* variables.

Function Arguments Function arguments are like local variables and are known throughout the function with which they are associated. The *scope* of an argument is the whole function.

STORAGE CLASS EXAMPLES Example 73.1, an example of storage classes:

```
/*                        program name:     storage1.c          */
#include <stdio.h>

extern  char        *error_descriptions [ ] ;            /*  line 1 */
extern  int         funct2();                            /*  line 2 */
char                common_area [ 512 ] ;                /*  line 3 */

static char         local_common [ 0x40 ] ;              /*  line 4 */

main()
{

register   int       i ;                                 /*  line 5 */

auto       int       err ;                               /*  line 6 */


      common_area [ 0 ] = 'a' ;                          /*  line 7 */

      err = function1( ) ;

      if ( err )
         printf( "%s\n" , error_descriptions [ err ] );   /*  line 8 */

}   /* end of main */

function1()
{

int        err ;                                         /* line 9 */

       err = funct2( common_area [ 0 ] );                 /* line 10 */

       return ( err ) ;

}   /* end of function1 */

/* end of module */
```

Line 1 This declaration tells the C compiler that this external variable is declared in another module, but used in this one. This must be declared ahead of the main.

Line 2 This external function definition is required of functions in other modules and libraries if they return a type other than *integer*. More on this subject is in Module 40, Functions, Part 2.

Line 3 This global variable (it is declared ahead of the main) can be accessed in any other module anywhere in the program. The word *global* is not necessary since it is declared ahead of the main.

Line 4 This *local global* variable is known by all functions within this module, but none outside it.

Line 5 This tells the compiler to place the *auto* variable into a register to speed program execution. This *register variable* is known only within the main.

Line 6 is an example of an *auto variable* with the auto included with the declaration. The word *auto* is optional and usually not used. This variable is known only within the main.

Line 7 This assigns a value to a global variable, one that later is accessed by another function where it is not passed as a parameter.

Line 8 is an example of using an *external variable*.

Line 9 shows that the name of a variable can be reused in another function – they are completely independent. There are no problems with using *automatic* and *register* variables having the same name.

Line 10 is an example of using the *static global variable* known only within this module.

Example 73.2 of storage classes:

```
/*                     program name:      storage2.c          */
#include <stdio.h>

char          *error_descriptions[] =                    /* line 11 */
              {
                 " no error  ",
                 " not a number error ",
                 "out of paper  error " ,
                 "printer not ready ",
              } ;

static char          local_common [ 0x40 ] ;             /* line 12 */

funct2 ( the_character )
char     the_character ;
{
     if ( the_character  > 0x39 || the_character < 0x30 )
          return ( 1 );

     return ( 0 ) ;

} /* end of function2 */

/* end of module */
```

Line 11 is another example of the declaration of a *global variable*. This variable is initialized by the compiler. Initialization is covered fully in Pointers Part 2.

Line 12 is an example of reusing a *module static variable*. Notice that the name is allowed to be the same as in the other function. This variable is known only within the *Example #2* module.

SCOPE EXAMPLES Example of scope for storage types:

The next example (scope1.c and scope2.c) shows the access to variables within and between modules. In this example, a plus sign (+) means that the variable can be accessed from that location within the modules. The X character means that the variable cannot be accessed from that location within the module. The question mark (?) means that there is an error, the variable is undefined when the program is linked.

```
/*                   program name:      scope1.c         */
#include <stdio.h>
extern  int  c  ;                                                         c
int          a  ;                                              a          +
static  int  b  ;                                        b     +          +
#define GLOBAL                                           +     +          +
main()                                                   +     +          +
{                                                        +     +          +
char       d  ;                                 d        +     +          +
int        e  ;                             e   +        +     +          +
        do                                  +   +        +     +          +
        {                                   +   +        +     +          +
             int   f ;                  f   +   +        +     +          +
             if ( e )                   +   +   +        +     +          +
             {                          +   +   +        +     +          +
                  int  d ;          d   +   +   X        +     +          +
                  int  c ;      c   +   +   +   X        +     +          X
                                +   +   +   +   X        +     +          X
                  /* code */    c   d   +   +   X        +     +          X
             }                          +   +   X        +     +          +
             else                       +   +   +        +     +          +
             {    int  e ;          e   +   X   +        +     +          +
                                    +   +   X   +        +     +          +
                  /* code */        e   +   X   +        +     +          +
              }                         +   X   +        +     +          +
                                        +   +   +        +     +          +
        }  while ( c );                 f   e   d        +     +          +
}                                                        +     +          +
                                                         +     +          +
function1 ( arg1 )          arg1                         +     +          +
char arg1 ;                    +                         +     +          +
{                              +                         +     +          +
       int    i ;           i  +                         +     +          +
                            +  +                         +     +          +
       /* code */           +  +                         +     +          +
                            i  +                         +     +          +
}                           arg1                         +     +          +
                                                         b     a          c
```

```
/*               program name:   scope2.c            */        +          +
#include "stdio.h                                              +          +
GLOBAL  int  c ;                                               +          c
extern  int  a ;                                               a          +
extern  int  b ;                                     b         +          +
static  int  g ;                   g                 ?         +          +
                                   +                 ?         +          +
function2 ( arg1 )          arg1   +                 ?         +          +
char  arg1 ;                   +   +                 ?         +          +
```

```
{                                  +   +                  ?       +       +
        int i ;                i   +   +                  ?       +       +
                               +   +   +                  ?       +       +
        /* code */             +   +   +                  ?       +       +
                               i   +   +                  ?       +       +
}                                 arg1 g                  b       a       c
```

The following example (scope3.c and scope4.c) shows the declaration of different storage classes. The comment on the line with the variable declaration gives the storage class of the variable.

```
/*                       program name:       scope3.c              */
#include <stdio.h>
#define GLOBAL

extern  int  c  ;      /* extern - defined outside of function */
        int  a  ;      /* global declared outside of function  */
static  int  b  ;      /* static declared outside of function  */

main()
{
           char       d   ;     /* auto declared inside of function */
register   int        e   ;     /* register declared inside of function */
          do
          {
                int   f ;  /* auto declared inside of block */
                if ( e )
                {
               register int  d ; /* retister declared inside of block */
               static   int  c ; /* static   declared inside of block */

                     /* code */
                }
                else
                {    int  e ;  /* auto declared inside of block */

                     /* code */
                 }

          }  while ( c );
}

static funct1 ( arg1 )             /* static function */
char arg1 ;                        /* auto argument   */
{
       int    i ;                  /* auto within function  */

       /* code */

}   /* end of function1 */
```

```
/*                      program name:     scope4.c            */
#include <stdio.h>
#define GLOBAL
GLOBAL  int   c ;       /* global declaration outside of function */
extern  int   a ;       /* extern - outside of function */
extern  int   b ;       /* extern - outside of function */
static  int   g ;       /* static outside of function   */
```

```
funct2 ( arg1 )              /* global function */
char  arg1 ;                 /* auto argument */
{
        int i ;              /* auto within function */

        /* code */

}    /* end of function2 */
```

SCOPE AND STORAGE CLASS SUMMARY The following chart summarizes scope and storage classes of variables.

SUMMARY OF STORAGE CLASSES and SCOPE

Storage Class	*Where Declared*	*Scope or Reference*	*Initialization & Comments*
auto & register variable	inside function/block	within function/block	Initialized each time function is executed, not default value. Arrays & structures cannot be initialized. Register type can only be passed by value. Auto is default if the storage class is not specified on variables declared inside a function or block.
auto	function argument	within function	Arguments cannot be initialized, and can be passed by value or reference.
static variable	inside function/block	within function/block	Initialized only once at start of program. Arrays & structures can be initialized. The default value is zero. Values retained all through program execution.
	outside function	within file	Static basic type variables are still passed by value.
static	function	within file	Static functions can only be called from within the file where they are declared.
GLOBAL variable	outside function	within function; within program with extern	Initialized only once at start of program. Arrays & structures can be initialized. The default value is zero. Values retained all through program execution. Global is default if storage class is not specified on variables declared outside of a function. To make global variables obvious use: #define GLOBAL
GLOBAL	function	within program	A function has global reference as a default.
extern variable	defined inside function/block	within function/block	External reference to global variable. Cannot be initialized when referenced here.
	defined outside function	within file	

Turn to Module 71 to continue the learning sequence.

Module 74

STRCAT
STRNCAT

```
NAME

     strcat    --   appends one string to the end of another
     strncat   --   appends one string to the end of another, but not
                    more than a specified number of characters

USAGE

    char   *strcat  (  char *tostring , char *fromstring ) ;
    char   *strncat (  char *tostring , char *fromstring , int n ) ;

PROTOTYPE in      string.h

ANSI Synopsis

    #include <string.h>
    char *strcat (noalias char *s1, const noalias char *s2 );
    char *strncat(noalias char *s1, const noalias char *s2, size_t n );

RETURNS

    returns the address of tostring
```

DESCRIPTION

The *strcat* function appends fromstring to tostring. *Strcat* searches tostring for the *end-of-string* character. When it finds it, *strcat* starts copying fromstring character by character to tostring, starting at the location occupied by the end-of-string character. You must make sure tostring is defined to be large enough to hold the contents of both tostring and fromstring.

The *strncat* function appends fromstring to tostring, but not more than n characters. *Strncat* searches tostring for the *end-of-string* character. When it finds it, *strncat* starts copying fromstring character by character to tostring, starting at the location occupied by the end-of-string character. You must make sure tostring is defined to be large enough to hold the contents of both tostring and fromstring, and this is usually done by specifing a value of n that prevents strncat from overflowing tostring's length.

An EOS ('\0') character is always appended to the end of the tostring when either function is complete.

Example 74.1, an example of strcat function:

```
/*                    program name:        strcat1.c       */
#include <string.h>
main()
{
    int     i  , count  ;
    char    string1 [ 9 ] ;
    char    string2 [ 9 ] ;

     for ( i=0 ; i < 8 ; i++ )
     {
         string1 [ i ] = ' '   ;
     }

     string1 [ 8 ]     = '\0' ;

     string1 [ 0 ] = 'G'  ;
     string1 [ 1 ] = 'O'  ;
     string1 [ 2 ] = '\0' ;

     string2 [ 0 ] = 'n'  ;
     string2 [ 1 ] = 'e'  ;
     string2 [ 2 ] = 'w'  ;
     string2 [ 3 ] = '1'  ;
     string2 [ 4 ] = '\0' ;

     strcat ( string1 , string2 );                          /* line 1 */

     printf ( "%s\n" , string1 );                           /* line 2 */

     count  = 8 ;                                           /* line 3 */
     count -= strlen ( string1 );                           /* line 4 */

     strncat ( string1 , string2 , count );                 /* line 5 */

     printf ( "%s\n" , string1 );                           /* line 6 */

}   /* end of main */
```

Line 1 is an example of the strcat function call.

Line 2 displays: GOnew1

Line 3 sets count to 8, which is the maximum number of characters that can be stored in string1.

Line 4 calculates the length of string1, which is 6, and substracts it from the value in count, leaving 2.

Line 5 is an example of the strncat function call. This call only appends 2 characters to string1 and then appends the '\0' character.

Line 6 displays: GOnew1ne

This is how memory looks before Line 1 executes:

string1

char	G	0	\0	0x20	0x20	0x20	0x20	0x20	\0	z
char#	0	1	2	3	4	5	6	7	8	9

string2

char	n	e	w	1	\0	x	x	x	y	m
char#	0	1	2	3	4	5	6	7	8	9

After Line 1 executes, memory looks like the following:

string1

char	G	0	n	e	w	1	\0	0x20	\0	z
char#	0	1	2	3	4	5	6	7	8	9

string2

char	n	e	w	1	\0	x	x	x	y	m
char#	0	1	2	3	4	5	6	7	8	9

Notice that string2 does not change. Also, the first two characters of string1 are still there. The '\0' character following the first two characters is gone and the next five characters of string1 are now the first five characters of string2. The '\0' was copied to string1 to mark the new end-of-string.

After Line 5 executes, memory looks like the following:

string1

char	G	0	n	e	w	1	n	e	\0	z
char#	0	1	2	3	4	5	6	7	8	9

The *strcat* function returns the address of string1 to the calling function. This is discussed further in Module 75.

SOURCE CODE FOR STRCAT FUNCTION The source code for the *strcat* function looks like this:

```
/*                              function name:     strcat.c
*/
#include <string.h>
char    *strcat ( to_string      , from_string )
```

```
char                to_string [ ] , from_string [ ] ;
{
        int     i , j ;

        for ( i = 0 ; to_string [ i ] ; i++ )               /* line 1 */
                  ;

        for ( j = 0 ; from_string [ j ] ; j++ , i++ )       /* line 2 */
        {
                  to_string [ i ] = from_string [ j ] ;
        }                                                   /* line 3 */

        to_string [ i ] = '\0' ;                            /* line 4 */

        return ( to_string );

}   /* end of strcat.c  */
```

Line 1 searches for the EOS character of the to_string.

Line 2 through line 3 move each character of the from_string onto the end of the to_string. Notice that the first character of the from_string overwrote the EOS character on the to_string.

Line 4 places the new EOS character at the end of the to_string.

APPLICATIONS

One common use of the string concatenate function is to combine strings together so that they can be manipulated as one string. An example again is the mailing list application. Here the city, state, and zipcode strings can be concatenated together to form one string, such that processing the single strings simplifies the function manipulating in one part of the mailing list application.

TYPICAL OPERATION

In this operation you enter, compile, and execute the program given in Example 74.1.

1. Begin at the DOS prompt, in your C source code directory. Invoke your text editor.
2. Type the C program given in Example 74.1, just like it is listed. Call the program STRCAT1.C.
3. Compile and link the program with your C compiler.
4. Type **STRCAT1** and press **Enter**. Notice the following output on your screen:

```
C:\C>STRCAT1
GOnew1
GOnew1ne
C:\C>_
```

5. Turn to Module 75 to continue the learning sequence.

Module 75

STRCMP
STRNCMP
MEMCMP

```
NAME

     strcmp    --   compares one string to another string
     strncmp   --   compares one string to another string, but not more
                    than the specified number of characters
     memcmp    --   compares one area of memory with another area of
                    memory, but not more than the specified number of
                    characters

USAGE

    int     strcmp  (  char *string1 , char *string2 ) ;
    int     strncmp (  char *string1 , char *string2 , int n ) ;
    int     memcmp  (  char *ptr1    , char *ptr2    , int n ) ;


ANSI Synopsis

   #include <string.h>
   int  strcmp(const noalias char *s1,const noalias char *s2);
   int strncmp(const noalias char *s1,const noalias char *s2, size_t n);
   int  memcmp(const noalias char *s1,const noalias char *s2, size_t n);

RETURNS

    strcmp and strncmp returns:
                      0  if string1 equals string2
                      positive number if string1 is greater than string2
                      negative number if string1 is less than string2

    memcmp returns:
                      0  if ptr1 equals ptr2
                      positive number if ptr1 is greater than ptr2
                      negative number if ptr1 is less than ptr2
```

DESCRIPTION

The *strcmp* function compares one string to another string. For two strings to compare equal they must have the same length and the same characters. Strings are compared until a difference in characters is found. When the difference occurs, the string whose character in that position has the largest binary value is greater.

The *strcmp* function returns one of three values:

1) It returns a 0 if the strings are equal.
2) It returns a positive number if string1 is greater than string2.
3) It returns a negative number if string1 is less than string2.

The *strncmp* function compares one string to another string, up to n characters. For two strings to compare equal they must have the same characters up to n characters. Strings are compared until a difference in characters is found or n characters are reached. If a difference occurs, the string whose character in that position has the largest binary value is greater.

The *memcmp* function compares one area of memory to another area, for up to n characters. For two areas to compare equal they must have each character the same for all n characters. The areas are compared until a difference in characters is found. When the difference occurs, the area with the character in that position that has the largest binary value is greater.

Example 75.1, an example using the strcmp function:

```
/*                      program name:        strcmp1.c        */
#include <string.h>
main()
{
    int     i   , count  ;

    char    string1 [ 9 ] ;
    char    string2 [ 9 ] ;
    char    string3 [ 9 ] ;
    char    string4 [ 9 ] ;

    strcpy ( string1 , "GO" );
    strcpy ( string2 , "GOx1" );
    string2 [ 2 ]    = '\0' ;

    strcpy ( string3 , "GOnew1" );
    strcpy ( string4 , "new1" );

    i = strcmp ( string1 , string2 );                    /* line 1 */
    printf ( "value returned = %d\n" , i );

    i = strcmp ( string3 , string4 );                    /* line 2 */
    printf ( "value returned = %d\n" , i );

    i = strncmp ( string1 , string3  , 2 );              /* line 3 */
    printf ( "value returned = %d\n" , i );

}   /* end of main */
```

Line 1 and Line 2 are examples of *strcmp* function calls.

Line 1 would return the value 0 because the strings are equal.

Line 2 would return a negative value since the first character of string3 is less than the first character of string4.

Line 3 is an example of the *strncmp* function call. Since the strings are equal in the first two characters, a value of 0 is returned.

Look at memory for the above example:

string1

char	G	O	\0	?	?	?	?	?	?	?
char#	0	1	2	3	4	5	6	7	8	9

string2

char	G	O	\0	1	\0	?	?	?	?	?
char#	0	1	2	3	4	5	6	7	8	9

In Line 1, *strcmp* returns a value of zero since the strings are equal. The strings are only compared up to the '\0' end-of-string character.

string3

char	G	O	n	e	w	1	\0	?	?	?
char#	0	1	2	3	4	5	6	7	8	9

string4

char	n	e	w	1	\0	?	?	?	?	?
char#	0	1	2	3	4	5	6	7	8	9

In Line 2, *strcmp* returns a negative number, since the first character of string1 is less than the first character of string2. The comparison stops as soon as a character in one string is not equal to a character in the other string, or when an end-of-string character is reached in one string.

SOURCE CODE FOR STRCMP FUNCTION The source code for the *strcmp* function looks like this:

```
/*                          function name:     strcmp.c
*/
#include <string.h>
int     strcmp ( char *string1 , char *string2  )
{
    int    i ;

     for ( i = 0 ; string1 [ i ] == string2 [ i ] ; i++ ) /* line 1 */
     {
```

```
        if ( string1 [ i ] == '\0' )                      /* line 2 */
            return ( 0 ) ;    /* equal */
    }

    if ( string1 [ i ]   <  string2 [ i ] )               /* line 3 */
       return ( -1 );           /* string1 less */

    return ( 1 );               /* string2 less */        /* line 4 */

}     /* end of strcmp.c    */
```

Line 1 compares the same element of both strings and remains in the *for* loop as long as the characters are equal.

Line 2 in the body of the *for* loop checks to see if the EOS character has been reached. If it is reached, that means that the strings are equal, and the function returns 0.

Line 3 receives control when the same element of both strings does not match. This statement compares the elements to see which is less. If string1 element is less than string2 element, it returns a −1 to mean string1 is less.

Line 4 returns a +1 to mean string2 is less than string1.

APPLICATIONS

The string compare function is useful in many programming applications. The most obvious is a spelling-checker program. Here words as strings are compared to strings in the dictionary. If the word is compared equal to a word in the dictionary, then it is spelled correctly.

TYPICAL OPERATION

In this operation you enter, compile, and execute the program given in Example 75.1.

1. Begin at the DOS prompt, in your C source code directory. Invoke your text editor.
2. Type the C program given in Example 75.1, just like it is listed. Call the program STRCMP1.C.
3. Compile and link the program with your C compiler.
4. Type **STRCMP1** and press **Enter**. Notice the following output on your screen:

```
C:\C>STRCMP1
value returned = 0
value returned = -1
value returned = 0
C:\C>_
```

5. Turn to Module 83 to continue the learning sequence.

Module 76

STRCPY
STRNCPY
MEMCPY
MEMMOVE

```
NAME

     strcpy    —   copies one string over another string
     strncpy   —   copies one string over another string, up to n
                   characters
     memcpy    —   copies one area of memory over another area, for n
                   characters, no overlapping fields
     memmove   —   copies one area of memory over another area, for n
                   characters, with overlapping fields

USAGE

    char   *strcpy  ( char *string1 , char *string2 ) ;
    char   *strncpy ( char *string1 , char *string2 , int n );
    void   *memcpy  ( void *ptr1    , void *ptr2    , int n );
    void   *memmove ( void *ptr1    , void *ptr2    , int n );


ANSI Synopsis

    #include <string.h>
    char *strcpy (noalias char *s1, const noalias char *s2);
    char *strncpy(noalias char *s1, const noalias char *s2, size_t n );
    void *memcpy (noalias void *s1, const noalias void *s2, size_t n );
    char *memmove(        void *s1, const         void *s2, size_t n );

RETURNS

    returns the address of string1 or ptr1
```

DESCRIPTION

The *strcpy* function copies string2 over string1. *Strcpy* copies every character from the start of string2 to string1 until it finds the end-of-string character in string2. It is your responsibility to make sure that string1 is defined to be big enough to hold string2.

The *strncpy* function copies string2 over string1, up to n characters. *Strncpy* copies every character from the start of string2 to string1 until it finds the end-of-string character in string2 or it reaches n characters. It is your responsibility to make sure that string1 is defined to be big enough to hold string2.

The *memcpy* function copies ptr2 over ptr1 for n characters. *Memcpy* copies every character from the start of ptr2 to ptr1 for n characters. It is your responsibility to make sure that ptr1 is defined to be big enough to hold ptr2. The two areas of memory cannot overlap.

The *memmove* function copies ptr2 over ptr1 for n characters. *Memmove* copies every character from the start of ptr2 to ptr1 for n characters. It is your responsibility to make sure that ptr1 is defined to be big enough to hold ptr2. The two areas of memory can overlap. The copying between areas of memory that overlap shall take place correctly.

Example 76.1, an example of strcpy and strncpy functions:

```
/*                    program name:       strcpy1.c        */
#include <string.h>
main()
{
    int     i , count  ;
    char    string1 [ 9 ] ;
    char    string2 [ 9 ] ;

     for ( i=0 ; i < 8 ; i++ )
     {
         string1 [ i ] = ' '   ;
     }

     string1 [ 8 ]      = '\0' ;

     string1 [ 0 ] = 'G'  ;
     string1 [ 1 ] = 'O'  ;
     string1 [ 2 ] = '\0' ;

     string2 [ 0 ] = 'n'  ;
     string2 [ 1 ] = 'e'  ;
     string2 [ 2 ] = 'w'  ;
     string2 [ 3 ] = '1'  ;
     string2 [ 4 ] = '\0' ;

     strncpy ( string1 , string2 , 3 );                   /* line 1 */
     printf ( "string = %s\n" , string1 );                /* line 2 */

     strcpy ( string1 , string2 );                        /* line 3 */

     printf ( "string = %s\n" , string1 );                /* line 4 */

}   /* end of main */
```

Line 1 is an example of the *strncpy* function call. Since the string is longer than 3 characters, only the first 3 characters are copied, and then the '\0' character is appended to string1.

Line 2 displays: string = new

Line 3 is an example of the *strcpy* function call. The whole string is copied to string1.

Line 4 displays: string = new1

Memory looks like the following before Line 1 executes:

string1 char	G	0	\0	0x20	0x20	0x20	0x20	0x20	\0	z
char#	0	1	2	3	4	5	6	7	8	9

string2 char	n	e	w	1	\0	x	x	x	y	m
char#	0	1	2	3	4	5	6	7	8	9

After Line 1 executes, memory looks like the following:

string1 char	n	e	w	\0	0x20	0x20	0x20	0x20	\0	z
char#	0	1	2	3	4	5	6	7	8	9

string2 char	n	e	w	1	\0	x	x	x	y	m
char#	0	1	2	3	4	5	6	7	8	9

Notice that string2 has not been changed at all. Notice that only the first four characters of string1 were changed, and that the '\0' was also copied to string1 to mark the new *end-of-string*.

After Line 3 executes, memory look like the following:

string1 char	n	e	w	1	\0	0x20	0x20	0x20	\0	z
char#	0	1	2	3	4	5	6	7	3	9

string2 char	n	e	w	1	\0	x	x	x	y	m
char#	0	1	2	3	4	5	6	7	8	9

Notice that string2 has not been changed at all. Notice that only the first five characters of string1 were changed, and that the '\0' was also copied to string1 to mark the new *end-of-string*.

The *strcpy* function returns the address of string1 to the calling function. This is discussed further in Module 74, so don't worry about it right now.

SOURCE CODE FOR STRCPY FUNCTION The source code for *strcpy* function looks like this:

```
/*                         function name:       strcpy.c
*/
char   *strcpy ( to_string    , from_string    )           /* line 1 */
char             to_string[] , from_string[] ;
{
    int    i ;

    for ( i = 0 ; from_string [ i ] ; i++ )                /* line 2 */
    {
         to_string [ i ] = from_string [ i ] ;
    }

    to_string [ i ] = '\0' ;                               /* line 3 */

    return ( to_string ) ;                                 /* line 4 */

}   /* end of strcpy.c    */
```

Line 2 is the *for* statement that copies each character from the source string into the same element of the destination string. It stops when it reaches the EOS character.

Line 3 places the EOS character at the end of the destination string.

Line 4 returns the address of the destination string to the calling function, as directed by line 1.

APPLICATIONS

The string copy function is used to make a copy of a string. One of the common uses for copying a string is in an input/edit function. Here the program makes a copy of the string and the string is displayed on the screen for the user to change, like changing the name or address in a mailing list program. Most edit routines allow an "undo" key which, if pressed, causes the changes made to be ignored. If the changes were made to the original data string then they could not be ignored. Since they are made to a copy of the original, it is a simple programming task to ignore the changes to the copy of the string.

TYPICAL OPERATION

In this operation you enter, compile, and execute the program given in Example 76.1.

1. Begin at the DOS prompt, in your C source code directory. Invoke your text editor.
2. Type the C program given in Example 76.1, just like it is listed. Call the program STRCPY1.C.
3. Compile and link the program with your C compiler.
4. Type **STRCPY1** and press **Enter**. Notice the following output on your screen:

```
C:\C>STRCPY1
string = new
string = new1
C:\C>_
```

5. Turn to Module 74 to continue the learning sequence.

Module 77
STRINGS — ARRAYS OF CHAR TYPE

DESCRIPTION

This module describes declaring, accessing, and storing *strings* in memory.

STRING DECLARATION A *strings* is an *array* of *char* type. Strings are declared like arrays, but they have one property that is different from normal arrays. Following the last character in a *string* is an *end-of-string* (EOS) marker, the '\0' character. When you declare a *string* you must allocate an extra character for this marker. The '\0' character cannot be stored as a character in a string since it is the EOS marker.

Example of a string declaration:

```
char    my_string[ 9 ] ;
```

This example is an array of 8 characters with one character position reserved for the *end-of-string* marker.

Since most strings vary in length, the *end-of-string* marker is used to determine the length of a string at any point in a program. The current length of a string is calculated by counting the number of characters in front of the EOS marker.

ACCESSING STRINGS The first character in a string is element zero, just like in all arrays in C. Each element in a string can be accessed just like elements in all arrays.

The names of the elements from the example above are:

```
my_string[ 0 ] , my_string[ 1 ] , . . . , my_string [ 8 ]
```

Example 77.1, an example of the use of string functions:

```
/* Program name:       string1.c      */
#include <stdio.h>
#include <string.h>
main()
{
    int    i  , count  ;
    char   my_string [ 9 ] ;

/*   initialize each element of the string equal to a space and then add
     the end-of-string marker.
*/
```

```
        for ( i=0 ; i < 8 ; i++ )                              /* line 1 */
        {
            my_string[ i ] = ' '  ;
        }
        my_string[ 8 ]      = '\0' ;                           /* line 2 */

    /*  To set the string equal to the word GO
    */

         my_string[ 0 ] = 'G'  ;                               /* line 3 */
         my_string[ 1 ] = 'O'  ;
         my_string[ 2 ] = '\0' ;                               /* line 4 */

         printf( "string = %s\n" , my_string );                /* line 5 */

    }   /* end of main */
```

Line 1 through line 2 initialize each element in the string to a space character and then place the EOS marker at the end of the string.

Line 3 through line 4 move a 'GO' into the first two elements in the string and then place the EOS marker into the element number 2 of the string. The other elements in the string are not changed at all.

Line 5 displays: string = GO
Only 11 characters are displayed on the terminal since the string is two characters long.

If the '\0' character is not at the end of the string, the *printf* function displays memory until it finds one. The EOS marker must be placed on the end of each string for the string functions to operate properly.

STRINGS IN MEMORY Typically, you do not care how data is stored in memory. But, in the case of *strings*, it helps to be able to see it on paper to visualize it a little better.

In the preceding example, the string variable my_string looks like this in memory when the *printf* function executes:

string char	G	O	\0	0x20	0x20	0x20	0x20	0x20	\0	don't know	...
char#	0	1	2	3	4	5	6	7	8	9	A ...

In the example (string.c):

Line 1 through line 2 move spaces into char# 0 through char# 7, and place the '\0' character into char# 8.

Line 3 through line 4 move the two characters 'GO' into char# 0 and 1 and then move the '\0' character into char# 2.

Line 5 displays GO, but memory looks like the above.

STRING FUNCTIONS IN THE STANDARD LIBRARY The string functions in the standard library usually include:

1. strlen — Function to measure the length of a string.
2. strcpy — Function to copy one string over another string.
3. strcat — Function to add one string to the end of another string (concatenate).
4. strcmp — Function to compare two strings.
5. atoi — Convert a number in a character string to an integer.

Each of these functions is covered in its own module in this text.

STRINGS IN CALENDAR PROGRAMS Algorithms concerning the calendar must be implemented on the computer in real world programming. These algorithms are fun and interesting and make good examples in text books. The following example to illustrate string usage uses calendar algorithms to determine the day of the week you were born. You input your birthday and the program calculates the day of the week on which you were born. This example is a subset of the complete day calculation routine, as this one is only for the Gregorian calendar for dates after the year 1752, when England converted from the Julian (Julius Caesar) calendar to the more accurate Gregorian. A leap year is a year evenly divisible by 4 but not by 100, or a year evenly divisible by 400. The day of the week which Jan. 1 comes on for any year since 1752 is calculated by taking the year number, adding 1 for every 4 years, subtracting 3 for every 400 years, and then doing a modulo 7 on the result. This yields a number from 0 to 6, where Sunday is 0, Monday is 1, etc. Add the number of days in the year previous to the birthday to the year calculation and modulo 7 produces the day on which a person was born, where Sunday is 0, Monday is 1, etc. Note that the year is not multiplied times 365 (number of days in a year) in this algorithm. It is in the more complete algorithm, but since "year modulo 7" is equal to "year*365 modulo 7" the multiplication is not necessary. Also if we did multiply by 365 we could not use integer variables.

One real application that requires the day-of-week algorithm is banking projects. Since banks are closed on weekends and holidays and banking customers have 10 days to renew Certificates of Deposit, when the renewal date falls on a holiday or the weekend, the last day for renewal is moved to the next business day.

Example 77.2, a programmed birthday example using strings:

```
/* Program Name:                      BIRTHDAY.C */
int daysinmonth ( int , int ) ;
#include <string.h>
main()
{
int     i , days , month , day , year ;
char    dayofweek [ 22 ]  ;                                    /* line 1 */
char    months [ 12 ][ 4 ] ;                                   /* line 2 */

        strcpy ( dayofweek , "SatSunMonTueWedThrFri" );        /* line 3 */
        name months ( months ) ;                               /* line 4 */
        printf( "Enter Month of birthday ... " );
        scanf ( "%d" , &month );
        printf( "Enter Day   of birthday ... " );
        scanf ( "%d" , &day   );
        printf( "Enter Year  of birthday ... " );
```

```
        scanf ( "%d" , &year  );
        if ( year < 1800 )
        {
           printf ( "Year less than 1800 ...  program stopped." );
           exit (0) ;
        }
        days  = year + ((year+3)/4);       /* add 1 day  for each   4 years */
        days -= (year - 1701 ) / 100 ;     /* sub 3 days for each 400 years */
        days += (year - 1601 ) / 400 ;
        for ( i = 1 ; i < month ; i++ )      /* add days in previous months */
            days += daysinmonth ( i , year );
        days += day ;                          /* add days in current month */
        days %= 7 ;                            /* mod 7 days per week       */
        printf ( "Your birthday %s %d, %d was on a %.3s" ,       /* line 5 */
           months [ month - 1 ] , day, year , &dayofweek [ days * 3 ]  );
}    /* end of main */


int daysinmonth ( int month , int year )
{
int days ;

        if ( month == 2 )
             if (     ( year % 4 == 0 && year % 100 != 0 )
                  || ( year % 400 == 0 )                 )
                 days = 29 ;    /* leap year */
             else days = 28 ;
        else  if ( month == 4 || month == 6 || month == 9 || month == 11 )
                days = 30 ;
            else days = 31 ;
        return ( days );
} /* end of daysinmonths */

void name_months ( months )
char                months [][4] ;                                  /* line 6 */
{
        strcpy ( months[0]  , "Jan" );    strcpy ( months[1]  , "Feb" ); /*7*/
        strcpy ( months[2]  , "Mar" );    strcpy ( months[3]  , "Apr" );
        strcpy ( months[4]  , "May" );    strcpy ( months[5]  , "Jun" );
        strcpy ( months[6]  , "Jul" );    strcpy ( months[7]  , "Aug" );
        strcpy ( months[8]  , "Sep" );    strcpy ( months[9]  , "Oct" );
        strcpy ( months[10] , "Nov" );    strcpy ( months[11] , "Dec" ); /*8*/
}
```

Line 1 is an example of declaring a string (array of char type). This string is declared to have 22 characters: 21 characters of data and one character reserved for the EOS (end-of-string) character.

Line 2 is an example of the declaring of a string with two dimensions. There are twelve months and each month name is 3 characters long. Note that one EOS character is reserved for each array element, i.e., month name.

Line 3 is an example of the use of the strcpy (string copy) function to initialize a string to a value.

Line 4 is an example of passing a string as a function parameter.

Line 5 is an example of displaying a string. In displaying the month name we display the whole string of three characters, therefore the %s works fine. In the second example we are only displaying a portion of the string. We start within the string and only display 3 characters; therefore, we must limit the string display length with the %.3s specifier.

Line 6 is an example of defining a function that has a string parameter. Note that the length of the array can only be not defined on the leftmost entry. The rest of the array sizes must be defined.

Line 7 through line 8 are examples of setting the elements of an array of strings equal to a value by the use of the strcpy function.

APPLICATIONS

String functions are fundamental to manipulating text. One of the most common applications using strings is the mailing list. In this application there are strings for name, address, city, state, zip code, and other data. The strings may be used to sort the mailing list by last name or by zip code. The strings are also manipulated to change any of the data fields.

The most common application of manipulating text is word processing, where characters are input and make words, and the words combine into lines, and lines combine into paragraphs, and paragraphs into chapters, and chapters into books. In word processing, strings of characters are manipulated; they are moved around, deleted, added to, and changed.

TYPICAL OPERATION

In this operation you enter, compile, and execute the programs given in Example 77.1 and Example 77.2.

1. Begin at the DOS prompt, in your C source code directory. Invoke your text editor.
2. Type the C program given in Example 77.1, just like it is listed. Call the program STRINGS1.C.
3. Compile and link the program with your C compiler.
4. Type **STRINGS1** and press **Enter**. Notice the following output on your screen:

```
C:\C>STRINGS1
string = GO
C:\C>_
```

5. Type the C program given in Example 77.2, just like it is listed. Call the program BIRTHDAY.C.
6. Compile and link the program with your C compiler.
7. Type **BIRTHDAY** and press **Enter**. Type **12** and press **Enter**, type **25** and press **Enter**, and type **1988** and press **Enter**. Notice the following output on your screen:

```
C:\C>BIRTHDAY
 Enter Month of birthday ... 12
 Enter Day   of birthday ... 25
 Enter Year  of birthday ... 1988
 Your birthday DEC 25, 1988 was on a Sun
C:\C>_
```

8. Turn to Module 78 to continue the learning sequence.

Module 78

STRLEN

```
NAME

     strlen    —    returns the length of a character string

USAGE

   unsigned  strlen (  char *string  ) ;

PROTOTYPE in      string.h

ANSI Synopsis

     #include <string.h>
     size_t strlen( const noalias char *s);

RETURNS

     returns the length of the string
```

DESCRIPTION

The *strlen* function searches the string, character by character, until it finds an *end-of-string* marker, the '\0' character. *Strlen* then returns the number of characters that are in front of the *end-of-string* marker. If the first character is the *end-of-string* marker, then "zero" is returned.

Example 78.1, an example of *strlen* function:

```
/*                        program name:       strlen1.c       */
#include <string.h>
main()
{
    int    i  , count  ;
    char   my_string [ 9 ] ;

     for ( i=0 ; i < 8 ; i++ )
     {
         my_string[ i ] = ' '  ;
     }
     my_string[ 3 ]     = '\0' ;
```

```
    my_string[ 0 ] = 'G'  ;
    my_string[ 1 ] = 'O'  ;
    my_string[ 2 ] = '\0' ;

    printf( "length = %d\n" , strlen( my_string ) );      /* line 1 */

}   /* end of main */
```

Line 1 would display: length = 2

Look at memory for Example 78.1:

string char	G	O	\0	0x20	0x20	0x20	0x20	0x20	\0	?
char#	0	1	2	3	4	5	6	7	8	9

The *strlen* function returns the value "2" to the calling function because there are two characters in front of the '\0' character.

SOURCE CODE FOR STRLEN FUNCTION The actual source code for the *strlen* function looks like this:

```
/*                        function name:        strlen.c          */
unsigned strlen (char *string )
{
    int     i ;

    for ( i = 0 ; string [ i ] ; i++ )                     /* line 1 */
        ;                                                  /* line 2 */

    return ( i );

}   /* end of strlen.c */
```

Line 1 searches the string for the EOS character. Since the EOS character '\0' has a value of zero, which is the same thing as false, the *for* loop terminates when it reaches the EOS character in the string. Notice the NULL statement in line 2.

APPLICATIONS

The string length (strlen) function is often used to get the length of a string where the length is the condition-parameter in a for loop. For example, in the following example the for loop executes the body of the for loop one time for each letter of the name that is present, not for the maximum number of characters allowed in the name field.

```
for ( i = 0 ; i < strlen ( name ) ; i++ )
{
     process_letter ( name[i] );
}
```

TYPICAL OPERATION

In this operation you enter, compile, and execute the program given in Example 78.1.

1. Begin at the DOS prompt, in your C source code directory. Invoke your text editor.
2. Type the C program given in Example 78.1, just like it is listed. Call the program STRLEN1.C.
3. Compile and link the program with your C compiler.
4. Type **STRLEN1** and press **Enter**. Notice the following output on your screen:

```
C:\C>STRLEN1
length = 2
C:\C>_
```

5. Turn to Module 76 to continue the learning sequence.

Module 79

STRUCTURES

DESCRIPTION

This module explains the declaration and use of structures.

A *structure* is a group of several variables, which usually have something in common. The variables are declared together as a group and are passed as a group when used as a function argument.

The different variables in a *structure* are called *members* of the *structure*. They do not have to be of the same data type.

Structures are declared with the other variables in a C program.

STRUCTURE DECLARATION The form for *structure declaration* is:

```
struct      struct_type                         /*  line 1 */
{                                               /*  line 2 */
  data_type        member1_name ;               /*  line 3 */
  data_type        member2_name ;               /*  line 4 */
}                                               /*  line 5 */
              struct_name ;                     /*  line 6 */
```

Line 1 shows that the key word struct is required to start the structure definition. This tells the C compiler a structure is being declared. Line 1 also shows that the structure can be given a type name. This name is optional. If you want to declare once what a structure looks like, but use the definition several times, then this is where you name the structure type.

Line 2 has the open brace to begin grouping the members of the structure.

Line 3 is an example of declaring a member of the structure. The member is declared just like a normal variable, with the variable data type and the variable name.

Line 4 is another example of declaring a member of the structure.

Line 5 is the close brace to mark the end of the group of structure members.

Line 6 shows how the structure name is assigned. This name is also optional. If the name is not present, then this is just the definition of a structure and not the declaration of a structure variable. A definition defines the form of the structure and does not declare a variable. A declaration declares a variable of the structure type. Line 6 also shows that the structure definition or declaration requires a terminating semicolon, like other variables.

ACCESSING STRUCTURE MEMBERS Structure members are accessed with the *dot operator*. This is the period character '.' used between the structure name and the member's name.

The appropriate structure name, followed by the dot operator, then the member name, is the name required to access a structure member in the module where the structure is declared.

Example 79.1, an example of structure definition, structure variable declaration, and accessing structure members:

```
/*                      program name:     struct1.c        */
#include <stdio.h>
main()
{
  struct      struct1_type                                /* line 1 */
  {
     int      a_field1 ;
     int      b_field1 ;
     float    c_field1 ;
  } ;                                                     /* line 2 */

  struct struct1_type       struct_record ;               /* line 3 */
  struct struct1_type       new_record ;                  /* line 4 */

  struct                                                  /* line 5 */
  {
     int      cust_no             ;
     char     cust_name[ 30 ]     ;
     float    cust_balance        ;
  }
                     customer_record ;                    /* line 6 */

  customer_record.cust_no       = 123 ;
  customer_record.cust_balance  = 230.66 ;
  strcpy ( customer_record.cust_name , "Mr. John Doe" );

  printf( "%d \n"   , customer_record.cust_no       );    /* line 7 */
  printf( "%s \n"   , customer_record.cust_name     );
  printf( "%.2f\n"  , customer_record.cust_balance  );    /* line 8 */

}   /* end of main */
```

Line 1 through Line 2 are an example of a structure definition. There is no structure name, since the space between the close brace and the semicolon is empty. This is simply a structure definition and not a structure variable declaration. No memory is set aside by the C compiler for this definition. The structure definition type was defined to be "struct1_type".

Line 3 and Line 4 both declare a structure variable and have the C compiler assign memory for the structure. Here, the key word struct is present first, followed by the name of the structure, then the name of the structure variable, and a closing semicolon. Both structure variables declared here are of the structure type defined by Line 1.

Line 5 through Line 6 show a structure definition, without assigning a structure type, and declare a structure variable at the same time.

Line 7 through Line 8 are an example of accessing structure members in the module in which the structure is declared.

The output of this example is:

```
123
Mr. John Doe
230.66
```

ARRAYS OF STRUCTURES Like other variables, an *array of structures* can be declared. The individual structures are elements of the array of structures and are accessible individually.

The declaration of the array of structures is like other array declarations.

Example 79.2, an example of an array of structures declaration:

```
/*                          program name:   struct2.c      */
#include <stdio.h>
main()
{

  struct                                                  /* line 1 */
  {
     int      cust_no          ;
     char     cust_name[ 30 ]  ;
     float    cust_balance     ;
  }
                    customer_record [ 20 ] ;              /* line 2 */

       strcpy( customer_record[ 2 ].cust_name , "C. Name" );

       customer_record[ 2 ].cust_no      = 1002 ;         /* line 3 */

       customer_record[ 2 ].cust_balance = 100.00 ;       /* line 4 */

       printf( "name= %s, no= %d, balance= %.2f\n",
               customer_record[ 2 ].cust_name ,
               customer_record[ 2 ].cust_no   ,
               customer_record[ 2 ].cust_balance );

}    /* end of main */
```

Line 1 through Line 2 show the definition of a structure (without assigning a structure type), declaring an array structure variable at the same time.

Line 3 through Line 4 show examples of accessing the members of an element in the array of structures.

The output of this example is:

```
name= C. Name, no= 1002, balance= 100.00
```

NESTED STRUCTURES A structure can be defined as an element of another structure. The structure to be included as part of another structure can be defined inside the structure definition or outside as an individual structure type. This is called nesting.

Example 79.3, an example of nested structures:

```
/*                   program name:    struct3.c      */
#include <stdio.h>
main()
{

  struct     struct1_type                                    /* line 1 */
  {
     float    new_bal    ;
     float    old_bal    ;
  } ;                                                        /* line 2 */


  struct
  {
   char                          name [ 30 ] ;
   struct struct1_type           balances ;                  /* line 3 */
  }
          account_record ;


       strcpy ( account_record.name , "C. Name" );

       account_record.balances.old_bal  = 100.00 ;           /* line 4 */
       account_record.balances.new_bal  = 200.00 ;           /* line 5 */

       printf( "name= %s, old= %.2f, new= %.2f\n",
            account_record.name ,
            account_record.balances.old_bal ,
            account_record.balances.new_bal  );

}   /* end of main */
```

Line 1 through Line 2 is the definition of a structure type.

Line 3 is an example of a member of a structure being another structure.

Line 4 through Line 5 are examples of accessing a member of a structure that is another structure. The structure members are referenced by the dot operator, even when nested together.

The output of this example is:

```
name= C. Name, old= 100.00, new= 200.00
```

APPLICATIONS

Structures always simplify the programs in which they are used. Fewer bugs are created when structures are used. A good illustration is the mailing list application. All the data for one person on a mailing list can be manipulated with one instruction since a structure is treated as a unit. The length of the structure can be determined and then that exact amount of data is read from disk and written back to disk with one instruction, so you know that all the data is always read and written back. Structures are wonderful, use them liberally.

TYPICAL OPERATION

In this operation you enter, compile, and execute the program given in Example 79.1.

1. Begin at the DOS prompt, in your C source code directory. Invoke your text editor.
2. Type the C program given in Example 79.1, just like it is listed. Call the program STRUCT1.C.
3. Compile and link the program with your C compiler.
4. Type **STRUCT1** and press **Enter**. Notice the following output on your screen:

```
C:\C>STRUCT1
123
Mr. John Doe
230.66
C:\C>_
```

5. Enter, compile, link, and execute the other examples in this module and verify the output screen with the output provided after each example.
6. Turn to Module 85 to continue the learning sequence.

Module 80

STRUCTURES — PART 2

DESCRIPTION

This module explains initializing of structures and passing structures as function arguments. Bit fields also are explained.

STRUCTURE INITIALIZATION The members of an *extern* or *static* structure can be initialized (set to a value) at compile time. The general form for initializing the structure is to place an equal sign after the structure declaration, followed by the values in braces. The generalized form for initializing a structure is presented in the next example. Normally there is one initialization value for each member of the structure. When not enough initialization values are given, the uninitialized fields in the structure are initialized to (set equal to) zero. A compiler error results if too many initialization values are given.

Example 80.1, an example of structure initialization:

```
/*                    program name:       struct21.c          */
#include <stdio.h>

  struct xx
  {
          float      z1 ;
          float      z2 ;
  } ;

  struct yy
  {
          char           x [ 30 ] ;
          int            y ;
          struct xx      z ;
  } ;

  struct yy   xyz_record =
  {
        "x_field",             /* init  x[30]  */          /* line 1 */
        1024 ,                 /* init  y      */          /* line 2 */
        2400.00 ,              /* init  z1     */          /* line 3 */
        5.66666                /* init  z2     */          /* line 4 */
  } ;

main()
{
```

```
        printf( "x[30] = %s\n", xyz_record.x     );
        printf( "y     = %d\n", xyz_record.y     );
        printf( "z1    = %f\n", xyz_record.z.z1 );
        printf( "z2    = %f\n", xyz_record.z.z2 );

    }  /* end of main */
```

Lines 1 through 4 initialize the xyz_record structure. The values are assigned to the structure members in the same sequence as they are declared. There are four structure members and four values, so each structure member is assigned a value. If Line 4 had not been included, then the value of z2 would be initialized to zero.

The output from this example is:

```
x[30] = x_field
y     = 1024
z1    = 2400.000000
z2    = 5.666660
```

STRUCTURES AS FUNCTION ARGUMENTS Structures, when passed as function arguments, are not always placed on the stack. Some compilers only allow a pointer to the structure to be passed as the function argument. This means that a copy of the structure is not placed onto the stack; therefore, the called function manipulates the actual structure. Some compilers support both methods.

Example 80.2, an example of structures as function arguments:

```
/*                    program name:     struct22.c         */
#include <stdio.h>

  struct       xyz_type
  {
            char            x [ 30 ] ;
            int             y   ;
  } ;

main()
{

      struct xyz_type       xyz_record ;


      xyz_record.y = 10 ;

      funct1( &xyz_record );                               /* line 1 */

      printf( " y = %d \n", xyz_record.y );                /* line 2 */

}   /* end of main */


funct1 ( xyz_record )
struct xyz_type          *xyz_record ;                     /* line 3 */
{
```

```
        xyz_record->y += 10 ;                           /* line 4 */

        funct2 ( xyz_record );                          /* line 5 */

    }   /* end of function1 */


    funct2 ( xyz_record )
    struct xyz_type        *xyz_record ;                /* line 6 */
    {

        xyz_record->y *= 2 ;                            /* line 7 */

    }   /* end of function2 */
```

Line 1 passes a structure as a function argument. The address operator is used because the address of the structure is passed. The value is not passed.

Line 2 displays: y = 40

Line 3 shows how to define a function argument when it is a pointer to a structure.

Line 4 accesses the structure members in the called function. The structure was passed as a pointer; therefore, the members are accessed with the *pointer operator*, the right arrow.

Line 5 passes the pointer to the structure as an argument in a function call. The pointer to a structure is treated like a basic variable type — no address operator is needed.

Line 6 shows how to define a function argument when it is a pointer to a structure.

Line 7 accesses the structure member y.

Example 80.3, an example of passing structures as function arguments:

```
/*                program name:    struct23.c         */
#include <stdio.h>

  struct  balances
  {
    float       curr_balance ;
    float       pastdue_balance    ;
    float      *cust_work     ;
  } ;

  struct  cust_struct
  {
     int                 cust_no ;
     char                cust_name[30] ;
     struct balances     cust_balances ;
     struct balances    *work_balances ;
  } ;

float             work, work2 ;
struct balances   bal ;
main()
{
```

```
   struct cust_struct   customer ;                                /* line 1 */
      show_cust ( customer );                                     /* line 2 */
      zero_cust   ( &customer );                                  /* line 3 */
} /* end of main */

show_cust  (            customer )
struct cust_struct   customer ;                                   /* line 4 */
{
     printf ( "CustNo %d's Name is %s\n",
            customer.cust_no, customer.cust_name ) ;             /* line 5 */
     printf ( "          Balance is %f\n"
            customer.cust_balances.curr_balance );
} /* end show_cust */

zero_cust  (            customer )
struct cust_struct  *customer ;                                   /* line 6 */
{
     customer->cust_no = 0 ;                                      /* line 7 */
     for ( i = 0 ; i < 30 ; i++ )
         customer->cust_name[i] =  ' ' ;                          /* line 8 */
     customer->cust_balances.curr_balance      = 0 ;              /* line 9 */
     customer->cust_balances.pastdue_balance   = 0 ;              /* line 10 */
     customer->cust_balances.cust_work         = &work ;          /* line 11 */
    *customer->cust_balances.cust_work         = 0 ;              /* line 12 */
     customer->work_balances                   = &bal ;           /* line 13 */
     customer->work_balances->curr_balance     = 0 ;              /* line 14 */
     customer->work_balances->pastdue_balance  = 0 ;              /* line 15 */
     customer->work_balances->cust_work        = &work2 ;         /* line 16 */
    *customer->cust_balances->cust_work        = 0 ;              /* line 17 */
} /* end zero_cust */
```

Line 1 is the declaration of a structure that will be passed both by reference and by value in this example.

Line 2 is an example of passing the whole structure as a parameter. Note here that if any value in the structure is changed it is only changed in the copy of the structure used within the called function. The original structure declared in Line 1 cannot be changed in this function.

Line 3 is an example of passing a pointer to a structure. If the called function changes any value in the parameter, it changes the original structure declared in Line 1, since a pointer to the original structure was passed as the parameter.

Line 4 shows how to declare a structure when passed as a function parameter when the whole structure is passed. Notice that the pointer indicator is not present in this declaration.

Line 5 shows how to access members of structures that are passed as function parameters when the whole structure is passed. They are accessed just as if the structure was defined in this function.

Line 6 shows how to declare a structure when passed as a function parameter when a pointer to the structure is passed. Notice that the pointer indicator (asterisk) is present in this declaration.

Line 7 shows how to modify an element in the original structure that is an integer via the pointer passed to this function.

Line 8 also shows modifying an element in the original structure that is an array of characters.

Line 9 and 10 illustrate modifying an element in the original structure that is a member of another structure declared within the original structure.

Line 11 shows the modifying of an element in the original structure that is a pointer.

Line 12 shows the modifying of a variable that is pointed to by an element in the original structure (which was initialized in Line 11).

Line 13 shows again the initialization of an element that is a pointer in the original structure.

Lines 14 thru 17 show the modifying of a variable that is pointed to by a pointer in the original structure.

BIT FIELDS C even allows the programmer to fiddle with bits in a formal manner. The smallest variable discussed so far is a byte, which is eight bits long. C allows bit variables that are from one bit to the number of bits in an integer type for the computer in use. Since the number of bits in *int* type varies from one computer to another, bit fields must be defined very carefully to preserve portability, which is described in Module 58.

The structure definition is used to describe and declare bit variables.

The form for declaring a bit variable is:

```
struct
{
  unsigned      bit_field_name  : bit_count ;
  unsigned      bit_field2_name : bit_count ;
  unsigned      bit_fieldN_name : bit_count ;

}               bit_variable_name ;
```

Bit Field Characteristics

1. The data type for a bit field is unsigned.
2. The bit_field_name can be any legal variable name in C.
3. The colon is what tells the C compiler that this is a bit field. It is required.
4. The bit_count can be from zero to the number of bits in an integer for the machine the program is running on.

A *field* is defined as a set of adjacent bits with a single *int*. This means a bit field cannot overlap an *int* boundary. The C compiler recognizes the fact that a bit field is going to overlap and it aligns the overlapping field into the next *int*. The programmer can tell the compiler to move the next field to the next *int* boundary by specifing a *bit field* with a bit width of zero.

Since bit fields occur in the middle of a byte, the address operator cannot be applied to them.

Example 80.4, an example of *bit* fields:

```
/*                  program name:     struct24.c        */
#include <stdio.h>
#define TRUE  1
#define FALSE 0

main()
{
      struct
      {
        unsigned     count     : 4 ;                    /* line 1 */
        unsigned     used_flag : 1 ;                    /* line 2 */
        unsigned     next_int1 : 0 ;                    /* line 3 */
        unsigned     error_no  : 8 ;                    /* line 4 */
      }
                     flags ;


        flags.count     = 4    ;                        /* line 5 */
        flags.used_flag = TRUE ;
        flags.error_no  = 222  ;


        if ( flags.used_flag == TRUE )                  /* line 6 */
             printf( "error number is %d \n" , flags.error_no );

}    /* end of main */
```

Line 1 declares a bit field. The range of unsigned values for this field is 0 to 15, since it is 4 bits wide.

Line 2 is a bit field one bit wide with a range of 0 thru 1, which is the right size of a TRUE or FALSE flag.

Line 3 shows how to tell the compiler to start the next bit field in the next integer boundary in memory.

Line 4 is a bit field 8 bits wide, with a range from 0 to 255.

Line 5 shows how to access bit fields like other structure members.

Line 6 also shows how bit fields can be treated just like any other variable.

APPLICATIONS

Example 80.3 is a typical example of passing a structure to a function. This example is appropriate for accounting applications, like accounts receivable and accounts payable. In these applications the customer's data is passed to the function with one parameter.

Another example is the common input routine for all menu answers in a program. One function accepts the keyboard input to answer all menu prompts in an application. A structure that contains the data for a simple input routine follows:

```
struct  menu_answer_struct
{
   int     row, column ;    /* screen row and column location for input   */
   int     length      ;    /* length of input                            */
   char    type        ;    /* input type: 0=numbers, 1=alpha, 2=any keys */
   char   *ans         ;    /* location to place keyboard input           */

} ;
```

This structure contains all the information necessary to input data from the keyboard. It specifies where on the screen to display the data as it is input. It also specifies how many characters to allow for this piece of data. It also indicates what particular characters are allowed in this field, whether just numbers are allowed, just alphabetic character are allowed, or any characters.

TYPICAL OPERATION

In this operation you enter, compile, and execute the program given in Example 80.1.

1. Begin at the DOS prompt, in your C source code directory. Invoke your text editor.
2. Type the C program given in Example 80.1, just like it is listed. Call the program STRUCT21.C.
3. Compile and link the program with your C compiler.
4. Type **STRUCT21** and press **Enter**. Notice the following output on your screen:

```
C:\C>STRUCT21
x[30] = x field
y     = 1024
z1    = 2400.000000
z2    = 5.666660
C:\C>_
```

5. Enter, compile, link, and execute the other examples in this module. Then verify the output of each example with the output provided in the text.
6. Turn to Module 57 to continue the learning sequence.

Module 81

SWITCH

```
NAME

   SWITCH — evaluates an expression and then
            transfer control to the following statement
            whose expression equals the evaluated expression.

USAGE
     switch ( expression )
     {
          case constant_expression1:       c-statement ;
          case constant_expression2:       c-statement ;
          default:                         c-statement ;
     }
```

DESCRIPTION

The *switch* statement evaluates the expression that follows it and then transfers control to the C statement following the case statement whose constant expression equals the result of the *switch* expression. The *switch* expression is converted to an integer value.

If no match is found and a default statement is present in the switch statement body, control transfers to the C statement following the default statement. If no match is found and there is no default statement, control transfers to the next statement following the switch statement body.

Once control transfers within the *switch* statement body, all statements from that point on in the body execute unless another statement transfers control. That is to say, all labels and constant expressions are ignored and have no further control of execution after the initial transfer. The break statement is normally the last statement in each case statement, to transfer control out of the *switch* body to the statement following the *switch* statement.

Example 81.1, example of *switch* statement:

```
/*                          program name:    switch1.c        */
main()
{

 char     answer ;
 int      yes = 0 , no = 0 , bad_answer = 0 ;
```

```
answer = 'y' ;

   switch ( answer )                                    /* line 1 */
   {
       case 'y':                                        /* line 2 */
       {      yes = yes + 1 ;   /* receives control if answer = y  */
              break ;           /* transfer control out of switch */
       }
       case 'n':                                        /* line 3 */
       {      no  = no  + 1 ;   /* receives control if answer = n  */
              break ;           /* transfer control out of switch */
       }
       default:                                         /* line 4 */
              bad_answer++ ;    /* receives control if answer not y or n */
   }

   printf( "yes=%d, no=%d, bad=%d\n",yes,no,bad_answer );  /* line 5 */

}    /* end of main */
```

The output of Example 81.1 is:

```
yes=1, no=0, bad=0
```

Line 1 is the *switch* statement. It evaluates the expression inside the parentheses. This time it is the value of the variable answer. The body of the *switch* statement is enclosed in braces.

Line 2 is one of the *case* statements within the switch statement. The value of the constant following the word *case* is compared to the result of the expression in the *switch* statement on line 1. If the result of the comparison is true then control transfers to the first statement following the *case* statement. Instructions from that point on execute unless control transfers again to another statement. The break statement transfers control to the statement following the closing brace of the *switch* statement.

Line 3 is another *case* statement. Execution can begin here in two ways. The first way is for none of the previous case statements to have matched the result of the *switch* expression and this case does. The second way is for a previous case to have received control but to have encountered a transfer instruction.

Line 4 is the *default case* statement. If no case statement matches the result of the *switch* statement then the body of this statement takes control. No *break* is needed, as this is the last body of statements to receive control, so control flows to the next statement following the closing brace for the *switch* statement.

Line 5 is the first statement following the *switch* statement. Control transfers to it if a break statement executes in one of the *case* statements, or if control falls through from the last *case* statement in the switch loop.

Example 81.2, another example of *switch* statement:

```
/*                          program name:    switch2.c         */
main()
{
int  score ;
char grade ;
```

```
        score = 96 ;
        switch ( score/10 )                                   /* line 1 */
        {
            case 10:                                          /* line 2 */
            case  9:   grade = 'A' ;   break ;                /* line 3 */
            case  8:   grade = 'B' ;   break ;                /* line 4 */
            case  7:   grade = 'C' ;   break ;                /* line 5 */
            case  6:   grade = 'D' ;   break ;                /* line 6 */
            default:   grade = 'F' ;   break ;                /* line 7 */
        }
        printf ( " grade = %c \n" , grade );                  /* line 8 */

    } /* end of main */
```

The output of Example 82.1 is:

```
grade = A
```

When line 1 is reached the value of score is 96. The switch statement then evaluates its expression. The value in this case is 9, since the value of a switch expression is always the size of an integer or less. In this case it is an integer which truncates to the value 9. Control is then transferred to the case statement that matches the value of the switch expression. Therefore control is transferred to line 3. After assigning the value of 'A' to grade, the next statement encountered by the program is a break which transfers control to line 8.

Note that control is passed in a switch statement to the case statement that matches the value of the switch expression. Execution begins there and continues until another control statement is encountered. If there had not been a break statement on line 3 then line 4 would have been executed next. Notice that line 2 has no statements and that this same rule applies to this condition also — when control is passed to line 2, next statement to execute is on line 3, which accomplishes what the program desires by assigning 'A' to grade.

APPLICATIONS

In contrast to the *if* statement, the *switch* statement is ideally suited for selecting one of many possible actions.

One typical application is in a program that edits an input field. The typical edit function allows an operator to input a certain number of characters to fill an input field. It also allows the operator to press the delete key to delete the last character typed or use the arrow keys to move within the input field for changing, adding, or deleting data. Note that this routine normally tests for an edit key (arrow, delete, etc.) and if it is not one of these keys, the routine assumes that the key pressed is data. The loop executes until the operator presses the Enter key. The segment of the code for this function that includes the switch statement usually resembles the following:

```
    while ( key != ENTER )
    {
        key = getchar() ;
        switch ( key )
        {
            case DELETE_KEY   : delete_function() ;
            case LEFT_ARROW   : left_arrow_function() ;
            case RIGHT_ARROW  : right_arrow_function() ;
            default           : insert_character_function() ;
        }
    }
```

TYPICAL OPERATION

In this operation you enter, compile, and execute the programs in Example 81.1 and Example 81.2.

1. Begin at the DOS prompt, in your C source code directory. Invoke your text editor.
2. Type the C program given in Example 81.1, just like it is listed. Call the program SWITCH1.C.
3. Compile and link the program with your C compiler.
4. Type **SWITCH1** and press **Enter**. Notice the following output on your screen:

```
C:\C>SWITCH1
yes=1, no=0, bad=0
C:\C>_
```

5. Type the C program given in Example 81.2, just like it is listed. Call the program SWITCH2.C.
6. Compile and link the program with your C compiler.
7. Type **SWITCH2** and press **Enter**. Notice the following output on your screen:

```
C:\C>SWITCH2
grade = A
C:\C>_
```

8. Turn to Module 12 to continue the learning sequence.

Module 82

TOLOWER

```
NAME

   tolower -- converts a character to lowercase if uppercase

USAGE

   int    tolower ( int c ) ;

PROTOTYPE in      ctype.h

ANSI Synopsis

    #include <ctype.h>
    int  tolower(int c);

RETURNS
        returns the converted character or the same character
```

DESCRIPTION

The *tolower* function converts the character argument to lowercase if the character is an uppercase character; otherwise it does not change it.

If it changes the character, it returns the new character; otherwise it returns the original character.

Example 82.1, an example using the *tolower* function:

```
/*                          program name:    tolower1.c      */
#include <ctype.h>
main()
{

        char    x = 'C' , y = 'O' ;

        printf( " x = %c, y = %c \n", tolower( x ),
                                      tolower( y ) );      /* line 1 */

}   /* end of main */
```

Line 1 displays: x = c, y = 0

The following example shows a function named *lower1*. The *lower* function converts any uppercase letter in the string to lowercase. The *lower* function quits as soon as it finds the marker for end-of-string, the '\0' character. *Lower* returns the address of the string.

Example 82.2, an example program using *lower* function:

```
/*                    program name:          lower1.c       */
#include <ctype.h>
char   *lower ( char *string  );
main()
{
    char    string [ 9 ] ;


    strcpy ( string , "1A3Bc    " );                          /* line 1 */

    lower ( string );                                         /* line 2 */

    printf ( "String returned = %s\n" , string );             /* line 3 */

}   /* end of main */

/*   Name:    lower
     Purpose: convert a string to lower case characters
*/
char   *lower ( char *string )
{
    int    i ;

    for ( i = 0 ; string [ i ] != '\0' ; i++ )                 /* line 4 */
    {
         if ( string [ i ] >= 'A' && string [ i ] <= 'Z' )    /* line 5 */
              string [ i ] += ( 'a' - 'A' );                  /* line 6 */
    }
    return ( string ) ;                                       /* line 7 */

}   /* end of lower.c */
```

Line 1 places a test value into the string.

Line 2 is an example of the *lower* function call.

Line 3 displays: String returned = 1a3bc

Line 4 checks to see if the EOS character has been found yet. If it has not then the body of the *for* executes.

Line 5 (in the body of the *for*) checks to see if the character in the string is an uppercase character. If it is, line 6 executes.

Line 6 converts the uppercase character to lowercase by adding the numeric difference between the uppercase 'A' and the lowercase 'a'.

Line 7 receives control when the EOS character is found and returns the address of the string to the calling function.

Look at memory, for the above example, as the program executes:

After Line 1 executes, memory for the string variable looks like:

string char	1	A	3	B	c	0x20	0x20	0x20	\0	Z
char#	0	1	2	3	4	5	6	7	8	9

After *lower* executes in Line 2, memory for the string variable is:

string char	1	a	3	b	c	0x20	0x20	0x20	\0	Z
char#	0	1	2	3	4	5	6	7	8	9

Notice that only the two uppercase characters within the string change to lowercase. Numbers and other characters remain the same, as do characters outside the string.

APPLICATIONS

A common use of the tolower function is to convert input from the computer user, like Y or N for yes or no to lowercase. The operator can input the value in either uppercase or lowercase, but the program converts it to lowercase. After an input value has been converted to lowercase, only one comparison is required to determine what character was input. This is particularly useful when the value is being continually tested throughout the program, as the program is simpler and shorter. Note that this is the same application note as for toupper. As you can tell, the program can convert the letters to either upper or lower case, as both work equally well. The one thing to remember is to be consistent throughout your program.

TYPICAL OPERATION

In this operation you enter, compile, and execute the programs given in Example 82.1 and Example 82.2.

1. Begin at the DOS prompt, in your C source code directory. Invoke your text editor.
2. Type the C program given in Example 82.1, just like it is listed. Call the program TOLOWER1.C.
3. Compile and link the program with your C compiler.
4. Type **TOLOWER1** and press **Enter**. Notice the following output on your screen:

```
C:\C>TOLOWER1
x = c, y = 0
C:\C>_
```

5. Type the C program given in Example 82.2, just like it is listed. Call the program LOWER1.C.
6. Compile and link the program with your C compiler.
7. Type **LOWER1** and press **Enter**. Notice the following output on your screen:

```
C:\C>LOWER1
String returned = 1a3bc
C:\C>_
```

8. Turn to Module 11 to continue the learning sequence.

Module 83
TOUPPER

```
NAME

   toupper — converts a character to uppercase if it is a
             lowercase

USAGE

   int    toupper ( int c );

PROTOTYPE in      ctype.h

ANSI Synopsis

    #include <ctype.h>
    int  toupper(int c);

RETURNS
     returns the converted character or the same character
```

DESCRIPTION

The *toupper* function converts the character argument to uppercase if the character is a lowercase character; otherwise it does not change it.

If it changes a character, it returns the new character; otherwise it returns the original character.

Example 83.1, an example using the *toupper* function:

```
/*                        program name:    toupper1.c        */
#include <ctype.h>
main()
{

        char    x = 'c' , y = '0' ;


        printf( " x = %c, y = %c \n", toupper( x ),
                                      toupper( y ) );      /* line 1 */

}   /* end of main */
```

Line 1 displays: x = C, y = 0

The following example shows a function named *upper*. The *upper* function converts any lowercase letter in the string to uppercase. The *upper* function quits as soon as it finds the marker for end-of-string, the '\0' character. *Upper* returns the address of the string.

Example 83.2, convert a string to upper case:

```
/*                    program name:          upper1.c       */
#include <ctype.h>
char    *upper ( char *string  ) ;

main()
{

    char   string [ 9 ] ;

    strcpy ( string , "1a3Bc    " );                        /* line 1 */

    upper ( string );                                       /* line 2 */

    printf ( "String returned = %s\n" , string );           /* line 3 */

}   /* end of main */

/* Name:       upper
   Purpose:    convert a string to upper case
*/
char    *upper ( char *string  )
{
    int     i ;

    for ( i = 0 ; string [ i ] != '\0' ; i++ )              /* line 4 */
    {
        if ( string [ i ] >= 'a' && string [ i ] <= 'z' )   /* line 5 */
             string [ i ] += ( 'A' - 'a' );                 /* line 6 */
    }

    return ( string ) ;                                     /* line 7 */

}   /* end of upper.c  */
```

Line 1 places a test value into the string.

Line 2 is an example of a call to the *upper* function.

Line 3 displays: String returned = 1A3BC

Line 4 checks to see if the EOS character has been found yet. If it has not then the body of the *for* executes.

Line 5 (in the body of the *for*) checks to see if the character in the string is a lowercase character. If it is, line 6 executes.

Line 6 converts the lowercase character to uppercase by adding the numeric difference between the uppercase 'A' and the lowercase 'a'.

Line 7 receives control when the EOS character is found and returns the address of the string to the calling function.

Look at memory for the above example:

After Line 1 executes, *string* looks like the following:

string char	1	A	3	B	C	0x20	0x20	0x20	\0	?
char#	0	1	2	3	4	5	6	7	8	9

After *upper* executes in Line 2, memory looks like the following:

string char	1	a	3	B	c	0x20	0x20	0x20	\0	?
char#	0	1	2	3	4	5	6	7	8	9

Only the two lowercase characters within the string change to uppercase. Numbers and other characters remain the same. Characters outside the string remain the same.

APPLICATIONS

A common use of the toupper function is to convert input from the computer user, like Y or N for yes or no to uppercase. The operator can input the value in either uppercase or lowercase, but the program converts it to uppercase. After an input value has been converted to upper case, only one comparison is required to determine what character was input. This is particularly useful when the value is being continually tested throughout the program, as the program is simpler and shorter.

TYPICAL OPERATION

In this operation you enter, compile, and execute the program given in Example 83.1.

1. Begin at the DOS prompt, in your C source code directory. Invoke your text editor.
2. Type the C program given in Example 83.1, just like it is listed. Call the program TOUPPER1.C.
3. Compile and link the program with your C compiler.
4. Type **TOUPPER1** and press **Enter**. Notice the following output on your screen:

```
C:\C>TOUPPER1
String returned = 1A3BC
C:\C>_
```

5. Turn to Module 82 to continue the learning sequence.

Module 84

UNGETC

```
NAME

   ungetc  -- puts a character back into input stream file

USAGE

   int    ungetc ( int c , FILE *stream ) ;

PROTOTYPE in      stdio.h

ANSI Synopsis

    #include <stdio.h>
    int   ungetc(int c, FILE *stream );

RETURNS
       returns the character put back, or -1 if an error
```

DESCRIPTION

The *ungetc* function puts a character back into the input stream file from which it was read. An EOF character cannot be written back. The next read function gets the character just written back to the stream file.

The *ungetc* function returns the character sent back. It returns EOF if an error occurs during the write.

The actual error number can be retrieved from *errno* if an error occurs using the *ungetc* function.

Example 84.1, an example using the *ungetc* function:

```
/*                    program name:      ungetc1.c      */
#include <stdio.h>
main()
{
    FILE    *stream ;
    char    c ;
    int     status ;
```

```
    stream = fopen ("ungetc1.c", "r" );    /* open for read */

    c  = getc ( stream );

    printf ( "character = %c\n" , c );

    status = ungetc ( c , stream );                  /* line 1 */
    if ( status == EOF )
         printf( "character not returned to file properly." );
    else
    {
        c  = getc ( stream );
        printf ( "character = %c\n" , c );
    }

}   /* end of main */
```

Line 1 is an example of an *ungetc* function call which returns a character to a stream that a character was read from.

Notice that the character read does not have to be the character returned to the stream. However, in this example if we changed it we would affect the compilation of our source code since we would be affecting the start of a comment.

APPLICATIONS

The ungetc function is used in functions that are looking ahead to see if the next character is a certain value, and if it is not, it puts the character back and continues processing. A typical function that performs this type of operation is a function that looks ahead to see if an abort key was pressed, and if not, it puts the regular key pressed back so it can be processed normally.

TYPICAL OPERATION

In this operation you enter, compile, and execute the program given in Example 84.1.

1. Begin at the DOS prompt, in your C source code directory. Invoke your text editor.
2. Type the C program given in Example 84.1, just like it is listed. Call the program UNGETC1.C.
3. Compile and link the program with your C compiler.
4. Type **UNGETC1** and press **Enter**. Notice the following output on your screen:

```
C:\C>UNGETC1
character = /
character = /
C:\C>_
```

5. Turn to Module 32 to continue the learning sequence.

Module 85
UNION

DESCRIPTION

This module explains the meaning and usage of a *union*.

A *union* is a variable that can hold data of different types at different times. The knowledge of the active object in the union at any one time must be maintained by the program, usually in another variable. This allows different kinds of data to be used in a single memory area.

Unions are very much like structures. The difference is that all members of a union share the same memory location. Therefore, only one member of a union is valid at any one time. It is the responsibility of the programmer to know which member of the union last had data stored in it.

The union is mainly used in advanced programming applications, but this introduction will at least make you aware of them.

UNION DECLARATION The *declaration of a union* is similar to the declaration of a structure. The different variables defined in a union are called *members* of the union. They do not have to be of the same data type.

The variables defined within a union share the same memory location. This means that only one member of a union is active at any one time. If one member contains the true value of the union and another member is assigned a value, then the true value of the union is destroyed.

The compiler allocates enough memory to hold the largest member of the union. Since the memory space is shared, this is one way to conserve memory or disk space.

Another use for a union is to be able to look at one piece of data from several viewpoints. For example, one time you may want to manipulate or use a variable named "date" as a whole entity; but, in another instance, you may want to manipulate or use the individual components of the variable, which are the month, day, and year.

The form for *union declaration* is:

```
union      union_type                       /*  line 1 */
{                                           /*  line 2 */
  data_type      member1_name ;             /*  line 3 */
  data_type2     member2_name ;             /*  line 4 */
}                                           /*  line 5 */
          union_name ;                      /*  line 6 */
```

Line 1 shows that the key word union is required to start the union definition. This tells the C compiler a union is being declared. Line 1 shows that the union can be given a type name. This name is optional. If you want to declare once what a union looks like, but use the definition several times, then this is where you name the union type.

Line 2 has the open brace to begin grouping the members of the union.

Line 3 is an example of declaring a member of the union. The member is declared just like a normal variable, with the variable data type and the variable name.

Line 4 is an example of declaring another member of the union. This variable shares the same memory as the first member. Usually only one of the two can be active at any one time, even though both can be referenced. Both are active if the variable is being looked at from two points of view.

Line 5 is the close brace to end grouping the union members.

Line 6 shows how the union name is assigned. This name is also optional. If the name is not defined, the union is usually just defined and not declared as a variable. If the name is present then, a union variable is declared and, therefore, its members can be used to store and manipulate data. Line 6 also shows that the union definition or declaration requires a terminating semicolon, like other variables.

The following is an example of a union declaration:

```
union union_type
{
    char     c ;
    int      i ;
    long     l ;
    float    f ;
} union_rec ;
```

The C compiler allocates enough memory to hold the longest member within a union. It only needs to allocate memory for the longest since the variables share the same memory locations.

The dot operator is used to access union members just like in structures. For example, to access members of the preceding example union:

```
union_rec.c = 'c' ;
union_rec.i = 10 ;
union_rec.l = 1234567 ;
union_rec.f = 12.456  ;
```

If you store something into the .f member of the union and then access the .i member, the value of .i is unpredictable. The programmer must know which union member contains the desired data. Since the variables use the same memory, only one member contains valid data at any one time.

Example 85.1, an example of a program using union:

```
/*                      program name:     union1.c              */
#include <stdio.h>
main()
{
    struct                                                /* line 1 */
    {
       char              record_type ;                    /* line 2 */
       union                                              /* line 3 */
       {
          char           name [ 30 ] ;
          float          balance ;
       }           union1 ;                               /* line 4 */
       union                                              /* line 5 */
       {
          char           date [ 7 ] ;
          struct
          {
             char        month1  ;
             char        month2  ;
             char        day1    ;
             char        day2    ;
             char        year1   ;
             char        year2   ;
          }              xdate   ;
       }           union2 ;                               /* line 6 */

     }           customer_record ;                        /* line 7 */

/*     A 'n' in record_type means name is active.
       A 'b' in record_type means balance is active. */

    strcpy ( customer_record.union1.name   , "C. Name" ) ; /* line 8 */

    customer_record.record_type = 'n' ;                   /* line 9 */

    strcpy ( customer_record.union2.date , "122584" );    /* line 10 */

    if ( customer_record.record_type == 'n' )             /* line 11 */
        printf( "name = %s \n", customer_record.union1.name );

    else  if ( customer_record.record_type == 'b')
                printf( "balance = %f \n", customer_record.union1.balance );
          else  printf( "record type is unknown\n" );     /* line 12 */

}    /* end of main */
```

Line 1 through line 7 is an example of a structure declaration with three members. Two members are unions.

Line 2 is one of the variables in the structure. In this example it is used to store a value which indicates which of the members in the union declared in Line 3 is active.

Line 3 through line 4 is the declaration of the structure variable that is a union. Either name or balance is active at any one time, and the variable record_type specifies which is active.

Line 5 through line 6 is the declaration of a union. Notice in this union there is no variable to store the active union member because the purpose of this union is just to look at the same data in two different ways.

Line 8 is an example of using a union member.

Line 9 is an example of how another member of a structure is used to store which union member is currently active.

Line 10 is a line that initializes one of the union members.

Line 11 through line 12 display the contents of a structure when one member is accessed to determine which of other members is active. Since record_type is 'n', the output is:

```
name = C. Name
```

If an inactive member of a union is used, the results are unpredictable. In the previous example, if the balance was displayed when the name was active, the program treats the characters in the name as a floating point number and displays it.

APPLICATIONS

The typical example for using union is in the storage of a date. In the following example of a union declaration for a date, the date can either be accessed as an array of 6 bytes, or each of the three members of the date (month, day, and year) can be accessed individually as two bytes each.

```
union date_union_type
{
    char     date[6] ;
    struct
    {
        char mo[2] ;
        char da[2] ;
        char yr[2] ;
    }                   modayr ;
}                       date_union_rec ;
```

TYPICAL OPERATION

In this operation you enter, compile, and execute the program given in Example 85.1.

1. Begin at the DOS prompt, in your C source code directory. Invoke your text editor.
2. Type the C program given in Example 85.1, just like it is listed. Call the program UNION1.C.
3. Compile and link the program with your C compiler.
4. Type **UNION1** and press **Enter**. Notice the following output on your screen:

```
C:\C>UNION1
name = C. Name
C:\C>_
```

5. Turn to Module 56 to continue the learning sequence.

Module 86

VARIABLES

DESCRIPTION

This module explains the use, declaration, and initialization of variables in a C program.

Variables are data objects that are manipulated in a program. Information can be stored in a variable and recalled later. Variables must be declared before they can be referenced in a program. Variables, for now, are defined immediately following the open brace and before the first coding statement in a function. The other places that variables can be declared in a program are explained in Module 73.

DECLARING VARIABLES The syntax for the declaration of a variable is:

```
data_type     variable_name ;
```

The data type of the variable is given first, followed by the variable name, and then the semicolon to end the variable declaration statement.

The following are valid variable declarations:

```
main()
{
   char     middle_initial , union_code ;
   int      num_dependents ;
   float    reg_hours , ot_hours , rate_of_pay ;
   double   gross_pay , net_pay ;
}
```

The following are invalid variable declarations:

```
main()
{
   integer      num_dependents ;           /* INVALID DATA TYPE  */
                reg_hours , ot_hours ;     /* NO DATA TYPE GIVEN */
   Double       gross_pay , net_pay ;      /* INVALID DATA TYPE, should
                                              be all lowercase   */
   char         union ;                    /* INVALID variable name, union
                                              it is a reserved word  */
}
```

Example 86.1, example of declaration of variables:

```
/*                        program name:    var1.c            */
main()
{
```

```
        char                    letter_grade ;
        int                     test_score ;
        float                   my_bank_balance ;
        double                  banks_total_deposits ;

        unsigned char           graphic_letter ;
        unsigned int            number_students_in_this_class ;
        short    int            number_of_silver_dollars_in_pocket ;
        long     int            metroplex_population ;

        long     float          total_credits ;

        short                   programmers_age_in_years ;       /* short    int */
        long                    age_of_programmer_in_hours ;     /* long     int */
        unsigned                my_age_in_hours ;                /* unsigned int */

     /*   code to manipulate variables goes here ....    */

  }   /* end of main */
```

INITIALIZING Most C compilers allow a variable to be assigned a value when it is declared. This is called *initialization*. It allows you to declare a variable and assign its value in the same statement, a good coding practice.

The syntax for variable *initialization* is:

```
data_type        data_name = expression ;
```

First the data type is given, followed by the variable name, an equal sign for value assignment, and then an expression or a number whose value is to be assigned to the variable. The expression must be able to be evaluated to a constant value when the program is compiled.

Example of variable declaration with initialization:

```
/*                          program name:     var2.c          */
#define monthly_rent_amount    500.00

main()
{
     int    months_in_a_year  = 12 ;                          /* line 1 */
     float  yearly_rent_cost  = 12 * monthly_rent_amount ;    /* line 2 */

/*  coding ....    */

}    /* end of main */
```

Line 1 shows the declaration of an *int* type variable, which is being assigned the value of 12.

Line 2 shows the declaration of a *float* type variable, which is assigned a value that is the result of an expression evaluation. Notice that the expression is being evaluated and assigned *by the compiler*. This calculation and assignment is made when the program is compiled, rather than when the program is executed.

ASSIGNING VALUES TO VARIABLES AND CONSTANTS Once you've defined the variables in the declarations, you will want to give a value to the variables. This is accomplished by a

C statement using the assignment operator (=). The value assigned is either a constant, a variable, or the result of an expression.

The following program demonstrates valid assignment statements:

```
main()
{
  char     middle_initial ;
  int      num_dependents ;
  float    reg_hours , ot_hours , rate_of_pay ;

         middle_initial =   'A' ;    /* see note below */
         num_dependents =    1  ;
         reg_hours      = 40.0  ;
         ot_hours       =    8  ;
         rate_of_pay    = 7.50  ;

}  /* end of main */
```

NOTE

The variable on the left of the equal sign is assigned the value on the right of the equal sign. The values on the right of the equal sign in this example are called *embedded* constants since their value cannot change during the execution of the program. The 'A' is a char constant, the 1 is an integer constant, and the rest are floating point constants.

sizeof Operator The sizeof operator is used to find the size, in bytes, of the object specified. A byte is the amount of memory required to store one character of information.

The following program illustrates the form and usage of the sizeof operator:

```
main()
{
  char     middle_initial ;
  int      num_dependents ;
  float    reg_hours , ot_hours , rate_of_pay ;
  int      length1, length2, length3, length4, length5, length6;

         length1 = sizeof ( middle_initial );    /* length1 =  1 */
         length2 = sizeof ( num_dependents );    /* length2 =  2 */
         length3 = sizeof ( reg_hours );         /* length3 =  4 */
         length4 = sizeof ( char );              /* length4 =  1 */
         length5 = sizeof ( int );               /* length5 =  2 */
         length6 = sizeof ( float );             /* length6 =  4 probably */
}
```

%d used with printf The printf function is used to display formatted data. This means that it can display the value of constants and variables. The %d is used to display integer values. When the data is output using printf, the %d is replaced by the value of the variable presented after the output string.

The other output specifiers will be covered soon.

The following program illustrates the form and usage of the %d output specifier used within printf:

```
main()
{
  int       num_dependents ;

         num_dependents =    1  ;

         printf ( "Number of dependents = %d" , num_dependents );
}
```

The output from the above program is:

```
Number of dependents = 1
```

HELPFUL HINTS / REMINDERS Some important points to remember about declarations are:

1. The declaration of a variable actually reserves a place in memory for its storage.
2. The size of the place reserved in memory is determined by the data type specified in the declaration.
3. All variables must be declared before being used in a statement.
4. Declarations must be placed at the beginning of a block.
5. You may specify more than one variable of the same type by listing them separated with commas.

APPLICATIONS

One of the real advantages of computer programs is the ability of the programmer to designate certain variables in the program and have the program manipulate them to produce a specified result. The computer needs to know two things about a variable: the name of the variable, and what kind of information the variable must contain. Variables require different amounts of memory, depending on the type of data they store.

TYPICAL OPERATION

In this operation you enter, compile and run the program in Example 86.1. This exercise is to confirm to you that your compiler understands the data types described in this book. If you can compile and link the example with no errors, your compiler accepts the data types used in the example, which should be the case.

1. Begin at the DOS prompt, in your C source code directory. Invoke your text editor.
2. Type the C program given in Example 86.1, just like it is listed. Name the program VAR1.C.
3. Compile and link the program with your C compiler.
4. Type **VAR1** and press **Enter** to execute the program. Note that there is no output from this program. You have accomplished the purpose of this operation when the example program compiles error free.
5. Turn to Module 17 to continue the learning sequence.

Module 87

VARIABLES — Part 2

DESCRIPTION

This module explains *mixed mode arithmetic* and *type casts.*

MIXING DATA TYPES When variables of unlike data types are combined to form expressions, the program must convert the values of the expressions into a common data type before it can evaluate the expression. C has rules that govern the assignment and conversion of numbers that are not of the same data type.

C is very free in its assumption that the types of data that are being combined and assigned are what the programmer really wants. In cases where data is converted to a type with higher precision, nothing is lost. If the data conversion is to a type with less precision, the values are truncated and some data may be lost.

DATA CONVERSION METHODS Conversion of data from one data type to another data type can involve the following changes to the data:

- zero-filling of bits
- truncating bits
- sign-extending of a value
- sign-extending on right shift
- no change in bit pattern

Examples of the data conversion methods follow.

Zero-filling Of Bits The *zero-filling of bits* is used when data of a shorter data type is being converted to a longer data type. The bits from the data in the shorter data type are moved into the corresponding bits of the data of the longer data type. The bits in the data of the longer data type that do not receive a bit value are zero-filled.

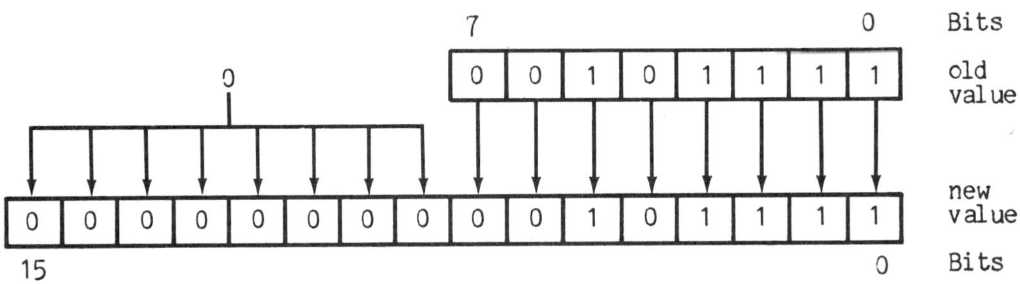

Truncate Bits The *truncating of bits* is used when data from a longer data type is moved to data of a shorter data type. The bits from the data in the longer data type are moved into the corresponding bits of the data of the shorter data type. The bits in the data of the longer data type that do not have a bit position to be moved into are truncated and lost.

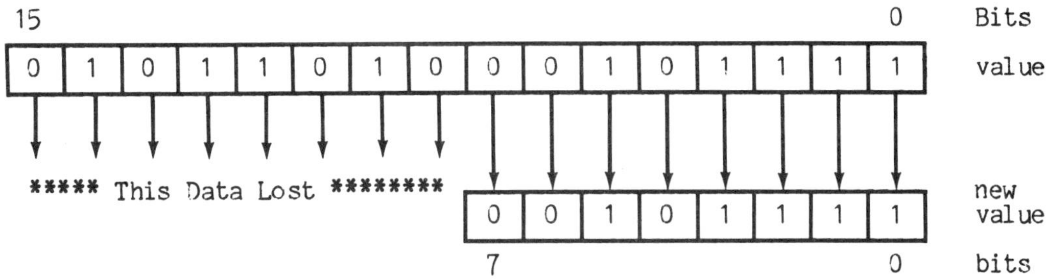

Sign Extending The *sign extending* is used when data from a shorter signed data type is moved to data of a longer signed data type. The bits from the data in the shorter signed data type are moved into the corresponding bits of the data of the longer signed data type. The bits in the data of the longer data type that do not receive a bit value have the sign bit from the shorter signed data type moved to them.

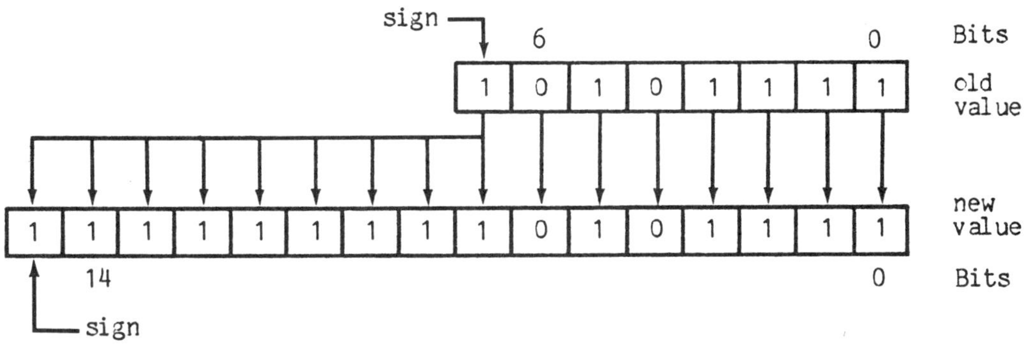

Shift-right with Sign Extending The *shift right with sign extending* is used when data from a signed data type is shifted and moved to data of another signed data type. The bits from the data in the source signed data type are shifted and moved into the correct bits of the data of the destination signed data type. The bits in the data of the destination data type that do not receive a bit value have the sign bit from the source signed data type moved to them.

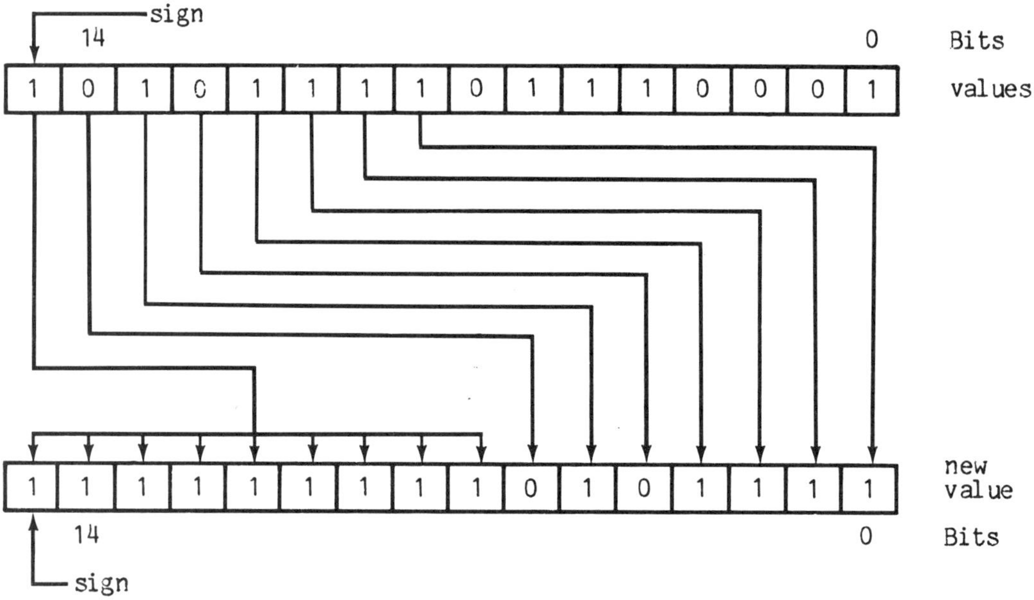

No Change in Bit Pattern The *no change in bit pattern* is used when data of the same length is moved from a signed data type to an unsigned data type or from an unsigned data type to a signed data type. The bit values in the data remain the same but the value of the data may change after the data is moved.

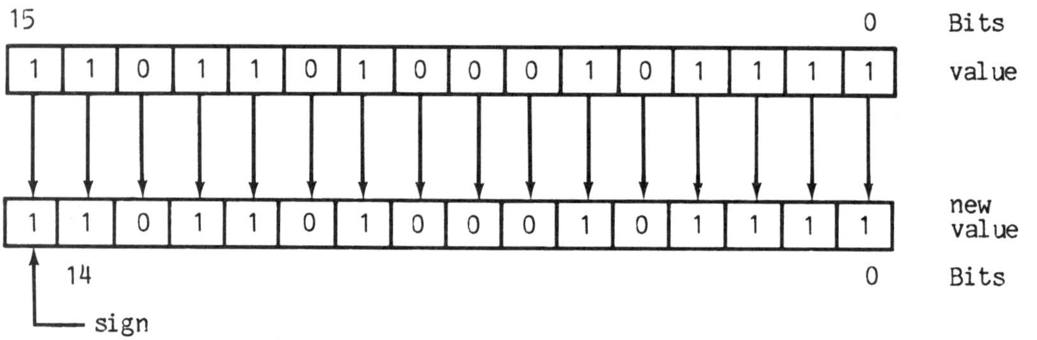

DATA CONVERSION CONVENTIONS Data type conversions take place in the following instances:

- mixed data types in expressions
- mixed data types in assignment operator
- mixed data types in function arguments
- an explicit data cast to another data type

Each instance of data type conversion is described in the following paragraphs.

Mixed Data Types in Expressions Before an expression is evaluated, all data involved is converted to the same data type. Smaller precision numbers are converted to higher precision and the result is expressed as higher precision. Signed numbers are sign-extended and retain the same value.

Mixed mode arithmetic is the use of more than one data type in an expression. C performs type conversions before the evaluating of an expression. The type conversions are always upward, giving a more precise result. Therefore, the application of the following rules increases the accuracy of the calculated results. The rules are applied to all expressions in the order listed:

1. First, if either operand has type long double, the other operand is converted to long double.
2. Otherwise, if either operand has type double, the other operand is converted to double.
3. Otherwise, if either operand has type float, the other operand is converted to float.
4. Otherwise, if either operand has type unsigned long int, the other operand is converted to unsigned long int.
5. Otherwise, if one operand has type long int and the other has type unsigned int, if a long int can represent all values of an unsigned int, the operand of type unsigned int is converted to long int; otherwise, both operands are converted to unsigned long int.
6. Otherwise, if either operand has type long int, the other operand is converted to long int.
7. Otherwise, if either operand has type unsigned int, the other operand is converted to unsigned int.
8. Otherwise, if either operand is not int, the operand is converted to int type.

Mixed Data Types in Assignment In assignment statements the value on the right side of the equal sign is converted to the data type of the operand on the left side of the equal sign. If the conversion is of a lower precision number being converted to higher precision number, the value is maintained without loss of data. If the conversion is of a higher precision number being converted to a lower precision number, then data can be lost because the data is truncated and the high-order bits are discarded.

In complex expressions, the value assigned to the operand on the left side of the equal sign is the value of this expression to be used in the next expression.

Mixed Data Types in Function Arguments When passing arguments to functions, the data types of the arguments must match the data types described in the function declaration. The data types can match by:

1. declaring variables of the same type
2. following the function argument data conversion rules
3. forcing the value of a variable to a specific type

Type conversion also occurs with function arguments. The data types that the compiler actually uses for a function argument can be different from the specified data type (without loss of data). Most C compilers pass the basic types as either *int* or *double*. These type conversions are done for many reasons, and it is important to understand the two following rules and the implications of using expressions in *function arguments*.

Data type conversion rules in function arguments:

1. The *char* and *short* types are converted to *int* type.
2. The *float* type is converted to *double*.

Explicit Data Type Cast The value of a variable or the result of an expression can be forced into a certain data type. The value of a variable is taken, converted to the desired type, and then used. One good use of this feature is to convert a variable to the proper type before passing it as an argument to another function. One advanced use in dynamic memory allocation is to declare the address of the allocated memory to be a pointer of a certain data or structure type.

The syntax of the data cast is:

```
(data_type) expression
```

The desired data type is placed in parentheses in front of the expression or variable. This forces the result of the expression or the value of the variable to be the specified type. The data cast operator has a high precedence and is in level 2 of the Precedence and Associativity Chart (see Appendix H).

Example 87.1, an example of explicit data type cast:

```
/*                  program name:      var21.c          */
#include <stdio.h>
function1( char var_char , double var_dbl );
main()
{

  char         var_char ;
  int          var_int  ;
  unsigned     var_uint ;

  float        var_float  ;
  double       var_double ;

     function1 ( var_char , (double) var_int ) ;      /* line 1 */

     var_float = var_char + var_int ;                 /* line 2 */

     var_double = 15000.2 ;
     var_int    = 30 ;

     var_int  =  var_char = var_double * var_int ;    /* line 3 */

     printf ( "results: var_char = %d, var_int = %d\n, var_char , var_int );
}   /* end of main */

function1( char var_char , double var_dbl )
{
       /* coding ... */

}   /* end of function1 */
```

Line 1 is a call to function1. The value of the var_char argument is converted to an integer value before being passed as an argument. The value of var_int is forced to a double-precision value before being passed as an argument.

Line 2 is an *assignment operation*. The expression on the right is evaluated first. The value of the var_char variable is converted to *int* type because the other value in the expression is *int* type. The new *int* value of var_char is added to the value of the var_int variable. Since the data type of the variable of the left side of the assignment statement is *float*, the result of the above addition is converted to *float*, which becomes the value of the expression on the right side of the equal sign, and replaces the value in the var_float variable.

Line 3 is a *complex assignment operation*. The evaluation will be from right to left per the *associativity* of the operator. Since one of the variables is *double*, the value of the var_int variable is converted to *double* and then multiplied by the value of the var_double variable. Since the variable on the left side of this expression is *char* type, the product is converted to *char* type and then assigned to var_char. Some data is more than likely lost and the result usually not predictable. But the program assumes the programmer desires this result and, therefore, converts the *double* type to *char* type. The *char* type is now the value of the expression. The left side of the next assignment statement is *int* type, so the program converts the current result (char type) to *int* type and assigns the result to var_int.

APPLICATIONS

Explicit data type casting is a good practice, even when assigning a pointer to another pointer of a different type. Most compilers generate a warning message when you assign a pointer to another pointer of a different type, but they generate the correct code and execute properly. It is preferable to not even have warning messages generated when a program is compiled, even if it does execute properly.

TYPICAL OPERATION

In this operation you enter, compile, and execute the program given in Example 87.1.

1. Begin at the DOS prompt, in your C source code directory. Invoke your text editor.
2. Type the C program given in Example 87.1, just like it is listed. Call the program VAR21.C.
3. Compile and link the program with your C compiler.
4. Type **VAR21** and press **Enter**. Notice the following output on your screen:

```
C:\C>VAR21
results: var_char = -43, var_int = -8747
C:\C>_
```

5. Explain why the two result values are different.
6. Turn to Module 54 to continue the learning sequence.

Module 88

WHILE

```
NAME

    while   -- executes a body of instructions as long as an
               expression remains true.

USAGE

       while ( expression )
       {
              /* code that execute as long as expression
                 in while remains true  */
       }
```

DESCRIPTION

The *while* statement is a loop statement that allows its body of instructions to be executed repeatedly as long as the test expression remains true. The body of instructions in a *while* loop does not execute if the expression is false (zero). The expression is evaluated prior to each execution of the body of the *while* statement.

The body of C statements that are executed is between the braces. If only one instruction is to be executed, then the braces are not required. A null statement can also be the statement to be executed. A null statement is just a semicolon.

Example 88.1, example of *while* statement:

```
/*                    program name:   while1.c                 */
main()
{
    int count , j = 0 ;


        count = 0 ;

        while ( count < 5 )                               /* line 1 */
        {                                                 /* line 2 */
                j = j + count ;
                count++ ;
        }                                                 /* line 3 */

        printf( "j = %d\n", j );

}   /* end of main */
```

Line 1 is an example of the *while* statement. C executes the body of statements that follows line 1 as long as the variable count is less than 5.

Line 2 through line 3 make up the body of statements that follow the *while* statement. They are executed as long as the variable count is less than 5.

The output from Example 88.1 is:

```
j = 10
```

Example 88.2, another example of while statement:

```
/*                      program name:   while2.c                  */
/* Purpose: sum the numbers from 1 to 10 */
main()
{
int sum    , number ;

      sum = 0 ;                                              /* line 1 */
      number = 1 ;                                           /* line 2 */
      while ( number <= 10 )                                 /* line 3 */
      {                                                      /* line 4 */
            sum += number ;                                  /* line 5 */
            number++ ;                                       /* line 6 */
      }                                                      /* line 7 */
      printf ( "sum = %d \n" , sum );                        /* line 8 */
}                                    /* end of main */
```

The first time line 3 executes, number equals 1. Since 1 is < = to 10, the body of the while executes, adding number to sum and then incrementing number. Control is then transferred back to line 3. Now number has the value of 2 which is also < = to 10, therefore, the body executes again. When the body of the while has executed 10 times, the value of number is 11 when control is transferred back to line 3. Now number 11 is not < = to 10 and control is passed to line 8 and the while statement is complete.

The output of Example 88.2 is:

```
sum = 55
```

WHILE STATEMENT FLOWCHART The following flowchart shows the sequence of events that occurs in the execution of a *while* statement.

```
WHILE    FLOWCHART
```

Form of while statement:

```
while  ( expression );
{
    body_of_while
}
```

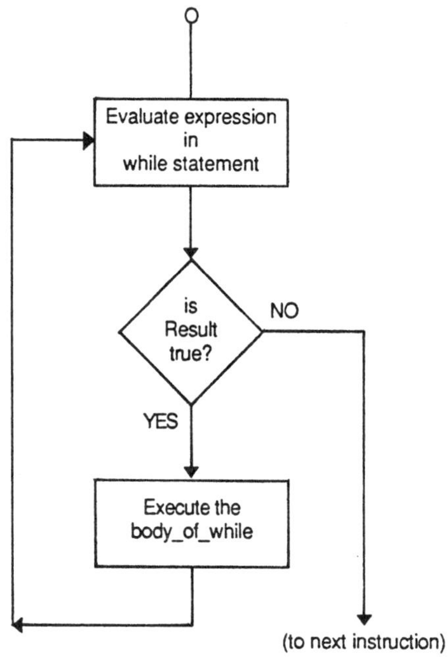

APPLICATIONS

Many times, when reading a disk file, you do not know exactly how many records or entries the file contains. C provides an end-of-file function that can be called to see if the end of the file occurred on a previous file-read function call. A typical application for this statement then is to set up a while loop with the expression being the test for end-of-file. The body of statements in the while both read and process the data, executing until end-of-file is reached.

TYPICAL OPERATION

In this operation you enter, compile, and execute the program in Example 88.1.

1. Begin at the DOS prompt, in your C source code directory. Invoke your text editor.
2. Type the C program in Example 88.1, just like it is listed. Call the program WHILE1.C.
3. Compile and link the program with your C compiler.
4. Type **WHILE1** and press **Enter**. Notice the following output on your screen:

```
C:\C>WHILE1
j = 10
C:\C>_
```

5. Type the C program in Example 88.2, just like it is listed. Call the program WHILE2.C.
6. Compile and link the program with your C compiler.
7. Type **WHILE2** and press **Enter**. Notice the following output on your screen:

```
C:\C>WHILE2
sum = 55
C:\C>_
```

8. Turn to Module 22 to continue the learning sequence.

Module 89

WRITE

```
NAME

   write  -- writes data to a low-level opened file

USAGE

  int    write ( int fd , void *buffer , int count ) ;

PROTOTYPE in      io.h

RETURNS
       returns the number of bytes written, or -1 to indicate
       an error
```

DESCRIPTION

The *write* low-level function writes the number of bytes specified by count from the buffer to the file associated with the file descriptor. Writing begins at the current file location, either from the last *write* or an *lseek* function. The *write* function returns the actual number of bytes written. It returns a − 1 if an error occurs.

Note that this is not an ANSI function.

Example 89.1, an example using the *write* function:

```
/*                 program name:        write1.c         */
#include <io.h>
#include <fcntl.h>
main()
{
    int     status , fd , mode ;
    char    buffer [ 512 ] ;

    mode = O_WRONLY ;                                  /* line 1 */

    fd = open ("filename", mode ) ;

    status = write ( fd , buffer , 512 ) ;             /* line 2 */

    if ( status == -1 )
        printf( "write was not done properly." );

}    /* end of main */
```

Line 1 sets the mode to write only for file access in this program.

Line 2 is an example of the *write* function call. It writes the buffer to the low-level opened file and returns the number of bytes written, unless an error occurs, in which case a –1 is returned.

Example 89.2, a program that copies a file using low-level functions:

```
/*                              program name:       lcopy.c

Purpose:    copy a file

Usage:      lcopy   source-file-name    destination-file-name

*/

#include <io.h>
#include <fcntl.h>                                          /* line 1 */

#define COUNT  512                                          /* line 2 */
main( argc , argv )                                         /* line 3 */
int    argc ;
char   *argv[] ;
{
    int     fd  ;           /* source file */
    int     fd2 ;           /* destination file */
    int     read_cnt  ;
    int     write_cnt ;
    char    buffer [ COUNT ] ;


    if ( argc < 3  || argc > 3 )                            /* line 4 */
    {
        fprintf( stderr , "Usage:\n" );
        fprintf( stderr , "      lcopy  source-file  destination-file\n\n" );
        exit(0);
    }

    fd = open ( argv[1] , O_RDONLY );                       /* line 5 */

    if ( fd == -1 )                                         /* line 6 */
    {
        fprintf( stderr , "Source file missing\n\n" );
        exit(0);
    }

    fd2 = open ( argv[2] , O_TRUNC );                       /* line 7 */

    if ( fd2 == -1 )                                        /* line 8 */
    {
        fprintf( stderr , "Cannot create Destination File\n\n" );
        close( fd );
        exit(0);
    }

    do                                                      /* line 9 */
    {
         read_cnt = read ( fd , buffer , COUNT );           /* line 10 */

         if ( read_cnt > 0 )                                /* line 11 */
```

```
            {
               write_cnt = write( fd2, buffer, read_cnt );   /* line 12 */

               if ( write_cnt != read_cnt )                  /* line 13 */
               {
                  fprintf( stderr, "file write error -- run stopped.\n\n" );
                  close( fd );
                  close( fd2 );
                  exit(0);
               }
            }

        } while ( read_cnt == COUNT ) ;                      /* line 14 */

        close ( fd );                                        /* line 15 */
        close ( fd2 );                                       /* line 16 */

        printf( "file copy complete.\n\n" );                 /* line 17 */

    }   /* end of lcopy */
```

Line 1 includes the file that contains the mode constants.

Line 2 defines the length of each data read, which is 512 for this example.

Line 3 is the *main* function name and includes the parameters for command line arguments, since this program receives the name of the file to copy on the command line when the program is run.

Line 4 tests to make sure 2 arguments plus the program name are on the command line when the program is run. If there are more than or less than 2 arguments, the program displays the proper command usage to run this program and then stops executing.

Line 5 opens the file specified in the first command line argument, the source file. This file is opened in the read only mode. The result of the *open* is assigned to variable fd1.

Line 6 tests the result of the open statement on the source file. If the resulting file descriptor is − 1, then the file was not on the disk or could not be opened, in which case an error message is displayed and the program stops executing.

Line 7 creates the file specified in the second command line argument and opens it in the write mode. Any data in an existing file by the same name is lost as this open sets the file length to 0. The result of the *open* is assigned to variable fd2.

Line 8 tests the result of the open statement on the destination file. If the resulting file descriptor is − 1, then the file was not opened, in which case an error message is displayed, the source file is closed, and the program stops executing.

Line 9 through line 14 contain the code that actually copies the file.

Line 10 reads a block of data from the source file, stores it into the buffer, and stores the number of characters read into a variable. A value of 0 is stored in the number of characters read when end-of-file is reached in the source file.

Line 11 tests the variable storing the number of characters read for EOF. If EOF is not reached, the body of the *if* is performed.

Line 12 writes the block of data just read to the destination file. The number of characters actually written is stored into a variable.

Line 13 tests to see if the whole buffer is written. If not, then an output error occurred, an error message is displayed, both the source and the destination files are closed, and the program stops executing.

Line 14 tests to see if the source file is at end-of-file. If the number of characters read is less than the number requested, then end-of-file is reached, the file is copied, and the program can leave the *do-while* loop.

Line 15 closes the source file.

Line 16 closes the destination file.

Line 17 displays a message that the copy is complete.

APPLICATIONS

The write function is used to write data to a file opened with the low-level open function. Always check the number of bytes actually written to the number of bytes you requested to be written to detect write errors. Refer to your C library reference manual when writing to text files, since the CONTROL-Z character is treated as an end-of-file indicator on some C compilers.

TYPICAL OPERATION

In this operation you enter, compile, and execute the program given in Example 89.2.

1. Begin at the DOS prompt, in your C source code directory. Invoke your text editor.
2. Type the C program given in Example 89.2, just like it is listed. Call the program LCOPY.C.
3. Compile and link the program with your C compiler.
4. Type **LCOPY LCOPY.C LCOPY1.C** and press **Enter**. Notice the following output on your screen:

```
C:\C>LCOPY LCOPY.C LCOPY1.C
file copy complete.
C:\C>_
```

5. Turn to Module 48 to continue the learning sequence.

Appendix A
RESERVED KEYWORDS IN C

Data Storage Classes	*Data Type Qualifiers*	*Data Types*	*C Statements*	*Other*
auto	long	char	break	void
extern	short	double	case	sizeof
register	unsigned	float	continue	typedef
static	signed	int	default	
	noalias	struct	do	
	volatile	union	else	
	const	enum	for	
			goto	
			if	
			return	
			switch	
			while	

NOTE

The above identifiers, always in lowercase, are reserved for use as keywords in C and cannot be used otherwise.

Appendix B

ASCII CODES

I. The Control (non-printable) ASCII characters:

hex	*abrev*	*description*	*hex*	*abrev*	*description*
00	NUL	Null character	11	DC1	Device control 1 (x-on)
01	SOH	Start of heading	12	DC2	Device control 2 (tape)
02	STX	Start of text	13	DC3	Device control 3 (x-off)
03	ETX	End of text	14	DC4	Device control 4
04	EOT	End of transmission	15	NAK	Negative acknowledge
05	ENQ	Enquiry	16	SYN	Synchronous idle
06	ACK	Acknowledge	17	ETB	End of trans block
07	BELL	Bell (sound)	18	CAN	Cancel
08	BS	Backspace	19	EM	End of medium
09	HT	Horizontal tab	1A	SUB	Substitute
0A	LF	Line feed	1B	ESC	Escape
0B	VT	Vertical tab	1C	FS	File separator
0C	FF	Form feed	1D	GS	Group separator
0D	CR	Carriage return	1E	RS	Record separator
0E	SO	Shift out	1F	US	Unit separator
0F	SI	Shift in			
10	DLE	Data line escape	7F	DEL	Delete (rub out)

II. The Graphic (printable) ASCII characters:

Hex	*Char*	*Hex*	*Char*	*Hex*	*Char*	*Hex*	*Char*	*Hex*	*Char*	*Hex*	*Char*
20	space	30	0	40	@	50	P	60	`	70	p
21	!	31	1	41	A	51	Q	61	a	71	q
22	"	32	2	42	B	52	R	62	b	72	r
23	#	33	3	43	C	53	S	63	c	73	s
24	$	34	4	44	D	54	T	64	d	74	t
25	%	35	5	45	E	55	U	65	e	75	u
26	&	36	6	46	F	56	V	66	f	76	v
27	'	37	7	47	G	57	W	67	g	77	w
28	(	38	8	48	H	58	X	68	h	78	x
29	)	39	9	49	I	59	Y	69	i	79	y
2A	*	3A	:	4A	J	5A	Z	6A	j	7A	z
2B	+	3B	;	4B	K	5B	[	6B	k	7B	{
2C	,	3C	<	4C	L	5C	\	6C	l	7C	|
2D	–	3D	=	4D	M	5D	]	6D	m	7D	}
2E	.	3E	>	4E	N	5E	^	6E	n	7E	~
2F	/	3F	?	4F	O	5F	_	6F	o		

Appendix C

HEX TO DECIMAL INTEGER CONVERSION CHART

Hex	*Decimal*	*Hex*	*Decimal*	*Hex*	*Decimal*
1	1	10	16	100	256
2	2	20	32	200	512
3	3	30	48	300	768
4	4	40	64	400	1 024
5	5	50	80	500	1 280
6	6	60	96	600	1 536
7	7	70	112	700	1 792
8	8	80	128	800	2 048
9	9	90	144	900	2 304
A	10	A0	160	A00	2 560
B	11	B0	176	B00	2 816
C	12	C0	192	C00	3 072
D	13	D0	208	D00	3 328
E	14	E0	224	E00	3 584
F	15	F0	240	F00	3 840

Hex	*Decimal*	*Hex*	*Decimal*	*Hex*	*Decimal*
1000	4 096	1 0000	65 536	10 0000	1 048 576
2000	8 192	2 0000	131 072	20 0000	2 097 152
3000	12 288	3 0000	196 608	30 0000	3 145 728
4000	16 384	4 0000	262 144	40 0000	4 194 304
5000	20 480	5 0000	327 680	50 0000	5 242 880
6000	24 576	6 0000	393 216	60 0000	6 291 456
7000	28 672	7 0000	458 752	70 0000	7 340 032
8000	32 768	8 0000	524 288	80 0000	8 388 608
9000	36 864	9 0000	589 824	90 0000	9 437 184
A000	40 960	A 0000	655 360	A0 0000	10 485 760
B000	45 056	B 0000	720 896	B0 0000	11 534 336
C000	49 152	C 0000	786 432	C0 0000	12 582 912
D000	53 248	D 0000	851 968	D0 0000	13 631 488
E000	57 344	E 0000	917 504	E0 0000	14 680 064
F000	61 440	F 0000	983 040	F0 0000	15 728 640

Appendix D

NUMBERS 0 to 255 IN DECIMAL, BINARY, OCTAL, HEX

Binary	*Octal*	*Decimal*	*Hex*	*Binary*	*Octal*	*Decimal*	*Hex*
0	0	0	0	11 0000	60	48	30
1	1	1	1	11 0001	61	49	31
10	2	2	2	11 0010	62	50	32
11	3	3	3	11 0011	63	51	33
100	4	4	4	11 0100	64	52	34
101	5	5	5	11 0101	65	53	35
110	6	6	6	11 0110	66	54	36
111	7	7	7	11 0111	67	55	37
1000	10	8	8	11 1000	70	56	38
1001	11	9	9	11 1001	71	57	39
1010	12	10	A	11 1010	72	58	3A
1011	13	11	B	11 1011	73	59	3B
1100	14	12	C	11 1100	74	60	3C
1101	15	13	D	11 1101	75	61	3D
1110	16	14	E	11 1110	76	62	3E
1111	17	15	F	11 1111	77	63	3F
1 0000	20	16	10	100 0000	100	64	40
1 0001	21	17	11	100 0001	101	65	41
1 0010	22	18	12	100 0010	102	66	42
1 0011	23	19	13	100 0011	103	67	43
1 0100	24	20	14	100 0100	104	68	44
1 0101	25	21	15	100 0101	105	69	45
1 0110	26	22	16	100 0110	106	70	46
1 0111	27	23	17	100 0111	107	71	47
1 1000	30	24	18	100 1000	110	72	48
1 1001	31	25	19	100 1001	111	73	49
1 1010	32	26	1A	100 1010	112	74	4A
1 1011	33	27	1B	100 1011	113	75	4B
1 1100	34	28	1C	100 1100	114	76	4C
1 1101	35	29	1D	100 1101	115	77	4D
1 1110	36	30	1E	100 1110	116	78	4E
1 1111	37	31	1F	100 1111	117	79	4F
10 0000	40	32	20	101 0000	120	80	50
10 0001	41	33	21	101 0001	121	81	51
10 0010	42	34	22	101 0010	122	82	52
10 0011	43	35	23	101 0011	123	83	53
10 0100	44	36	24	101 0100	124	84	54
10 0101	45	37	25	101 0101	125	85	55
10 0110	46	38	26	101 0110	126	86	56
10 0111	47	39	27	101 0111	127	87	57
10 1000	50	40	28	101 1000	130	88	58
10 1001	51	41	29	101 1001	131	89	59
10 1010	52	42	2A	101 1010	132	90	5A
10 1011	53	43	2B	101 1011	133	91	5B
10 1100	54	44	2C	101 1100	134	92	5C
10 1101	55	45	2D	101 1101	135	93	5D
10 1110	56	46	2E	101 1110	136	94	5E
10 1111	57	47	2F	101 1111	137	95	5F

NUMBERS 0 to 255 IN DECIMAL, BINARY, OCTAL, HEX (Continued)

Binary	Octal	Decimal	Hex	Binary	Octal	Decimal	Hex
110 0000	140	96	60	1001 0000	220	144	90
110 0001	141	97	61	1001 0001	221	145	91
110 0010	142	98	62	1001 0010	222	146	92
110 0011	143	99	63	1001 0011	223	147	93
110 0100	144	100	64	1001 0100	224	148	94
110 0101	145	101	65	1001 0101	225	149	95
110 0110	146	102	66	1001 0110	226	150	96
110 0111	147	103	67	1001 0111	227	151	97
110 1000	150	104	68	1001 1000	230	152	98
110 1001	151	105	69	1001 1001	231	153	99
110 1010	152	106	6A	1001 1010	232	154	9A
110 1011	153	107	6B	1001 1011	233	155	9B
110 1100	154	108	6C	1001 1100	234	156	9C
110 1101	155	109	6D	1001 1101	235	157	9D
110 1110	156	110	6E	1001 1110	236	158	9E
110 1111	157	111	6F	1001 1111	237	159	9F
111 0000	160	112	70	1010 0000	240	160	A0
111 0001	161	113	71	1010 0001	241	161	A1
111 0010	162	114	72	1010 0010	242	162	A2
111 0011	163	115	73	1010 0011	243	163	A3
111 0100	164	116	74	1010 0100	244	164	A4
111 0101	165	117	75	1010 0101	245	165	A5
111 0110	166	118	76	1010 0110	246	166	A6
111 0111	167	119	77	1010 0111	247	167	A7
111 1000	170	120	78	1010 1000	250	168	A8
111 1001	171	121	79	1010 1001	251	169	A9
111 1010	172	122	7A	1010 1010	252	170	AA
111 1011	173	123	7B	1010 1011	253	171	AB
111 1100	174	124	7C	1010 1100	254	172	AC
111 1101	175	125	7D	1010 1101	255	173	AD
111 1110	176	126	7E	1010 1110	256	174	AE
111 1111	177	127	7F	1010 1111	257	175	AF
1000 0000	200	128	80	1011 0000	260	176	B0
1000 0001	201	129	81	1011 0001	261	177	B1
1000 0010	202	130	82	1011 0010	262	178	B2
1000 0011	203	131	83	1011 0011	263	179	B3
1000 0100	204	132	84	1011 0100	264	180	B4
1000 0101	205	133	85	1011 0101	265	181	B5
1000 0110	206	134	86	1011 0110	266	182	B6
1000 0111	207	135	87	1011 0111	267	183	B7
1000 1000	210	136	88	1011 1000	270	184	B8
1000 1001	211	137	89	1011 1001	271	185	B9
1000 1010	212	138	8A	1011 1010	272	186	BA
1000 1011	213	139	8B	1011 1011	273	187	BB
1000 1100	214	140	8C	1011 1100	274	188	BC
1000 1101	215	141	8D	1011 1101	275	189	BD
1000 1110	216	142	8E	1011 1110	276	190	BE
1000 1111	217	143	8F	1011 1111	277	191	BF

NUMBERS 0 to 255 IN DECIMAL, BINARY, OCTAL, HEX (Continued)

Binary	Octal	Decimal	Hex	Binary	Octal	Decimal	Hex
1100 0000	300	192	C0	1110 0000	340	224	E0
1100 0001	301	193	C1	1110 0001	341	225	E1
1100 0010	302	194	C2	1110 0010	342	226	E2
1100 0011	303	195	C3	1110 0011	343	227	E3
1100 0100	304	196	C4	1110 0100	344	228	E4
1100 0101	305	197	C5	1110 0101	345	229	E5
1100 0110	306	198	C6	1110 0110	346	230	E6
1100 0111	307	199	C7	1110 0111	347	231	E7
1100 1000	310	200	C8	1110 1000	350	232	E8
1100 1001	311	201	C9	1110 1001	351	233	E9
1100 1010	312	202	CA	1110 1010	352	234	EA
1100 1011	313	203	CB	1110 1011	353	235	EB
1100 1100	314	204	CC	1110 1100	354	236	EC
1100 1101	315	205	CD	1110 1101	355	237	ED
1100 1110	316	206	CE	1110 1110	356	238	EE
1100 1111	317	207	CF	1110 1111	357	239	EF
1101 0000	320	208	D0	1111 0000	360	240	F0
1101 0001	321	209	D1	1111 0001	361	241	F1
1101 0010	322	210	D2	1111 0010	362	242	F2
1101 0011	323	211	D3	1111 0011	363	243	F3
1101 0100	324	212	D4	1111 0100	364	244	F4
1101 0101	325	213	D5	1111 0101	365	245	F5
1101 0110	326	214	D6	1111 0110	366	246	F6
1101 0111	327	215	D7	1111 0111	367	247	F7
1101 1000	330	216	D8	1111 1000	370	248	F8
1101 1001	331	217	D9	1111 1001	371	249	F9
1101 1010	332	218	DA	1111 1010	372	250	FA
1101 1011	333	219	DB	1111 1011	373	251	FB
1101 1100	334	220	DC	1111 1100	374	252	FC
1101 1101	335	221	DD	1111 1101	375	253	FD
1101 1110	336	222	DE	1111 1110	376	254	FE
1101 1111	337	223	DF	1111 1111	377	255	FF

Appendix E

POWERS OF TWO

2^n	n	hex 2^n	2^{-n}
1	0	1	1.0
2	1	2	.5
4	2	4	.25
8	3	8	.125
16	4	10	.062 5
32	5	20	.031 25
64	6	40	.015 625
128	7	80	.007 812 5
256	8	100	.003 906 25
512	9	200	.001 953 125
1 024	10	400	.000 976 562 5
2 048	11	800	.000 488 281 25
4 096	12	1000	.000 244 140 625
8 192	13	2000	.000 122 070 312 5
16 384	14	4000	.000 061 035 156 25
32 768	15	8000	.000 030 517 578 125
65 536	16	1 0000	.000 015 258 789 062 5
131 072	17	2 0000	.000 007 629 394 531 25
262 144	18	4 0000	.000 003 814 697 265 625
524 288	19	8 0000	.000 001 907 348 632 812 5
1 048 576	20	10 0000	.000 000 953 674 316 406 25
2 097 152	21	20 0000	.000 000 476 837 158 203 125
4 194 304	22	40 0000	.000 000 238 418 579 101 562 5
8 388 608	23	80 0000	.000 000 119 209 289 550 781 25
16 777 216	24	100 0000	.000 000 059 604 644 775 390 625
33 554 432	25	200 0000	.000 000 029 802 322 387 695 312 5
67 108 864	26	400 0000	.000 000 014 901 161 193 847 656 25
134 217 728	27	800 0000	.000 000 007 450 580 596 923 828 125
268 435 456	28	1000 0000	.000 000 003 725 290 298 461 914 062 5
536 870 912	29	2000 0000	.000 000 001 862 645 149 230 957 031 25
1 073 741 824	30	4000 0000	.000 000 000 931 322 574 615 478 515 625
2 147 483 648	31	8000 0000	.000 000 000 465 661 287 307 739 257 812 5

Appendix F

POWERS OF SIXTEEN (IN BASE 10)

16^n	n	$hex\ 16^n$	16^{-n}
1	0	1	1.0
16	1	10	.062 5
256	2	100	.003 906 25
4 096	3	1000	.000 244 140 625
65 536	4	1 0000	.000 015 258 789 062 5
1 048 576	5	10 0000	.000 000 953 674 316 406 25
16 777 216	6	100 0000	.000 000 059 604 644 775 390 625
268 435 456	7	1000 0000	.000 000 003 725 290 298 461 914 062 5

POWERS OF TEN (IN BASE 16)

$HEX\ 10^n$	n	10^n	$HEX\ 10^{-n}$
1	0	1	1.0
A	1	10	.1999 9999 9999 999A
64	2	100	.28F5 C28F 5C28 F5C3 $\times 16^{-1}$
3E8	3	1 000	.4189 374B C6A7 EF9E $\times 16^{-2}$
2710	4	10 000	.68DB 8BAC 710C B296 $\times 16^{-3}$
1 86A0	5	100 000	.A7C5 AC47 1B47 8423 $\times 16^{-4}$
F 4240	6	1 000 000	.10C6 F7A0 B5ED 8D37 $\times 16^{-4}$
98 9680	7	10 000 000	.1AD7 F29A BCAF 4858 $\times 16^{-5}$

Appendix G

ADDITION FACTS FOR BINARY, OCTAL, AND HEX

Facts for Octal:

+	0	1	2	3	4	5	6	7
0	0	1	2	3	4	5	6	7
1	1	2	3	4	5	6	7	10
2	2	3	4	5	6	7	10	11
3	3	4	5	6	7	10	11	12
4	4	5	6	7	10	11	12	13
5	5	6	7	10	11	12	13	14
6	6	7	10	11	12	13	14	15
7	7	10	11	12	13	14	15	16

Facts for Binary:

+	0	1
0	0	1
1	1	10

Facts for Hex:

+	0	1	2	3	4	5	6	7	8	9	A	B	C	D	E	F
0	0	1	2	3	4	5	6	7	8	9	A	B	C	D	E	F
1	1	2	3	4	5	6	7	8	9	A	B	C	D	E	F	10
2	2	3	4	5	6	7	8	9	A	B	C	D	E	F	10	11
3	3	4	5	6	7	8	9	A	B	C	D	E	F	10	11	12
4	4	5	6	7	8	9	A	B	C	D	E	F	10	11	12	13
5	5	6	7	8	9	A	B	C	D	E	F	10	11	12	13	14
6	6	7	8	9	A	B	C	D	E	F	10	11	12	13	14	15
7	7	8	9	A	B	C	D	E	F	10	11	12	13	14	15	16
8	8	9	A	B	C	D	E	F	10	11	12	13	14	15	16	17
9	9	A	B	C	D	E	F	10	11	12	13	14	15	16	17	18
A	A	B	C	D	E	F	10	11	12	13	14	15	16	17	18	19
B	B	C	D	E	F	10	11	12	13	14	15	16	17	18	19	1A
C	C	D	E	F	10	11	12	13	14	15	16	17	18	19	1A	1B
D	D	E	F	10	11	12	13	14	15	16	17	18	19	1A	1B	1C
E	E	F	10	11	12	13	14	15	16	17	18	19	1A	1B	1C	1D
F	F	10	11	12	13	14	15	16	17	18	19	1A	1B	1C	1D	1E

Appendix H

PRECEDENCE AND ASSOCIATIVITY OF THE OPERATORS IN C

	Operator	*Description*	*Associativity*
1.	( )	Function call	left to right
	[ ]	Array element	
	- >	Pointer to structure member	
	.	Structure member	
2.	!	Logical negation operator	right to left
	~	One's complement	
	+ +	Increment	
	- -	Decrement	
	-	Unary minus (negate)	
	(type)	Cast (forced type conversion)	
	*	Indirection	
	&	Address	
	sizeof	Size of an object	
3.	*	Multiplication	left to right
	/	Division	
	%	Modulo (remainder)	
4.	+	Addition	left to right
	-	Subtraction	
5.	< <	Left shift	left to right
	> >	Right shift	
6.	<	Less than	left to right
	< =	Less than or equal to	
	>	Greater than	
	> =	Greater than or equal to	
7.	= =	Equality	left to right
	! =	Inequality	
8.	&	Bitwise AND	left to right
9.	^	Bitwise exclusive OR (XOR)	left to right
10.	¦	Bitwise inclusive OR	left to right
11.	&&	Logical AND	left to right
12.	¦ ¦	Logical OR	left to right
13.	?:	Conditional expression	right to left
14.	=	Assignment	right to left
	* = / = % = + =	Assignment (compound form)	
	& = ¦ = ^ = < - =		
	< < = > > =		
15.	,	Comma separator	left to right

Appendix I
FORMATTED OUTPUT CHARTS

The general form of an output format specification field is:

```
%[flag][width][.precision][L]type
```

Flags for Data Output Field

Character	*Flag*	*Output Format*
–	justification flag	The data is left-justified when the minus sign is present.
+	sign flag	The data value is always to be displayed with plus or minus sign.
0	zero padded on left side flag	The data is zero-padded on left and not space-padded.
space	sign conversion	If signed data field and a positive number, use space for sign character.
#	alternate form	Don't remove trailing zeroes from G type. Include decimal on E, F, G types. Place 0x on hexadecimal type. Put 0 in front of octal numbers.
*	minimum field width	The asterisk specifies that the next argument to the print function indicates the minimum number of positions to be used to output data value.
L	argument is long type flag	The input argument is a long data type.
.	next field is precision field	The next field in the specifier is the precision field.
1 to n	precision field	The precision field specifies the maximum number of characters to output for *d,u,o,x* type. This is exact number of characters to output float and double.
*	precision field	The asterisk specifies that the next argument to the print function indicates the number of decimal places after decimal point.

Output Data Type Field

Character	*Input Type*	*Output Format*
d	integer	The argument is output in signed decimal notation.
u	integer	The argument is output in unsigned decimal notation.
o	integer	The argument is output in unsigned octal notation with a leading zero.
x	integer	The argument is output in unsigned hexadecimal notation with the 0x.
c	character	Output is a single character.
p	pointer	Output is a pointer.
s	string of characters	The argument is output until either the \0 character is reached in the string or the precision is reached.
e	floating point	Output is in exponential format of the form [–]m.nnnnnnE[+ –]xx, where n is the precision; default is 6.
f	floating point	Output is in signed decimal notation of the form [–]mmm.nnnnnn, where n is the precision; default is 6.
g	floating point	Output uses either the %e or %f notation, whichever is shorter. Insignificant zeros are not shown.

Appendix J
SUMMARY OF STORAGE CLASSES AND SCOPE

Storage Class	*Where Declared*	*Scope or Reference*	*Initialization & Comments*
auto & register variable	inside function/block	within function/block	Initialized each time function is executed, no default value. Arrays & structures can not be initialized. Register type can only be passed by value. Auto is default if the storage class is not specified on variables declared inside a function or block.
auto	function argument	within function	Arguments cannot be initialized, and can be passed by value or reference.
static variable	inside function/block	within function/block	Initialized only once at start of program. Arrays & structures can be initialized. The default value is zero. Values retained all through program execution.
	outside function	within file	Static basic type variables are still passed by value.
static	function	within file	Static functions can only be called from within the file where they are declared.
GLOBAL variable	outside function	within function; within program with extern	Initialized only once at start of program. Arrays & structures can be initialized. The default value is zero. Values retained all through program execution. Global is default if storage class is not specified on variables declared outside of a function. To make global variables obvious use: #define GLOBAL
GLOBAL	function	within program	A function has global reference as a default.
extern variable	defined inside function/block	within function/block	External reference to global variable. Cannot be initialized when referenced here.
	defined outside function	within file	

Appendix K

MICROSOFT C VERSION 5.1 STANDARD HEADER FILES

<assert.h>		<stddef.h>
<ctype.h>	<math.h>	<stdio.h>
<errno.h>	<setjmp.h>	<stdlib.h>
<float.h>	<signal.h>	<string.h>
<limits.h>	<stdarg.h>	<time.h>

```
/***
*assert.h - define the assert macro
*
*   Copyright (c) 1985-1988, Microsoft Corporation.  All rights reserved.
*
*Purpose:
*   Defines the assert(exp) macro.
*   [ANSI/System V]
*
*******************************************************************************/


#ifndef _ASSERT_DEFINED

#ifndef NDEBUG

static char _assertstring[] = "Assertion failed: %s, file %s, line %d\n";

#define assert(exp) { \
    if (!(exp)) { \
        fprintf(stderr, _assertstring, #exp, __FILE__, __LINE__); \
        fflush(stderr); \
        abort(); \
        } \
    }

#else

#define assert(exp)

#endif /* NDEBUG */

#define _ASSERT_DEFINED

#endif /* _ASSERT_DEFINED */
```

```
/***
*ctype.h - character conversion macros and ctype macros
*
*   Copyright (c) 1985-1988, Microsoft Corporation.  All rights reserved.
*
*Purpose:
*   Defines macros for character classification/conversion.
*   [ANSI/System V]
*
******************************************************************************/
#ifndef NO_EXT_KEYS /* extensions enabled */
    #define _CDECL  cdecl
    #define _NEAR   near
#else /* extensions not enabled */
    #define _CDECL
    #define _NEAR
#endif /* NO_EXT_KEYS */

/*
 * This declaration allows the user access to the ctype look-up
 * array _ctype defined in ctype.obj by simply including ctype.h
 */

extern unsigned char _NEAR _CDECL _ctype[];

/* set bit masks for the possible character types */

#define _UPPER       0x1      /* upper case letter */
#define _LOWER       0x2      /* lower case letter */
#define _DIGIT       0x4      /* digit[0-9] */
#define _SPACE       0x8      /* tab, carriage return, newline, */
                              /* vertical tab or form feed */
#define _PUNCT       0x10     /* punctuation character */
#define _CONTROL     0x20     /* control character */
#define _BLANK       0x40     /* space char */
#define _HEX         0x80     /* hexadecimal digit */

/* the character classification macro definitions */

#define isalpha(c)      ( (_ctype+1)[c] & (_UPPER|_LOWER) )
#define isupper(c)      ( (_ctype+1)[c] & _UPPER )
#define islower(c)      ( (_ctype+1)[c] & _LOWER )
#define isdigit(c)      ( (_ctype+1)[c] & _DIGIT )
#define isxdigit(c)     ( (_ctype+1)[c] & _HEX )
#define isspace(c)      ( (_ctype+1)[c] & _SPACE )
#define ispunct(c)      ( (_ctype+1)[c] & _PUNCT )
#define isalnum(c)      ( (_ctype+1)[c] & (_UPPER|_LOWER|_DIGIT) )
#define isprint(c)      ( (_ctype+1)[c] & (_BLANK|_PUNCT|_UPPER|_LOWER|_DIGIT) )
#define isgraph(c)      ( (_ctype+1)[c] & (_PUNCT|_UPPER|_LOWER|_DIGIT) )
#define iscntrl(c)      ( (_ctype+1)[c] & _CONTROL )

#define toupper(c)      ( (islower(c)) ? _toupper(c) : (c) )
#define tolower(c)      ( (isupper(c)) ? _tolower(c) : (c) )

#define _tolower(c)     ( (c)-'A'+'a' )
#define _toupper(c)     ( (c)-'a'+'A' )

#define isascii(c)      ( (unsigned)(c) < 0x80 )
#define toascii(c)      ( (c) & 0x7f )
/* MS C version 2.0 extended ctype macros */

#define iscsymf(c)      (isalpha(c) || ((c) == '_'))
#define iscsym(c)       (isalnum(c) || ((c) == '_'))
```

```
/***
*errno.h - system wide error numbers (set by system calls)
*
*   Copyright (c) 1985-1988, Microsoft Corporation.  All rights reserved.
*
*Purpose:
*   This file defines the system-wide error numbers (set by
*   system calls).  Conforms to the XENIX standard.  Extended
*   for compatibility with Uniforum standard.
*   [System V]
*
*******************************************************************************/

#define  EZERO      0
#define  EPERM      1
#define  ENOENT     2
#define  ESRCH      3
#define  EINTR      4
#define  EIO        5
#define  ENXIO      6
#define  E2BIG      7
#define  ENOEXEC    8
#define  EBADF      9
#define  ECHILD    10
#define  EAGAIN    11
#define  ENOMEM    12
#define  EACCES    13
#define  EFAULT    14
#define  ENOTBLK   15
#define  EBUSY     16
#define  EEXIST    17
#define  EXDEV     18
#define  ENODEV    19
#define  ENOTDIR   20
#define  EISDIR    21
#define  EINVAL    22
#define  ENFILE    23
#define  EMFILE    24
#define  ENOTTY    25
#define  ETXTBSY   26
#define  EFBIG     27
#define  ENOSPC    28
#define  ESPIPE    29
#define  EROFS     30
#define  EMLINK    31
#define  EPIPE     32
#define  EDOM      33
#define  ERANGE    34
#define  EUCLEAN   35
#define  EDEADLOCK 36
```

```
/***
*float.h - constants for floating point values
*
*   Copyright (c) 1985-1988, Microsoft Corporation.  All rights reserved.
*
*Purpose:
*   This file contains defines for a number of implementation dependent
*   values which are commonly used by sophisticated numerical (floating
*   point) programs.
*   [ANSI]
*
*******************************************************************************/


#ifndef NO_EXT_KEYS /* extensions enabled */
    #define _CDECL  cdecl
#else /* extensions not enabled */
    #define _CDECL
#endif /* NO_EXT_KEYS */

#define DBL_DIG         15                      /* # of decimal digits of precision */
#define DBL_EPSILON     2.2204460492503131e-016 /* smallest such that 1.0+DBL_EPSILON != 1.0 */
#define DBL_MANT_DIG    53                      /* # of bits in mantissa */
#define DBL_MAX         1.797693134862315Be+308 /* max value */
#define DBL_MAX_10_EXP  308                     /* max decimal exponent */
#define DBL_MAX_EXP     1024                    /* max binary exponent */
#define DBL_MIN         2.2250738585072014e-308 /* min positive value */
#define DBL_MIN_10_EXP  -307                    /* min decimal exponent
#define DBL_MIN_EXP     -1021                   /* min binary exponent */
#define DBL_RADIX       2                       /* exponent radix */
#define DBL_ROUNDS      0                       /* addition rounding: chops */

#define FLT_DIG         6                       /* # of decimal digits of precision */
#define FLT_EPSILON     1.192092896e-07         /* smallest such that 1.0+FLT_EPSILON != 1.0 */
#define FLT_GUARD       0
#define FLT_MANT_DIG    24                      /* # of bits in mantissa */
#define FLT_MAX         3.402823466e+38         /* max value */
#define FLT_MAX_10_EXP  38                      /* max decimal exponent */
#define FLT_MAX_EXP     128                     /* max binary exponent */
#define FLT_MIN         1.175494351e-38         /* min positive value */
#define FLT_MIN_10_EXP  -37                     /* min decimal exponent */
#define FLT_MIN_EXP     -125                    /* min binary exponent */
#define FLT_NORMALIZE   0
#define FLT_RADIX       2                       /* exponent radix */
#define FLT_ROUNDS      0                       /* addition rounding: chops */

#define LDBL_DIG        DBL_DIG                 /* # of decimal digits of precision */
#define LDBL_EPSILON    DBL_EPSILON             /* smallest such that 1.0+LDBL_EPSILON != 1.0 */
#define LDBL_MANT_DIG   DBL_MANT_DIG            /* # of bits in mantissa */
#define LDBL_MAX        DBL_MAX                 /* max value */
#define LDBL_MAX_10_EXP DBL_MAX_10_EXP          /* max decimal exponent */
#define LDBL_MAX_EXP    DBL_MAX_EXP             /* max binary exponent */
#define LDBL_MIN        DBL_MIN                 /* min positive value */
#define LDBL_MIN_10_EXP DBL_MIN_10_EXP          /* min deimal exponent
#define LDBL_MIN_EXP    DBL_MIN_EXP             /* min binary exponent */
#define LDBL_RADIX      DBL_RADIX               /* exponent radix */
#define LDBL_ROUNDS     DBL_ROUNDS              /* addition rounding: chops */


/*
 *  8087/80287 math control information
 */
```

```
/* User Control Word Mask and bit definitions.
 * These definitions match the 8087/80287
 */

#define     MCW_EM          0x003f      /* interrupt Exception Masks */
#define     EM_INVALID      0x0001      /*   invalid */
#define     EM_DENORMAL     0x0002      /*   denormal */
#define     EM_ZERODIVIDE   0x0004      /*   zero divide */
#define     EM_OVERFLOW     0x0008      /*   overflow */
#define     EM_UNDERFLOW    0x0010      /*   underflow */
#define     EM_INEXACT      0x0020      /*   inexact (precision) */

#define     MCW_IC          0x1000      /* Infinity Control */
#define     IC_AFFINE       0x1000      /*   affine */
#define     IC_PROJECTIVE   0x0000      /*   projective */

#define     MCW_RC          0x0c00      /* Rounding Control */
#define     RC_CHOP         0x0c00      /*   chop */
#define     RC_UP           0x0800      /*   up */
#define     RC_DOWN         0x0400      /*   down */
#define     RC_NEAR         0x0000      /*   near */

#define     MCW_PC          0x0300      /* Precision Control */
#define     PC_24           0x0000      /*    24 bits */
#define     PC_53           0x0200      /*    53 bits */
#define     PC_64           0x0300      /*    64 bits */


/* initial Control Word value */

#define CW_DEFAULT  ( IC_AFFINE + RC_NEAR + PC_64 + EM_DENORMAL + EM_UNDERFLOW + EM_INEXACT )


/* user Status Word bit definitions */

#define SW_INVALID          0x0001      /*   invalid */
#define SW_DENORMAL         0x0002      /*   denormal */
#define SW_ZERODIVIDE       0x0004      /*   zero divide */
#define SW_OVERFLOW         0x0008      /*   overflow */
#define SW_UNDERFLOW        0x0010      /*   underflow */
#define SW_INEXACT          0x0020      /*   inexact (precision) */


/* invalid subconditions (SW_INVALID also set) */

#define SW_UNEMULATED       0x0040      /* unemulated instruction */
#define SW_SQRTNEG          0x0080      /* square root of a neg number */
#define SW_STACKOVERFLOW    0x0200      /* FP stack overflow */
#define SW_STACKUNDERFLOW   0x0400      /* FP stack underflow */


/*  Floating point error signals and return codes */

#define FPE_INVALID         0x81
#define FPE_DENORMAL        0x82
#define FPE_ZERODIVIDE      0x83
#define FPE_OVERFLOW        0x84
#define FPE_UNDERFLOW       0x85
#define FPE_INEXACT         0x86
```

```
#define FPE_UNEMULATED      0x87
#define FPE_SQRTNEG         0x88
#define FPE_STACKOVERFLOW   0x8a
#define FPE_STACKUNDERFLOW  0x8b

#define FPE_EXPLICITGEN     0x8c    /* raise( SIGFPE ); */

/* function prototypes */

unsigned int _CDECL _clear87(void);
unsigned int _CDECL _control87(unsigned int,unsigned int);
void _CDECL _fpreset(void);
unsigned int _CDECL _status87(void);
```

```
/***
*limits.h - implementation dependent values
*
*   Copyright (c) 1985-1988, Microsoft Corporation.  All rights reserved.
*
*Purpose:
*   contains defines for a number of implementation dependent values
*   which are commonly used in C programs.
*   [ANSI]
*
*******************************************************************************/

#ifndef _CHAR_UNSIGNED
#define CHAR_MAX         127            /* maximum char value */
#define CHAR_MIN        -127            /* mimimum char value */
#else
#define CHAR_MAX         255
#define CHAR_MIN        0
#endif
#define SCHAR_MAX        127            /* maximum signed char value */
#define SCHAR_MIN       -127            /* minimum signed char value */
#define UCHAR_MAX        255            /* maximum unsigned char value */
#define CHAR_BIT        8               /* number of bits in a char */
#define USHRT_MAX        0xffff         /* maximum unsigned short value */
#define SHRT_MAX         32767          /* maximum (signed) short value */
#define SHRT_MIN        -32767          /* minimum (signed) short value */
#define UINT_MAX         0xffff         /* maximum unsigned int value */
#define ULONG_MAX        0xffffffff     /* maximum unsigned long value */
#define INT_MAX          32767          /* maximum (signed) int value */
#define INT_MIN         -32767          /* minimum (signed) int value */
#define LONG_MAX         2147483647     /* maximum (signed) long value */
#define LONG_MIN        -2147483647     /* minimum (signed) long value */
```

```
/***
*math.h - definitions and declarations for math library
*
*   Copyright (c) 1985-1988, Microsoft Corporation.  All rights reserved.
*
*Purpose:
*   This file contains constant definitions and external subroutine
*   declarations for the math subroutine library.
*   [ANSI/System V]
*
*******************************************************************************/


#ifndef NO_EXT_KEYS /* extensions enabled */
    #define _CDECL   cdecl
#else /* extensions not enabled */
    #define _CDECL
#endif /* NO_EXT_KEYS */

/* definition of exception struct - this struct is passed to the matherr
 * routine when a floating point exception is detected
 */

#ifndef _EXCEPTION_DEFINED
struct exception {
    int type;           /* exception type - see below */
    char *name;   /* name of function where error occured */
    double arg1;        /* first argument to function */
    double arg2;        /* second argument (if any) to function */
    double retval;      /* value to be returned by function */
    } ;
#define _EXCEPTION_DEFINED
#endif


/* definition of a complex struct to be used by those who use cabs and
 * want type checking on their argument
 */

#ifndef _COMPLEX_DEFINED
struct complex {
    double x,y;     /* real and imaginary parts */
    } ;
#define _COMPLEX_DEFINED
#endif

/* Constant definitions for the exception type passed in the exception struct
 */

#define DOMAIN      1   /* argument domain error */
#define SING        2   /* argument singularity */
#define OVERFLOW    3   /* overflow range error */
#define UNDERFLOW   4   /* underflow range error */
#define TLOSS       5   /* total loss of precision */
#define PLOSS       6   /* partial loss of precision */

#define EDOM        33
#define ERANGE      34


/* definitions of HUGE and HUGE_VAL - respectively the XENIX and ANSI names
 * for a value returned in case of error by a number of the floating point
```

```
 * math routines
 */

extern double HUGE;
#define HUGE_VAL HUGE

/* function prototypes */

int    _CDECL abs(int);
double _CDECL acos(double);
double _CDECL asin(double);
double _CDECL atan(double);
double _CDECL atan2(double, double);
double _CDECL atof(const char *);
double _CDECL cabs(struct complex);
double _CDECL ceil(double);
double _CDECL cos(double);
double _CDECL cosh(double);
int    _CDECL dieeetomsbin(double *, double *);
int    _CDECL dmsbintoieee(double *, double *);
double _CDECL exp(double);
double _CDECL fabs(double);
int    _CDECL fieeetomsbin(float *, float *);
double _CDECL floor(double);
double _CDECL fmod(double, double);
int    _CDECL fmsbintoieee(float *, float *);
double _CDECL frexp(double, int *);
double _CDECL hypot(double, double);
double _CDECL j0(double);
double _CDECL j1(double);
double _CDECL jn(int, double);
long   _CDECL labs(long);
double _CDECL ldexp(double, int);
double _CDECL log(double);
double _CDECL log10(double);
int    _CDECL matherr(struct exception *);
double _CDECL modf(double, double *);
double _CDECL pow(double, double);
double _CDECL sin(double);
double _CDECL sinh(double);
double _CDECL sqrt(double);
double _CDECL tan(double);
double _CDECL tanh(double);
double _CDECL y0(double);
double _CDECL y1(double);
double _CDECL yn(int, double);
```

```
/***
*setjmp.h - definitions/declarations for setjmp/longjmp routines
*
*   Copyright (c) 1985-1988, Microsoft Corporation.  All rights reserved.
*
*Purpose:
*   This file defines the machine-dependent buffer used by
*   setjmp/longjmp to save and restore the program state, and
*   declarations for those routines.
*   [ANSI/System V]
*
*******************************************************************************/


#ifndef NO_EXT_KEYS /* extensions enabled */
    #define _CDECL  cdecl
#else /* extensions not enabled */
    #define _CDECL
#endif /* NO_EXT_KEYS */


/* define the buffer type for holding the state information */

#define _JBLEN  9  /* bp, di, si, sp, ret addr, ds */

#ifndef _JMP_BUF_DEFINED
typedef  int  jmp_buf[_JBLEN];
#define _JMP_BUF_DEFINED
#endif


/* function prototypes */

int _CDECL setjmp(jmp_buf);
void _CDECL longjmp(jmp_buf, int);



/***
*signal.h - defines signal values and routines
*
*   Copyright (c) 1985-1988, Microsoft Corporation.  All rights reserved.
*
*Purpose:
*   This file defines the signal values and declares the signal functions.
*   [ANSI/System V]
*
*******************************************************************************/

#ifndef NO_EXT_KEYS /* extensions enabled */
    #define _CDECL  cdecl
#else /* extensions not enabled */
    #define _CDECL
#endif /* NO_EXT_KEYS */

#ifndef _SIG_ATOMIC_T_DEFINED
typedef int sig_atomic_t;
#define _SIG_ATOMIC_T_DEFINED
#endif

#define NSIG 23     /* maximum signal number + 1 */
```

```
/* signal types */
/* SIGINT, SIGFPE, SIGILL, SIGSEGV, and SIGABRT are recognized on DOS 3.x */

#define SIGINT       2   /* interrupt - corresponds to DOS 3.x int 23H */
#define SIGILL       4   /* illegal instruction - invalid function image */
#define SIGFPE       8   /* floating point exception */
#define SIGSEGV      11  /* segment violation */
#define SIGTERM      15  /* Software termination signal from kill */
#define SIGUSR1      16  /* User defined signal 1 */
#define SIGUSR2      17  /* User defined signal 2 */
#define SIGUSR3      20  /* User defined signal 3 */
#define SIGBREAK     21  /* Ctrl-Break sequence */
#define SIGABRT      22  /* abnormal termination triggered by abort call */

/* signal action codes */
/* SIG_DFL and SIG_IGN are recognized on DOS 3.x */

#define SIG_DFL (void (*)())0 /* default signal action */
#define SIG_IGN (void (*)())1 /* ignore */
#define SIG_SGE (void (*)())3 /* signal gets error */
#define SIG_ACK (void (*)())4 /* error if handler not setup */

/* signal error value (returned by signal call on error) */

#define SIG_ERR (void (*)())-1    /* signal error value */

/* function prototypes */

void (_CDECL * _CDECL signal(int, void (_CDECL *)()))();
int _CDECL raise(int);
```

```
/***
*stdarg.h - defines ANSI-style macros for variable argument functions
*
*   Copyright (c) 1985-1988, Microsoft Corporation.  All rights reserved.
*
*Purpose:
*   This file defines ANSI-style macros for accessing arguments
*   of functions which take a variable number of arguments.
*   [ANSI]
*
*******************************************************************************/

#ifndef _VA_LIST_DEFINED
typedef char *va_list;
#define _VA_LIST_DEFINED
#endif

#define va_start(ap,v) ap = (va_list)&v + sizeof(v)
#define va_arg(ap,t) ((t *)(ap += sizeof(t)))[-1]
#define va_end(ap) ap = NULL
```

```
/***
*stddef.h - definitions/declarations for common constants, types, variables
*
*   Copyright (c) 1985-1988, Microsoft Corporation.  All rights reserved.
*
*Purpose:
*   This file contains definitions and declarations for some commonly
*   used constants, types, and variables.
*   [ANSI]
*
*******************************************************************************/


#ifndef NO_EXT_KEYS /* extensions enabled */
    #define _CDECL  cdecl
    #define _NEAR   near
#else /* extensions not enabled */
    #define _CDECL
    #define _NEAR
#endif /* NO_EXT_KEYS */


/* define NULL pointer value */

#if (defined(M_I86SM) || defined(M_I86MM))
#define  NULL    0
#elif (defined(M_I86CM) || defined(M_I86LM) || defined(M_I86HM))
#define  NULL    0L
#endif


/* declare reference to errno */

extern int _NEAR _CDECL errno;


/* define the implementation dependent size types */

#ifndef _PTRDIFF_T_DEFINED
typedef int ptrdiff_t;
#define _PTRDIFF_T_DEFINED
#endif

#ifndef _SIZE_T_DEFINED
typedef unsigned int size_t;
#define _SIZE_T_DEFINED
#endif
```

```
/***
*stdio.h - definitions/declarations for standard I/O routines
*
*   Copyright (c) 1985-1988, Microsoft Corporation.  All rights reserved.
*
*Purpose:
*   This file defines the structures, values, macros, and functions
*   used by the level 2 I/O ("standard I/O") routines.
*   [ANSI/System V]
*
****************************************************************************/


#ifndef _SIZE_T_DEFINED
typedef unsigned int size_t;
#define _SIZE_T_DEFINED
#endif

#ifndef _VA_LIST_DEFINED
typedef char *va_list;
#define _VA_LIST_DEFINED
#endif

#ifndef NO_EXT_KEYS /* extensions enabled */
    #define _CDECL  cdecl
    #define _NEAR   near
#else /* extensions not enabled */
    #define _CDECL
    #define _NEAR
#endif /* NO_EXT_KEYS */


/* buffered I/O macros */

#define  BUFSIZ  512
#define  _NFILE  20
#define  EOF     (-1)

#ifndef _FILE_DEFINED
#define  FILE    struct _iobuf
#define _FILE_DEFINED
#endif

/* P_tmpnam: Directory where temporary files may be created.
 * L_tmpnam size =  size of P_tmpdir
 *      + 1 (in case P_tmpdir does not end in "\\")
 *      + 6 (for the temp number string)
 *      + 1 (for the null terminator)
 */

#define  P_tmpdir "\\"
#define  L_tmpnam sizeof(P_tmpdir)+8

#define  SEEK_CUR 1
#define  SEEK_END 2
#define  SEEK_SET 0

#define  SYS_OPEN 20
#define  TMP_MAX  32767


/* define NULL pointer value */
```

```
#if (defined(M_I86SM) || defined(M_I86MM))
#define  NULL    0
#elif (defined(M_I86CM) || defined(M_I86LM) || defined(M_I86HM))
#define  NULL    0L
#endif


/* define file control block */

#ifndef _IOB_DEFINED
extern FILE {
    char *_ptr;
    int   _cnt;
    char *_base;
    char  _flag;
    char  _file;
    } _NEAR _CDECL _iob[];
#define _IOB_DEFINED
#endif

#define  fpos_t  long   /* file position variable */

#define  stdin  (&_iob[0])
#define  stdout (&_iob[1])
#define  stderr (&_iob[2])
#define  stdaux (&_iob[3])
#define  stdprn (&_iob[4])

#define  _IOREAD    0x01
#define  _IOWRT     0x02

#define  _IOFBF     0x0
#define  _IOLBF     0x40
#define  _IONBF     0x04

#define  _IOMYBUF   0x08
#define  _IOEOF     0x10
#define  _IOERR     0x20
#define  _IOSTRG    0x40
#define  _IORW      0x80

#define getc(f)         (--(f)->_cnt >= 0 ? 0xff & *(f)->_ptr++ : _filbuf(f))
#define putc(c,f)       (--(f)->_cnt >= 0 ? 0xff & (*(f)->_ptr++ = (char)(c)) \
                        :  _flsbuf((c),(f)))
#define getchar()       getc(stdin)
#define putchar(c)      putc((c),stdout)

#define feof(f)         ((f)->_flag & _IOEOF)
#define ferror(f)       ((f)->_flag & _IOERR)
#define fileno(f)       ((f)->_file)


/* function prototypes */

int _CDECL _filbuf(FILE *);
int _CDECL _flsbuf(int, FILE *);
void _CDECL clearerr(FILE *);
int _CDECL fclose(FILE *);
int _CDECL fcloseall(void);
FILE * _CDECL fdopen(int, char *);
int _CDECL fflush(FILE *);
```

```
int _CDECL fgetc(FILE *);
int _CDECL fgetchar(void);
int _CDECL fgetpos(FILE *, fpos_t *);
char * _CDECL fgets(char *, int, FILE *);
int _CDECL flushall(void);
FILE * _CDECL fopen(const char *, const char *);
int _CDECL fprintf(FILE *, const char *, ...);
int _CDECL fputc(int, FILE *);
int _CDECL fputchar(int);
int _CDECL fputs(const char *, FILE *);
size_t _CDECL fread(void *, size_t, size_t, FILE *);
FILE * _CDECL freopen(const char *, const char *, FILE *);
int _CDECL fscanf(FILE *, const char *, ...);
int _CDECL fsetpos(FILE *, const fpos_t *);
int _CDECL fseek(FILE *, long, int);
long _CDECL ftell(FILE *);
size_t _CDECL fwrite(const void *, size_t, size_t, FILE *);
char * _CDECL gets(char *);
int _CDECL getw(FILE *);
void _CDECL perror(const char *);
int _CDECL printf(const char *, ...);
int _CDECL puts(const char *);
int _CDECL putw(int, FILE *);
int _CDECL remove(const char *);
int _CDECL rename(const char *, const char *);
void _CDECL rewind(FILE *);
int _CDECL rmtmp(void);
int _CDECL scanf(const char *, ...);
void _CDECL setbuf(FILE *, char *);
int _CDECL setvbuf(FILE *, char *, int, size_t);
int _CDECL sprintf(char *, const char *, ...);
int _CDECL sscanf(const char *, const char *, ...);
char * _CDECL tempnam(char *, char *);
FILE * _CDECL tmpfile(void);
char * _CDECL tmpnam(char *);
int _CDECL ungetc(int, FILE *);
int _CDECL unlink(const char *);
int _CDECL vfprintf(FILE *, const char *, va_list);
int _CDECL vprintf(const char *, va_list);
int _CDECL vsprintf(char *, const char *, va_list);


/***
*stdlib.h - declarations/definitions for commonly used library functions
*
*   Copyright (c) 1985-1988, Microsoft Corporation.  All rights reserved.
*
*Purpose:
*   This include file contains the function declarations for
*   commonly used library functions which either don't fit somewhere
*   else, or, like toupper/tolower, can't be declared in the normal
*   place (ctype.h in the case of toupper/tolower) for other reasons.
*   [ANSI]
*
*******************************************************************************/


#ifndef _SIZE_T_DEFINED
typedef unsigned int size_t;
#define _SIZE_T_DEFINED
#endif
```

```
#ifndef NO_EXT_KEYS /* extensions enabled */
    #define _CDECL  cdecl
    #define _NEAR   near
#else /* extensions not enabled */
    #define _CDECL
    #define _NEAR
#endif /* NO_EXT_KEYS */


/* definition of the return type for the onexit() function */

#ifndef _ONEXIT_T_DEFINED
typedef int (_CDECL * _CDECL onexit_t)();
#define _ONEXIT_T_DEFINED
#endif


/* Data structure definitions for div and ldiv runtimes. */

#ifndef _DIV_T_DEFINED

typedef struct {
    int quot;
    int rem;
} div_t;

typedef struct {
    long quot;
    long rem;
} ldiv_t;

#define _DIV_T_DEFINED
#endif

/* Maximum value that can be returned by the rand function. */

#define RAND_MAX 0x7fff


/* min and max macros */

#define max(a,b)     (((a) > (b)) ? (a) : (b))
#define min(a,b)     (((a) < (b)) ? (a) : (b))


/* sizes for buffers used by the _makepath() and _splitpath() functions.
 * note that the sizes include space for 0-terminator
 */

#define _MAX_PATH      144      /* max. length of full pathname */
#define _MAX_DRIVE   3      /* max. length of drive component */
#define _MAX_DIR       130      /* max. length of path component */
#define _MAX_FNAME   9      /* max. length of file name component */
#define _MAX_EXT     5      /* max. length of extension component */

/* external variable declarations */

extern int _NEAR _CDECL errno;               /* XENIX style error number */
extern int _NEAR _CDECL _doserrno;           /* MS-DOS system error value */
extern char * _NEAR _CDECL sys_errlist[];    /* perror error message table */
extern int _NEAR _CDECL sys_nerr;            /* # of entries in sys_errlist table */
```

```
extern char ** _NEAR _CDECL environ;        /* pointer to environment table */

extern unsigned int _NEAR _CDECL _psp;      /* Program Segment Prefix */

extern int _NEAR _CDECL _fmode;             /* default file translation mode */

/* DOS major/minor version numbers */

extern unsigned char _NEAR _CDECL _osmajor;
extern unsigned char _NEAR _CDECL _osminor;

#define DOS_MODE    0   /* Real Address Mode */
#define OS2_MODE    1   /* Protected Address Mode */

extern unsigned char _NEAR _CDECL _osmode;


/* function prototypes */

double _CDECL atof(const char *);
double _CDECL strtod(const char *, char * *);
ldiv_t _CDECL ldiv(long, long);

void   _CDECL abort(void);
int    _CDECL abs(int);
int    _CDECL atexit(void (_CDECL *)(void));
int    _CDECL atoi(const char *);
long   _CDECL atol(const char *);
void * _CDECL bsearch(const void *, const void *, size_t, size_t, int (_CDECL *)(const vo:
void * _CDECL calloc(size_t, size_t);
div_t  _CDECL div(int, int);
char * _CDECL ecvt(double, int, int *, int *);
void   _CDECL exit(int);
void   _CDECL _exit(int);
char * _CDECL fcvt(double, int, int *, int *);
void   _CDECL free(void *);
char * _CDECL gcvt(double, int, char *);
char * _CDECL getenv(const char *);
char * _CDECL itoa(int, char *, int);
long   _CDECL labs(long);
unsigned long _CDECL _lrotl(unsigned long, int);
unsigned long _CDECL _lrotr(unsigned long, int);
char * _CDECL ltoa(long, char *, int);
void   _CDECL _makepath(char *, char *, char *, char *, char *);
void * _CDECL malloc(size_t);
onexit_t _CDECL onexit(onexit_t);
void   _CDECL perror(const char *);
int    _CDECL putenv(char *);
void   _CDECL qsort(void *, size_t, size_t, int (_CDECL *)(const void *, const void *));
unsigned int _CDECL _rotl(unsigned int, int);
unsigned int _CDECL _rotr(unsigned int, int);
int    _CDECL rand(void);
void * _CDECL realloc(void *, size_t);
void   _CDECL _searchenv(char *, char *, char *);
void   _CDECL _splitpath(char *, char *, char *, char *, char *);
void   _CDECL srand(unsigned int);
long   _CDECL strtol(const char *, char * *, int);
unsigned long _CDECL strtoul(const char *, char * *, int);
void   _CDECL swab(char *, char *, int);
int    _CDECL system(const char *);
char * _CDECL ultoa(unsigned long, char *, int);
```

```
#ifndef tolower         /* tolower has been undefined - use function */
int _CDECL tolower(int);
#endif  /* tolower */

#ifndef toupper         /* toupper has been undefined - use function */
int    _CDECL toupper(int);
#endif  /* toupper */



/***
*string.h - declarations for string manipulation functions
*
*   Copyright (c) 1985-1988, Microsoft Corporation.  All rights reserved.
*
*Purpose:
*   This file contains the function declarations for the string
*   manipulation functions.
*   [ANSI/System V]
*
*******************************************************************************/


#ifndef _SIZE_T_DEFINED
typedef unsigned int size_t;
#define _SIZE_T_DEFINED
#endif

#ifndef NO_EXT_KEYS /* extensions enabled */
    #define _CDECL  cdecl
#else /* extensions not enabled */
    #define _CDECL
#endif /* NO_EXT_KEYS */


/* function prototypes */

void * _CDECL memccpy(void *, void *, int, unsigned int);
void * _CDECL memchr(const void *, int, size_t);
int _CDECL memcmp(const void *, const void *, size_t);
int _CDECL memicmp(void *, void *, unsigned int);
void * _CDECL memcpy(void *, const void *, size_t);
void * _CDECL memmove(void *, const void *, size_t);
void * _CDECL memset(void *, int, size_t);
void _CDECL movedata(unsigned int, unsigned int, unsigned int, unsigned int, unsigned int);

char * _CDECL strcat(char *, const char *);
char * _CDECL strchr(const char *, int);
int _CDECL strcmp(const char *, const char *);
int _CDECL strcmpi(const char *, const char *);
int _CDECL stricmp(const char *, const char *);
char * _CDECL strcpy(char *, const char *);
size_t _CDECL strcspn(const char *, const char *);
char * _CDECL strdup(const char *);
char * _CDECL _strerror(char *);
char * _CDECL strerror(int);
size_t _CDECL strlen(const char *);
char * _CDECL strlwr(char *);
char * _CDECL strncat(char *, const char *, size_t);
int _CDECL strncmp(const char *, const char *, size_t);
```

```
int _CDECL strnicmp(const char *, const char *, size_t);
char * _CDECL strncpy(char *, const char *, size_t);
char * _CDECL strnset(char *, int, size_t);
char * _CDECL strpbrk(const char *, const char *);
char * _CDECL strrchr(const char *, int);
char * _CDECL strrev(char *);
char * _CDECL strset(char *, int);
size_t _CDECL strspn(const char *, const char *);
char * _CDECL strstr(const char *, const char *);
char * _CDECL strtok(char *, const char *);
char * _CDECL strupr(char *);



/***
*time.h - definitions/declarations for time routines
*
*   Copyright (c) 1985-1988, Microsoft Corporation.  All rights reserved.
*
*Purpose:
*   This file has declarations of time routines and defines
*   the structure returned by the localtime and gmtime routines and
*   used by asctime.
*   [ANSI/System V]
*
****************************************************************************/


#ifndef NO_EXT_KEYS /* extensions enabled */
    #define _CDECL  cdecl
    #define _NEAR   near
#else /* extensions not enabled */
    #define _CDECL
    #define _NEAR
#endif /* NO_EXT_KEYS */


/* define the implementation defined time type */

#ifndef _TIME_T_DEFINED
typedef long time_t;              /* time value */
#define _TIME_T_DEFINED           /* avoid multiple def's of time_t */
#endif

#ifndef _CLOCK_T_DEFINED
typedef long clock_t;
#define _CLOCK_T_DEFINED
#endif

#ifndef _TM_DEFINED
struct tm {
    int tm_sec;         /* seconds after the minute - [0,59] */
    int tm_min;         /* minutes after the hour - [0,59] */
    int tm_hour;        /* hours since midnight - [0,23] */
    int tm_mday;        /* day of the month - [1,31] */
    int tm_mon;         /* months since January - [0,11] */
    int tm_year;        /* years since 1900 */
    int tm_wday;        /* days since Sunday - [0,6] */
    int tm_yday;        /* days since January 1 - [0,365] */
    int tm_isdst;       /* daylight savings time flag */
    };
```

```
#define _TM_DEFINED
#endif

#define CLK_TCK 1000


/* extern declarations for the global variables used by the ctime family of
 * routines.
 */

extern int _NEAR _CDECL daylight;     /* non-zero if daylight savings time is used */
extern long _NEAR _CDECL timezone;    /* difference in seconds between GMT and local time
extern char * _NEAR _CDECL tzname[2]; /* standard/daylight savings time zone names */


/* function prototypes */

char * _CDECL asctime(const struct tm *);
char * _CDECL ctime(const time_t *);
clock_t _CDECL clock(void);
double _CDECL difftime(time_t, time_t);
struct tm * _CDECL gmtime(const time_t *);
struct tm * _CDECL localtime(const time_t *);
time_t _CDECL mktime(struct tm *);
char * _CDECL _strdate(char *);
char * _CDECL _strtime(char *);
time_t _CDECL time(time_t *);
void _CDECL tzset(void);
```

Appendix L

BORLAND TURBO C VERSION 1.5 STANDARD HEADER FILES

<assert.h>		<stddef.h>
<ctype.h>	<math.h>	<stdio.h>
<errno.h>	<setjmp.h>	<stdlib.h>
<float.h>	<signal.h>	<string.h>
<limits.h>	<stdarg.h>	<time.h>

```
/*       assert.h

         assert macro

         Copyright (c) Borland International 1987
         All Rights Reserved.
*/

#if      !defined(NDEBUG)
#define assert(p)   if(!(p)){fprintf(stderr,\
                    "Assertion failed: %s, file %s, line %d\n",\
                    #p, __FILE__, __LINE__);abort();}
#else
#define assert(p)
#endif
/*       ctype.h

         Defines the ctype macros.

         Copyright (c) Borland International 1987
         All Rights Reserved.
*/
#if __STDC__
#define _Cdecl
#else
#define _Cdecl      cdecl
#endif

#define _IS_SP      1                           /* is space */
#define _IS_DIG     2                           /* is digit indicator */
#define _IS_UPP     4                           /* is upper case */
#define _IS_LOW     8                           /* is lower case */
#define _IS_HEX     16                          /* [A-F or [a-f] */
#define _IS_CTL     32                          /* Control */
#define _IS_PUN     64                          /* punctuation */

extern   char _Cdecl _ctype[];         /* Character type array */
```

```
#define isalnum(c)  (_ctype[(c) + 1] & (_IS_DIG | _IS_UPP | _IS_LOW))
#define isalpha(c)  (_ctype[(c) + 1] & (_IS_UPP | _IS_LOW))
#define isascii(c)  ((unsigned)((c) + 1) < 0x81)
#define iscntrl(c)  (_ctype[(c) + 1] & _IS_CTL)
#define isdigit(c)  (_ctype[(c) + 1] & _IS_DIG)
#define isgraph(c)  ((c) >= 0x21 && (c) <= 0x7e)
#define islower(c)  (_ctype[(c) + 1] & _IS_LOW)
#define isprint(c)  ((c) >= 0x20 && (c) <= 0x7e)
#define ispunct(c)  (_ctype[(c) + 1] & _IS_PUN)
#define isspace(c)  (_ctype[(c) + 1] & _IS_SP)
#define isupper(c)  (_ctype[(c) + 1] & _IS_UPP)
#define isxdigit(c) (_ctype[(c) + 1] & (_IS_DIG | _IS_HEX))
#define _toupper(c) ((c) + 'A' - 'a')
#define _tolower(c) ((c) + 'a' - 'A')
#define toascii(c)  ((c) & 0x7f)

int       _Cdecl tolower(int ch);
int       _Cdecl toupper(int ch);
/*        errno.h

          Defines the system error variable errno and the error
          numbers set by system calls. Errors which exist in Unix(tm)
          but not MSDOS have value 0.

          Copyright (c) Borland International 1987
          All Rights Reserved.
*/
#if __STDC__
#define _Cdecl
#else
#define _Cdecl     cdecl
#endif


/*  Dos Error Codes */

#define EZERO       0               /* Error 0                         */
#define EINVFNC     1               /* Invalid function number   */
#define ENOFILE     2               /* File not found            */
#define ENOPATH     3               /* Path not found            */
#define ECONTR      7               /* Memory blocks destroyed   */
#define EINVMEM     9               /* Invalid memory block address */
#define EINVENV 10           /* Invalid environment          */
#define EINVFMT 11           /* Invalid format          */
#define EINVACC 12           /* Invalid access code          */
#define EINVDAT 13           /* Invalid data                 */
#define EINVDRV 15           /* Invalid drive specified  */
#define ECURDIR 16           /* Attempt to remove CurDir  */
#define ENOTSAM 17           /* Not same device          */
#define ENMFILE 18           /* No more files            */

#define ENOENT      2               /* No such file or directory */
#define EMFILE      4               /* Too many open files             */
#define EACCES      5               /* Permission denied               */
#define EBADF       6               /* Bad file number           */
#define ENOMEM      8               /* Not enough core           */
#define ENODEV     15               /* No such device            */
#define EINVAL     19               /* Invalid argument          */
#define E2BIG      20               /* Arg list too long               */
#define ENOEXEC 21           /* Exec format error            */
#define EXDEV      22               /* Cross-device link               */
#define EDOM       33               /* Math argument             */
#define ERANGE     34               /* Result too large          */
```

```
#define EFAULT      -1                /* Unknown error          */
#define EPERM       -1                /* UNIX - not MSDOS       */
#define ESRCH       -1                /* UNIX - not MSDOS       */
#define EINTR       -1                /* UNIX - not MSDOS       */
#define EIO         -1                /* UNIX - not MSDOS       */
#define ENXIO       -1                /* UNIX - not MSDOS       */
#define ECHILD      -1                /* UNIX - not MSDOS       */
#define EAGAIN      -1                /* UNIX - not MSDOS       */
#define ENOTBLK -1          /* UNIX - not MSDOS       */
#define EBUSY       -1                /* UNIX - not MSDOS       */
#define EEXIST      -1                /* UNIX - not MSDOS       */
#define ENOTDIR -1          /* UNIX - not MSDOS       */
#define EISDIR      -1                /* UNIX - not MSDOS       */
#define ENFILE      -1                /* UNIX - not MSDOS       */
#define ENOTTY      -1                /* UNIX - not MSDOS       */
#define ETXTBSY -1          /* UNIX - not MSDOS       */
#define EFBIG       -1                /* UNIX - not MSDOS       */
#define ENOSPC      -1                /* UNIX - not MSDOS       */
#define ESPIPE      -1                /* UNIX - not MSDOS       */
#define EROFS       -1                /* UNIX - not MSDOS       */
#define EMLINK      -1                /* UNIX - not MSDOS       */
#define EPIPE       -1                /* UNIX - not MSDOS       */
#define EUCLEAN -1          /* UNIX - not MSDOS       */


#define _sys_nerr 34                  /* highest defined system error number */

extern   int      _Cdecl   errno;
extern   int      _Cdecl   _doserrno;

/*       float.h

         Defines implementation specific macros for dealing with
         floating point.

         Copyright (c) Borland International 1987
         All Rights Reserved.
*/
#if __STDC__
#define _Cdecl
#else
#define _Cdecl     cdecl
#endif

#define FLT_RADIX                 2
#define FLT_ROUNDS                1
#define FLT_GUARD                 1
#define FLT_NORMALIZE                       1

#define DBL_DIG                             14
#define FLT_DIG                             6
#define LDBL_DIG                  14

#define DBL_MANT_DIG                        53
#define FLT_MANT_DIG                        24
#define LDBL_MANT_DIG                       53

#define DBL_EPSILON               2.2204460492503131E-16
#define FLT_EPSILON               1.19209290E-07F
#define LDBL_EPSILON                        2.2204460492503131E-16
```

```
#define DBL_MIN                          2.225073858507201E-16
#define FLT_MIN                          1.17549435E-38F
#define LDBL_MIN                 2.225073858507201E-16

#define DBL_MAX                          1.797693134862316E+308
#define FLT_MAX                          3.40282347E+38F
#define LDBL_MAX                 1.797693134862316E+308

#define DBL_MAX_EXP              +1024
#define FLT_MAX_EXP              +128
#define LDBL_MAX_EXP                     +1024

#define DBL_MAX_10_EXP                   +308
#define FLT_MAX_10_EXP                   +38
#define LDBL_MAX_10_EXP                  +308

#define DBL_MIN_10_EXP                   -307
#define FLT_MIN_10_EXP                   -37
#define LDBL_MIN_10_EXP                  -307

#define DBL_MIN_EXP              -1021
#define FLT_MIN_EXP              -125
#define LDBL_MIN_EXP                     -1021

unsigned int _Cdecl _clear87(void);
unsigned int _Cdecl _control87(unsigned int new, unsigned int mask);
void           _Cdecl _fpreset(void);
unsigned int _Cdecl _status87(void);

/* 8087/80287 Status Word format   */

#define SW_INVALID          0x0001   /* Invalid operation              */
#define SW_DENORMAL         0x0002   /* Denormalized operand           */
#define SW_ZERODIVIDE                0x0004   /* Zero divide                    */
#define SW_OVERFLOW         0x0008   /* Overflow                       */
#define SW_UNDERFLOW                 0x0010   /* Underflow                      */
#define SW_INEXACT          0x0020   /* Precision (Inexact result)     */

/* 8087/80287 Control Word format */

#define MCW_EM                       0x003f   /* interrupt Exception Masks */
#define      EM_INVALID              0x0001   /*   invalid                      */
#define      EM_DENORMAL             0x0002   /*   denormal                     */
#define      EM_ZERODIVIDE  0x0004   /*   zero divide          */
#define      EM_OVERFLOW             0x0008   /*   overflow                     */
#define      EM_UNDERFLOW   0x0010   /*   underflow                 */
#define      EM_INEXACT              0x0020   /*   inexact (precision)       */

#define MCW_IC                       0x1000   /* Infinity Control          */
#define      IC_AFFINE               0x1000   /*   affine                       */
#define      IC_PROJECTIVE  0x0000   /*   projective                */

#define MCW_RC                       0x0c00   /* Rounding Control          */
#define      RC_CHOP                 0x0c00   /*   chop                    */
#define      RC_UP          0x0800   /*   up                        */
#define      RC_DOWN                 0x0400   /*   down                    */
#define      RC_NEAR                 0x0000   /*   near                    */

#define MCW_PC                       0x0300   /* Precision Control                  */
#define      PC_24          0x0000   /*   24 bits                   */
#define      PC_53          0x0200   /*   53 bits                   */
#define      PC_64          0x0300   /*   64 bits                   */
```

```
/* 8087/80287 Initial Control Word */
/* should be same as in rules.asi  */

#define CW_DEFAULT (RC_NEAR+PC_64+EM_DENORMAL+EM_UNDERFLOW+EM_INEXACT)

/*        limits.h

          Defines implementation specific limits on type values.

          Copyright (c) Borland International 1987
          All Rights Reserved.
*/
#if __STDC__
#define _Cdecl
#else
#define _Cdecl     cdecl
#endif

#define CHAR_BIT                        8

#if (((int)((char)0x80)) < 0)
#define CHAR_MAX                        0x7F
#define CHAR_MIN                        0x80
#else
#define CHAR_MAX                        0xFFU
#define CHAR_MIN                        0x00
#endif

#define SCHAR_MAX                       0x7F
#define SCHAR_MIN                       0x80
#define UCHAR_MAX                       0xFFU

#define SHRT_MAX                        0x7FFF
#define SHRT_MIN                        ((int)0x8000)
#define USHRT_MAX                       0xFFFFU

#define INT_MAX                                   0x7FFF
#define INT_MIN                                   ((int)0x8000)
#define UINT_MAX                        0xFFFFU

#define LONG_MAX                        0x7FFFFFFFL
#define LONG_MIN                        ((long)0x80000000L)
#define ULONG_MAX                       0xFFFFFFFFUL

/*        math.h

          Definitions for the math floating point package.

          Copyright (c) Borland International 1987
          All Rights Reserved.
*/
#if   STDC__
#define _Cdecl
#else
#define _Cdecl     cdecl
#endif

#ifndef   _MATH_H
#define   _MATH_H 1
```

```
#define EDOM        33                  /* Math argument */
#define ERANGE      34                  /* Result too large */

#define HUGE_VAL    (_huge_val())
double    _Cdecl _huge_val(void);

int       _Cdecl abs   (int x);
double    _Cdecl acos  (double x);
double    _Cdecl asin  (double x);
double    _Cdecl atan  (double x);
double    _Cdecl atan2 (double y, double x);
double    _Cdecl atof  (const char *s);
double    _Cdecl ceil  (double x);
double    _Cdecl cos   (double x);
double    _Cdecl cosh  (double x);
double    _Cdecl exp   (double x);
double    _Cdecl fabs  (double x);
double    _Cdecl floor (double x);
double    _Cdecl fmod  (double x, double y);
double    _Cdecl frexp (double x, int *exponent);
long      _Cdecl labs  (long x);
double    _Cdecl ldexp (double x, int exponent);
double    _Cdecl log   (double x);
double    _Cdecl log10 (double x);
double    _Cdecl modf  (double x, double *ipart);
double    _Cdecl pow   (double x, double y);
double    _Cdecl sin   (double x);
double    _Cdecl sinh  (double x);
double    _Cdecl sqrt  (double x);
double    _Cdecl tan   (double x);
double    _Cdecl tanh  (double x);

struct    exception
{
          int      type;
          char   *name;
          double   arg1, arg2, retval;
};

int _Cdecl matherr (struct exception *e);

#if !__STDC__
double    cdecl hypot (double x, double y);
double    cdecl poly  (double x, int degree, double coeffs []);
double    cdecl pow10 (int p);

struct complex         /* as used by "cabs" function */
{
    double  x, y;
};

#define cabs(z)      (hypot ((z).x, (z).y))

/*  The customary matherr() exception handler for maths functions is
    not compatible with the x3j11 draft standard for C.  _matherr() is
    provided as a compromise.
*/
```

```
typedef enum
{
    DOMAIN = 1,     /* argument domain error -- log (-1)         */
    SING,    /* argument singularity  -- pow (0,-2))     */
    OVERFLOW,          /* overflow range error  -- exp (1000)       */
    UNDERFLOW,         /* underflow range error -- exp (-1000)      */
    TLOSS,             /* total loss of significance -- sin(10e70) */
    PLOSS,             /* partial loss of signif. -- not used       */
}   _mexcep;

double _Cdecl _matherr (_mexcep why, char *fun, double  *arg1p,
                             double  *arg2p, double  retval);

/* Constants rounded for 18 decimals. */

#define M_E                  2.71828182845904524
#define M_LOG2E              1.44269504088896341
#define M_LOG10E   0.434294481903251828
#define M_LN2                0.693147180559945309
#define M_LN10               2.30258509299404568
#define M_PI                 3.14159265358979324
#define M_PI_2               1.57079632679489662
#define M_PI_4               0.785398163397448310
#define M_1_PI               0.318309886183790672
#define M_2_PI               0.636619772367581343
#define M_1_SQRTPI 0.564189583547756287
#define M_2_SQRTPI 1.12837916709551257
#define M_SQRT2              1.41421356237309505
#define M_SQRT_2   0.707106781186547524

#endif    /* __STDC__ */

#endif

/*         setjmp.h

           Defines typedef and functions for setjmp/longjmp.

           Copyright (c) Borland International 1987
           All Rights Reserved.
*/
#if __STDC__
#define _Cdecl
#else
#define _Cdecl     cdecl
#endif

#ifndef _SETJMP
#define _SETJMP
typedef struct {
         unsigned  j_sp;
         unsigned  j_ss;
         unsigned  j_flag;
         unsigned  j_cs;
         unsigned  j_ip;
         unsigned  j_bp;
         unsigned  j_di;
         unsigned  j_es;
         unsigned  j_si;
         unsigned  j_ds;
}        jmp_buf[1];
```

```
void      _Cdecl longjmp(jmp_buf jmpb, int retval);
int       _Cdecl setjmp(jmp_buf jmpb);
#endif

/*        Signal.H

          Definitions For Software Signalling Mechanism.

          Copyright (c) Borland International 1987
          All Rights Reserved.
*/
#if __STDC__
#define _Cdecl
#else
#define _Cdecl     cdecl

#endif

#define SIG_DFL ((int(*)())0)                      /* Default action */
#define SIG_IGN ((int(*)())1)                      /* Ignore action */
#define SIG_ERR ((int(*)())-1)                     /* Error return */

#define SIGABRT 1
#define SIGFPE     2                               /* Floating point trap */
#define SIGILL     3                               /* Illegal instruction */
#define SIGINT     4
#define SIGSEGV 5                        /* Memory access violation */
#define SIGTERM 6

typedef int        sig_atomic_t;                   /* atomic entity type */

#if !__STDC__
int cdecl gsignal(int sig);
int (*cdecl ssignal(int sig, int (*action)())) ();
#endif

/*        stdarg.h

          Definitions for accessing parameters in functions that accept
          a variable number of arguments.

          Copyright (c) Borland International 1987
          All Rights Reserved.
*/
#if __STDC__
#define _Cdecl
#else
#define _Cdecl     cdecl
#endif

#if       !defined(__STDARG)
#define __STDARG

typedef void       *va_list;

#define va_start(ap, parmN)  (ap = ...)
#define va_arg(ap, type)     (*((type *)(ap))++)
#define va_end(ap)
#define _va_ptr                       (...)
#endif
```

```
/*        stddef.h

          Definitions for common types, NULL, and errno.

          Copyright (c) Borland International 1987
          All Rights Reserved.
*/
#if __STDC__
#define _Cdecl
#else
#define _Cdecl     cdecl
#endif

#ifndef _STDDEF
#define _STDDEF
#ifndef _PTRDIFF_T
#define _PTRDIFF_T

#if       defined(__LARGE__) || defined(__HUGE__) || defined(__COMPACT__)
typedef long        ptrdiff_t;
#else
typedef int         ptrdiff_t;
#endif
#endif
#ifndef _SIZE_T
#define _SIZE_T
typedef unsigned size_t;
#endif

#ifndef NULL
#if defined(__TINY__) || defined(__SMALL__) || defined(__MEDIUM__)
#define NULL        0
#else
#define NULL        0L
#endif
#endif

extern   int        _Cdecl errno;

#endif

/*       stdio.h

         Definitions for stream input/output.

         Copyright (c) Borland International 1987
         All Rights Reserved.
*/
#if __STDC__
#define _Cdecl
#else
#define _Cdecl  cdecl
#endif

#if     !defined(__STDIO_DEF_)
#define __STDIO_DEF_

#ifndef _SIZE_T
#define _SIZE_T
typedef unsigned size_t;
#endif
```

```
#ifndef NULL
#   if defined(__TINY__) || defined(__SMALL__) || defined(__MEDIUM__)
#   define      NULL    0
#   else
#   define      NULL    0L
#   endif
#endif

#if     !defined(__STDARG)
#include        <stdarg.h>
#endif

/* Definition of the file position type
*/
typedef long    fpos_t;

/* Definition of the control structure for streams
*/
typedef struct  {
        short           level;          /* fill/empty level of buffer */
        unsigned        flags;          /* File status flags    */
        char            fd;             /* File descriptor      */
        unsigned char   hold;           /* Ungetc char if no buffer */
        short           bsize;          /* Buffer size          */
        unsigned char   *buffer;        /* Data transfer buffer */
        unsigned char   *curp;          /* Current active pointer */
        unsigned        istemp;         /* Temporary file indicator */
        short           token;          /* Used for validity checking */
}       FILE;                           /* This is the FILE object */

/* Bufferisation type to be used as 3rd argument for "setvbuf" function
*/
#define _IOFBF  0
#define _IOLBF  1
#define _IONBF  2

/*      "flags" bits definitions
*/
#define _F_RDWR 0x0003                  /* Read/write flag      */
#define _F_READ 0x0001                  /* Read only file       */
#define _F_WRIT 0x0002                  /* Write only file      */
#define _F_BUF  0x0004                  /* Malloc'ed Buffer data */
#define _F_LBUF 0x0008                  /* line-buffered file   */
#define _F_ERR  0x0010                  /* Error indicator      */
#define _F_EOF  0x0020                  /* EOF indicator        */
#define _F_BIN  0x0040                  /* Binary file indicator */
#define _F_IN   0x0080                  /* Data is incoming     */
#define _F_OUT  0x0100                  /* Data is outgoing     */
#define _F_TERM 0x0200                  /* File is a terminal   */

/* End-of-file constant definition
*/
#define EOF     (-1)                    /* End of file indicator */

/* Number of files that can be open simultaneously
*/
#define OPEN_MAX 20                     /* Total of 20 open files */
#define SYS_OPEN 20

/* Default buffer size use by "setbuf" function
*/
#define BUFSIZ  512                     /* Buffer size for stdio */
```

```
/* Size of an arry large enough to hold a temporary file name string
*/
#define L_ctermid       5               /* CON: plus null byte */
#define L_tmpnam        13              /* tmpnam buffer size */

/* Constants to be used as 3rd argument for "fseek" function
*/
#define SEEK_CUR        1
#define SEEK_END        2
#define SEEK_SET        0

/* Number of unique file names that shall be generated by "tmpnam" function
*/
#define TMP_MAX         0xFFFF

/* Standard I/O predefined streams
*/
extern  FILE    _Cdecl _streams[];

#define stdin   (&_streams[0])
#define stdout  (&_streams[1])
#define stderr  (&_streams[2])
#define stdaux  (&_streams[3])
#define stdprn  (&_streams[4])

void     _Cdecl clearerr (FILE *fp);
int      _Cdecl fclose   (FILE *fp);
int      _Cdecl fflush   (FILE *fp);
int      _Cdecl fgetc    (FILE *fp);
int      _Cdecl fgetpos  (FILE *fp, fpos_t *pos);
char    *_Cdecl fgets    (char *s, int n, FILE *fp);
FILE    *_Cdecl fopen    (const char *filename, const char *mode);
int      _Cdecl fprintf  (FILE *fp, const char *format, ...);
int      _Cdecl fputc    (int c, FILE *fp);
int      _Cdecl fputs    (const char *s, FILE *fp);
size_t   _Cdecl fread    (void *ptr, size_t size, size_t n, FILE *fp);
FILE    *_Cdecl freopen  (const char *filename, const char *mode,
                          FILE *oldfile);
int      _Cdecl fscanf   (FILE *fp, const char *format, ...);
int      _Cdecl fseek    (FILE *fp, long offset, int whence);
int      _Cdecl fsetpos  (FILE *fp, const fpos_t *pos);
long     _Cdecl ftell    (FILE *fp);
size_t   _Cdecl fwrite   (const void *ptr, size_t size, size_t n,
                          FILE *fp);
char    *_Cdecl gets     (char *s);
void     _Cdecl perror   (const char *s);
int      _Cdecl printf   (const char *format, ...);
int      _Cdecl puts     (const char *s);
int      _Cdecl rename   (const char *oldname, const char *newname);
void     _Cdecl rewind   (FILE *fp);
int      _Cdecl scanf    (const char *format, ...);
void     _Cdecl setbuf   (FILE *fp, char *buf);
int      _Cdecl setvbuf  (FILE *fp, char *buf, int type, size_t size);
int      _Cdecl sprintf  (char *buffer, const char *format, ...);
int      _Cdecl sscanf   (const char *buffer, const char *format, ...);
char    *_Cdecl strerror (int errnum);
FILE    *_Cdecl tmpfile  (void);
char    *_Cdecl tmpnam   (char *s);
int      _Cdecl ungetc   (int c, FILE *fp);
int      _Cdecl vfprintf (FILE *fp, const char *format, va_list arglist);
int      _Cdecl vfscanf  (FILE *fp, const char *format, va_list arglist);
```

```
int      _Cdecl vprintf  (const char *format, va_list arglist);
int      _Cdecl vscanf   (const char *format, va_list arglist);
int      _Cdecl vsprintf (char *buffer, const char *format, va_list arglist);
int      _Cdecl vsscanf  (const char *buffer, const char *format, va_list arglist);

#if !__STDC__
int      _Cdecl fcloseall(void);
FILE    *_Cdecl fdopen   (int handle, char *type);
int      _Cdecl fgetchar (void);
int      _Cdecl flushall (void);
int      _Cdecl fputchar (int c);
int      _Cdecl getw     (FILE *fp);
int      _Cdecl putw     (int w, FILE *fp);
char    *_Cdecl _strerror(const char *string);
int      _Cdecl unlink   (const char *filename);

#endif

int      _Cdecl _fgetc   (FILE *fp);              /* used by getc() macro */
int      _Cdecl _fputc   (char c, FILE *fp);      /* used by putc() macro */

/*      The following macros provide for common functions */

#define ferror(f)        ((f)->flags & _F_ERR)
#define feof(f)          ((f)->flags & _F_EOF)
#define fileno(f)        ((f)->fd)
#define remove(filename) unlink(filename)

#define getc(f) \
  ((--((f)->level) >= 0) ? (unsigned char)(++(f)->curp)[-1] : _fgetc (f))
#define putc(c,f) \
  ((++((f)->level) < 0) ? (unsigned char)((++(f)->curp)[-1]=(c)) : \
  _fputc ((c),f))
#define getchar()  getc(stdin)
#define putchar(c) putc((c), stdout)

#define ungetc(c,f)     ungetc((c),f)   /* traditionally a macro */

#endif

/*      stdlib.h

        Definitions for common types, variables, and functions.

        Copyright (c) Borland International 1987
        All Rights Reserved.
*/
#if __STDC__
#define _Cdecl
#else
#define _Cdecl  cdecl
#endif

#if     !defined(__STDLIB)
#define __STDLIB

#ifndef _SIZE_T
#define _SIZE_T
typedef unsigned size_t;
#endif
```

```
#ifndef _DIV_T
#define _DIV_T
typedef struct {
        int     quot;
        int     rem;
} div_t;
#endif

#ifndef _LDIV_T
#define _LDIV_T
typedef struct {
        long    quot;
        long    rem;
} ldiv_t;
#endif

#define EXIT_SUCCESS 0
#define EXIT_FAILURE 1

/* Maximum value returned by "rand" function
*/
#define RAND_MAX 0x7FFF

typedef void _Cdecl (* atexit_t)(void);

void     _Cdecl abort  (void);
int      _Cdecl abs    (int x);
int      _Cdecl atexit (atexit_t func);
double   _Cdecl atof   (const char *s);
int      _Cdecl atoi   (const char *s);
long     _Cdecl atol   (const char *s);
void    *_Cdecl bsearch(const void *key, const void *base,
                        size_t nelem, size_t width,
                        int _Cdecl (*fcmp)(const void *, const void *));
void    *_Cdecl calloc (size_t nitems, size_t size);
div_t    _Cdecl div    (int numer, int denom);
void     _Cdecl exit   (int status);
void     _Cdecl free   (void *block);
char    *_Cdecl getenv (const char *name);
long     _Cdecl labs   (long x);
ldiv_t   _Cdecl ldiv   (long numer, long denom);
void    *_Cdecl malloc (size_t size);
void     _Cdecl qsort  (void *base, size_t nelem, size_t width,
                        int _Cdecl (*fcmp)(const void *, const void *));
int      _Cdecl rand   (void);
void    *_Cdecl realloc(void *block, size_t size);
void     _Cdecl srand  (unsigned seed);
double   _Cdecl strtod (const char *s, char **endptr);
long     _Cdecl strtol (const char *s, char **endptr, int radix);
unsigned long _Cdecl strtoul (const char *s, char **endptr, int radix);
int      _Cdecl system (const char *command);

#if !__STDC__

#ifndef NULL
#if defined(__TINY__) || defined(__SMALL__) || defined(__MEDIUM__)
#define NULL    0
#else
#define NULL    0L
#endif
#endif
```

```
/* Variables */
extern  int             _Cdecl _doserrno;
extern  char          **_Cdecl environ;
extern  int             _Cdecl errno;
extern  int             _Cdecl _fmode;
extern  unsigned char   _Cdecl _osmajor;
extern  unsigned char   _Cdecl _osminor;
extern  unsigned        _Cdecl _psp;
extern  char           *_Cdecl sys_errlist[];
extern  int             _Cdecl sys_nerr;
extern  unsigned int    _Cdecl _version;

int     _Cdecl __abs__(int x);          /* This is an in-line function */
#define abs(x)          __abs__(x)
#define atoi(s)         ((int) atol (s))

#define max(a,b)        (((a) > (b)) ? (a) : (b))
#define min(a,b)        (((a) < (b)) ? (a) : (b))

#define random(num)     (rand() % (num))
#define randomize()     srand((unsigned)time(NULL))

char   *_Cdecl ecvt     (double value, int ndig, int *dec, int *sign);
void    _Cdecl _exit    (int status);
char   *_Cdecl fcvt     (double value, int ndig, int *dec, int *sign);
char   *_Cdecl gcvt     (double value, int ndec, char *buf);
char   *_Cdecl itoa     (int value, char *string, int radix);
void   *_Cdecl lfind    (const void *key, const void *base,
                         size_t *num, size_t width,
                         int _Cdecl (*fcmp)(const void *, const void *));

unsigned long _Cdecl _lrotl(unsigned long val, int count);
unsigned long _Cdecl _lrotr(unsigned long val, int count);

void   *_Cdecl lsearch  (const void *key, void *base,
                         size_t *num, size_t width,
                         int _Cdecl (*fcmp)(const void *, const void *));
char   *_Cdecl ltoa     (long value, char *string, int radix);
int     _Cdecl putenv   (const char *name);

unsigned _Cdecl _rotl   (unsigned value, int count);
unsigned _Cdecl _rotr   (unsigned value, int count);

void    _Cdecl swab     (char *from, char *to, int nbytes);
char   *_Cdecl ultoa    (unsigned long value, char *string, int radix);
#endif

#endif

/*      string.h

        Definitions for memory and string functions.

        Copyright (c) Borland International 1987
        All Rights Reserved.
*/
#if __STDC__
#define _Cdecl
#else
#define _Cdecl     cdecl
#endif
```

```
#ifndef _SIZE_T
#define _SIZE_T
typedef unsigned size_t;
#endif

void     *_Cdecl memccpy    (void *dest, const void *src, int c, size_t n);
void     *_Cdecl memchr     (const void *s, int c, size_t n);
int       _Cdecl memcmp     (const void *s1, const void *s2, size_t n);
void     *_Cdecl memcpy     (void *dest, const void *src, size_t n);
int       _Cdecl memicmp    (const void *s1, const void *s2, size_t n);
void     *_Cdecl memmove    (void *dest, const void *src, size_t n);
void     *_Cdecl memset     (void *s, int c, size_t n);
void      _Cdecl movedata(unsigned srcseg, unsigned srcoff, unsigned dstseg,
                           unsigned dstoff, size_t n);
char     *_Cdecl stpcpy     (char *dest, const char *src);
char     *_Cdecl strcat     (char *dest, const char *src);
char     *_Cdecl strchr     (const char *s, int c);
int       _Cdecl strcmp     (const char *s1, const char *s2);
char     *_Cdecl strcpy     (char *dest, const char *src);
size_t    _Cdecl strcspn    (const char *s1, const char *s2);
char     *_Cdecl strdup     (const char *s);
char     *_Cdecl strerror(int errnum);
int       _Cdecl stricmp    (const char *s1, const char *s2);
size_t    _Cdecl strlen     (const char *s);
char     *_Cdecl strlwr     (char *s);
char     *_Cdecl strncat    (char *dest, const char *src, size_t maxlen);
int       _Cdecl strncmp    (const char *s1, const char *s2, size_t maxlen);
char     *_Cdecl strncpy    (char *dest, const char *src, size_t maxlen);
int       _Cdecl strnicmp(const char *s1, const char *s2, size_t maxlen);
char     *_Cdecl strnset    (char *s, int ch, size_t n);
char     *_Cdecl strpbrk    (const char *s1, const char *s2);
char     *_Cdecl strrchr    (const char *s, int c);
char     *_Cdecl strrev     (char *s);
char     *_Cdecl strset     (char *s, int ch);
size_t    _Cdecl strspn     (const char *s1, const char *s2);
char     *_Cdecl strstr     (const char *s1, const char *s2);
char     *_Cdecl strtok     (char *s1, const char *s2);
char     *_Cdecl strupr     (char *s);

/* compatibility with other compilers */

#define strcmpi(s1,s2)              stricmp(s1,s2)
#define strncmpi(s1,s2,n)    strnicmp(s1,s2,n)

#if !__STDC__
char      *_Cdecl _strerror (const char *s);
#endif

/*      time.h

        Struct and function declarations for dealing with time.

        Copyright (c) Borland International 1987
        All Rights Reserved.
*/
#if __STDC__
#define _Cdecl
#else
#define _Cdecl     cdecl
#endif
```

```
#ifndef _TIME_T
#define _TIME_T

typedef long        time_t;

struct   tm        {
         int       tm_sec;
         int       tm_min;
         int       tm_hour;
         int       tm_mday;
         int       tm_mon;
         int       tm_year;
         int       tm_wday;
         int       tm_yday;
         int       tm_isdst;
};

char      *_Cdecl  asctime   (const struct tm *tblock);
char      *_Cdecl  ctime     (const time_t *timer);
double     _Cdecl  difftime(time_t time2, time_t time1);
struct tm *_Cdecl gmtime(const time_t *timer);
struct tm *_Cdecl localtime(const time_t *timer);
time_t     _Cdecl  time      (time_t *timer);

#if !__STDC__
extern int           _Cdecl daylight;
extern long          _Cdecl timezone;

int        _Cdecl stime(time_t *tp);
void       _Cdecl tzset(void);
#endif

#endif
```

Appendix M

REPRESENTATIVE C DATA TYPE CONVERSIONS

Conversion of char type to:

1.	unsigned char	There is no change in bit pattern, it is a direct move of bits. The sign bit remains and becomes a data bit.
2.	short	The value is sign-extended, no data value is lost.
3.	unsigned short	The value is sign-extended as a short, and the sign bit becomes a data bit.
4.	int	The value is sign-extended, no data value is lost.
5.	unsigned int	The value is sign-extended as an int type, and the sign bit becomes a data bit.
6.	long	The value is sign-extended, no data value is lost.
7.	unsigned long	The value is sign-extended as long type, and the sign bit becomes a data bit.
8.	float	The value is sign-extended, no data value is lost.
9.	double	The value is sign-extended, no data value is lost.

NOTE

This conversion is representative of data conversions on full C compilers. Refer to your C manual for actual data conversions for your compiler.

This based on: char = 8 bit, short = 16 bit, int = 16 bit, long = 32 bit.

Conversion of unsigned short type to:

1.	char	Truncate high-order bits, data bit becomes sign bit. Data may be lost.
2.	unsigned char	Truncate high-order bits. Data may be lost.
3.	short	There is no change in bit pattern, with the high-order bit becoming the sign bit.
4.	int	There is no change in bit pattern, with the new bits being zero-filled, including the sign bit.
5.	unsigned int	There is no change in bit pattern, with the new bits being zero-filled.
6.	long	There is no change in bit pattern, with the new bits being zero-filled, including the sign bit.

7. unsigned long	There is no change in bit pattern, with the new bits being zero-filled.
8. float	The value is assumed to be short type, with the high-order bit being a sign bit, and the value is then sign-extended to float type.
9. double	The value is assumed to be short type, with the high-order bit being a sign bit, and the value is then sign-extended to double type.

Conversion of short type to:

1. char	Truncate high-order bits, data bit becomes sign bit. Data may be lost.
2. unsigned char	Truncate high-order bits. Data may be lost.
3. unsigned short	There is no change in bit pattern, and the sign bit becomes a data bit.
4. int	The value is sign-extended, no data value is lost.
5. unsigned int	The value is sign-extended as an int type, and the sign bit becomes a data bit.
6. long	The value is sign-extended, no data value is lost.
7. unsigned long	The value is sign-extended as long type, and the sign bit becomes a data bit.
8. float	The value is sign-extended, no data value is lost.
9. double	The value is sign-extended, no data value is lost.

Conversion of unsigned char type to:

1. char	There is no change in bit pattern, it is a direct move of bits. The high-order bit becomes the sign bit, value may become negative.
2. short	There is no change in bit pattern, with the new bits being zero-filled, including the sign bit.
3. unsigned short	There is no change in bit pattern, with the new bits being zero-filled.
4. int	There is no change in bit pattern, with the new bits being zero-filled, including the sign bit.
5. unsigned int	There is no change in bit pattern, with the new bits being zero-filled.
6. long	There is no change in bit pattern, with the new bits being zero-filled, including the sign bit.
7. unsigned long	There is no change in bit pattern, with the new bits being zero-filled.
8. float	The value is assumed to be char type, with the high-order bit being a sign bit, and the value is then sign-extended to float type.
9. double	The value is assumed to be char type, with the high-order bit being a sign bit, and the value is then sign-extended to double type.

Conversion of int type to:

1. char	Truncate high-order bits, data bit becomes sign bit. Data may be lost.
2. unsigned char	Truncate high-order bits. Data may be lost.
3. short	Truncate high-order bits, data bit becomes sign bit. Data may be lost.
4. unsigned short	Truncate high-order bits. Data may be lost.
5. unsigned int	The bits move across, and the sign bit becomes a data bit.
6. long	The value is sign-extended, no data value is lost.
7. unsigned long	The value is sign-extended as long type, and the sign bit becomes a data bit.
8. float	The value is sign-extended, no data value is lost.
9. double	The value is sign-extended, no data value is lost.

Conversion of unsigned int type to:

1. char	Truncate high-order bits, data bit becomes sign bit. Data may be lost.
2. unsigned char	Truncate high-order bits. Data may be lost.
3. short	Truncate high-order bits, data bit becomes sign bit. Data may be lost.
4. unsigned short	Truncate high-order bits. Data may be lost.
5. int	There is no change in bit pattern, with the high-order bit becoming the sign bit.
6. long	There is no change in bit pattern, with the new bits being zero-filled, including the sign bit.
7. unsigned long	There is no change in bit pattern, with the new bits being zero-filled.
8. float	The value is assumed to be int type, with the high-order bit being a sign bit, and the value is then sign-extended to float type.
9. double	The value is assumed to be int type, with the high-order bit being a sign bit, and the value is then sign-extended to double type.

Conversion of long type to:

1. char	Truncate high-order bits, data bit becomes sign bit. Data may be lost.
2. unsigned char	Truncate high-order bits. Data may be lost.
3. short	Truncate high-order bits, data bit becomes sign bit. Data may be lost.
4. unsigned short	Truncate high-order bits. Data may be lost.
5. int	Truncate high-order bits, data bit becomes sign bit. Data may be lost.

6. unsigned int — Truncate high-order bits. Data may be lost.
7. unsigned long — There is no change in bit pattern, and the sign bit becomes a data bit.
8. float — The value is sign-extended. Usually no data value is lost, however some computers do lose some precision.
9. double — The value is sign-extended. Usually no data value is lost, however some computers do lose some precision.

Conversion of unsigned long type to:

1. char — Truncate high-order bits, data bit becomes sign bit. Data may be lost.
2. unsigned char — Truncate high-order bits. Data may be lost.
3. short — Truncate high-order bits, data bit becomes sign bit. Data may be lost.
4. unsigned short — Truncate high-order bits. Data may be lost.
5. int — Truncate high-order bits, data bit becomes sign bit. Data may be lost.
6. unsigned int — Truncate high-order bits. Data may be lost.
7. long — There is no change in bit pattern, with the high-order bit becoming the sign bit.
8. float — The value is assumed to be long type, with the high-order bit being a sign bit, and the value is then sign extended to float type. Some computers lose some precision.
9. double — The value is assumed to be long type, with the high-order bit being a sign bit, and the value is then sign extended to double type. Some computers lose some precision.

Conversion of float type to:

1. long — The value is truncated at the decimal point. If the resultant value is too large to fit into a long, then the value is unpredictable, usually not even close. If the value fits, it is used.
2. double — The value is sign-extended. No data value is lost.
3. Other types — For the other types the value is first converted to long type. Then the rules for long type conversions are followed.

Conversion of double type to:

1. float — If the value is too large to fit into a float, then the value is unpredictable, usually not even close. If the value fits, it is used.
2. Other types — For the other types the value is first converted to float type. Then the rules for float type conversions are followed.

Appendix N
EXERCISES

1. About This Book
   a. How are the modules organized in this book?
   b. How is the Recommended Learning Sequence used?

2. C Overview
   a. Compare the stengths of C with the strengths of another programming language that you are familiar with.
   b. List the reasons why was C standarized.

3. Basic Elements of a C Program
   a. List the items that make up the form of a C program.
   b. List the major aspects concerning the syntax of C source programs.
   c. What defines where a C program starts executing?

4. Your First Real C Program
   a. Enter, compile, and run your first C program, Example 4.1, listed at the front of Module 4.
   b. Modify this example C program to display your name on the computer.
   c. Enter, compile, and run the C program, Example 4.2, listed at the front of Module 4.
   d. Modify this example C program to print your name with the computer.

5. Standard Library Functions
   a. Describe the purpose of the standard library.
   b. Summarize the functions in the standard library.

6. Naming in C
   a. Describe the *naming* rules in C.
   b. What is the significance of the keywords in C?

7. abort
   a. Write and compile a program that demonstrates the use of the *abort* function.

8. abs
   a. Input and compile the Example 8.1 source code for the *abs* function. Write and compile a program to prove that the code is correct. Note: change the name to make sure that this function is executed and not the function in the standard library.

9. Arrays
   a. Write and compile a program that contains an array and a multidimentional array. Assign values to elements in the multidimentional array and display them in your program.
10. Arrays — Part 2
    a. Modify and compile the program arrays21.c to verify that the array initialization is performed properly.
    b. Modify and compile the program arrays22.c to verify that arrays are not placed on the stack.
11. atoi, atol, atof
    a. Enter, compile, and run the program atoi1.c that uses the *atoi* function to verify for yourself that the values returned are the values presented in this book.
12. break
    a. Write and compile a program that demonstrates and proves that the *break* transfers control as described in this module for the *do*, *for*, *switch*, and *while* statements.
13. calloc
    a. Describe the difference between the *malloc* function and the *calloc* function.
14. clearerr
    a. Write and compile a program to demonstrate that the *clearerr* function does clear the error flag.
15. close
    a. Name three things that will cause the *close* function to return an error.
16. Command Line Arguments
    a. Determine if the command line redirection fields can be accessed as command line arguments.
    b. Write and compile a program that demonstrates that argc and argv are stored in memory as presented in this module.
17. Constants
    a. Write and compile a program that contains one of each constant explained in this module.
    b. Describe the significance and effect of the backslash in both character and string constants.
18. continue
    a. Write and compile a program that demonstrates and proves that the *continue* statement transfers control as described in this module for the *do*, *for*, and *while* statements.
    b. Write and compile a program that demonstrates and proves that the *continue* statement transfers control as described in this module for nested *do*, *for*, and *while* statements.
19. creat
    a. Write and compile a program that uses the *creat* function to create a new file and to open and truncate an existing file to prove the *creat* function works as described in this module.

20. Data Types
    a. Describe the six basic data types.
    b. Describe the qualifiers for the basic data types.
    c. What is the criteria for selecting the data type of a variable or constant?

21. Data Types — Part 2
    a. Modify and compile the program data2.c to demonstrate the assigning and displaying of values of variable declared with a *typedef*.
    b. Use the *increasing spiral rule* to prove that the two following declarations are equal:
        1) char *argv[]
        2) char **argv

22. do-while
    a. Write and compile a program that demostrates the use of the *do-while* statement.
    b. Write and compile a program that proves the *do-while* flowchart is correct.

23. eof
    a. Enter and compile the program in this module to demonstrate that the *eof* works as described in this module.

24. exit
    a. Write and compile a program that demonstrates the *exit* statement.

25. fclose
    a. Modify and compile the program in this module to such that the *fclose* function returns an error.

26. ferror
    a. Modify and compile the program in this module such that an error condition is created so that the *ferror* function will return an error value.

27. fgetc
    a. Modify and compile the program in this module to accept the filename on the command line and then display the file on the *stdout* stream file.

28. fgets
    a. Modify and compile the program in this module to accept the filename from the command line and then display the file on the *stdout* stream file.
    b. Write the program to remove the new-line character at the end of each line input in this example.

29. File Input/Output
    a. Compare in your own words the low-level and the high-level disk functions.
    b. Write an explanation for each generalized program flow for all high-level and low-level functions diagramed in this module.

30. fopen
    a. Write and compile a program that performs a *fopen* function in the three modes (read, write, and append) to files that both exist and do not exist. Display any appropriate error messages.

31. for
    a. Write and compile a program that demonstrates the use of the *for* statement.
    b. Write and compile a program that proves the *for* flowchart is correct.

32. fprintf, vfprintf
    a. Write and compile a program using the *fprintf* statement with all data types, varying the flags, width, precision, and output data types.

33. fputc
    a. Modify and compile the *fputc.c* program in this module to accept the filename from the command line and then to use the *fputc* function to display the file on *stdout*.

34. fputs
    a. Modify and compile the *fputs.c* program in this module to accept the filename from the command line and to use the *fputs* function to display the file on *stdout*.

35. fread
    a. Enter and compile the program in this module to prove the *fread* function works as described in this module.

36. free
    a. Write and compile a program to prove that memory allocated and then freed is reused.
    b. Modify your program to free an area of memory not allocated. Does it return an error?

37. fscanf
    a. Write and compile a program that uses each of the basic data types to prove that all of them can be used with the *fscanf* function.

38. fseek
    a. Write and compile a program that uses the *fseek* function call to position the file to the three possible locations and to write to the file at those locations. Display the modified file to verify that the writes occured at the desired locations.

39. Functions
    a. List the advantages of using functions.
    b. List the advantages of using prototypes.
    c. Write and compile a program that demonstates that all basic data types can be passed to and from functions.

40. Functions — Part 2
    a. Write and compile a program that passes a variable of each basic data type by both value and by reference.

41. fwrite
    a. Enter and compile the *fcopy.c* program that copies a stream file. Verify that the program copies the exact file, no more and no less.

42. getc
    a. Modify and compile the program in this module to accept the filename from the command line and display the file on the *stdout* stream file.

43. getchar
   a. Explain why in Example 43.1 the character returned from the *getchar* function is assigned to an integer variable instead of a character type variable.

44. gets
   a. Modify and enter the program in this module to prove that the *gets* function does not place the newline character into the input buffer.

45. goto
   a. Write and compile a program that demonstrates the use of the *goto* statement.
   b. Rewrite and compile the Example 45.1 program such that the *goto* statement is not necessary. Give an instance of when a *goto* is absolutely necessary and cannot be avoided.

46. if-else
   a. Explain the principle usage of the *if* statement.
   b. Write and compile a program demonstrating the usage of the *if-else* statement.
   c. Write and compile a program that proves that the *if* flowchart is correct.

47. is_____
   a. Write and compile a program that demonstates the use of each *is*_____ function.
   b. Modify the program from Example 47.1 to prove that several characters within and outside the limits of the function return the proper value.

48. lseek
   a. Write and compile a program that uses the *lseek* low-level function to position to the three possible locations within the file and write a record. Display the file to prove that the records were written at the proper locations.

49. malloc
   a. Modify the program in this module to display the values stored in the allocated area of memory.
   b. Modify the program in this module to continually allocate memory till an error occurs to test the error exit.

50. memset
   a. Modify the example in this module to prove that the memset function works as described.

51. Numbering Systems
   a. Convert the decimal numbers 250, 583, and 333 to Binary, Octal, and Hex.
   b. Convert the results of the previous exercise back to decimal to verify your conversions.
   c. Add the numbers 250 and 333 in each base and compare to the conversion of 583 as a second verification of your conversions.

52. open
   a. Explain the difference between the *creat* function and the *open* function.

53. Operators
    a. Write and compile a program demonstrating the differences between the bit-wise and logical *and* and *or* operators.
    b. Write and compile a program that uses each operator presented in this module.
54. Operators — Part 2
    a. Write and compile a program that determines the length of each basic data type for your C compiler.
    b. Describe the difference between *lvalue* and *rvalue*.
55. perror
    a. Modify and compile the program in this module such that the perror function is called to display the last disk function error.
56. Pointers
    a. Write and compile a program that includes a pointer to all the basic data types, to an array, to a structure, and to a union. Assign and display the value of each variable pointed to by the pointers in your program.
57. Pointers — Part 2
    a. Draw a memory map of the data defined in the program pointr23.c.
    b. Write and compile a program that uses a pointer to a pointer to display a value in a ragged array.
    c. Write and compile a program demonstrating pointer arithmetic.
58. Portability
    a. Write and compile a program that will confirm the storage byte order described in this module for your particular processor.
59. Precedence in Expressions
    a. Write and compile a program that proves the precedence and associativity for all 15 precedence levels.
60. Preprocessor Directives
    a. Write and compile a program that uses each preprocessor command described in this module.
61. printf, vprintf
    a. Write and compile a program using the *printf* statement with all data types, varing the flags, width, precision, and output data types.
62. putc
    a. Explain how an error can occur using putc.
63. putchar
    a. Explain why the *putchar* function returns an integer type value.
64. puts
    a. Explain how an error can occur using the *puts* function.

65. read
    a. Enter and compile the program in this module to prove the *read* function works as described in this module.

66. remove
    a. Modify the program in this module to accept the filename from the command line and delete that file from the filing system on the disk. Be sure and test this program on test files that contain no valuable data as the data in the files are destroyed.

67. return
    a. Write and compile a program that demonstrates the *return* statement.

68. scanf
    a. Write and compile a program that uses each of the basic data types to prove that all of them can be used with the *scanf* function.

69. sprintf, vsprintf
    a. Write and compile a program using the *sprintf* statement with all data types, varing the flags, width, precision, and output data types.

70. sscanf
    a. Write and compile a program with each basic data type to prove that all of them can be used with the *sscanf* function.

71. Stack
    a. Modify the example in this module to prove that the arguments in funct1 and funct2 use the same memory address. Refer to your C compiler manual for instructions on how to display a pointer.

72. stdin, stdout, stderr
    a. What is the main purpose and use of the *stdin*, *stdout*, and *stderr* files?
    b. Write and compile a program that demonstrates the use of the *stdin*, *stdout*, and *stderr* files.

73. Storage Classes
    a. From memory summarize all storage classes.

74. strcat, strncat
    a. Input and compile the Example 74.1 source code for the *strcat* function. Write and compile a program to prove that the code is correct. Note: change the name to make sure that this function is executed and not the function in the standard library.

75. strcmp, strncmp, memcmp
    a. Input and compile the Example 75.1 source code for the *strcmp* function. Write and compile a program to prove that the code is correct. Note: change the name to make sure that this function is executed and not the function in the standard library.

76. strcpy, strncpy, memcpy, memmove
    a. Input and compile the Example 76.1 source code for the *strcpy* function. Write and compile a program to prove that the code is correct. Note: change the name to make sure that this function is executed and not the function in the standard library.

77. Strings — Arrays of Char Type
    a. Write and compile a program that assigns and displays your name from a string.
78. strlen
    a. Input and compile the Example 78.1 source code for the *strlen* function. Write and compile a program to prove that the code is correct. Note: change the name to make sure that this function is executed and not the function in the standard library.
79. Structures
    a. Describe the advantages of using structures.
    b. Enter and compile the programs in this module. Add *printf* statements to the programs to prove the members of the structures contain the values assigned.
80. Structures — Part 2
    a. Modify and compile the program struct21.c to prove the structure initialization is performed properly.
81. switch
    a. Write and compile a program that demonstrates the use of the *switch* statement.
    b. Write and compile a program without the *break* statements to demonstrate that they are usually necessary. Give an example of when the *break* statement is not necessary.
82. tolower
    a. Write and compile a function that performs the same as the *tolower* function. Write and compile a program to prove your code is correct. Note: change the name to make sure that your function is executed and not the function in the standard library.
83. toupper
    a. Write and compile a function that performs the same as the *toupper* function. Write and compile a program to prove your code is correct. Note: change the name to make sure that your function is executed and not the function in the standard library.
84. ungetc
    a. Write and compile a program that uses the *ungetc* function. Prove that the character returned to the file does not have to be the character read from the file.
85. Union
    a. Describe the advantages of using *unions*.
    b. Enter and compile the examples in this module. Modify the examples to assign and display values for each union member in the examples.
86. Variables
    a. Write a C program that contains a variable of each basic data type and each basic data type with qualifiers.
    b. Modify the C program in exercise 1 by initializing each variable and printing the length of each variable.

87. Variables — Part 2
    a. Write and compile a program that demonstrates the following data conversions when assigning one variable to another: 1) zero-filling of bits, 2) truncating bits, 3) sign-extending, 4) no change in bit pattern.
    b. Describe when explicit data type cast are necessary.

88. while
    a. Write and compile a program demonstrating the use of the *while* statement.
    b. Write and compile a program that proves the *while* flowchart is correct.

89. write
    a. Enter and compile the *lcopy.c* program that copies a file with low-level functions. Verify that the program copies the exact file, no more and no less.

Index

WORDWARE'S BOOKS ON PROGRAMMING LANGUAGES

Advanced Programming Techniques in Turbo Pascal $21.95
2nd Edition 1-55622-123-1
Tanik/Pooch/Urdas

Use these techniques to improve your applications and increase your speed in writing programs. Detailed instructions provide a toolkit of skills to build custom-designed programs. The Pascal user can get up to speed on Turbo Pascal with a special section paralleling the two. The usages of Turbo Pascal language constructs are featured. A diskette of the source code from the book is available.

Illustrated QuickBASIC 4.0 $19.95
Hari Venkateswaran, Murat Tanik, and Udo Pooch 1-55622-067-7

Make full use of major performance and feature enhancements available with this fascinating integrated program. This complete handbook fully demonstrates the ease of moving among compiling, debugging, and editing functions without switching programs or diskettes. This comprehensive tutorial provides an excellent reference tool to menu bar selections, new language constructs, recursive programming, and more.

Illustrated Turbo C $21.95
Version 2.0 1-55622-117-7
Michael Yester

Start by learning C language basics, then discover how C interfaces with this powerful software development tool. Hands-on demonstrations introduce the new Break/Watch menu entry and the expanded debug and run menus that make Turbo C such a versatile C compiler. Programming tips and applications use the expanded set of functions, Turbo editor, and superb graphics library. Clear, complete explanations make writing, editing, and compiling programs a snap.

Illustrated Turbo Pascal 5.0 $21.95
Paul Schlieve 1-55622-107-X

Newly updated with the expanded features of 5.0, including source-level debugging, this language reference-tutorial provides hands-on instruction and sound advice for both the novice and expert Turbo Pascal user. Program examples make excellent models for your programming needs. Original and expanded features are demonstrated with short, easy-to-perform activities, which are easily found for quick reference.

Library of Turbo Pascal Programs $21.95
2nd Edition 1-55622-150-9
Tanik/Pooch/Urdas

Eliminate guesswork by adapting these extensive Turbo Pascal listings to your own programming needs. This book provides extensions which make the programs more practical while demonstrating the use of Pascal constructs. Real-life system applications such as inventory control and cost-benefit analysis are used. Each program is thoroughly described and illustrated. Companion diskettes are available.

ILLUSTRATED BOOKS FROM WORDWARE PUBLISHING, INC.

ARTIFICIAL INTELLIGENCE

Illustrated Turbo Prolog 2.04 $21.95
Mick McAllister 0-915381-97-4

Advance at your own pace to learn the latest Artificial Intelligence techniques required for programming in Prolog. Sound advice and detailed directions teach programming of customized knowledge bases, natural language interfaces, and smart information management systems. An indispensable learning and teaching tool that becomes an easy-to-use, quick reference.

Illustrated VP-Expert $19.95
Wallace E. Wang and John Mueller 1-55622-057-X

Explore the power of artificial intelligence with little, if any, knowledge of a programming language. Examples serve as models for designing expert systems on anything ranging from financial planning to medical diagnoses. Learn to use the full-screen text editor, a word processor, or pop-up utility to create and edit expert systems. Effectively store and retrieve data to provide problem-solving advice.

COMPUTER-AIDED DRAFTING

Illustrated AutoCAD $23.95
Release 10 1-55622-064-2
Tom W. Berghauser and Paul Schlieve

Create, edit, and copy a variety of drawings as easily as a word processor manipulates text. Learn to use line types, cross-hatch patterns, layer names, and text fonts/styles effectively. Define and modify screen and tablet menus, components, and shape libraries. Novice users will find that clear illustrated examples provide the key to this Computer-Aided Drafting (CAD) based system. This book is an excellent reference tool for drafting design experts. It covers versions 2.17 through Release 10.

Illustrated AutoSketch 1.04 $21.95
Paul Schlieve and Tom Berghauser 1-55622-113-4

The authors of the popular *Illustrated AutoCAD* bring you detailed information on this entry-level, full-functioned, precision drawing tool. This complete AutoSketch introduction gets you up and running in about one hour. Hands-on activities step through the easy-to-use pull-down menus and dialog boxes that control sophisticated graphics manipulation functions. Details on how to import AutoSketch drawings to AutoCAD for additional refinements are included.

Call Wordware Publishing, Inc. for the names of bookstores in your area
(214) 423-0090

ILLUSTRATED BOOKS FROM WORDWARE PUBLISHING, INC.

Illustrated Paradox Volume II 3.0 $21.95
Paradox Application Language (PAL) 1-55622-108-8
Debbie and Doug Stone

This better-than-ever relational database manager combines ease of use with power and sophistication. Even the beginner will find himself up and running after learning a few basic commands. Learn how to make Paradox 3.0 a sophisticated multiuser product. This step-by-step learning guide becomes an indispensable alphabetical reference to the commands that make this program so versatile.

Illustrated VP-Info 1.4 $19.95
Mick McAllister 1-55622-070-7

This definitive introduction and reference handbook makes it easy for novice and experienced computer users to learn this high-speed, multi-dimensional management system. It contains a complete source of detailed, inside information including the latest 1.4 updates. Emphasis is placed on the numerous enhanced features, commands, and functions added to many original dBASE utilities. An indispensable tool for using VP-Info.

SPREADSHEET/INTEGRATED

Illustrated Framework III $21.95
Debbie Stone 1-55622-114-2

This timely update includes the newest capabilities of Framework III. Learn to use a keyboard and mouse to access E-Mail, Thesaurus, and the other color-supported features that make Framework III better than ever. Master skills to use the improved spreadsheet features for seamless integration of dBASE and Lotus files into Framework's database, spreadsheet, and word processing modules.

Illustrated Lotus 1-2-3 $19.95
Ralph Mylius 0-915381-67-2

Expanded to include the most up-to-date features of this top-selling worksheet program. Designed for first-time and experienced users, this book includes all features and functions of Lotus 1-2-3. Learn to create, edit, and print useful worksheets and graphs simply by following the detailed instructions and illustrated examples. Easy-to-follow procedures are included for using Lotus 1-2-3 files with Symphony and new macro commands. A comprehensive learning and reference tool.

Call Wordware Publishing, Inc. for the names of bookstores in your area
(214) 423-0090

Other Books from Wordware Publishing, Inc.

Artificial Intelligence
Artificial Ingelligence Programming Techniques in BASIC
Illustrated Turbo Prolog 2.0
Illustrated VP-Expert

Computer-Aided Drafting
Illustrated AutoCAD (Release 9)
Illustrated AutoCAD (Release 10)
Illustrated AutoSketch 1.04
Illustrated GenericCAD

Database Management
The DataFlex Developer's Handbook
Illustrated dBASE II (2nd Ed.)
Illustrated dBASE III Plus
Illustrated dBASE IV
Illustrated Paradox Volume I 1.2
Illustrated Paradox Volume II 1.2
Illustrated Paradox Volume II 2.0
Illustrated VP-Info 1.2
Illustrated VP-Info 1.4

Desktop Publishing
Desktop Publisher's Dictionary
Handbook of Desktop Publishing
Illustrated PageMaker 3.0
Illustrated Ready, Set, Go! 4.5 (Macintosh)
Illustrated Ventura 1.1
Illustrated Ventura 2.0

General Advanced Topics
The Complete Communications Handbook
Consulting Handbook for the High-Tech Professional
Illustrated Dac Easy Accounting 2.0
Illustrated Dac Easy Accounting 3.0
Illustrated Novell NetWare
Managing Your Megabytes

Programming Languages
Advanced Programming Techniques in Turbo Pascal
Illustrated C Programming (ANSI)
The FOCUS Developer's Handbook
From BASIC to 8086/8088 Assembly Language
Library of Turbo Pascal Programs
Illustrated PC/FOCUS
Illustrated QuickBASIC 4.0
Illustrated RM/COBOL
Illustrated Turbo Pascal 3.01

Programming Languages cont.
Illustrated Turbo Pascal 4.0
Illustrated Turbo Pascal 5.0

Spreadsheet/Integrated
Illustrated Framework II
Illustrated Framework III
Illustrated Lotus 1-2-3 2.01
Illustrated Microsoft Excel 2.01 (IBM)
Illustrated Microsoft Excel 1.5 (Macintosh)
Illustrated Multiplan 2.0
Illustrated Q & A
Illustrated Quattro
Illustrated Symphony 1.2

Systems and Operating Guides
Illustrated Microsoft Windows 2.0
Illustrated MS/PC-DOS 3.3
Illustrated MS/PC-DOS 4.0
Illustrated OS/2

Word Processing
Illustrated DisplayWrite 4
Illustrated Microsoft Word 5.0
Illustrated Sprint
Illustrated WordPerfect 1.0 (Macintosh)
Illustrated WordPerfect 4.2
Illustrated WordPerfect 5.0
Illustrated WordStar 3.3
Illustrated WordStar Professional (Rel. 4)
Illustrated WordStar Professional (Rel. 5)
The New WordStar Customizing Guide 4.0
WordPerfect: Advanced Applications Handbook
The WordStar Customizing Guide 3.3

Business-Professional Books
Business Emotions
How to Win Pageants
Innovation, Inc.
Investor Beware
MegaTraits
Occupying the Summit
Steps to Strategic Management

Regional
This Dog'll Hunt
100 Days in Texas — The Alamo Letters
Exploring the Alamo Legends
Wit and Wisdom
Forget the Alamo
Rainy Day Workbook, Texas Edition

Call Wordware Publishing, Inc. for names of the bookstores in your area.
(214) 423-0090